The Writing Cure

The Writing Cure

How Expressive Writing Promotes Health
and Emotional Well-Being

Edited by

Stephen J. Lepore and **Joshua M. Smyth**

American Psychological Association • Washington, DC

First Printing April 2002
Second Printing August 2002
Third Printing April 2003

Published by
American Psychological Association
750 First Street, NE
Washington, DC 20002
www.apa.org

To order
APA Order Department
P.O. Box 92984
Washington, DC 20090-2984

Tel: (800) 374-2721, Direct: (202) 336-5510
Fax: (202) 336-5502, TDD/TTY: (202) 336-6123
Online: www.apa.org/books/
Email: order@apa.org

In the U.K., Europe, Africa, and the Middle East, copies may be ordered from
American Psychological Association
3 Henrietta Street
Covent Garden, London
WC2E 8LU England

Typeset in Goudy by EPS Group Inc., Easton, MD

Printer: United Books, Baltimore, MD
Cover designer: Naylor Design, Washington, DC
Technical/Production Editor: Casey Ann Reever

The opinions and statements published are the responsibility of the authors, and such opinions and statements do not necessarily represent the policies of the American Psychological Association.

Library of Congress Cataloging-in-Publication Data
The writing cure : how expressive writing promotes health and emotional well-being / edited by Stephen J. Lepore, Joshua M. Smyth
    p. cm
Includes bibliographical references and index.
ISBN 1-55798-910-9
    1. Diaries—Authorship—Psychological aspects.   2. Diaries—Therapeutic use.
I. Lepore, Stephen J.   II. Smyth, Joshua M.
PN4390 .W75 2002
808'.06692—dc21

                                                                2002018509

British Library Cataloguing-in-Publication Data
A CIP record is available from the British Library.

Printed in the United States of America

For Stefanie and Brianna, my inspiration.

Stephen J. Lepore

Maiorum consuetudini deditus.

Joshua M. Smyth

CONTENTS

CONTRIBUTORS

Roger J. Booth, MSc, PhD, Department of Molecular Medicine and Pathology, University of Auckland, New Zealand

Michelle Bruno, BA, Department of Psychology, Graduate Center of the City University of New York, New York

Ellie Buteau, MA, Social–Personality Psychology, Graduate Center of the City University of New York, New York

Delwyn Catley, PhD, Department of Preventative Medicine, University of Kansas Medical Center, Kansas City

Colette Daiute, EdD, Professor of Psychology, Graduate Center of the City University of New York, New York

Sharon Danoff-Burg, PhD, Department of Psychology, State University of New York, Albany

Elizabeth David, MA, Sudbury, MA

Karina Davidson, PhD, Department of Cardiology, Mount Sinai School of Medicine, New York

William Gerin, PhD, Department of Cardiology, Mount Sinai School of Medicine, New York

Melanie A. Greenberg, PhD, Department of Psychology, Alliant International University, San Diego, CA

Roy Kern, PhD, Department of Counseling and Psychological Services, Georgia State University, Atlanta

Laura A. King, PhD, Department of Psychological Sciences, University of Missouri, Columbia

Kitty Klein, PhD, Department of Psychology, North Carolina State University, Raleigh

Luciano L'Abate, PhD, Department of Psychology, Georgia State University, Atlanta

Alfred Lange, PhD, Department of Clinical Psychology, University of Amsterdam, The Netherlands

Stephen J. Lepore, PhD, Department of Psychology, Brooklyn College and Graduate Center of the City University of New York, New York

Mark A. Lumley, PhD, Department of Psychology, Wayne State University, Detroit, MI

Susan K. Lutgendorf, PhD, Department of Psychology, University of Iowa, Iowa City

Debra J. Macklem, MEd, Department of Psychology, Wayne State University, Detroit, MI

Ronald S. McCord, MD, Department of Medicine, East Tennessee State University, Johnson City

James W. Pennebaker, PhD, Department of Psychology, University of Texas at Austin

Keith J. Petrie, PhD, DipClinPsych, Department of Health Psychology, University of Auckland, New Zealand

Mirjam Schoutrop, PhD, Center 45, Noordwijkerhout, The Netherlands

Bart Schrieken, MA, Department of Clinical Psychology, University of Amsterdam, The Netherlands

Amy R. Schwartz, SB, Department of Medicine, Stanford University School of Medicine, Stanford, CA

Carolyn E. Schwartz, ScD, Department of Family Medicine and Community Health, University of Massachusetts Medical School, Worchester

David Sheffield, PhD, Department of Psychology, Staffordshire University, Stoke-on-Trent, England

Joshua M. Smyth, PhD, Department of Psychology, Syracuse University, Syracuse, NY

Annette L. Stanton, PhD, Department of Psychology, University of Kansas, Lawrence

Tina M. Tojek, MA, Department of Psychology, Wayne State University, Detroit, MI

Philip Ullrich, MA, Department of Psychology, University of Iowa, Iowa City

Jean-Pierre van de Ven, MA, Department of Clinical Psychology, University of Amsterdam, The Netherlands

I

INTRODUCTION

1

THE WRITING CURE: AN OVERVIEW

STEPHEN J. LEPORE AND JOSHUA M. SMYTH

Primitive cuneiform signs impressed on clay tablets by Sumerians 5,000 years ago were the precursors to one of humankind's most potent tools for expressing meaning: the written word. Throughout history, writing has had a profound influence on the feelings, thoughts, and behaviors of individuals and entire societies. The effects have not always been desirable, but there is no disputing that writing has permeated and shaped every sphere of private and public life, be it spiritual, commercial, political, educational, artistic, or vocational. This book examines the power of writing to positively shape, or reshape, human experiences, in the context or aftermath of stressful life experiences. The contributors to this volume pose important questions about whether, when, for whom, and how writing can be used as a therapeutic tool to reduce the harmful effects of stress and trauma on health and well-being.

The application of writing for therapeutic ends seems to have emerged from the psychotherapeutic tradition of using expressive therapies to relieve ailments associated with traumatic experiences (Smyth & Greenberg, 2000). Diverse psychotherapies have at their core techniques that promote identification, exploration, and expression of stress-related thoughts and feelings. Early psychotherapies were based on abreaction theory. In brief, abreaction theory maintained that keeping traumatic experiences out of consciousness had adverse health effects that could be reversed by recovering the original memories of a trauma through techniques such as free association, talking, and releasing the appropriate affect associated with the trauma (Breuer & Freud, 1895/1966). Thus was born the so-called "talking cure."

Other theorists and clinicians extended these early ideas. For instance, Janet (1919) argued that very stressful life experiences can undermine health, but his model emphasized cognitive processes, particularly the cognitive integration of stress-related information. He asserted that memories of stressful events are organized at the perceptual level, as fragmented and disorganized sensations: sounds, images, and feeling states that are similar to, and as distressing as, those accompanying the original event. Janet claimed that transforming perceptual-level memories into cohesive narrative accounts would mitigate the unhealthy effects of traumatic experiences. This work was important for implicating both cognitive and emotional mechanisms in expressive therapies. Several contributors to this volume further elaborate on how cognitive and emotional processes mediate the health effects of writing about stressful experiences.

Interest in the therapeutic effects of writing has risen dramatically over the last few years among researchers, the public, and clinicians. We attribute this surge of interest to several factors. First, there is the tremendous success of the writing intervention pioneered by James Pennebaker and colleagues (Pennebaker, 1989). In Pennebaker's "expressive writing" manipulation, people write several times for about 20–30 minutes on their deepest thoughts and feelings related to a stressful event. This brief intervention often produces highly revealing, and sometimes poignant, personal accounts of stressful life events (see Exhibit 1.1). Findings from numerous experiments suggest that the writing exercises also confer a wide array of benefits, including improved lung functioning in asthma patients and reduced symptoms in rheumatoid arthritis patients (Smyth, Stone, Hurewitz, & Kaell, 1999), reductions in emotional and physical health complaints (Greenberg & Stone, 1992; Lepore, 1997; Pennebaker, Colder, & Sharp, 1990), and enhanced social relationships and role functioning (Lepore & Greenberg, in press; Spera, Buhrfeind, & Pennebaker, 1994).

Second, it may provide the sort of low-cost treatment that many clinicians and health care professionals are seeking in today's environment of health management and strict cost controls. Despite accumulating evidence on the effectiveness of behavioral medicine interventions, barriers to the integration of behavioral and biomedical treatments remain (Friedman, Sobel, Myers, Caudill, & Benson, 1995). Accordingly, the development and validation of inexpensive behavioral treatments is critical, especially as the economic benefits of behavioral medicine treatments in health care have been documented more generally (Friedman et al., 1995).

Third, although individuals often want to discuss stressful experiences

EXHIBIT 1.1
Writing Sample From Mary-Jean Becker, Participant in a Research
Study on the Role of Expressive Writing in Women's Adjustment
to Breast Cancer

I view the diagnosis of breast cancer as an inconvenience in my normally orderly and well-planned life. The positive biopsy results were reported to me two days before the start of the '96–'97 school year. I am a fourth grade teacher who had spent the week before preparing the classroom for the arrival of my new students as well as packing with my only child to send him off to begin his freshman year at State University. I am used to being in control of events in my life; my mind began buzzing with the extent to which I would have to turn responsibilities over to another adult. After discussing options with my surgeon, it was explained to me that the cancer had probably been with me for 8–10 years, so I was safe in postponing the surgery for two weeks, giving me enough time to begin the school year, organize my lesson plans to permit time between surgery and recovery, and to attend a "Meet the Teacher Night" when I could formally present fourth grade curriculum expectations to an auditorium full of some 80 parents.

This night was emotionally difficult for me because I knew about my condition but chose not to share this information with children's parents so as not to alarm them about the possibility of long term or intermittent absences from school. I did not yet know the extent of cancer involvement so I would not have been able to answer long term care questions they might want to ask. I was also upset by some very trivial concerns parents had in light of my life-threatening situation. They were asking things such as what is best to send to school for a birthday treat for their child—cookies, drinks, a cake? One birthday was to be celebrated while I knew I would be away for surgery but I made myself take their concerns seriously and advise them accordingly. Many parents wanted to speak to me about personal concerns for their children: she is shy, he is disorganized, do not place him near this particular child because they do not get along. All of these concerns which were of the most importance to parents began swimming around in my mind as more information to pass on to a substitute in my absence, when all the while I thought about setting priorities in life. Compared to what I was facing, how important was the decision whether to send cookies or cake?

Once it was determined that lumpectomy surgery would take place two weeks after school began, I felt that the medical community was working with me to help me restore order to my life. My husband and I planned on visiting my son at State University for Labor Day weekend. This would take place since it was prior to surgery. A big decision was whether to tell our son about the diagnosis and impending surgery. We decided to say nothing because we did not have any details about the extent of involvement. We did know that the tumor was not considered small. I remember thinking about my son as I was being wheeled into surgery. The last thing they tie onto the cot is a toe tag with the patient's name in case I had died in surgery. Even with that knowledge, I thought it was best to wait to tell him after surgery.

Following surgery on a Monday, my husband and I had planned to attend a State University football game on the following Saturday and to renew our wedding vows on the campus of State University where we had met as students and married twenty five years ago. This had all been planned prior to the diagnosis. During the visit, our son read an excerpt from the Velveteen Rabbit by Margery Williams, a reading that had been a part of our wedding ceremony 25 years before. After the reading and renewal of our vows, during which my husband had tears in his eyes at the "till death do us part" stage, I told our son I had something to talk to him about. I repeated the excerpt from the Velveteen

Exhibit continues

EXHIBIT 1.1   (*Continued*)

Rabbit where the once beautiful rabbit was bald in patches and ragged in the seams because of his long life, as a best loved stuffed animal. The message is that being loved is the most important thing, not how we look after so many years of being loved. I told my son that like the Velveteen Rabbit, I was ragged in the seams, but more ragged in one seam than any other because I had undergone surgery for breast cancer. Then I told him that with chemotherapy, the cure rate was ninety five percent and like the Velveteen Rabbit, for a while I might be bald in patches but that whatever I had to endure was worth going through to save my life. I told him I did not want him to worry or feel that he had to come home often to visit me; life as a college freshman requires an uninterrupted period of adjustment. I explained that we had waited two weeks to explain things to him because if we had told him at first, we would only have had a diagnosis, not a prognosis report which turned out to be very favorable.

I met with an oncologist in late September and expressed my wish to continue teaching if possible. He arranged my treatment schedule so that I could remain in school as much as possible. I again felt that he was helping me gain as much control over my life and priorities as was possible. Fortunately, I have experienced minimal side effects except for hair loss. I bought a beautiful wig and am working nearly every day. I plan to tell parents about my situation during spring conferences. A diagnosis of breast cancer does not mean the end of the world. One can set priorities and go on with life as in the past. I am optimistic about the future but cautious, knowing that cancer can come back. I see the present as the best time of my life and will continue to live in the present. Knowing that our 25th anniversary was approaching, my husband and I had selected a two-carat diamond anniversary band prior to the diagnosis. After learning that I had cancer, I asked what my husband wanted to do about the ring. He said we would just have to pick it up early and he knew I would be wearing it for a very long time.

with others, various factors can limit such discussion. Social constraints, problems in mobility, lack of access to adequate services, or personal inhibitions may greatly reduce the likelihood that a person discusses stressful or traumatic experiences with others (Lepore, Silver, Wortman, & Wayment, 1996; Pennebaker & Harber, 1993). Writing overcomes many of these barriers by providing a method for expressing stress-related thoughts and feelings nearly anywhere and without social repercussions.

Writing about stressful life events and associated confusion and negative emotions is, of course, not new. In addition to drawing on traumatic life experiences as a source of inspiration, poets and novelists for centuries have viewed writing as a way of transforming trauma and healing themselves and others (DeSalvo, 1999). Expressive writing techniques also are not new to the therapeutic community. Ira Progoff (1977) popularized "journaling" as a method of psychic healing decades ago. Today, writing assignments are often given as "homework" in the context of ongoing psychotherapy. Only recently, however, have investigators used controlled, scientific studies to evaluate the therapeutic benefits of writing. As noted above, controlled studies strongly suggest that writing about a stressful experience can confer health benefits. Of course, not all studies show positive effects of writing, and not all persons who write show benefit (cf. Smyth et al., 1999). Some scholars have, in fact, been forthright in their skepticism about the benefits of writing (e.g., Greenlaugh, 1999). It is both appropriate and desirable to maintain some skepticism, especially in an area of research that is relatively new and rapidly expanding. Thus, one important aim in this book is to examine the health effects of writing and to clarify which claims are, and which are not, supported by research.

We have three major goals. Our first goal is to present cutting-edge theory and research on expressive writing and health outcomes. This information advances basic scientific understanding on why expressive writing influences health, what health outcomes it affects, and the conditions under which it is most and least beneficial. Our second goal is to point students and scientists to new avenues of research, by highlighting critical themes and gaps in knowledge. Our third goal is to share how clinicians are beginning to translate basic research findings into practical applications. This information will be helpful to those who are interested in adding expressive writing to their arsenal of therapeutic techniques. Although the book is divided into parts, readers will clearly see links among parts and a great deal of cross-referencing.

WRITING AND ADJUSTMENT TO LIFE STRESSORS: EXAMPLES OF CURRENT RESEARCH

Part II of the book examines the role of expressive writing in physical and emotional recovery from life stressors, invasive medical procedures, and chronic illness. This part of the book introduces readers to both the power and limitations of expressive writing, the potential range of health outcomes influenced by expressive writing, and the important individual differences in response to expressive writing.

The expression and nonexpression of emotion have long been implicated in chronic illnesses, such as heart disease and cancer, and in the quality of life of people living with or recovering from these illnesses and their treatments. Davidson and colleagues (chapter 2) review evidence linking emotional expression to elevated blood pressure, a principal risk factor for cardiovascular disease and death. The authors discuss preliminary findings linking expressive writing to reductions in blood pressure and consider how this intervention might benefit persons with hypertension. They also consider how expressive writing might be useful in combating high blood pressure in persons who have difficulty regulating anger and intrusive thoughts about stressors. This work suggests useful ways for clinicians to identify and intervene with persons at high risk for cardiovascular disease.

Stanton and Danoff-Burg (chapter 3) evaluate the evidence linking emotional expression to health-related quality of life in cancer survivors. They also present results from a novel clinical trial comparing the effects of different kinds of writing exercises on psychological and physical health outcomes in cancer patients. It appears that writing following the instructions used in Pennebaker's (1989) approach, with the emphasis on confronting negative thoughts and emotions, reduced physical symptoms and medical visits for cancer-related morbidity. It is interesting that writing about positive aspects of the cancer experience also resulted in health benefits. These findings are important and relevant to clinicians interested in applying the writing technique. It has been found that the traditional writing instructions, in which writers tend to focus on negative thoughts and emotions, can produce residual, short-term distress. For persons in a state of crisis or with high levels of distress, clinicians might be concerned that expressive writing could exacerbate harm. In such instances, this alternative approach, which enables a person to adjust by focusing on positive aspects of a stressor, might be most beneficial (see also King, chapter 7).

The bulk of research on writing and health focuses on adult populations, but it is clear that children can benefit, too. In addition, schools might be a good venue for administering the intervention. Writing is already part of the core curriculum at any school. However, it is mostly viewed as a tool for assessing learning rather than promoting it. Dauite and Buteau (chapter 4) argue that writing is not just a product of children's inner thought processes, but rather actively shapes children's thoughts. They assert that written narratives influence children's social identity and conflict negotiation strategies in a positive way, thus protecting them from dangerous situations. They support their conclusions using findings from their ongoing research on the use of narratives in violence prevention interventions conducted with New York City school children. This work provides researchers with a novel approach to coding written narratives, and it illustrates how writing can reduce health risks by promoting social–cognitive and social–emotional development.

It is obviously important to know what outcomes are affected by expressive writing, but also, it is critical to know who is most and least likely to benefit from this intervention. Lumley, Tojek, and Macklem (chapter 5) examine individual differences in responses to expressive writing and other expressive therapies. They discuss how individual differences in emotional awareness, comprehension, and expression can moderate the effects of expressive interventions on health outcomes. The benefits of expressive techniques, including expressive writing, have been demonstrated primarily among relatively healthy and psychologically sophisticated persons. Yet, as Lumley and colleagues note, expressive techniques undoubtedly are useful for people who lack emotional awareness, comprehension, and expression skills. Their chapter suggests that individuals may need some degree of emotional awareness and sophistication to benefit from expressive writing tasks.

In summary, the chapters in Part II of the book suggest that expressive writing is being applied in exciting ways to a variety of health problems. It also raises critical questions about boundary conditions and the underlying mechanisms linking expressive writing to health outcomes. These chapters suggest, among other things, that expressive writing can produce benefits without explicitly addressing painful thoughts and memories and that multiple behavioral, psychological, and physiological mechanisms might be at play. The chapters in Part III examine questions about the potential mechanisms of action in greater detail.

EMOTIONAL, COGNITIVE, AND BIOLOGICAL PROCESSES

Part III is designed to stimulate current thought and future investigations into the influences of expressive writing on physical and mental health. Contributors present diverse yet often complementary perspectives and data on mechanisms of adaptation, which involve affective, cognitive, and biological systems. There is abundant evidence that the inhibition of thoughts, feelings, and behavior requires physiological work, which can result in low-level autonomic arousal. Also, it has been noted that such arousal, if persistent over a period of time, can undermine biological mechanisms of adaptation and increase health risks (e.g., McEwen, 1998). Many early researchers on expressive writing assumed that dis-inhibition accounted for most of the effects of expressive writing on health, that is, that the act of no longer inhibiting one's thoughts, feelings, or behaviors reduces arousal and disease risk. Evidence for this explanation, however, is somewhat sparse, thus prompting the search for other pathways through which writing influences health and well-being.

The chapters by Lepore and colleagues (chapter 6) and King (chapter 7) suggest that expressive writing facilitates self-regulation, which, in turn, enhances psychological and physical health. Although both of these chapters examine self-regulation, they emphasize different aspects of the process. The work of Lepore and colleagues is grounded in emotion regulation theory, which has received a great deal of attention by developmental and clinical psychologists. Beginning with the observation that dysregulated emotion—either excessively controlled or excessively uncontrolled emotion—is associated with poorer health outcomes, they argue that expressive writing confers health benefits by regulating extreme emotional responses. They evaluate the evidence linking expressive writing to emotion regulation processes, such as attention, habituation, and cognitive reappraisals, as well as the evidence that these processes can have a positive impact on emotional responses in three channels: subjective, physiological, and behavioral.

King's work, on the other hand, is grounded in cybernetic and control theories, with an emphasis on feedback loops that facilitate maintenance or change in goal pursuit. She argues that writing can be used, among other things, to help individuals to learn about themselves, their priorities, and the meaning of the emotions they experience. Through this process, individuals can adjust their behaviors to maintain goal-driven behaviors or, perhaps, develop new goals around which their life can be centered. Thus, King's work is focused on the self and the role of writing in constructing a positive self (see also Daiute & Buteau, chapter 4). Like Stanton and Danoff-Burg (chapter 3), King's work is original in its positive focus (i.e., possible, positive future selves) and suggests exciting new directions for clinicians interested in applying expressive writing in their practice with their more emotionally fragile patients.

Although much of the work on expressive writing and health tends to focus on symptoms, such as depressive symptoms or upper respiratory illness symptoms, an important aspect of health is one's ability to function effectively in everyday life. Basic aspects of cognitive functioning, such as our ability to perceive, process, and remember information in the environment, are critical to daily role functioning and health. For example, lapses in memory, attention, and judgment can be the cause of serious accidents, influence adherence to medical regimens, and interfere with effective modes of coping with life stress. Klein (chapter 8) presents a detailed analysis of how expressive writing influences underlying cognitive processes, particularly working memory. She presents compelling evidence that stressful life events undermine cognitive processes and that expressive writing can restore these processes. Furthermore, she introduces creative ways to assess underlying cognitive processes. Until now, researchers in this field have been greatly hampered by the challenges of measuring cognitive processes.

In addition to identifying the upstream emotional and cognitive processes that mediate the effects of writing on health, it is important to identify the downstream biological and physiological mediators. Booth and Petrie (chapter 9) and Lutgendorf and Ullrich (chapter 10) tackle the question of whether and how expressive techniques, including expressive writing, influence physiological processes implicated in health and illness. Booth and Petrie review the evidence linking expressive writing to neuroendocrine and immune system functioning, and they argue that writing modifies emotion-based stress responses that influence these systems. They advise readers not to overinterpret current findings, because the clinical significance of observed immune system changes in expressive writing studies is not known. They further caution against reducing the benefits of expressive writing to neuroendocrine or immune processes, because the effects of writing on these processes are likely to be dependent on characteristics of writers and their broader psychosocial milieu.

Lutgendorf and Ullrich demonstrate that characteristics of writers and their writing do indeed play a critical role in the ultimate biological effects of writing. The heart of their chapter focuses on the "experiential model" of disclosure, which is closely aligned with Janet's (1919) theory of trauma and health. They argue that a critical task in recovery from stressful events is the successful cognitive integration of emotions, thoughts, and sensations associated with the stressful event (also see chapters 6 and 12). They provide convincing evidence that *depth of processing*, or the degree to which individuals are able to reexperience stress-related emotions, thoughts, and sensations, is critical for these recovery processes, with greater depth of processing being associated with better psychological and immune system functioning.

In summary, the chapters in this part suggest multiple, intersecting, and interactive pathways linking expressive writing to different health outcomes. Early models that focused on dis-inhibition of trauma-related thoughts and feelings are not adequate to account for the myriad benefits of expressive writing. It is clear that expressive writing modulates activity in emotional, cognitive, and physiological systems, although the precise manner in which it does so, the clinical significance of these various changes, and who is affected in this way have yet to be fully determined. The chapters in this part give us promising leads for understanding how expressive writing influences health and well-being. The ways in which information from the first two parts can be translated into clinical applications are addressed in the next part of the book.

NEW DIRECTIONS AND CLINICAL APPLICATIONS OF EXPRESSIVE WRITING

Part IV presents views on translating basic research findings into practical applications and discusses some novel clinical applications of expressive writing, including writing interventions that are Internet-based or used in conjunction with group therapy. We expect that the next wave of research in this area will very likely head where these investigators have already tread.

Smyth and Catley (chapter 11) begin this part by sensitizing researchers to the need to move from laboratory demonstrations of efficacy to clinical demonstrations of effectiveness. Much of the evidentiary basis of the effects of expressive writing on health consists of highly controlled, laboratory-based experiments, often with healthy college populations. One strength of these studies is that they eliminate many confounding factors that could create spurious results. However, this strength is also a liability, in that it is not clear that the results generalize to the real world, which can constrain, amplify, or otherwise distort the effects of expressive writing on health. New studies are underway, including some reported in this book, that are finding promising results with expressive writing interventions with clinical populations and are identifying the characteristics of persons who are likely to benefit the most and least from expressive writing interventions. More of these studies are needed to determine the true value of this tool.

Other chapters in this part introduce specific ways in which writing can be used to facilitate physical and mental health among patients who are coping with stressful or traumatic life experiences. One approach is to use expressive writing as a primary clinical tool for ameliorating psychological suffering. Lange and colleagues (chapter 12) provide a detailed discussion of their ongoing program of research, The Amsterdam Writing Project, which includes clinical trials of expressive writing interventions and a novel Internet-based approach ("Interapy") for delivering mental health services that was born out of these trials. Similarly, L'Abate and Kern (chapter 13) promote the use of the Internet for delivering mental health services using structured writing assignments called *workbooks*. They argue that their approach has several advantages over face-to-face therapies, including ease of access and low costs to patients. They also discuss some of the potential limitations of using writing and the Internet in this way.

Schwartz and David (chapter 14) discuss the use of writing as an adjuvant to group-based therapies, as opposed to individual-based therapies for persons with a serious illness. Group therapy and support groups are becoming increasingly popular for people coping with traumatic life events, particularly chronic and terminal illnesses. Schwartz and David argue that combining writing with other treatments, such as relaxation therapies, can produce synergistic benefits. In addition to promoting individual growth, they suggest that writing can facilitate group processes by having people share some of their writings within a group. Thus, whereas writing is essentially a private act, it can have strong social influences, some of which reverberate back to the writer, who gets feedback from the audience. Writing also can be used to extend therapeutic processes through "homework" assignments, which may help people to stay mentally engaged in their therapy between group meetings or even between individual therapy sessions.

In summary, this part of the book sets an agenda for clinical research using expressive writing and it shows the exciting and original ways in which writing is being implemented in clinical practice. Some of these applications have not yet been fully validated. As a result, the authors in this part continue to collect data on these approaches, point out the limitations of their findings, and note precautions to observe. At the same time, contributors to this part are eager to provide some relief to individuals who cannot access or do not benefit fully from traditional therapies, and they have had some measured success in doing so.

The book concludes with an epilogue by James Pennebaker, the seminal figure in the recent scientific investigation of the health effects of expressive writing. Pennebaker provides an interesting reflection on both his personal contributions to this field and the evolving theories and new data offered by the contributors to this book. By weaving the findings and basic themes discussed in this book with his own original insights and research findings, he maps a challenging course for future research. He also makes the case for additional, bold explorations into the clinical utility of expressive writing for promoting health and well-being.

REFERENCES

Breuer, J., & Freud, S. (1966). *Studies on hysteria.* New York: Avon Books. (Original work published 1895)

DeSalvo, L. (1999). *Writing as a way of healing: How telling our stories transforms our lives.* San Francisco: Harper.

Friedman, R., Sobel, D., Myers, P., Caudill, M., & Benson, H. (1995). Behavioral medicine, clinical health psychology, and cost offset. *Health Psychology, 14,* 509–518.

Greenberg, M. A., & Stone, A. A. (1992). Emotional disclosure about traumas and its relation to health: Effects of previous disclosure and trauma severity. *Journal of Personality and Social Psychology, 63,* 75–84.

Greenlaugh, T. (1999). Writing as therapy. *British Medical Journal, 319,* 270–271.

Janet, P. (1919). *Les medications psychologiques* [The Medication Psychological] (Vols. 1–3). Paris: Alcan.

Lepore, S. J. (1997). Expressive writing moderates the relation between intrusive thoughts and depressive symptoms. *Journal of Personality and Social Psychology, 7,* 1030–1037.

Lepore, S. J., & Greenberg, M. A. (in press). Mending broken hearts: Effects of expressive writing on mood, cognitive processing, social adjustment, and health following a relationship breakup. *Psychology and Health.*

Lepore, S. J., Silver, R. C., Wortman, C. B., & Wayment, H. A. (1996). Social constraints, intrusive thoughts, and depressive symptoms among bereaved mothers. *Journal of Personality and Social Psychology, 70,* 271–282.

McEwen, B. S. (1998). Protective and damaging effects of stress mediators. *New England Journal of Medicine, 338,* 171–179.

Pennebaker, J. W. (1989). Confession, inhibition, and disease. In L. Berkowitz (Ed.), *Advances in experimental social psychology* (Vol. 22, pp. 211–244). New York: Springer-Verlag.

Pennebaker, J. W., Colder, M., & Sharp, L. K. (1990). Accelerating the coping process. *Journal of Personality and Social Psychology, 58,* 528–537.

Pennebaker, J. W., & Harber, K. (1993). A social stage model of collective coping: The Loma Prieta earthquake and the Persian Gulf War. *Journal of Social Issues, 49,* 125–146.

Progoff, I. (1977). *At a journal workshop: The basic text and guide for using the intensive journal process.* New York: Dialogue H.

Smyth, J. M., & Greenberg, M. A. (2000). Scriptotherapy: The effects of writing about traumatic events. In J. Masling & P. Duberstein (Eds.), *Empirical studies in psychoanalytic theories: Vol. 9. Psychoanalytic perspectives on health psychology* (pp. 121–164). Washington, DC: American Psychological Association.

Smyth, J. M., Stone, A. A., Hurewitz, A., & Kaell, A. (1999). Effects of writing about stressful experiences on symptom reduction in patients with asthma or rheumatoid arthritis. *Journal of the American Medical Association, 281,* 1304–1329.

Spera, S., Buhrfeind, E., & Pennebaker, J. W. (1994). Expressive writing and job loss. *Academy of Management Journal, 37,* 722–733.

II

WRITING AND ADJUSTING TO LIFE STRESSORS: EXAMPLES OF CURRENT RESEARCH

2

EXPRESSIVE WRITING AND BLOOD PRESSURE

KARINA DAVIDSON, AMY R. SCHWARTZ, DAVID SHEFFIELD,
RONALD S. MCCORD, STEPHEN J. LEPORE, AND WILLIAM GERIN

The role of emotional expression in health has been debated since the advent of psychosomatic medicine. Some have argued (Alexander, 1950) that emotional expression improves health by alleviating underlying psychological tensions, whereas others have argued that it undermines health by increasing social strains and discord in one's self-concept. The issues are more complex than this, and new questions about the relation between emotional expression and health have arisen because of provocative findings linking "expressive writing" to health (Pennebaker, 1989; Smyth & Pennebaker, 2001). In the expressive writing intervention, individuals are asked to write about personally upsetting experiences for 20 to 30 minutes each day for several days. In randomized controlled trials, the intervention has been found to produce positive effects on diverse aspects of physical and mental health, including reductions in health center visits, self-reported illness, and depressive symptoms and improvements in immune system and role functioning (Smyth, 1998).

This research was partially supported by National Institutes of Health Grants HL04458, HL47540, and HL65720.

In this chapter, we do not consider the myriad pathways through which expressive writing influences diverse physical and mental health outcomes. Instead, we focus on two questions: How might expressive writing influence blood pressure? Can expressive writing be used to control blood pressure in patients with hypertension? Blood pressure problems present a significant health threat, so it is critical to develop ways to effectively control blood pressure—especially noninvasive, easy-to-administer interventions that patients are likely to use. Chronically high blood pressure, or *hypertension*, is the principle risk factor for cardiovascular disease, accounts for 10% of deaths in the United States, and has an age-adjusted prevalence of 23% for Caucasians and 37% for African Americans (American Heart Association, 1999). High blood pressure increases the risk of atherosclerosis, left-ventricular hypertrophy, cardiovascular disease, and stroke (The Joint National Committee on Prevention, Detection, Evaluation, and Treatment of High Blood Pressure, 1997).

There are few direct tests of the effects of expressive writing on blood pressure. However, strong theoretical reasons for expecting beneficial effects of expressive writing on blood pressure are available, largely derived from the general literature on emotional expression and blood pressure. Thus, we begin our chapter with an overview of the literature linking emotional expression to blood pressure. We then discuss cognitive and emotional processes that link emotional expression to blood pressure. We next present preliminary data relating expressive writing to reductions in blood pressure. Finally, we discuss the potential benefits of expressive writing for patients with high blood pressure and future research directions.

NONEXPRESSION OF EMOTION AND ELEVATED BLOOD PRESSURE: A HISTORICAL OVERVIEW

Alexander (1939, 1950) introduced the psychosomatic hypothesis by proposing that blocking the experience or expression of specific emotions caused specific health difficulties. He suggested that chronic inhibition of rage would lead to chronic blood pressure elevation. How to test such a hypothesis, however, has not been clear, because of conceptual fuzziness about the construct of emotion inhibition. At times, Alexander's writings suggested that the inhibition of negative emotions was an unconscious process (also see Dunbar, 1935; Wolff, 1937). This raises obvious measurement problems. Theorists and researchers have dealt with the consciousness problem by asserting that emotional inhibition is never completely successful, and so identifiable signs of inhibition always exist, such as tension in the body, slips of the tongue, and so on. On self-report scales, emotionally inhibited persons may report little anger, anxiety, or hostility and may be indistinguishable from those persons who genuinely experience small amounts of these negative emotions (see Shedler, Mayman, & Manis, 1993, for further discussion). However, those who are unconsciously inhibiting the negative emotions would have elevated blood pressure compared to persons who genuinely do not have negative emotions.

Alexander's early writings (1939, 1950) also suggested that knowingly blocking or withholding negative emotions could lead to disease. In this case, inhibiting the expression (as opposed to the experience) of negative emotions leads to disease. This type of inhibition can be self-reported. Consequently, researchers adopting this perspective have sought to identify persons who can report when they have experienced aversive events and emotional states and also persons who knowingly inhibit expression of their emotions.

Although these two interpretations of emotion inhibition exist within the original psychosomatic formulations of the relation of the nonexpression of emotion to hypertension, they are not clearly differentiated. Indeed, at certain points it appears that Alexander (1939) used the terms *emotion experience* and *emotion expression* interchangeably. Given the variants of meanings previously associated with the term *emotion inhibition* and the measurement difficulty in ascertaining whether inhibition is conscious or unconscious, we use the term *nonexpression of emotion* to indicate that emotion is not being expressed (whether consciously or unconsciously). Furthermore, consideration of causes of hypertension in early psychosomatic writings mainly focused on emotional processes and did not refer to cognitive processes to any great extent. Although this is the history of the field, later studies and conceptualizations suggest that cognitive content, load, and intrusions of cognitions are very likely also involved in the ultimate model of how expressive writing may affect hypertension.

ANGER EXPRESSION, REGULATION, AND BLOOD PRESSURE

Much of the research on the nonexpression of emotion and blood pressure has focused on anger expression. Does keeping one's anger in, or letting that anger emerge, have a positive effect on blood pressure? Again, this formulation of the question has turned out to be overly simplistic. Most studies of the effect of nonexpression of emotion on blood pressure have focused on the anger–hostility–aggression complex, which, for simplicity, we refer to here as *anger*. Originally, anger expression was conceptualized as a unidimensional construct: Persons could be classified as expressing their anger (anger-out) or as not expressing their anger (anger-in; Funkenstein, King, & Drolette, 1954). However, Spielberger and colleagues (1985) created a self-report measure of anger expression and found that anger-in and anger-out items comprised two separate and independent factors rather than a single dimension.

Despite other ambiguities in his writings, Alexander (1950) clearly predicted that anger expression would lead to lower resting blood pressure levels and that the nonexpression of anger would promote hypertension. However, in the contemporary literature two seemingly contradictory hypotheses have emerged. In the original psychosomatic hypothesis (the *psychosomatic model*), anger-in is conceptualized as health damaging because it causes short, heightened, states of autonomic arousal, which, over time, are hypothesized to lead to increased resting blood pressure. A prediction of this model is that expression of anger would reduce blood pressure. However, a contrasting perspective is embodied in the *hostility–aggression model*, which posits that the outward expression of anger is detrimental to health because it causes acute, heightened autonomic arousal. This model predicts that repeated anger expression and exposure to associated increases in arousal would, over time, lead to an upward drift in resting blood pressure. The second model also suggests that anger expression may increase social conflict and erode social support—factors that could further increase blood pressure. Thus, both the psychosomatic and the hostility–aggression models suggest that frequent, acute episodes of heightened autonomic arousal can lead to elevated resting blood pressure (Davidson, 1996).

In a meta-analytic review, Suls, Wan, and Costa (1995) examined the relation between resting blood pressure and measures of anger and anger expression. In random samples, anger-out, as measured by the Spielberger inventory (Spielberger et al., 1985), was significantly related to lower resting systolic blood pressure, and anger-in, assessed with the Spielberger and another self-report measure by Goldstein, Edelberg, Meier, and Davis (1988), was significantly related to higher resting systolic and diastolic blood pressure. In a later meta-analytic review, Jorgensen, Johnson, Kolodziej, and Schreer (1996) confirmed the finding that the nonexpression of anger was associated with higher resting blood pressure and that anger expression was related to lower resting blood pressure. Overall, the meta-analytic reviews support the psychosomatic model and not the hostility–aggression model. However, some investigators have found a positive relation between anger expression (anger-out) and high blood pressure (Linden & Lamensdorf, 1990), and they have argued that the relation between anger expression and blood pressure is not linear. The social conflict model (Linden & Feuerstein, 1981) posits that adaptive anger expression lies somewhere between aggression and passivity. The model also suggests that the relation between anger expression and blood pressure is best described as a U-shaped curve: Individuals with extreme anger-out tendencies, as well as those exhibiting excessive anger-in behavior, are thought to generate social or psychological conflict as a consequence, and they may be at the greatest risk for developing high blood pressure (Linden & Lamensdorf, 1990). Persons who fall somewhere between the two extreme styles of anger expression tend to have the lowest blood pressures.

Persons who are not extreme on the anger-in or the anger-out dimensions have been described as *reflective anger copers* (Gentry, Chesney, Gary, Hall, & Harburg, 1982; Harburg, Blakelock, & Roeper, 1979), and several studies have provided support for the social conflict model (Davidson, MacGregor, Stuhr, Dixon, & MacLean, 2000; Everson et al., 1999). For example, Everson and her colleagues reported hypertension incidence as a function of anger expression style in a large community sample, and they found the lowest rates among reflective anger copers. Davidson and her colleagues have described an anger expression style called *constructive anger behavior–verbal* (CAB–V), which is similar to reflective anger coping. They found that persons who tend to express their anger, but in a constructive and reflective manner, have lower resting blood pressure levels. Thus, there is some evidence that moderate anger expression may be the most beneficial for blood pressure levels, although clearly more research is needed in this area. We further speculate: If expressive writing operates on health variables through emotion regulation, instead of or in addition to emotion expression, then expressive writing, by increasing emotion regulation, may lead to more constructive, or reflective, anger coping, which in turn may lead to less autonomic arousal, and ultimately, lower blood pressure (see Figure 2.1). For a discussion of the effects of expressive writing on emotion regulation, see chapter 6, this volume.

COGNITIVE PROCESSES AND BLOOD PRESSURE

As noted above, early psychosomatic models of hypertension emphasized emotional processes and virtually ignored cognitive processes. There is reason to believe, however, that cognitive processes, particularly those related to stressful experiences, can influence blood pressure. Researchers have hypothesized that cognitive processes, such as the persistence of trauma-related thoughts, memories, and images, or attempts to avoid such

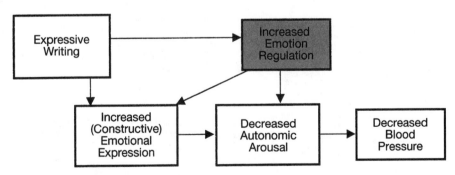

Figure 2.1. Emotion Regulation Mediator added to the Expressive Writing and Blood Pressure Model.

intrusive thoughts, can result in increased arousal, psychological distress, and illness (e.g., Creamer, Burgess, & Pattison, 1992; Lepore, Silver, Wortman, & Wayment, 1996). Intrusive thoughts about emotion-provoking experiences are presumed to result from incomplete or unsuccessful cognitive integration of stressful events (e.g., Lepore, 1997; Lepore et al., 2000). We speculate further that in addition to thought intrusion, the inability to understand a personal tragedy, or lack of cognitive integration, could increase anger and associated arousal, and eventually blood pressure.

There is evidence that cognitive integration is related to intrusive thoughts and that intrusive thoughts are related to health risks, including elevations in blood pressure (see Figure 2.2). For example, DiSavino and colleagues (1992) analyzed victims' trauma-related narratives and found that increasing narrative organization over time was associated with decreased intrusive thoughts and psychological distress. In another study, investigators found that getting people to recall an anger-provoking event increased their negative mood and blood pressure and that having intrusive thoughts about the event impeded blood pressure recovery (Schwartz et al., 2000). The investigators showed that providing people with some distraction after an anger-recall task helped them to reduce their intrusive thoughts about the anger-provoking event and subsequently to return more quickly to their resting level of blood pressure. The investigators also found that persons who were prone to ruminate (*trait ruminators*) had the greatest delays in blood pressure recovery in the no distraction condition. Taken together, these findings suggest that intrusive thoughts reflect unsuccessful cognitive integration of stressful experiences, can cause elevations in blood pressure, and can sustain blood pressure elevations in the absence of the original triggering event.

The findings by Schwartz and colleagues (2000) suggest that distraction is an effective technique for reducing intrusive thoughts and, thereby, attenuating the effects of such thoughts on blood pressure. However, some caution must be used in interpreting these results or in translating them

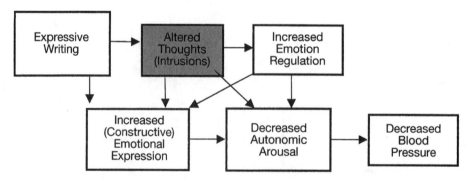

Figure 2.2. Thought Intrusion Mediator added to the Expressive Writing and Blood Pressure Model.

into practice. Although distraction might help persons to rid themselves of intrusive thoughts in the short term, it appears that actively trying to inhibit certain thoughts can have the paradoxical effect of exacerbating those thoughts at a later point in time (Wegner, Schneider, Carter, & White, 1987). In addition to distraction, expressive techniques can be beneficial to persons experiencing stress-related intrusive thoughts. Lepore, Ragan, and Jones (2000) found that when persons were encouraged to talk about a stressful film, they experienced fewer intrusive thoughts about the film and less psychological stress when they were re-exposed to the film. Their analyses suggested that the reduction of intrusive thoughts mediated the positive effects of verbal expression on psychological stress. Other investigators (see chapters 8 and 12, this volume) have found that writing about personal traumas also results in fewer trauma-related intrusive thoughts. However, Lepore (1997) found that writing about impending professional school examinations (e.g., MCAT, LSAT, GRE) did not reduce the frequency of intrusive thoughts but that it did reduce the association between intrusive thoughts and depressive symptoms (see also Lepore & Greenberg, in press). Thus, it is possible that expressive techniques, including expressive writing, can reduce both the frequency and the impact of intrusive thoughts on psychological and physiological outcomes. To the extent that expressive techniques facilitate cognitive integration, they should reduce the frequency of intrusive thoughts; to the extent that these techniques promote habituation to stressful stimuli, they should attenuate the impact of intrusive thoughts on many outcomes (see Lepore, 1997; Lepore et al., 2000). However, little research has been conducted in this area.

A CLINICAL FRAMEWORK FOR STUDYING EXPRESSIVE WRITING AND BLOOD PRESSURE

We have discussed a variety of ways that emotional expression, particularly the expression of negative emotions and anger associated with stressful life experiences, could influence blood pressure. From this review, we hypothesize that expressive writing should influence blood pressure, particularly for persons who are under stress and have not adequately cognitively integrated their stressful experience. Expressive writing could reduce blood pressure by helping persons to moderate their expression of negative emotions, particularly anger. To the extent that expressive writing helps persons to eliminate extreme levels of anger inhibition or expression (or both), this decrease in anger levels should reduce blood pressure in people prone to anger. It also could reduce blood pressure indirectly by helping persons to maintain positive, supportive social relationships and to avoid social conflicts. That is, to the extent that writing helps persons to decrease their anger experience and thereby moderate their anger expression, it could improve their social interactions. In addition to emotion regulation functions, we hypothesize that expressive writing might reduce blood pressure by diminishing the frequency or impact of stress-related cognitions, or intrusive thoughts. A decrease in intrusive cognitions might lead to improved anger control and more constructive emotional expression. Finally, any or all of these alterations may lead to less chronic autonomic arousal and so have a favorable impact on blood pressure. However, as can be seen by this review, there are currently far more mechanisms and speculations than there are studies to support them.

We turn now to the basic question that must be addressed in this research line: Does expressive writing affect blood pressure? Only one study has addressed this question. Crow, Pennebaker, and King (2001) randomly assigned 52 participants (29 women, 23 men; mean age 41 years) to an expressive writing or a control condition. Two casual blood pressure readings were taken using an electronic home monitor (Omron Healthcare, Inc., Vernon Hills, IL), and the two readings were averaged to provide a baseline measure. Participants were then assigned to a condition: Those in the expressive writing condition were asked to write about some issues in their lives, which could include traumatic events; those in the control condition were asked to write about a trivial, nonemotional topic. Participants wrote on their respective topics for 20 minutes, on three consecutive days, and then returned to the laboratory approximately 6 weeks after the final writing day. Again, two blood pressure measurements were taken and averaged to comprise the postintervention measure.

On average, the 26 participants assigned to the expressive writing condition experienced a drop in both systolic and diastolic pressure of almost 3 mm Hg (systolic pressure went from 127.9 to 125.2; diastolic dropped from 81.8 to 78.6). The overall group differences were somewhat stronger (a difference of 5.6 mm Hg systolic and of 3.4 mm Hg diastolic); however, the differences were partly due to an unanticipated increase in both systolic and diastolic pressure in the control condition. The difference in diastolic blood pressure was significant ($p < .05$), but the difference in systolic blood pressure was only marginally significant ($p < .07$). However, even small reductions in blood pressure can reduce the risk for future events such as myocardial infarction and stroke (American Heart Association, 1999).

Crowe and colleagues' findings are encouraging but must be regarded as preliminary. The study was intended to be a pilot test, and therefore the sample size was small, and ordinarily one would not expect an increase in blood pressure in the control participants during a short time span. In addition to replicating these findings, it is important to examine the effects of expressive writing on persons who have hypertension or hypertension risk factors. We propose that mildly hypertensive patients with poorly controlled blood pressure are a viable population in which to examine the effects of expressive writing on blood pressure. Several studies have demonstrated that behavioral interventions may lower resting blood pressure in individuals with poorly controlled mild hypertension (Linden & Chambers, 1994). In contrast, a population of well-controlled hypertensive patients (diastolic pressure below 90) and normotensives may have "floor" effects and may therefore be expected to show much smaller changes. Thus, the small reductions in blood pressure reported by Crowe and colleagues may underestimate the potential blood pressure reducing effects that might be found in individuals with mild hypertension.

Another reason that hypertensive patients in particular might benefit from the expressive writing intervention concerns the putative personality characteristics of the hypertensive population that may distinguish it from the normotensive population. Many researchers have hypothesized that persons who are prone to certain stable trait characteristics are at greater risk to develop hypertension (Harburg, Julius, McGinn, McLeod, & Hoobler, 1964). Researchers in this area have suggested that individuals with hypertension may score high on "submissiveness," which may reflect the tendency to view past and future events as uncontrollable. Such a perception could lead to a "threat" perception, more passive coping, and, physiologically, more autonomic arousal. Expressive writing might be helpful in reducing perceived threat and feelings of helplessness (Greenberg, Wortman, & Stone, 1996). Furthermore, some persons including those with the "hypertensive personality" are thought to be more "repressive" and more likely to withdraw from social interactions when stressed than those without this personality disorder (Repetti, 1992). For example, repressive persons tend to be less emotionally expressive and engage in fewer self-disclosure behaviors that are likely to elicit reciprocation (King & Emmons, 1990) and are more likely to be concerned about social approval, thus delaying and reducing the chances of successful support recruitment (Repetti, 1992). So, when repression is socially motivated, writing might be especially beneficial because it minimizes social processes such as the need for approval.

Written expression might serve an important social function by providing an outlet for cognitive restructuring and emotional expression without social repercussions. In this transactional model, persons who engage in extreme inhibition or expression of emotions are likely to actively structure their worlds in ways that decrease both the frequency and the intensity of their social interactions so as to avoid destructive emotion outbursts (Smith, 1994, 1995). This may make expressive writing ideal for these specific persons, because it might allow them to preserve social relationships (Zuroff & Mongrain, 1987) and reduce negative, stressful social interactions. Thus, hostile individuals, for example, might be able to write and thereby avoid venting to others who might, in turn, react negatively toward them (Smith & Christensen, 1992). Thus, by helping patients regulate negative emotions (like anger) outside of their social relationships, expressive writing might help reduce stressful interactions and preserve social relationships.

CONCLUSION: FUTURE DIRECTIONS

It is interesting that the very origins of psychosomatic medicine began with the hypothesis that expressing one's deepest thoughts and emotions would lower one's blood pressure. It is part of the interesting story of behavioral science that we have come full circle, for the original notions, rooted in Freud's core psychoanalytic theories (Alexander, 1950), fell into disfavor. Although speculations on the pathways by which expressive writing affects psychological and physiological processes have changed, the basic intuitions that exercised so much influence over the origins of the field of psychosomatic medicine remain viable, and it is to the field's credit that it has not discarded them wholly but has become flexible in testing them.

At present, it is worthwhile to pursue the research on the effects of expressive writing on blood pressure. Although there is little direct evidence on the effects of the intervention on resting blood pressure, the underlying models and pathways have some indirect support, and the pilot data by Crow et al. (2001), though preliminary, are encouraging. Hypertension remains a huge public health problem in the United States, with vast costs in terms of mortality, morbidity, and dollars. The expressive writing intervention may be a cost-effective means of dealing with this problem. What direction, then, should future studies in this area take?

We concur with the recommendations of Suls and colleagues (1995) that in future studies blood pressure should be measured on multiple occasions, and, possibly, with ambulatory blood pressure technology. This is crucial, because blood pressure measured in the physician's office, or taken only once or twice by a laboratory assistant, might be a poor indicator of the person's true resting blood pressure level. We further recommend that measures of alternative mechanisms be considered; it is certainly possible that, if indeed the intervention does have positive effects on blood pressure, it might do so through multiple pathways. It also is important to examine physiological mechanisms in more minute detail. For instance, it is possible to study noninvasively the underlying hemodynamics that produce changes in blood pressure. Investigators can differentiate the source of blood pressure changes, which may stem from more central mechanisms (e.g., cardiac output, which is the amount of blood being ejected from the heart each minute) or from more peripheral mechanisms (such as total peripheral resistance, a measure of peripheral vasoconstriction). One reason to incorporate these techniques in expressive writing studies is that different mechanisms of action appear to be associated with different underlying psychological states. At least one of these measures, total peripheral resistance, has been associated with emotional expression (Mendes, Seery, Blascovitch, & Reis, 1999). Next, the expressive writing and blood pressure will suffer from some of the same limitations as other areas of behavioral medicine. First, blood pressure reactivity—one of the underlying mechanisms posited here—has not been shown definitively to lead to higher levels of resting blood pressure (Pickering & Gerin, 1990). Next, without clear evidence that expressive writing has a clinically significant impact on blood pressure, we must question the utility of ascertaining the mechanisms by which expressive writing might affect blood pressure. Finally, we suggest that researchers attempt to identify subgroups of persons for whom the intervention may be more or less successful and that these attempts be based on validated individual differences, which use behavioral observation as well as paper-and-pencil instruments as a means of assessment.

REFERENCES

Alexander, F. (1939). Emotional factors in essential hypertension. *Psychosomatic Medicine, 1*, 173–179.

Alexander, F. (1950). *Psychosomatic medicine. Its principles and applications.* New York: Norton.

American Heart Association. (1999). *2000 Heart and stroke statistical update.* Dallas, TX: Author.

Creamer, M., Burgess, P., & Pattison, P. (1992). Reaction to trauma: A cognitive processing model. *Journal of Abnormal Psychology, 101*, 452–459.

Crow, D. M., Pennebaker, J. W., & King, L. A. (2001). *Effects of writing about stress in an organization setting.* Manuscript submitted for publication.

Davidson, K. W. (1996). Self- and expert-reported emotion inhibition: On the utility of both data sources. *Journal of Research in Personality, 30*, 535–549.

Davidson, K. W., MacGregor, M. W., Stuhr, J., Dixon, K., & MacLean, D. (2000). Constructive anger verbal behavior predicts blood pressure in a population-based sample. *Health Psychology, 19*, 55–64.

DiSavino, P., Turk, E., Massie, E., Riggs, D., Penkower, D., Molnar, C., & Foa, E. (1992, November). *The content of traumatic memories: Evaluating treatment efficacy by analysis of verbatim descriptions of the rape scene.* Paper presented at the 27th annual meeting of the Association for the Advancement of Behavior Therapy, Atlanta, GA.

Dunbar, H. F. (1935). *Emotions and bodily changes. A survey of literature on psychosomatic interrelationships, 1920–1933.* New York: Columbia University Press.

Everson, S. A., Kaplan, G. A., Goldberg, D. E., Lakka, T. A., Sivenius, J., & Salonen, J. T. (1999). Anger expression and incident stroke: Prospective evidence from the Kuopio ischemic heart disease study. *Stroke, 30*, 523–528.

Funkenstein, D. H., King, S. H., & Drolette, M. (1954). The direction of anger during a laboratory stress-inducing situation. *Psychosomatic Medicine, 16,* 404–413.

Gentry, W. D., Chesney, A. P., Gary, H. E., Jr., Hall, R. P., & Harburg, E. (1982). Habitual anger-coping styles: I. Effect on mean blood pressure and risk for essential hypertension. *Psychosomatic Medicine, 44,* 195–202.

Goldstein, H. S., Edelberg, R., Meier, C. F., & Davis, L. (1988). Relationship of resting blood pressure and heart rate to experienced anger and expressed anger. *Psychosomatic Medicine, 50,* 321–329.

Greenberg, M. A., Wortman, C. B., & Stone, A. A. (1996). Emotional expression and physical health: Revising traumatic memories or fostering self-regulation. *Journal of Personality and Social Psychology, 71,* 588–602.

Harburg, E., Blakelock, E. H., & Roeper, P. J. (1979). Resentful and reflective coping with arbitrary authority and blood pressure: Detroit. *Psychosomatic Medicine, 41,* 189–202.

Harburg, E., Julius, S., McGinn, N. F., McLeod, J., & Hoobler, S. W. (1964). Personality traits and behavioral patterns associated with systolic blood pressure levels in college males. *Journal of Chronic Diseases, 17,* 405–414.

Jorgensen, R. S., Johnson, B. T., Kolodziej, M. E., & Schreer, G. E. (1996). Elevated blood pressure and personality: A meta-analytic review. *Psychological Bulletin, 120,* 293–320.

King, L. A., & Emmons, R. A. (1990). Conflict over emotional expression: Psychological and physical correlates. *Journal of Personality and Social Psychology, 58,* 864–877.

Lepore, S. J. (1997). Expressive writing moderates the relation between intrusive thoughts and depressive symptoms. *Journal of Personality and Social Psychology, 73,* 1030–1037.

Lepore, S. J., & Greenberg, M. A. (in press). Mending broken hearts: Effects of expressive writing on mood, cognitive processing, social adjustment, and health following a relationship breakup. *Psychology and Health.*

Lepore, S. J., Ragan, J. D., & Jones, S. (2000). Talking facilitates cognitive–emotional processes of adaptation to an acute stressor. *Journal of Personality and Social Psychology, 78,* 499–508.

Lepore, S. J., Silver, R. C., Wortman, C. B., & Wayment, H. A. (1996). Social constraints, intrusive thoughts, and depressive symptoms among bereaved mothers. *Journal of Personality and Social Psychology, 70,* 271–282.

Linden, W., & Chambers, L. A. (1994). Clinical effectiveness of non-drug therapies for hypertension: A meta-analysis. *Annals of Behavioral Medicine, 16,* 35–45.

Linden, W., & Feuerstein, M. (1981). Essential hypertension and social coping behavior. *Journal of Human Stress, 7,* 28–34.

Linden, W., & Feuerstein, M. (1993). Essential hypertension and social coping behavior. *Journal of Human Stress, 9,* 22–31.

Linden, W., & Lamensdorf, A. M. (1990). Hostile affect and casual blood pressure. *Psychology and Health, 4,* 343–349.

Mendes, W. B., Seery, M. D., Blascovitch, J., & Reis, H. (1999, October). *Emotional expression and suppression as challenge and threat.* Abstract presented at the 39th annual meeting of the Society for Psychophysiological Research. Grenada, Spain.

Pennebaker, J. W. (1989). Confession, inhibition, and disease. In L. Berkowitz (Ed.), *Advances in experimental and social psychology* (Vol. 22, pp. 211–244). Orlando, FL: Academic Press.

Pickering, T. G., & Gerin, W. (1990). Cardiovascular reactivity in the laboratory and the role of behavioral factors in hypertension: A critical review. *Annals of Behavioral Medicine, 12,* 3–16.

Repetti, R. L. (1992). Social withdrawal as a short-term coping response to daily stressors. In H. Friedman (Ed.), *Hostility, coping, and health* (pp. 151–165). Washington, DC: American Psychological Association.

Schwartz, A. R., Gerin, W., Christenfeld, N., Glynn, L., Davidson, K. W., & Pickering, T. G. (2000). Effects of an anger-recall task on poststress rumination and blood pressure recovery in men and women. *Psychophysiology, 37*(Suppl. 1), S12–S13.

Shedler, J., Mayman, M., & Manis, M. (1993). The illusion of mental health. *American Psychologist, 48,* 1117–1131.

Smith, T. W. (1994). Concepts and methods in the study of anger, hostility, and health. In A. W. Siegman & T. W. Smith (Eds.), *Anger, hostility, and the heart* (pp. 23–42). Hillsdale, NJ: Erlbaum.

Smith, T. W. (1995). Assessment and modification of coronary-prone behavior: A transactional view of the person in social context. In A. Goreczny (Ed.), *Handbook of health and rehabilitation psychology* (pp. 197–217). New York: Plenum Press.

Smith, T. W., & Christensen, A. J. (1992). Hostility, health, and social contexts. In H. S. Friedman (Ed.), *Hostility, coping, and health* (pp. 33–48). Washington, DC: American Psychological Association.

Smyth, J. M. (1998). Written emotional expression: Effect sizes, outcome types, and moderating variables. *Journal of Consulting and Clinical Psychology, 66,* 174–184.

Smyth, J. M., & Pennebaker, J. W. (2001). What are the health effects of disclosure? In A. Baum, T. A. Revenson, & J. E. Singer (Eds.), *Handbook of health psychology* (pp. 339–348). Hillsdale, NJ: Erlbaum.

Spielberger, C. D., Johnson, E. H., Russell, S. F., Crane, R. J., Jacobs, G. A., & Worden, T. J. (1985). The experience and expression of anger: Construction and validation of an anger expression scale. In M. A. Chesney & R. H. Rosenman (Eds.), *Anger and hostility in cardiovascular and behavioral disorders* (pp. 5–30). New York: Hemisphere.

Suls, J., Wan, C. K., & Costa, P. T., Jr. (1995). Relationship of trait anger to resting blood pressure: A meta-analysis. *Health Psychology, 14,* 444–456.

The Joint National Committee on Prevention, Detection, Evaluation, and Treatment of High Blood Pressure. (1997). The sixth report of the Joint National Committee on Prevention, Detection, Evaluation, and Treatment of High Blood Pressure. *Archives of Internal Medicine, 157,* 2413–2446.

Wegner, D. M., Schneider, D. J., Carter, S. R., & White, T. L. (1987). Paradoxical effects of thought suppression. *Journal of Personality and Social Psychology, 53,* 5–13.

Wolff, H. G. (1937). Personality features and reactions of subjects with migraine. *Archives of Neurology and Psychiatry, 37,* 895–921.

Zuroff, D. C., & Mongrain, M. (1987). Dependency and self-criticism: Vulnerability factors for depressive affective states. *Journal of Abnormal Psychology, 96,* 14–22.

3

EMOTIONAL EXPRESSION, EXPRESSIVE WRITING, AND CANCER

ANNETTE L. STANTON AND SHARON DANOFF-BURG

"Until cancer, 'stoic' used to be my middle name. Now I've realized how important it is to acknowledge to myself and to others my fears, hopes, sadnesses."

* * *

"A friend of mine who had cancer could hardly say the word. It's so much easier to just talk about what you're up against and how you feel. When I need to have a good cry, I feel better afterward, and I can take up the fight again."

These sentiments, expressed by our research participants, highlight the importance of expressive disclosure in the adjustment process for some women diagnosed with cancer. Such salutary consequences are consistent with positive effects well documented in the literature on experimentally induced written emotional expression (Pennebaker, 1993). In a meta-analysis of 13 studies of written expressive disclosure, Smyth (1998) obtained an overall effect size of .47, representing an improvement of 23% in experimental groups compared with controls. Expressive writing produced significant beneficial effects on self-reported health, psychological well-being, physiological indices (e.g., immune function), and general functioning (e.g., grade point average, reemployment after layoff). With notable exceptions, participants in these studies were college students in sound physical and psychological health.

Does expressive disclosure carry similar benefits for those who are undergoing health-related adversity? Our primary goal is to address this question, with particular attention to the role of emotional expression and processing in adaptation to cancer. Because published studies on written expressive disclosure in medical populations are rare, we broaden our focus to examine the role of emotional expression in cancer patients as evidenced through other methods, including correlational studies and psychological intervention trials. We go on to describe findings on written emotional disclosure in medical populations in general and in women with breast cancer specifically. We conclude with directions for research and application.

EMOTIONAL EXPRESSION AND CANCER: EVIDENCE FROM CORRELATIONAL RESEARCH

Researchers have posed two broad questions relevant to emotional expression and cancer. First, does emotional expression play a role in the initiation or progression of the disease? Second, does emotional expression facilitate or hinder adjustment in those who confront a cancer diagnosis? Although the second question is more pertinent to our goals for this chapter, the first has generated substantial scrutiny, and we briefly devote attention to it.

Emotional (Non)expression in the Initiation and Progression of Cancer

Cancer, a collection of diseases characterized by uncontrolled cell proliferation, may be catalyzed by various endogenous (e.g., genetic) and exogenous (e.g., smoking) factors. A controversial hypothesis is that stable personality dispositions constitute one class of influences on cancer initiation and progression. One attribute that has received considerable attention is emotional expressiveness, such that individuals who are dispositionally nonexpressive are hypothesized to be cancer prone (e.g., the Type C personality, Temoshok & Dreher, 1992). Research methods in this area all involve a comparison of samples with and without cancer (Bleiker & van der Ploeg, 1999). Retrospective studies comparing cancer patients with healthy controls are plagued by the serious limitation of confounding the extant cancer diagnosis with participants' reports of expressiveness. Quasi-prospective studies typically involve examination of individuals referred for definitive diagnosis after detection of a suspicious lesion, with comparison of those who subsequently receive a malignant versus a benign diagnosis. A methodological problem arises in the evidence that the majority of patients who undergo biopsy may be able to identify their ultimate diagnosis accurately (Schwartz & Geyer, 1984), again confounding reaction to potential diagnosis with report of expressiveness. In the methodologically sound prospective design, individuals without a diagnosis of chronic disease are assessed on the personality construct of interest and followed over a period of years to detect differences between those who subsequently do or do not receive a cancer diagnosis.

Reviewers of this literature have come to dramatically different conclusions. Eysenck (1994) concluded that links between suppression of emotion and cancer initiation and progression are strongly supported by research. In contrast, two groups of researchers (Bleiker & van der Ploeg, 1999; Mulder, van der Pompe, Spiegel, Antoni, & de Vries, 1992) have suggested that extant research provides no definitive answer. Garssen and Goodkin (1999) concluded that the evidence regarding suppression of negative emotions is stronger for its role in cancer progression than in initiation.

To our knowledge, only one quantitative review has addressed the link between psychosocial factors and cancer development, and this review was specific to breast cancer (McKenna, Zevon, Corn, & Rounds, 1999). The authors located 46 studies yielding 99 effect sizes in which women diagnosed with cancer were compared with women who received a benign diagnosis or healthy controls. Eight constructs were examined, including denial–repression coping (indicating failure to express emotions). Of the significant effect sizes, that for denial–repression coping (15 studies, of which the assessment occurred before biopsy in 13) was the largest (Hedges's g = .38). Thus, the average woman with breast cancer was more likely to attempt to control unpleasant feelings than were 65% of controls. The fail-safe sample size indicated that 218 studies with negative findings would be required to reduce the relation's significance. Studies of older women and of smaller samples were more likely to yield this relation than were studies of younger women or larger samples. Effects were not influenced by a number of other potential moderators (e.g., participants' and investigators' knowledge of the diagnosis). Other significant effect sizes emerged for separation and loss, stressful life events, and conflict-avoidant personality (although this effect was not robust). Again, most of the studies were quasi-prospective, and we cannot rule out the possibility that women's awareness of their probable diagnosis before biopsy influenced their responses. Furthermore, conceptual clarity for the construct of interest was lacking or not consistent across studies (e.g., definitional problems regarding conscious suppression of emotion vs. presumably unconscious repression).

Methodological and conceptual limitations preclude definitive conclusions from this literature, and even truly prospective studies cannot rule out the possibility that some third variable caused both nonexpressivity and cancer development. However, the McKenna et al. (1999) meta-analysis suggests that the relation is sufficiently robust to warrant additional, methodologically sound investigation and identification of mechanisms for the obtained effects. Such mechanisms for cancer initiation (e.g., chronic physiological activation, immunosuppression, health behaviors such as smoking; Garssen & Goodkin, 1999; Greer & Watson, 1985) may be distinct from those for cancer progression (e.g., nonadherence to treatment). Only through careful, theory-driven (see Andersen, Kiecolt-Glaser, & Glaser, 1994) documentation of mechanisms can a convincing case be advanced for the role of emotional suppression in cancer initiation and progression.

Emotional Expression and Adjustment to Cancer

Correlational research varies in its demonstration of positive or negative relations between emotional expression and adjustment to cancer in accordance with how expression is conceptualized and measured. In a sample of 80 breast cancer patients followed from diagnosis to 6 months after diagnosis, Compas and colleagues (1999) found that emotional ventilation used as a coping strategy was associated with greater distress, when distress at a previous assessment point was controlled statistically (although ventilation assessed at a prior point did not predict change in adjustment across time). However, the measure of emotional ventilation contained items reflecting a cathartic approach involving discharge of negative affect (e.g., "My feelings were overwhelming and they just exploded"). In contrast to the negative effects of cathartic expression, the researchers suggested that "expression of affect in response to a breast cancer that leads to greater regulation and understanding of emotions is likely to be adaptive" (p. 202).

When assessed with measures that are unconfounded with distress and that represent more intentionally elected strategies, emotional expression has predicted more positive adjustment in individuals with cancer. For example, Phipps and Mulhern (1995) found that parent-perceived family expressiveness predicted better adjustment across time in children who underwent bone marrow transplant (primarily for leukemia). In a longitudinal study of 92 women followed from completion of primary medical treatment for breast cancer through 3 months (Stanton, Danoff-Burg, et al., 2000), we were interested in the influence of coping through emotional approach, which involves purposive emotional processing and expression under stressful conditions (Stanton, Kirk, Cameron, & Danoff-Burg, 2000), on women's adjustment to the disease. We conceptualize *emotional processing* as active, intentional attempts to acknowledge, explore meanings, and come to an understanding of one's emotions and *emotional expression* as active, intentional attempts to express one's emotions regarding a stressor, which may take both intrapersonal (e.g., journal writing) and interpersonal forms (Stanton, Kirk, Cameron, & Danoff-Burg, 2000). We found that women who expressed emotions surrounding cancer at study entry had fewer medical appointments for cancer-related morbidities (e.g., pain), enhanced self-perceived physical health and vigor, and decreased distress during the subsequent 3 months relative to less expressive women. These relations held when age, other coping strategy scores (e.g., seeking social support), and initial values on dependent variables were controlled statistically. Emotionally expressive coping also was related to improved quality of life for women who viewed their social contexts as highly receptive.

In contrast with positive findings regarding coping through emotional expression, coping through emotional processing was associated only with one dependent variable reflecting greater distress over time. The strong and consistent findings for emotional expression relative to emotional processing in this study may reflect the lesser utility of emotional processing as a stressor persists. Women on average had been diagnosed with cancer approximately 6 months before study entry, and high scores on coping through emotional processing may have reflected in part either an inability to come to a satisfactory understanding of their feelings surrounding cancer or rumination, which has been shown to exacerbate distress (e.g., Morrow & Nolen-Hoeksema, 1990). It also is possible that distress is diminished only to the extent that emotional processing is coupled with emotional expression (Stanton, Danoff-Burg, et al., 2000).

Additional analyses suggested that coping through approaching emotion may facilitate goal clarification and pursuit, as revealed by significant mediated and moderated relations of emotionally expressive coping with dispositional hope, a construct involving a sense of goal-directed determination and ability to generate plans to achieve goals (Snyder et al., 1991). For example, through expressing feelings regarding the loss of control prompted by a cancer diagnosis, a woman may begin to distinguish what she can and cannot control in her experience of cancer and her life more generally, to attempt pursuit of attainable goals, and to work toward active acceptance of the less controllable facets of her experience.

Indirect evidence of the utility of emotional expression lies in research regarding the relation of emotional suppression or avoidance more generally with adjustment. In a study of women with metastatic or recurrent breast cancer, Classen, Koopman, Angell, and Spiegel (1996) found that high control of emotional expression was associated with greater distress (see also Watson et al., 1991). Studying emotional expression in men with prostate cancer, Helgeson and Lepore (1997) found that agency, a personality construct involving a positive focus on the self manifested in independence and self-confidence, was related to comfort expressing emotions, which in turn was related to more positive general mental health and cancer-related adjustment (e.g., communication with doctor, intimacy with spouse, sexual interest). On the other hand, unmitigated agency, involving a focus on the self to the exclusion of others, was related to greater difficulty in expressing emotions (e.g., "It is difficult to admit that I am afraid"), which in turn was associated with negative general and cancer-related adjustment. In a study of testicular cancer survivors, Rieker, Edbril, and Garnick (1985) also reported that emotional concealment was related to more pronounced sexual impairment. These three studies suggest a link between emotional suppression and poorer adjustment, with the caveat that their cross-sectional designs preclude causal inference.

Numerous studies of avoidance-oriented coping also provide indirect evidence that strategies geared more toward approaching than avoiding cancer-related cognitions and emotions may confer greater benefit. Although studies with noncancer patient samples suggest that avoidance of emotions may be useful under some conditions (e.g., Bonanno, Znoj, Siddique, & Horowitz, 1999), longitudinal studies (Carver et al., 1993; Stanton & Snider, 1993) of breast cancer patients have revealed that avoidance-oriented coping predicts increased distress across time. Just what the individual is attempting to avoid is at question here but is likely to involve a constellation of distressing emotions (e.g., fear, sadness) and thoughts (e.g., mortality salience). Taken together, correlational studies, and particularly those that are longitudinal in design, reveal that intentional attempts by persons with cancer to approach their emotions through expression are associated with benefits. We now turn to findings generated in experimental designs, which provide stronger evidence of causal priority.

EMOTIONAL EXPRESSION AND CANCER: EVIDENCE FROM CONTROLLED EXPERIMENTAL RESEARCH

Two domains of experimental studies provide evidence regarding the link between emotional expression and positive outcomes in cancer patients: randomized, controlled trials of psychological interventions and investigations of experimentally induced emotional expression through writing. We review both here, and we expand our discussion of writing interventions to include studies with other medical patient samples.

Psychological Intervention Trials for Cancer Patients

Researchers who have conducted randomized, controlled trials have documented that psychological interventions for cancer patients may enhance quality of life (see Andersen, 1992, for a review), improve immune function (Fawzy et al., 1990), and even promote longer survival (Fawzy et al., 1993; Spiegel, Bloom, Kraemer, & Gottheil, 1989). The structured psychological interventions used in these randomized trials typically have been multifaceted, including components such as coping skills training, social support, emotional expression, and techniques for stress management or pain control. Such interventions may benefit a large number of patients by casting a wide net, but their multimodal structure does not reveal which intervention elements are responsible for positive outcomes. Dismantling studies, which isolate the critical components of interventions by comparing a full treatment with pared down versions of the treatment, would be useful in determining the effectiveness of emotional expression relative to other elements (also see chapter 11, this volume).

In their meta-analysis of randomized, controlled outcome studies of psychosocial interventions for groups of adults with cancer, Meyer and Mark (1995) addressed the question of whether effectiveness depends on the intervention content. Forty-five studies were included; patients were predominantly White women from the United States. Effect sizes showed beneficial effects on emotional ($d = .24$) and functional ($d = .19$) adjustment and on treatment- and disease-related physical symptoms ($d = .26$), but not on medical measures ($d = .17$). Significant differences among types of treatment (e.g., cognitive–behavioral, social support) did not emerge, a finding that may result from low statistical power. It is likely that emotional expression was common to several of the treatment categories.

The best-known research on psychological intervention with cancer patients involves an explicit emotional expression component that is central to the treatment package. Spiegel's supportive–expressive group therapy, used with metastatic breast cancer patients and, more recently, with HIV patients (Classen, Diamond, & Spiegel, 1999), involves encouraging group members to express feelings openly and fully about their illness and its effect on their lives. In addition to sharing emotions, group members discuss topics such as physical problems, communication with physicians, family relations, finding meaning in life, and facing death.

More than a decade ago, Spiegel and colleagues (1989) reported results of a 10-year follow-up of women with metastatic breast cancer who had participated in their psychotherapy outcome research. Patients in the intervention and control groups had received routine oncological care, and the groups did not differ significantly in age, marital status, treatment, or staging. Earlier reports had documented that following the weekly, year-long intervention, patients randomized to group therapy had significantly less mood disturbance and those whose treatment included hypnosis had less pain (Spiegel & Bloom, 1983; Spiegel, Bloom, & Yalom, 1981). Although the intervention was not designed to influence survival as such, the 10-year follow-up showed that women in the intervention group ($n = 50$) lived on average twice as long (36.6 vs. 18.9 months from study entry to death) as women in the control group ($n = 36$; Spiegel et al., 1989). The research has been criticized and the mechanisms underlying the effect remain unknown; the investigators discussed social support, compliance with medical regimens, health behavior change, and neuroendocrine and immune function as potential mediators.

In conclusion, the evidence from randomized, controlled trials suggests that multimodal interventions including induction of emotional expression yield positive outcomes among cancer patients, but we cannot conclude that emotional expression is an active ingredient. Research designed to identify mechanisms underlying positive effects is needed; this will allow the design of interventions that are clinically successful and cost-effective. Given the relatively homogenous demographic composition of the groups of patients enrolled in randomized controlled trials, future studies also must consider whether the effects of structured, emotional expression-based interventions for cancer patients differ as a function of gender, race, and ethnicity.

Expressive Disclosure Experiments

Only a handful of studies have been published with medical populations using the expressive writing paradigm (Pennebaker & Beall, 1986) or a similar method. Kelley, Lumley, and Leisen (1997) randomly assigned 72 rheumatoid arthritis patients (mean age = 56.6 years; 83% women) to an emotional disclosure condition in which participants spoke into an audiorecorder for 15 minutes on each of four consecutive days about their deepest feelings regarding events they identified as stressful or about the content of neutral pictures. They were assessed at a clinic visit an average of 3 months following the experimental task. Patients in the emotional disclosure condition reported less affective disturbance and better physical functioning in daily activities than did control participants. No significant main effect of disclosure emerged on pain reports or on joint condition as rated by a physician. However, those who experienced larger increases in negative mood immediately after the disclosure task had greater joint improvement.

Patients with asthma (n = 58; mean age = 41 years; 73% women) and rheumatoid arthritis (n = 49; mean age = 51 years; 71% women) comprised the sample in an experimental trial of the writing paradigm (Smyth, Stone, Hurewitz, & Kaell, 1999). Participants wrote over three sessions either about the most stressful event of their lives or emotionally neutral topics. Physical function was assessed before the writing induction and at 2-week, 8-week, and 16-week follow-up. As compared with control participants whose health outcomes did not change significantly, asthma patients in the disclosure condition evidenced significantly improved lung function as assessed through spirometry at the 4-month follow-up (as well as at 2-week and 8-week follow-up), and rheumatoid arthritis patients demonstrated significant improvement in overall disease activity as indicated in clinical examinations performed by a rheumatologist (at 4-month follow-up only). Overall, 47% of disclosure condition participants demonstrated clinically significant improvement, whereas only 24% of control patients evidenced improvement at 4 months.

Two trials of the expressive disclosure paradigm focused specifically on women with breast cancer. Walker, Nail, and Croyle (1999) randomly assigned women with Stage I or II breast cancer (mean age = 54 years) to one of the following conditions: a single-session attentional control condition, in which they talked with the researcher on their final day of radiation therapy about events and plans unrelated to cancer, or a 1-session (on the final treatment day or the following day) or 3-session (during the last week of treatment) 30-minute writing intervention. Participants in the disclosure conditions were instructed to write about their deepest thoughts and feelings regarding their cancer experience. Fourteen women completed the control condition, 11 completed the one-session writing condition, and 14 completed the three-session writing intervention. Follow-up telephone interviews were completed at 1, 4–6, 16, and 28 weeks after radiation therapy, in which measures of negative and positive mood and intrusiveness and avoidance of cancer-related thoughts were administered. Trait negative affectivity and treatment side effect severity were used as covariates. No significant main effects of condition or Condition × Time interactions emerged on any dependent variable. Inspection of means at the final 28-week follow-up revealed that participants in the expressive disclosure conditions reported slightly higher negative and positive mood, as well as slightly higher avoidance and intrusiveness of cancer-related thoughts, than did control participants. In addition to suggesting the possibility that expressive writing simply was not effective for these participants, the negative findings might be attributed to the small sample size or the relatively positive adjustment reported by participants, particularly on the positive affect measure. It also should be noted that the researchers did not assess physical health outcomes.

We conducted a randomized trial of expressive writing in 60 women who recently had completed primary medical treatment for Stage I or II breast cancer (Stanton et al., in press). In addition to testing effects on psychological and physical health-related outcomes of writing about deepest thoughts and feelings against a control condition in which women wrote about the facts of their cancer experience, our goal was to assess effects of encouraging participants to write about the benefits in their experience of cancer. Descriptive studies reveal that many individuals who confront serious adversity report extracting benefits from their experience, often including perceptions of positive personality change (e.g., increased empathy, self-esteem), enhanced personal relationships, and renewed commitments to life priorities (e.g., Affleck & Tennen, 1996). Furthermore, naturally elected benefit finding is associated with positive adjustment across time (Affleck & Tennen, 1996).

A finding that experimentally induced benefit finding produces valuable outcomes may imply that invoking painful feelings is not a necessary prerequisite for positive change in the expressive writing paradigm (see also King & Miner, 2000). Although it is possible that induced benefit finding would lead women to feel constrained in the full range of emotional expression and thus produce untoward effects, we reasoned that most women would have had ample opportunity to express negative emotions by the time they had completed medical treatment. Accordingly, we hypothesized that both experimentally induced expressive disclosure and benefit finding would carry positive effects on well-being (i.e., health-related quality of life, affect) and physical health (i.e., medical appointments for cancer-related morbidities, self-reported physical symptoms) relative to a control condition in which women wrote solely about facts of their experience with cancer. We also explored whether effects of the writing conditions would vary as a function of participants' self-reported avoidance of cancer-related thoughts and feelings, reasoning that women low on avoidance might benefit more from emotional disclosure than would high-avoidant women, for whom induced emotional disclosure might be difficult.

Women (mean age = 50 years; mean time since diagnosis duration = 28 weeks) were assigned randomly to the three conditions and completed four, 20-minute writing sessions within a 3-week period. Trained research assistants conducted the sessions in the participants' homes or a laboratory room. Because they conveyed writing instructions to participants, research assistants were aware of condition assignment for each participant, but they were unaware of study hypotheses and read instructions from a standard script. Exhibit 3.1 presents the instructions that were given to participants in the first writing session. In subsequent sessions, instructions were repeated in briefer form. Participants were not led to expect any particular benefit from the writing.

Writing samples were transcribed, and an independent judge was asked to indicate the experimental condition assignment for each transcribed essay, ordered randomly. The judge's determination was correct for 95% of the 240 individual essays, confirming excellent adherence to experimental instructions. As shown in Exhibit 3.2, samples from the essays of participants in the benefit-finding and expressive-disclosure conditions illustrate the range of responses engendered by the task.

Self-reported physiological arousal and positive affect did not differ significantly among groups immediately following the writing sessions. However, expressive writing and control participants reported significantly increased distress after writing compared with participants induced to focus on the benefits of their experience. Increased distress evidenced by control participants is not typical in this paradigm (Smyth, 1998) and most likely reflects participants' focus on the factual details of their cancer experience rather than the trivial topics (e.g., contents of one's closet) typically addressed in control writing conditions. Increased distress following expressive writing, however, is a typical finding in this literature (Smyth, 1998). A number of women commented on the ultimate benefit of this sometimes painful writing task. One woman stated, "It has caused me to think in my own words about what went on this past year. It also made me think of where my life is and where I want it to go. I feel all of these thoughts are difficult but overall a positive experience." Another participant reported,

EXHIBIT 3.1
Experimental Condition Instructions

EXPRESSIVE DISCLOSURE

What I would like you to write about for these four sessions are your deepest thoughts and feelings about your experience with breast cancer. I realize that women with breast cancer experience a full range of emotions, and I want you to focus on any and all of them. In your writing, I want you to really let go and explore your very deepest emotions and thoughts. You might think about all the various feelings and changes that you experienced before being diagnosed, after diagnosis, during treatment, and now. Whatever you choose to write, it is critical that you really focus on your deepest thoughts and feelings. Ideally, I would like you to focus on feelings, thoughts, or changes that you have not discussed in great detail with others. You might also tie your thoughts and feelings about your experiences with cancer to other parts of your life—your childhood, people you love, who you are, or who you want to be. Again, the most important part of your writing is that you really focus on your deepest emotions and thoughts. The only rule we have is that you write continuously for the entire time. If you run out of things to say, just repeat what you have already written. Don't worry about grammar, spelling, or sentence structure. Don't worry about erasing or crossing things out. Just write.

BENEFIT FINDING

What I would like you to write about for these four sessions are any POSITIVE thoughts and feelings about your experience with breast cancer. I realize that women with breast cancer experience a full range of emotions that often includes some positive emotions, thoughts, and changes, and in this writing exercise I want you to focus only on the positive thoughts and feelings that you have experienced over the course of your cancer. [Instructions continue as above, with the modifier of "positive" thoughts and feelings]

FACT CONTROL

What I would like you to write about for these four sessions is a detailed account of facts regarding your breast cancer and its treatment. I am interested in how the specifics of detection, diagnosis, and treatment differ among women with breast cancer; therefore, it is critical that you provide an extremely detailed account of all that happened to you with regard to having breast cancer. I realize that women with breast cancer experience many emotions, but in your writing I want you to focus only on the facts, not on your emotions. No fact is too big or too small. You might write about when your cancer was discovered and who discovered it, appointments that you had with doctors or other people about your cancer, information you were given, and what treatment was chosen. You might recount your experience from beginning to present day, including all the factual details you can think of. Again the most important part of your writing is that you focus on the facts and try to reconstruct what happened in as great factual detail as possible. The only other rule . . . [Instructions continue as above].

Note. These instructions are taken from "Randomized, Controlled Trial of Written Emotional Expression and Benefit Finding in Breast Cancer Patients," Stanton et al., in press. Reprinted with permission.

"Writing about my cancer brought out feelings that I hadn't dealt with. My understanding of these feelings brought many, many conversations with my husband and close friends which in turn brought out things they were feeling and were afraid to say. I feel that all of this has brought us all a lot

EXHIBIT 3.2
Sample Expressive-Disclosure and Benefit-Finding Writing

EXPRESSIVE DISCLOSURE

Looking back, I realize that last year, when I was in treatment, I had the feeling that yeah, it was scary, inconvenient, pretty horrible. But I thought that at the end I'd be finished with it. May hair has not come back; I don't like the way I look anymore. When I'm naked I don't like my breast.

When I was in the room waiting to go for surgery, it all kind of hit me. Was there going to be more than they thought? Are they going to have to remove my breast? Am I going to have to undergo chemotherapy? I was not so concerned about not waking up, but about what I would be facing in the weeks and months ahead. I think with cancer, the unknown is the hardest, for you have had friends who have experienced great illness and prolonged struggle. However, I have always had this deep feeling that we would all be okay.

Now every little thing has me petrified! Any ache means the cancer is back . . . but then I worry that if part of my mind still believes the cancer will come back, maybe it will. Just trying to think positively can cause stress. I think the hardest part of this week has been the sense of loss I've felt being finished with treatment. You spend so many months doing everything you can to fight the disease, even just relaxing to fight it, and then the doctors have completed all your treatments. How do I pick up the pieces?

BENEFIT FINDING

It probably made me evaluate my life, realize that I have many blessings to count. It made me appreciate my family, my friends, and my church.

I knew I had a strong marriage and a wonderful husband. He was very compassionate, understanding, and helpful. My mother was able to stay with me for a couple of weeks and help with laundry and housework. She has been of great support also. I have always had a good positive attitude about all things and that has really helped me during this time. I found that I was strong if not even stronger than I thought I was.

I have learned to be more patient and take some time for people and things. I still find myself getting hurried and upset at things. Then I stop to realize, "This is not important, slow down, focus on the important things in life." It is great to have this new perspective on life in general. It makes you focus on friends and family, happiness, quality of life, and your true feelings. I have found that I think I am an even better friend.

There really are positive things that come out of bad situations. Every day I look at life so much differently. I have encountered many new people because of my cancer, and they have been such positive influences in my life. I have felt the power of prayer, the power of God, and His strength more than ever. My life has been so richly blessed.

Note. These quotations are taken from "Randomized, Controlled Trial of Written Emotional Expression and Benefit Finding in Breast Cancer Patients," Stanton et al., in press. Reprinted with permission.

closer and opened a door wider for conversations." Despite the positive reports of many participants, however, at 1-month and 3-month follow-up assessments, the psychological outcomes revealed no significant main effects for writing condition. In general, participants reported relatively positive quality of life, low distress, and high vigor compared with other cancer patient samples. A significant interaction of participants' self-reported cancer-related avoidance and experimental condition did emerge on distress, however. Expressive disclosure produced decreased distress for women low in avoidance, but not for more avoidant women. In contrast, women high in avoidance tended to profit most from the benefit-finding condition.

With regard to physical health-related outcomes, the groups did not differ on self-reported somatic symptoms at 1 month. At 3 months, however, the expressive writing group evidenced a significant decrease in physical symptoms as compared with the control group, and benefit-finding participants' scores fell between the other groups. Prospectively recorded medical appointments for cancer-related morbidities (e.g., lymphedema) during the 3 months following writing also evidenced significant between-group differences. Women in the expressive writing (M = 0.40) and benefit-finding (M = 0.90) conditions had significantly fewer medical visits for cancer-related morbidities than did control participants (M = 2.20) during the 3 months following study completion. No condition × avoidance interactions emerged on physical health outcomes. Thus, a central finding of this research is that benefits with regard to physical health echoed those reported by Smyth et al. (1999) for other medical samples.

Another important finding in this experiment is that patients apparently need not address painful thoughts and feelings in their writings to profit from them. Like expressive disclosure participants, women assigned to write about the benefits of their experience with cancer had fewer appointments for cancer-related morbidities in the subsequent 3 months than did control-writing participants (Stanton et al., in press). Expressive disclosure participants did evidence slightly greater benefit with regard to these medical appointments and self-reported physical symptoms than did women who wrote about positive aspects of their experience. However, women in the benefit-finding condition reported slightly greater advantage than expressive disclosure participants with regard to self-perceived enhanced understanding of their experience, value of the project, and long-lasting positive effects of the writing (Stanton et al., in press). King and Miner (2000) also have documented the salutary consequences of experimentally induced benefit finding (see also chapter 7, this volume). They found in a sample of 118 undergraduates that writing about one's deepest thoughts and feelings or about benefits produced by traumatic events reduced health center visits in the following 3 and 5 months relative to a control condition. Our findings also are consistent with those of Pennebaker, Mayne, and Francis (1997). Their analysis of six experiments on written emotional disclosure revealed that participants' use of words indicating positive emotion was associated with health benefits.

We have advised caution in prescribing benefit finding as an intervention for individuals confronting adversity (e.g., Stanton, Tennen, Affleck, & Mendola, 1992). Indeed, exhorting individuals to "look on the bright side" or to focus on a specific advantage in their misfortune is likely to be interpreted as minimizing or not understanding their plight. We believe that the benefit-finding induction in this sample produced positive results as a consequence of at least three aspects of the experimental design. First, we did not suggest to participants that they focus on particular benefits; rather, women had control over the benefits they cited and explored. Second, even though we did not induce participants in the benefit-finding condition to focus on both the positive and negative aspects of their experience, we have evidence that they had processed negative thoughts and feelings in other venues. A number of women commented that focusing on benefits was a refreshing addition to their ongoing confrontation of more painful emotions. For example, one woman stated, "The first time I was asked to write about the positive aspects for 20 minutes, I thought, 'Are you kidding?!' Then as I started thinking about it I was amazed at all of the things that came to mind!". Another participant wrote, "When I first thought about this project, I thought I was going to talk about my pain and hurt feelings that occurs with diagnosis. I was not prepared to write about the positive aspects of cancer. I am glad that it ended up that way. It was a jolt to have to look at what good could come out of this." Thus, participants in this condition did not seem to fall prey to the "tyranny of positive thinking" (Holland & Lewis, 2000, p. 14) that may impose pressure on cancer patients to present a cheerful face to the world, lest their cancer recur or they encounter social rejection. Rather, the condition may have yielded balanced expression of positive and negative emotions. Finally, the experiment was conducted following the completion of primary medical treatment. In our opinion, performing the trial shortly after cancer diagnosis may have yielded very different and perhaps harmful effects. The ability to find benefit in the diagnosis of a life-threatening illness and its adaptive advantages may be more likely to accrue only after one has addressed the attendant negative emotions and has come to make sense of one's experience (e.g., Janoff-Bulman & Frantz, 1997).

A final point regarding Stanton et al. (in press) is that, although the benefit-finding condition produced positive outcomes with regard to medical use, some evidence remains that expressive writing was the more useful than the benefit-finding condition in its promotion of nonsignificantly fewer self-reported physical symptoms and medical appointments for cancer-related morbidities. Furthermore, two participants in the benefit-finding condition reported that writing solely about their positive experience felt constraining and reflected only "part of the story" of their experience. Although prompting greater immediate distress, expressing the full range of thoughts and emotions surrounding cancer appeared to yield maximal benefit in this sample. The relative risks and benefits of various forms of expressive writing require further investigation.

Although not entirely consistent, findings from these four randomized experiments are promising with regard to the potential of the expressive writing paradigm as applied to medical patient populations. All three trials (Kelley et al., 1997; Smyth et al., 1999; Stanton et al., in press) that assessed self-reported or objective physical health indicators revealed important benefits of expressive writing. (Kelley et al. revealed positive effects on one health-related outcome but not others.) Positive effects emerged on physical health-related outcomes including self-reported physical symptoms as well as medical care use for cancer-related morbidities (Stanton et al., in press) in women with breast cancer, disease activity (Smyth et al., 1999) and physical functioning in daily activities (Kelley et al., 1997) in rheumatoid arthritis patients, and lung function in asthma patients (Smyth et al., 1999). Such outcomes carry both medical relevance and functional import for individuals diagnosed with disease.

Findings with regard to psychological health were more mixed. Expressive writing participants in Kelley et al.'s study (1997) reported less affective disturbance than did control participants. Smyth et al. (1999) did not assess psychological outcomes, Walker et al. (1999) found no significant between-group effects on psychological variables, and Stanton et al. (in press) found that psychological benefits of the two writing conditions varied as a function of participants' self-reported avoidance of cancer-related thoughts and feelings. Psychological improvement may have been difficult to detect in these samples. The women in Stanton et al. (in press) reported more positive life quality at study outset than did other cancer patient samples, and Walker et al. (1999) noted that mean scores on a scale assessing positive emotions were close to the scales' ceiling (and that sample was the smallest among the four trials). Perhaps medical samples experiencing more distress would reap greater psychological benefit from expressive writing. In addition, Stanton et al.'s findings suggest that expressive writing may have variable effects on psychological outcomes, dependent on the writer's pre-existing psychological attributes.

CONCLUSIONS FROM THE RESEARCH ON EMOTIONAL EXPRESSION AND CANCER

To summarize, both correlational and experimental evidence provides preliminary support for the important role of emotional expression for individuals who confront a cancer diagnosis. With regard to cancer initiation, the meta-analysis of McKenna et al. (1999) suggests that nonexpressiveness may pose a risk. However, none of the studies reviewed by McKenna et al. were truly prospective, calling the implied causality into question. We would argue that distinct mechanisms may be relevant for initiation and progression of cancer, that more methodologically sound research is needed, and that we need to take great care in concluding that personality factors are relevant in light of the potential for victim blaming.

Addressing the question of whether emotional expression promotes psychological adjustment to cancer, cross-sectional and longitudinal correlational studies indicate that uncontrolled discharge of negative emotion may be associated with poorer adjustment (Compas et al., 1999), whereas intentional efforts to express emotion may result in positive outcomes (Stanton, Danoff-Burg, et al., 2000). Psychological intervention trials (e.g., Spiegel et al., 1989) also suggest that emotional expression in a supportive context may confer benefit for cancer patients, although the multimodal nature of these therapies precludes strong conclusion. Perhaps the strongest evidence that emotional disclosure is adaptive comes from studies of experimental induction of this process through writing in both cancer patients (Stanton et al., in press) and other medical samples (Kelley et al., 1997; Smyth et al., 1999). However, findings are not entirely consistent (e.g., Walker et al., 1999); they may be stronger for outcomes associated with physical health than for psychological functioning, and few studies with medical populations have been accomplished thus far. Findings from research using the expressive writing paradigm prompt many questions, and it is to these that we now turn.

FUTURE DIRECTIONS FOR THE EXPRESSIVE WRITING PARADIGM AS APPLIED TO CANCER PATIENTS

The most obvious question regarding the effects of expressive writing on psychological and physical health outcomes in individuals with cancer is whether the extant findings are reliable. Currently, only one of two trials of expressive writing with breast cancer patients has yielded health benefits (Stanton et al., in press). Positive findings obtained with other medical populations (Kelley et al., 1997; Smyth et al., 1999) and with healthy samples (see Smyth, 1998) promote confidence in the reliability and validity of these results. However, continued study of the writing paradigm in individuals with cancer is warranted. Also in question is the generalizability of effects to cancer patients with diverse characteristics. In healthy samples, effects of expressive writing are somewhat stronger for men than women (Smyth, 1998). Furthermore, evidence suggests benefits of emotional expression in men with cancer, particularly within a receptive social context (Lepore, 2001; Lepore & Helgeson, 1998), and in men in infertile couples (Berghuis & Stanton, in press; see Stanton, Danoff-Burg, Cameron, & Ellis, 1994, for contrasting findings in undergraduate men). Do positive effects of expressive writing generalize to men with cancer, to individuals with other cancers, to the loved ones of cancer patients? Do benefits emerge for those with advanced disease and for individuals at various points in the treatment trajectory? The most interesting questions regarding expressive writing for cancer patients involve delineating for whom, under what conditions, and how expressive writing confers benefit. A number of researchers in this volume address these questions regarding moderators of and mechanisms for the effects of expressive writing.

Another question relates to whether the power of the expressive writing paradigm can be enhanced. Perhaps building into the instructions for the intervention some of the ingredients presumed to be mechanisms for its benefits, such as narrative coherence, causal thinking, and positive emotion (e.g., Pennebaker et al., 1997), would yield even more robust results. Cameron and Nicholls (1998) found that engaging in written emotional disclosure was effective in reducing health center visits for optimists but not for pessimists, for whom expressive writing was successful only if accompanied by explicit instruction in self-regulation. Because women low in optimism have been demonstrated to be at risk for poorer adjustment surrounding breast cancer diagnosis (Carver et al., 1993; Stanton & Snider, 1993), such instruction might be a promising addition to the writing paradigm for cancer patients.

Another avenue for research involves comparison of the standard expressive writing paradigm to other writing instructions. We have preliminary evidence that focusing on benefits in stressful experiences can be useful (King & Miner, 2000; Stanton et al., in press). Other writing instructions deserve study. For example, anticipating difficulties and constructing coping plans may be a useful writing strategy for individuals newly diagnosed with cancer. Findings of comparative trials are instructive not only in understanding which interventions are most beneficial for patients but also in elucidating the processes underlying their effects.

Final questions relate to whether expressive writing carries therapeutic potential over the long term and whether it can be teamed productively with other therapeutic strategies of known efficacy for cancer patients. Whether the proximal effects of expressive writing promote distal benefits, such as enhanced quality of life or more positive health status over greater than several months, remains an open question. Furthermore, expressive writing may prove to be a useful adjunct to effective psychosocial interventions. Certainly, the potential of research on this paradigm lies in its illumination of theoretical mechanisms for therapeutic change as well as its real-world application to individuals facing profound health challenges.

REFERENCES

Affleck, G., & Tennen, H. (1996). Construing benefits from adversity: Adaptational significance and dispositional underpinnings. *Journal of Personality, 64,* 899–922.

Andersen, B. (1992). Psychological interventions for cancer patients to enhance quality of life. *Journal of Consulting and Clinical Psychology, 60,* 552–568.

Andersen, B. L., Kiecolt-Glaser, J. K., & Glaser, R. (1994). A biobehavioral model of cancer stress and disease course. *American Psychologist, 49,* 389–404.

Berghuis, J. P., & Stanton, A. L. (in press). Adjustment to a dyadic stressor: A longitudinal study of coping and depressive symptoms in infertile couples over an insemination attempt. *Journal of Consulting and Clinical Psychology.*

Bleiker, E. M. A., & van der Ploeg, H. M. (1999). Psychosocial factors in the etiology of breast cancer: Review of a popular link. *Patient Education and Counseling, 37,* 201–214.

Bonanno, G. A., Znoj, H., Siddique, H. I., & Horowitz, M. J. (1999). Verbal-autonomic dissociation and adaptation to midlife conjugal loss: A follow-up at 25 months. *Cognitive Therapy and Research, 23,* 605–624.

Cameron, L. D., & Nicholls, G. (1998). Expression of stressful experiences through writing: Effects of a self-regulation manipulation for pessimists and optimists. *Health Psychology, 17,* 84–92.

Carver, C. S., Pozo, C., Harris, S. D., Noriega, V., Scheier, M. F., Robinson, D. S., Ketcham, A. S., Moffat, F. L., & Clark, K. C. (1993). How coping mediates the effect of optimism on distress: A study of women with early stage breast cancer. *Journal of Personality and Social Psychology, 65,* 375–390.

Classen, C., Diamond, S., & Spiegel, D. (1999). Supportive–expressive group therapy for cancer and HIV patients. In L. VandeCreek & T. L. Jackson (Eds.), *Innovations in clinical practice: A source book* (Vol. 17, pp. 119–134). Sarasota, FL: Professional Resource Press.

Classen, C., Koopman, C., Angell, K., & Spiegel, D. (1996). Coping styles associated with psychological adjustment to advanced breast cancer. *Health Psychology, 15,* 434–437.

Compas, B. E., Stoll, M. F., Thomsen, A. H., Oppedisano, G., Epping-Jordan, J. E., & Krag, D. N. (1999). Adjustment to breast cancer: Age-related differences in coping and emotional distress. *Breast Cancer Research and Therapy, 54,* 195–203.

Eysenck, H. J. (1994). Cancer, personality and stress: Prediction and prevention. *Advances in Behaviour Research and Therapy, 16,* 167–215.

Fawzy, F. I., Fawzy, N. W., Hyun, C. S., Elashoff, R., Guthrie, D., Fahey, J. L., & Morton, D. L. (1993). Malignant melanoma: Effects of an early structured psychiatric intervention, coping, and affective state on recurrence and survival 6 years later. *Archives of General Psychiatry, 50,* 681–689.

Fawzy, F. I., Kemeny, M. E., Fawzy, N. W., Elashoff, R., Morton, D., Cousins, N., & Fahey, J. L. (1990). A structured psychiatric intervention for cancer patients: II. Changes over time in immunological measures. *Archives of General Psychiatry, 47,* 729–735.

Garssen, B., & Goodkin, K. (1999). On the role of immunological factors as mediators between psychosocial factors and cancer progression. *Psychiatry Research, 85,* 51–61.

Greer, S., & Watson, M. (1985). Towards a psychobiological model of cancer: Psychological considerations. *Social Science and Medicine, 20,* 773–777.

Helgeson, V. S., & Lepore, S. J. (1997). Men's adjustment to prostate cancer: The role of agency and unmitigated agency. *Sex Roles, 37,* 251–267.

Holland, J. C., & Lewis, S. (2000). *The human side of cancer: Living with hope, coping with uncertainty.* New York: HarperCollins.

Janoff-Bulman, R., & Frantz, C. M. (1997). The impact of trauma on meaning: From meaningless world to meaningful life. In M. Power & C. R. Brewin (Eds.), *The transformation of meaning in psychological therapies* (pp. 91–106). New York: Wiley.

Kelley, J. E., Lumley, M. A., & Leisen, J. C. C. (1997). Health effects of emotional disclosure in rheumatoid arthritis patients. *Health Psychology, 16,* 331–340.

King, L. A., & Miner, K. N. (2000). Writing about the perceived benefits of traumatic events: Implications for physical health. *Personality and Social Psychology Bulletin, 26,* 220–230.

Lepore, S. J. (2001). A social–cognitive processing model of emotional adjustment to cancer. In A. Baum & B. Andersen (Eds.), *Psychosocial interventions for cancer* (pp. 99–118). Washington, DC: American Psychological Association.

Lepore, S. J., & Helgeson, V. S. (1998). Social constraints, intrusive thoughts, and mental health after prostate cancer. *Journal of Social and Clinical Psychology, 17,* 89–106.

McKenna, M. C., Zevon, M. A., Corn, B., & Rounds, J. (1999). Psychosocial factors and the development of breast cancer: A meta-analysis. *Health Psychology, 18,* 520–531.

Meyer, T. J., & Mark, M. M. (1995). Effects of psychosocial interventions with adult cancer patients: A meta-analysis of randomized experiments. *Health Psychology, 14,* 101–108.

Morrow, J., & Nolen-Hoeksema, S. (1990). Effects of responses to depression on the remediation of depressive affect. *Journal of Personality and Social Psychology, 58,* 519–527.

Mulder, C. L., van der Pompe, G., Spiegel, D., Antoni, M. H., & de Vries, M. J. (1992). Do psychosocial factors influence the course of breast cancer? A review of recent literature, methodological problems and future directions. *Psycho-oncology, 1,* 155–167.

Pennebaker, J. W. (1993). Putting stress into words: Health, linguistic, and therapeutic implications. *Behaviour Research and Therapy, 31,* 539–548.

Pennebaker, J. W., & Beall, S. (1986). Confronting a traumatic event: Toward an understanding of inhibition and disease. *Journal of Abnormal Psychology, 95,* 274–281.

Pennebaker, J. W., Mayne, T. J., & Francis, M. E. (1997). Linguistic predictors of adaptive bereavement. *Journal of Personality and Social Psychology, 72,* 863–871.

Phipps, S., & Mulhern, R. K. (1995). Family cohesion and expressiveness promote resilience to the stress of pediatric bone marrow transplant: A preliminary report. *Developmental and Behavioral Pediatrics, 16,* 257–263.

Rieker, P. P., Edbril, S. D., & Garnick, M. B. (1985). Curative testis cancer therapy: Psychosocial sequelae. *Journal of Clinical Oncology, 3,* 1117–1126.

Schwartz, R., & Geyer, S. (1984). Social and psychological differences between cancer and noncancer patients: Cause or consequence of the disease? *Psychotherapy and Psychosomatics, 41,* 195–199.

Smyth, J. M. (1998). Written emotional expression: Effect sizes, outcome types, and moderating variables. *Journal of Consulting and Clinical Psychology, 66,* 174–184.

Smyth, J. M., Stone, A. A., Hurewitz, A., & Kaell, A. (1999). Effects of writing about stressful experiences on symptom reduction in patients with asthma or rheumatoid arthritis: A randomized trial. *Journal of the American Medical Association, 281,* 1304–1309.

Snyder, C. R., Harris, C., Anderson, J. R., Holleran, S. A., Irving, L. M., Sigmon, S. T., Yoshinobu, L., Gibb, J., Langelle, C., & Harney, P. (1991). The will and the ways: Development and validation of an individual-differences measure of hope. *Journal of Personality and Social Psychology, 60,* 570–585.

Spiegel, D., & Bloom, J. R. (1983). Group therapy and hypnosis reduce metastatic breast carcinoma pain. *Psychosomatic Medicine, 45,* 333–339.

Spiegel, D., Bloom, J. R., Kraemer, H. C., & Gottheil E. (1989). Effect of psychosocial treatment on survival of patients with metastatic breast cancer. *Lancet, ii,* 888–891.

Spiegel, D., Bloom, J. R., & Yalom, I. (1981). Group support for patients with metastatic cancer: A randomized outcome study. *Archives of General Psychiatry, 38,* 527–533.

Stanton, A. L., Danoff-Burg, S., Cameron, C. L., Bishop, M., Collins, C. A., Kirk, S. B., Sworowski, L. A., & Twillman, R. (2000). Emotionally expressive coping predicts psychological and physical adjustment to breast cancer. *Journal of Consulting and Clinical Psychology, 68,* 875–882.

Stanton, A. L., Danoff-Burg, S., Cameron, C. L., & Ellis, A. P. (1994). Coping through emotional approach: Problems of conceptualization and confounding. *Journal of Personality and Social Psychology, 66,* 350–362.

Stanton, A. L., Danoff-Burg, S., Sworowski, L. A., Collins, C. A., Branstetter, A. D., Rodriguez-Hanley, A., Kirk, S. B., & Austenfeld, J. L. (in press). Randomized, controlled trial of written emotional expression and benefit finding in breast cancer patients. *Journal of Clinical Oncology.*

Stanton, A. L., Kirk, S. B., Cameron, C. L., & Danoff-Burg, S. (2000). Coping through emotional approach: Scale construction and validation. *Journal of Personality and Social Psychology, 78,* 1150–1169.

Stanton, A. L., & Snider, P. (1993). Coping with a breast cancer diagnosis: A prospective study. *Health Psychology, 12,* 16–23.

Stanton, A. L., Tennen, H., Affleck, G., & Mendola, R. (1992). Coping and adjustment to infertility. *Journal of Social and Clinical Psychology, 11,* 1–13.

Temoshok, L., & Dreher, H. (1992). *Type C behavior and cancer.* New York: Random House.

Walker, B. L., Nail, L. M., & Croyle, R. T. (1999). Does emotional expression make a difference in reactions to breast cancer? *Oncology Nursing Forum, 26,* 1025–1032.

Watson, M., Greer, S., Rowden, L., Gorman, C., Roberston, B., Bliss, J. M., & Tunmore, R. (1991). Relationships between emotional control, adjustment to cancer and depression and anxiety in breast cancer patients. *Psychological Medicine, 21,* 51–57.

4

WRITING FOR THEIR LIVES: CHILDREN'S NARRATIVES AS SUPPORTS FOR PHYSICAL AND PSYCHOLOGICAL WELL-BEING

COLETTE DAIUTE AND ELLIE BUTEAU

Environmental conditions and social stresses pose serious health threats to children living in urban settings. Crowding, inadequate resources, and high population turnover are associated with violence, which accounts for one third of the injury deaths of young people in the United States and for the chronic physical and psychological problems that plague survivors of violence (Hamburg, 1998; Laub & Lauritsen, 1998). Because aggression and violence resulting in physical and psychological harm to young people tend to occur as fights in school settings (Laub & Lauritsen, 1998), social conflict among young people is an especially important context for research on protective processes. Research on expressive communication about trauma is a fertile knowledge source to link to research on social development for insights about youth conflict and associated risks.

Ethics and prevention programs have created opportunities for dis-

This work was supported in part by the William T. Grant Foundation and The Rockefeller Foundation Bellagio Study and Conference Center.

cussing the social issues that most often provoke violent conflicts, like discrimination (Samples & Aber, 1998; Walker, 1998). Such programs provide opportunities for expressive communication about traumas related to social conflict and instruction on strategies for dealing with them. Social supports, like those from teachers and parents, have proved to be crucial to the well-being of children who are exposed to violence (Kliewer, Lepore, Oskin, & Johnson, 1998). Social issues programs provide forums where teachers and children can acknowledge, analyze, understand, and (sometimes) resolve traumatic and routine conflicts. Although some violence prevention programs promote step-by-step procedures for dealing with conflicts among young peers, like "walking away" or "telling an adult," others move beyond formulas to explore the thoughts and feelings of those involved in institutional and interpersonal social strife, thereby validating the expression of affective experience.

The study described here is a step toward linking narrative writing with risks of physical injury. Research on protective aspects of children's writing can contribute to the quickly advancing practice of addressing psychophysical health in school settings and can add to knowledge about the role of writing in health. We take a different approach to examining writing in health and well-being than the other contributors to the book, in part through our focus on children (a seldom-studied population in expressive writing research) and in part by conducting research in the field, where the strict experimental controls typical of the Pennebaker-type (1997) writing paradigm are impossible to implement. We explain how social aspects of narrative writing may be protective and explore this idea through systematic analyses of narratives and measures of social problem behaviors, like fighting, which lead to physical or psychological harm.

EXPRESSIVE WRITING AND HEALTH

Analyses of writing as a healing process have been grounded in assumptions about psychodynamic processes. Theoretical explanations within this writing paradigm have identified psychological functions of verbal expression that unblock repressed traumas that stress healthy physical and psychological systems (Pennebaker & Beall, 1986). Research has focused in particular on mechanisms of emotional release and emotion regulation in relation to writing about painful experiences. Cognitive processes, such as attention and emotion regulation, have been explored as healing mechanisms by virtue of disclosure during expressive writing (Lepore, 1997; chapter 6, this volume). Self-regulative functions of expressive writing have, moreover, been conceptualized as registering and adjusting to feedback in the process of pursuing goals. King's (chapter 7, this volume) theory of self-regulation posits that, during the emotionally liberating process of writing about painful experiences, individuals register feedback, disrupting habitual reactions to traumas and thus revising central beliefs and values. When self-regulation involves the formulation of a narrative of one's best self, the protective aspects of this process are dramatic.

Designed to disclose feelings strong and deep enough to have caused physical and psychological problems, the paradigm invites uncensored written expression repeatedly over short periods of time (Pennebaker, 1997; Smyth, 1998). Measures of emotion words, causal connectors, and other linguistic indicators of affective expression have been established and related systematically to a range of health outcomes, including outcomes in autonomic and social processes such as "grade point average" and "absenteeism from work" (Pennebaker, 1997). Results have been attributed to freedom of expression in the private nonjudgmental setting of the laboratory. Although social aspects of self-regulation have not yet been explored sufficiently, these processes seem consistent with sociocultural and discursive theories that could shed new light on the role of expressive writing in health.

Theoretical explanations of the role of expressive narrative writing in the context of a classroom-based violence prevention program share with the Pennebaker-type writing paradigm assumptions about the need to discuss traumatic experience for emotional release, to provide processes for increased self-knowledge through writing about traumatic experiences, and to use that knowledge to strengthen one's relationships with others through increasingly positive self-presentations. Methodologically, our inquiry is consistent with the writing paradigm in its invitation to write about traumatic events, in this case social conflicts, repeatedly over short periods of time, as well as across longer periods. Because experimental control is not feasible in field settings like classrooms, numerous writing sessions in similar circumstances provide data for systematic analysis. Analyses of writing in our paradigm, as in the traditional writing paradigm, include identifying emotionally laden linguistic devices in texts and reports of behaviors associated with health risks.

Among several unique features of this study is the conceptualization of social aspects of protective processes. Theory about the social nature of expressive communication in writing incorporates assumptions about the importance of emotional release and self-regulative functions but interprets these processes as essentially social relational. The social issues curriculum was designed to support self-expression around issues of conflict through writing, promoting values such as the importance of authors' and characters' feelings and the need to work on relationships by sharing feelings, even when there are problems. Another difference is that specific outcome measures—children's social behaviors—are relevant to the population and circumstances of this study. Finally, our narrative writing measures augmented expressive elements used in previous studies with measures to account for social-relational representations and narrative structure.

NARRATIVE WRITING AS PRESENTATION OF SELF IN SOCIETY

Writing is a symbolic process under a person's control yet at the same time utterly social. Discourse theories explain how individual writers are involved in social interaction as they enact cultural values and practices toward some meaningful end from their unique perspectives (Billig, 1999). Sociocultural theorists explain that persons develop and grow as they become members of a culture through symbolic means like writing (Wertsch, 1991), and children as young as 7 years use writing to transform cultural symbols through complex interpretive processes (Daiute, 1998). Psychodynamic theory explains that symbolic processes mask as well as express intentions and behavior (Billig, 1999).

Beyond mere reporting, narrative serves in identity development (Hermans & Hermans-Jansen, 1995) and learning (Daiute & Griffin, 1993). Children adopt the mores, practices, and affects of their cultures largely through narrative means (Nelson, 1993). Narrative elements like coherence have been linked to well-being (Baerger & McAdams, 1999), yet narrative is also a context for critical reflection and resistance, which serve developmental needs (Daiute, 1998). Because narrative writing is also a form of social positioning, addressed to audiences and to one's self (Nystrand & Wiemelt, 1993), children can use it to perform their identities or to reflect on them. Young persons can craft self-representations in narrative writing—trying on and revising identities and creating motivations for engagement in social life. With adequate support, children can, thus, use writing to create healthy orientations to life. Writing about stressful events can, therefore, be a self-regulative process, in which writers represent themselves handling challenging experiences, and, over time, crafting effective selves that, whether true or not, are the basis for ongoing self-reflection and motivation.

Socially protective processes are integrated within the narrative genre. Narratives express references to real-world events and evaluative meanings —discourse strategies with which the narrator conveys why the story is being told (Labov & Waletzky, 1997). This evaluative meaning, thus, links narrator and audience—the explanation and the context of the story respectively. The brief narrative "The child ran home, and his sister said that his friends had called," for example, is a social communication referring to characters (child, sister, friends) and events (ran, called), which becomes a purposeful and revealing interaction between narrator and reader when it is transformed evaluatively, as in "The child ran home oh, so very quickly, and his sister said that his friends had just called a minute ago." Evaluative devices like the adjectival phrase "oh, so very quickly" and "just . . . a minute ago" augment referential meanings with information about urgency that hints at why the narrator might have told the story.

Embedding the self in society through narrative writing positions the author as someone whose experiences are worth recounting and reading; someone whose interpretations give meaning to mere events; someone who deserves a response; someone who is preserved into the future through written artifacts; someone who can be imagined, interpreted, and even revered through readings by others as well as the self. When writings contend with specific conflicts in the narrator's experience, this social-interpretive function of writing can promote healing.

A violence prevention program, like any curriculum, conveys a particular version of reality—a social script—which children use in complex ways. For example, social scripts in narratives by children in a violence prevention program transformed from fight scripts to socially responsible conflict scripts, and children from diverse backgrounds demonstrated the ability to adapt social scripts to different contexts (Daiute, Buteau, & Rawlins, 2001; Daiute & Jones, in press). The following two stories are examples of a shift in social script from a conflict framed as a fight (first story) to a more socially negotiated disagreement (second story).

The Computer Fight
My friend wanted to use my computer at school. She pushed on my seat.
I pushed her away. And I said get your own computer. She said okay.

In contrast, the following narrative presents a very differently organized conflict, described as a problem by both participants with equal responsibilities for the conflict and rights to have it resolved and a socially mediated tool, the schedule, to call on.

The Bike Fight
One day me and my friend had an argument. We had an argument about
my bike. He alwaysed hoged it allot and I never got to ride it. Since I never
got to ride it we made a time schechuite. He had it outside for 1 hour and
I had it for 1 hour.

Because there is evidence that social scripts organize perception and action, transforming fight stories into socially responsible stories could have something to do with prosocial actions in the future. Like therapies that guide people to renarrate events in their lives as a means for changing their orientations to future events (Hermans & Hermans-Jansen, 1995), writing about social interactions in a supported educational context could also serve developmental purposes.

In summary, narrative writing is a symbolic space for imagining diverse social relational options in the context of a conflict plot. Cultural expectations and practices are, for example, always embedded in narratives, and children may explore those by defying them, such as when they write violent stories in the context of a violence prevention program forbidding violence, or they may rewrite experiences to mimic cultural mores. A detailed analysis of texts by children over time in the context of a violence prevention program explores these ideas about the protective function of narrative writing.

SOCIAL SKILLS AND URBAN HEALTH

Exposure to violence leads to myriad forms of stress in children, including difficulty concentrating, intrusive thinking, anxiety, and depression, especially if they lack adequate social supports, such as positive relationships with parents and other significant adults (Kliewer et al., 1998). When families lack adequate physical resources or suffer social oppression, children facing such circumstances need social relational maturity, self-determination, and healthy connections. Some children's lives can depend on their abilities to recognize and buffer racist threats (Boyd-Franklin & Franklin, 2000). Children who have ample resources face different sorts of challenges to identity and interpersonal relations, leading, for example, to alienation and risk taking (Lightfoot, 1998).

Violence prevention programs are contexts where educators can guide young people to examine social issues in relation to conflicts in their lives and in the communities where they live. The major prevention programs examine social problems like racial, ethnic, and sexual discrimination and teach children to deal with such problems through conflict negotiation processes (Samples & Aber, 1999; Walker, 1998). Most prevention programs conceptualize domains of change in knowledge (i.e., what children say they know about conflict) and behavior (i.e., whether and how much they engage in aggressive or violent conflicts). Research has begun to suggest the effectiveness of prevention programs in reducing physical and psychological health risks (Samples & Aber, 1998), but researchers have also identified the need to examine how youth conceptualize challenging environments (Daiute, 2001); how they resist, transform, and conform to values conveyed in prevention programs (Daiute, Stern, & Lelutiu-Weinberger, in press); and how children unjustly identified as sources of crime cope with extreme environmental threats (Cross & Strauss, 1998). What seems to be missing in models of violence prevention is a mechanism of personal meaning which, presumably, links knowledge and behavior across contexts (Levitt & Selman, 1996).

Narrative writing is a site of personal meaning making because it is a symbolic process by which individuals control cultural tools, including language and values, for social and personal purposes. Writing narratives about one's life, for example, is an activity involving the presentation of self in social context, as well as an emotional release. Young people can use this context to connect program-based social values with their own experiences and imaginative processes.

WRITING AS A MEANS OF VIOLENCE PREVENTION

Based on the psychosocial function of narrative writing, teachers and students participating in a violence prevention program read and discussed high-quality children's literature about social conflicts (Walker, 1998). Literature with culturally authentic examples of discrimination conflicts was the basis for discussions about characters' motivations, actions, and ways of dealing with their conflicts. For example, third grade classes studied the discrimination conflict in *Angel Child, Dragon Child* (Surat, 1983), a story about Hoa, a recently immigrated Vietnamese girl who was the object of discriminatory teasing. The fifth grades studied *Mayfield Crossing* (Nelson, 1993), a story in which the main characters are a group of African Americans in the 1960s South, where the small predominantly Black middle school closes, sending the children from that school to a mostly White school in another town. A teacher's guide provided the framework for theory-based activities. The guide suggests, for example, that before reading the book aloud, teachers set the scene with a story from their own lives and present information about the socio-historical context in which the book was written. Activities included reading the books aloud and using interpretive discussion questions to engage children in thinking about how social situations in the characters' lives escalated into conflicts and how characters resolved their differences, all the while paying attention to characters' emotions. The intervention also engaged children in writing three sets of narratives, including a fictional story, an autobiographical conflict story, and an original ending to the novel, which children wrote with small groups of peers.

Narrative writing activities were designed as opportunities for children to analyze social problems raised in the literary selections, to consider how such problems might occur in their own lives, and to imagine effective and healthy ways of dealing with such conflicts.

CONTEXT AND RESEARCH DESIGN

This study involved gathering writing samples and risk-behavior reports from children in the fall and spring of the year they were involved in the literacy-based violence prevention program. Writing was done as part of classroom practice, which asked children to compose two fictional narratives and two autobiographical narratives, spaced alternately across the year.

The autobiographical narrative (AN) writing task asked children to write about a social conflict they had experienced: *Write about a time when you or someone you know had a disagreement or conflict with a friend, a classmate, or someone else your age. What happened? How did the people involved think and feel about it? How did it all turn out?* This task was based on the idea that the actual experience would provide a link between social skills instruction and children's experiences. In this way, the autobiographical narrative could provide a personally meaningful context for transforming conflict analysis and resolution strategies. Nevertheless, pressures to conform and perhaps to conceal experiences that might not match the ones idealized in instruction could have minimized the expressive value of the autobiographical narrative, so we also collected fictional narrative about conflicts.

Before any curriculum activities and after all had been completed, teachers assigned a fictional narrative (FN) writing task: *Imagine this scene in a story called "Three." "Jama and Max were best friends. Pat moved in next to Max, and they began to spend lots of time together. One day, Jama saw Max and Pat walking together and laughing." What happened next? Continue this story about how the friends got along. What happened? How did they all think and feel about the events? How did it all turn out?* This FN task served for assessment outside prescribed curriculum activities and, more importantly, provided information about conflict representations that were or could be presented as fictional.

The purpose of this study was to build on psychosocial theory of writing and examine its relationship to behavioral factors that risk children's health. Relating narratives and self-reports of problem behaviors is a first step to examining whether and how symbolic processes in writing might relate to children's behaviors. Research questions focus specifically on relationships between changes in narrative social relations variables and changes in reports of problem behaviors, with an hypothesis that changes toward social relational orientations promoted in the curriculum would predict decreases in reports of problem behaviors over time. Questions include "How are shifts in narrative social relational scripts related to shifts in reports of problem behaviors?" and "What role, in particular, do shifts toward patterns of integrated self-determination and connection play in decreases in problem behaviors?"

Method

Data and Narrative Analysis

Data for this study include 316 narratives by 3rd and 5th graders (*n* = 79), 158 narratives written in response to the curriculum-based FN task in the fall and the spring, and 158 narratives written in response to the

AN task in the fall and spring. These narratives were written by equal numbers of girls and boys from a range of racial and ethnic backgrounds, including 33% European-American, 33% Latino and Latina, 20% African American, 5% Asian American, and 9% recent immigrants (European, Caribbean). The children all lived in a large northeastern city, where the public schools serve families with poor to low-middle economic situations (i.e., approximately 50% came from families living below the poverty level). Many of the children lived in low-income housing projects with relatively high rates of crime. Study inclusion criteria were (a) obtaining parental consent and child assent, (b) having written two FNs and two ANs, and (c) having filled out both the fall and spring behavioral report data. Copies of the narratives as written were coded after all individual, class, and school identifiers were removed.

The primary data analytic task for this study was to identify the range of social representations across these narrative tasks. *Social representations* are conceptualized as portrayals of characters and relationships among characters, including character perspectives, conflicts, conflict resolution strategies, and other social issues and organizations. Narrative social representations occur with written narrative skills, so we created a parallel coding scheme to account for narrative structure. Exhibit 4.1 outlines the narratives social relations and narrative structure phases of this coding scheme.

The narrative structure phase of the coding scheme was designed to identify basic narrative elements from research on oral language development in English-speaking children (Peterson & McCabe, 1983; Stein & Albro, 1997) and in writing (Daiute & Griffin, 1993). As shown in Exhibit 4.1, this identifies the inclusion of character, action, setting, character and plot developments, and various types of plot structures. The narrative structure coding captures several features of the following text by 3rd grader George. Children's original spellings and wordings are included in all examples (except when letters or words are added in brackets to facilitate reading).

> Friends Fight
> *one day in Music I was working with Alexis. Tyronne got Mad a[t] Me Because I did not work with him. but then we came Friends. So I worked with Tyronne. but then Alxis got mad at me. But then I [work] with both of them. We all became friends.*

The narrative structure phase of coding notes that this text establishes the characters ("I, Alexis"), action ("was working"), setting ("one day in music"), and resolution, although not in a developed way. Like George with this "Friends Fight" story, most of the children were able to construct basic narratives in both the FN and AN contexts.

The narrative social relations phase of the coding, which is unique among narrative analysis systems, is the focus of the present study. This

EXHIBIT 4.1
Narrative Structure, Codes, and Variables

NARRATIVE STRUCTURE

Total narrative elements (sum of three possible subcategories below)

1. Establishes focal character
2. Action: Story set in motion; picks up on prompt
3. Setting

Characters included (sum of three possible subcategories below)

1. Focal character–protagonist
2. Other (multiple characters)
3. Self included

Character development (sum of five possible subcategories below)

1. Physical description and traits
2. Personality traits
3. Personality traits
4. Context
5. Motivations

Literary plot resolution (sum of four possible categories below)

1. Magical resolution
2. Major issue addressed minimally
3. Major issue resolved more fully

Significance (sum of three possible subcategories below)

1. Explicit reflection about story
2. Social significance of story
3. Cultural import

NARRATIVE SOCIAL RELATIONS

Characters: In autobiographical narratives: Focal (protagonist), Other 1 (antagonist), Other 2, 3

In fictional narratives: Jama (or protagonist), Max, Pat, Other

Character actions (sum across characters)
Character words (sum across characters)
Character psychological states (sums across characters and different psychological states)

1. Cognitions (*think, know, believe* . . .);
2. Intentions (*intend, tried to, was going to* . . .);
3. Feelings (*want, hope, feel sad, happy* . . .);
4. Perceptions (*saw, noticed, heard, listened*)

Conflict negotiation strategies (sum of six possible subcategories below)

1. Magical ("we became friends" but how not indicated)
2. Verbal steps ("said I was sorry"; talked it through; agreed; etc.)
3. Physical steps (hugged; gave the toy back; shared; etc.)
4. Mental steps ("I wanted to say I was sorry"; etc.)
5. Conflicting character perspectives recognized, empathized, acknowledged
6. Mediated or appealed (establish rule; persuade; persist; give up)

Agent(s) of conflict negotiation strategies (sum of four possible subcategories below)

1. Fate
2. One conflict participant played major role

EXHIBIT 4.1   (*Continued*)

3. Major conflict participants involved
4. Conflict observer–arbiter decided
5. Conflict observer–arbiter facilitated

Significance (sum of three possible subcategories below)

1. Reflect on conflict
2. Reflect on interpersonal consequences
3. Set in social, cultural context

Note. Information about coding is available from Colette Daiute, Graduate Center, The City University of New York, 365 Fifth Avenue, New York, NY.

coding identifies interpersonal and intergroup interactions among characters, characters' feelings and thoughts about these interactions, the nature of interaction difficulties, processes related to these difficulties, and the social and political organization of the narrative. The narrative social relations identify psychosocial relationships through various markers, including internal states (e.g., cognitions, intentions, feelings, perceptions) and a range of social-relational descriptions.

The narrative social relations coding of George's story indicates that the conflict revolved around character perspectives and entitlement (to the author's collaboration). The focal character "I" engaged in several actions which are described as prompting various psychological states—feeling "mad," cognition offering reason, "because ..." in another character, Alexis. In addition, narrative social relations codings identify the psychosocial representations across a range of voices in and around a narrative, including the author as narrator and as character. For example, even in the relatively brief text by George, two nonauthor characters' psychosocial states are represented ("Tyronne got mad ..." "then Alexis got mad"). The protagonist's psychosocial states are expressed through the causal justifications of other characters' states ("got mad at me because I did not work with him"); of his actions ("So I worked with Tyronne"; ... "But then I worked with both of them"). In addition, the author–protagonist conveys his assumptions about the other characters' internal states through the solution, "if I work with them both they won't be mad," implying that the conflict stems from his two friends' desire for his company. The conflict resolution strategy is primarily physical ("then I worked with both of them") but resolved to achieve social relational harmony ("We all became friends") rather than for the benefit of any individual character's desires. Describing interpersonal states and social relational systems in this way is a relatively novel narrative analytic approach. Both the FN and AN tasks were coded for narrative social relations and narrative structure with at least 80% reliability across three to four coders.

To assess relationships between social representations and narrative structure, we correlated the overall narrative social relations and narrative structure codes. Across time and tasks (FN, AN), the correlations were low to moderate, with higher correlation coefficients in the spring than in the fall. Narrative social relations and narrative structure correlations for the FN in the fall were .35 and the spring .51. Narrative social relations and narrative structure correlations for the AN in the fall were .48 and the spring .52. These correlations indicate that representing social relations in narratives captures something unaccounted for in narrative structure, which is important in justifying the new narrative social relations measurement and to establish that social relational analysis did not overly rely on a specific kind of European American narrative structure used in U.S. schools.

Narrative element codes indicated either the presence or absence of a category in a text. The dichotomous items were summed to account for the sums across codes, yielding variables including "Total character actions," "Total character words," "Total psychological states," "Total character cognitions," "Total character feelings," and so on. Similarly, enumerations of various perspective resolution strategies and different agents are compiled into "(Total) perspective resolution strategies" and "(Total) agents of resolution strategies."

Measures of Narrative Social Relations

Sums for 21 variables were used as measures of children's narrative writing. Summary variables for the FN and AN tasks in the fall were subtracted from sums for those variables in the spring. The resulting scores in narrative representations were then related through regression analyses to the presence of and changes in problem behaviors that put children at risk for traumatic or chronic injury or social isolation.

We examined both sets of FN and AN variables in relation to the problem behavior measures and did so separately on the basis of several assumptions about the use of fiction and autobiographical contexts for emotional release and self-development. The AN narratives were elicited for children's actual conflict experiences, crafted interpretively for salient issues at the time. Analyzing the explicitly fictional writings separately offers information about whether the issue of disclosures about personal conflicts (and children's presumptions about consequences of such disclosures to their reputations or grades) affects relationships between narrative writing and problem behaviors. The FN context provides the option of veiled personae within which children can explore what they may feel are shameful disclosures and to explore alternative selves, for example, by situating their own self perspective in one of the fictional characters. The AN, in contrast, is potentially a more public disclosure of issues that may be healing because they maintain details presented directly.

Measures of Problem Behavior

At the beginning and end of the school year, children involved in our study were asked to fill out a problem behavior questionnaire indicating the number of times during the past year they had been in a fight, sent to the Principal's office, and suspended from school (Schultz & Selman, 2000). The response options for these items included a choice of 0 times, 1 time, and then pairs of numbers, such as 2–3 times up to 12 or more times for the number of fights, and 4 or more times for the number of principal visit and suspensions.

The questionnaire indicates children's reports of their participation in events that (we theorized) put them at risk for injury, chronic physical problems, and threats to their psychological well-being because the behaviors involve social isolation and stigma. Although these may not be objective measures of actual fighting, trips to the Principal, or suspensions, these self-reports represent the children's perceptions or projections, so how they co-vary with social representations in narratives is relevant to the examination of the healing function of narrative writing.

Repeated fighting in school environments is also related to disciplinary procedures, such as being sent to the Principal, who might then suspend a child if something he or she did was against a major school policy. Being disciplined, especially by being suspended from school, then puts the child further at risk because being out of school increases learning problems, which put the child further out of the social mainstream. Reports of fights were more common than reports of principal visits, which were more frequent than reports of suspensions. Because these three variables relate to one another, they were combined into dichotomous variables for groups of children depending on presence or absence of problem behaviors at the points of measurement. By creating groups whose data were analyzed as a group, we examined behavioral change focusing on those children who did report problems in the fall but not in the spring.

Results

To predict change in problem behaviors over time from changes in narrative writing over time, a dichotomous outcome variable was used to separate data for the children who reported problems in the fall but not in the spring (coded as 1) from those that did not report problems in the fall but did in the spring or stayed the same over time (coded as 0). Following the inclusion criteria discussed above, the sample consisted of 79 children. See Table 4.1 for the gender and school grade composition of this sample. Analyses for the FN and AN writings were run separately because these contexts offered children different options for disclosure and privacy, as discussed above. A separate logistic regression was run for each narrative predictor.

TABLE 4.1
Gender and Grade Composition of Sample (*n* = 79; in Percentages)

Occurrence of problem behaviors	Gender		Grade	
	Boys	Girls	3rd	5th
In fall				
Yes	45	55	62	38
No	44	56	47	53
In spring				
Yes	42	58	58	42
No	48	52	52	48

Analyses of fictional narratives revealed that an increase over time in the number of agents of resolution strategies, total number of resolution strategies, and highest level of narrative social relations was associated with an increasing probability of problem behaviors decreasing over time. For example, a child whose narratives exhibit no change over time in the number of agents of resolution strategies has a .15 probability of showing this decrease in problematic behaviors over time. A child who reported one more agent in the spring than in the fall, and who reported problem behaviors in the fall, has a probability of .31 of exhibiting no problem behaviors in the spring. If this same child reported one less agent in the spring than the fall, this probability would decrease to .06. This same pattern of relationship holds for changes over time in the total number of resolution strategies and highest level of narrative social relations.

With regard to the highest level of narrative social relations reached, the children with increases or no change over time in problem behaviors began with higher means on this narrative variable in the fall than those children who reported problems in the fall but not in the spring. However, those children who reported problems in the fall but not the spring actually surpassed the other children in the level of writing reached by the spring (see Table 4.2).

This dichotomous problem behavior outcome was also significantly predicted by changes over time in the autobiographical narratives in reflections on the significance and consequence of conflict on social relationships and in number of agents of resolution strategies. The probability of a child who exhibits problem behaviors in the fall showing no problems in the spring is .16 when this child shows no change over time in reflections on the significance and consequence of conflict on social relationships. When this child's narrative reflecting increases by one point from fall to spring, the probability of the child reporting no problem behaviors in the spring rises to .37; if this child demonstrates less reflection in the spring, this probability decreases to .06. The pattern of results for the total number of agents of resolution strategies in the autobiographical narratives

TABLE 4.2
Narrative Variable Means (*n* = 79)

Narrative type: Variable	Fall		Spring	
	M	*SD*	*M*	*SD*
Fictional: Sum of agents of resolution strategies				
Increase problems or stayed the same	.70	.55	.83	.63
Decrease problem behaviors	.27	.46	.80	.56
Fictional: Highest level of social relations reached				
Increase problems or stayed the same	3.55	1.05	3.70	1.05
Decrease problem behaviors	2.53	1.19	3.80	.77
Fictional: Sum of resolution strategies				
Increase problems or stayed the same	1.14	.91	1.19	.97
Decrease problem behaviors	.47	.74	1.20	.86
Autobiographical: Significance or consequence on social relations				
Increase problems or stayed the same	.14	.35	.16	.37
Decrease problem behaviors	.07	.26	.47	.64
Autobiographical: Sum of agents of resolution strategies				
Increase problems or stayed the same	.63	.70	.91	.64
Decrease problem behaviors	.40	.63	1.13	.52

is similar to this pattern for reflections. The children who decreased in problem behaviors over time began the fall with lower means on both of these variables and ended with higher means in the spring than the children who increased or stayed the same in problem behaviors (see Table 4.2).

Writing about resolution strategies appears to be an important focus for children, in the realm of problematic behaviors. In particular, similarities in increases in representations of conflict resolutions and agents of resolutions related to decreases in reports of problem behaviors underscore common narrative functions across fictional and autobiographical contexts. The specific narrative variables demonstrating this relationship, moreover, capture complex social relational orientations. The unique AN result of increases in comments about the significance of conflicts suggests a power in relevance to real situations, whereas the unique FN increase in highest level of social relations suggests a power in idealization in fiction.

Of the 21 summary variables tested in these logistic regression analyses, the 3 that related most significantly to changes in social risk behaviors capture safe conflict resolution strategies. Total resolution strategies is a sum of narrative representations of different kinds of resolutions strategies taught in the curriculum, including "walking away" (which is sometimes the most appropriate response in a threatening conflict), "talking it out," "compromising," "physical connections (like hugging)," "finding a new solution," and "mental strategies," such as imagining or intending a resolution. Increases in agents of resolutions are also a socially desired and wise strategy because this variable accounts for representations of conflict resolutions that call on facilitators (parents, teachers, peers, etc.) to help when tensions arise. Finally, increases in the highest level of narrative social relations achieved capture an overall tendency toward social negotiation represented in the narrative, because higher levels denote strategies conceptualized as most mature. One of the highest points on the scale is for including in a narrative a character's or the author's explicit reflection about the consequences of the conflict on social and cultural relationships, which is also related to decreases in problem behavior reports. This study was not intended as a program evaluation, but to gain some insight into the issue of maturation in social aspects of narrative writing, data collected from a comparison group illustrate the interactive nature of narrative writing with social context.[1]

An example illustrates how the healing function of writing presents itself. Dianna, a fifth grader who identifies her race–ethnicity as Jamaican, was one of the children who reported fewer problem behaviors in the spring (2) than in the fall (10). Dianna's two autobiographical conflict narratives, presented below, show the kinds of changes in writing that are related to decreases in reports of problem behaviors. In the story she wrote in the fall, "My Conflicts by: Dianna," Dianna wrote about a conflict with her friend Serena.

> My Conflict by: Dianna
>
> I had a conflict with my friend Serena in the park. She was calling me names and hiting me. I was walking away but she following me. But I was'nt calling her names to start with. I was feeling mad but a little sad, because of what she said to me. But I knew that it was not true.

This description of Dianna and Serena's fight is characteristic of narratives earlier in the year, in particular because of the predominance of the author-as-protagonist and victim point of view. Dianna was called names, hit, and felt bad. Dianna hints that she engaged in name calling, but only in retaliation, "I was'nt calling her names to start with." There is, moreover, no description of attempts to resolve the conflict. In contrast, Dianna's spring narrative, "The Fight," reports resolution strategies and a reflection about the conflict.

> My friend and I were whtching a movie and we saw the movie before so we played fight. I hurt her badly and she got mad so she hurt me

---

[1]Repeated measures analyses of variance were used to examine the impact of curriculum involvement on the fictional writing task. The comparison group included children from the same school and similar backgrounds but not involved in the same violence prevention curriculum. Analyses of changes in the means of 21 narrative variables across fictional narratives written by the group discussed in the present study and the comparison group at two points earlier and later in the school year revealed several significant Time × Group interactions. Of the 21 narrative variables, the comparison group decreased representations on all the narrative social relations variables for which the focal group showed increases.

badly and we had a fight. She hit me and I hit her back. She sat on me and I could not get out. I got out and kicked her she got hurt by my kick and she slapped me and I cry. I tried not to let her see. I could not stop. It hurt a lot, and I slapped her back and it did not hurt her at all. So we foght some more and I cried and I went home and she called and said, "Sorry. Fighting does not help." I said "Sorry." and made up.

It is interesting that Dianna reports that her friend was the one who initiated the conflict resolution by calling and apologizing. After Dianna responded in kind, they made up. The resolution strategy also embeds a reflection on the conflict when Dianna's friend points out that "Fighting does not help."

In addition to illustrating the dynamic narrative features in relation to decreases in problem behavior, these stories by Dianna also illustrate the nature of protective aspects of narrative writing. Narrative writing does not obliterate all reports of aggressive and violent behavior, as illustrated by the more detailed and protracted fight reported in the spring story. Instead, these events are reported within a different social script. It is impossible to locate "The Fight" in time in relation to the previous story, to the time of writing, to the fighting events in Dianna's life, or to those reports of them. What is clear, however, is the change in how physical conflicts are reported and that the more prosocial way Dianna narrates conflict is around the same time as she reported fewer problem behaviors in her life.

The connections between increasingly "prosocial" conflict resolutions and decreases in reports of problem behaviors may be based on changes in the physical world or in children's orientations to the physical world. In other words, children's reports of fighting and so on may be changing as "narratives" of their behavior just as their conflict narratives change. If children change the social scripts with which they organize narratives in ways similar to how they change social scripts with which they fill out behavioral questionnaires, a link between realms of discourse and action is a significant step toward our conceptualizations of variables for research.

A distinction between feelings and emotions described by Vygotsky is relevant to explain uses of writing characterized by increasing narrative evaluation (as in the variables for resolutions, agents, and significance) compared to increasing referential reports (as in the variable for character action), which were not isolated in relation to decreases in reports of problem behaviors.

> Despite the apparent similarity between feelings and emotions, these processes have different roles in mental life. Compare the [wo]man who is aware of a danger and arms [her]self in advance with the [wo]man who is not aware and is attacked, or compare the [wo]man who can run with the [wo]man who discovers the danger by surprise. In other words, compare the person who can find an adequate exit from the

situation to one who cannot. The psychological processes that are involved in the two situations are very different. (Vygotsky, 1987, p. 335)

He goes on to explain, "What is [a problem] in this system is not the intellectual or emotional processes themselves, but their relationship" (Vygotsky, 1987, p. 337). What we think we have begun to illustrate here is that the evaluative phase of narrative writing, in particular, with its social–emotional qualities is a powerful protective tool.

Discussion

Conflict resolution skills require mature understanding and control in young children, and this study illustrates how narrative writing can provide supports for such developments. On the basis of our theoretical framework, we argue that changes in orientation and self-reported-action are changes that place Dianna and other children in this study in a different position in social life. Shifts in psychosocial orientation may make an important, even life-saving, difference for a child at some point when a less resourceful orientation might involve her in interactions leading to irreparable harm.

This relatively novel inquiry thus establishes baseline descriptions and relationships between narrative writing and health-risk measures in systematic ways that connect to the writing paradigm and offer insights for extensions in future research. By defining narrative as a social process of self presentation in a social context, the study we described in this chapter explores the healing function of writing as the integration of social–cognitive–emotional life, which influences some aspects of living in stressful environments that might be under a person's control.

Although this study is a preliminary and descriptive examination of the impact of narrative writing, the nature and development of expression of psychological states in conflictual social relations suggests the value of such writing in educational and clinical settings. Writing narratives about conflict repeatedly over time is not a common practice in educational or child counseling settings. Contemporary writing process approaches actually frown on assigning writing topics, so asking children to write about conflicts or any specific issue like painful experiences might seem inauthentic or controlling. The wide range of representations that children make in response to the prompts for social conflict narratives offers evidence to the contrary. Moreover, in the context of a curriculum, practices can be established to guide kind and fair listening among children and teachers and to provide referrals for any extreme expressions. The social and emotional richness of the children's narrative writing discussed here can, moreover, be added to arguments to maintain curricula that are being omitted from school practice, because they do not directly support improved performance on standardized tests. More work on social issues in school could eliminate the need for some counseling or could allow counselors to begin at a higher level of intervention with students who have had the chance to express their pain. This study indicates that by Grade 3 (7–8 years old), children can sustain and use narrative writing for personal gains, and insights from the narrative social relations coding scheme described here could be useful to clinicians and counselors as tools they can use with children for self-reflection.

Our purpose was to understand the restorative functions of writing. We are not implying that responsibility lies mostly with the individual, especially when those at risk are children who should be able to count on environments to support their health and well-being. Given contemporary realities, we researchers identify supports children can use for self-determination, social connection, and, when necessary, protection. What we identify in research can then be applied to educational, clinical, and social service practices and policies, as well as to future research. We hope that soon we are able to study the expansive functions of writing—functions related to children's thriving and leadership.

REFERENCES

Baerger, D. R., & McAdams, D. P. (1999). Life story coherence and its relation to psychological well being. *Narrative Inquiry, 9,* 69–96.

Billig, M. (1999). *Freudian repression: Conversation creating the unconscious.* New York: Cambridge University Press.

Boyd-Franklin, N., & Franklin, A. J. (2000). *Boys into men: Raising our African-American teenage sons.* New York: Dutton.

Cross, W. E., & Strauss, L. (1998). The everyday functions of African American identity. In J. Swim & C. Stangor (Eds.), *Prejudice: The targets perspective* (pp. 268–278). New York: Academic Press.

Daiute, C. (1998). Points of view in children's writing. *Language Arts, 75,* 138–149.

Daiute, C. (2000). Narrative sites for youths' construction of social consciousness. In M. Fine & L. Weis (Eds.), *Construction sites: Excavating class, race, gender, and sexuality among urban youth* (pp. 211–234). New York: Teachers College Press.

Daiute, C. (2001). Social relational knowing in writing development. In E. Amsel & J. Byrnes (Eds.), *Language, literacy, and cognitive development* (pp. 193–229). Mahwah, NJ: Erlbaum.

Daiute, C., Buteau, E., & Rawlins, C. (2001). Social relational wisdom: Developmental diversity in children's written narratives about social conflict. *Narrative Inquiry, 11*(2), 1–30.

Daiute, C., & Griffin, T. M. (1993). The social construction of written narrative.

In C. Daiute (Ed.), *The development of literacy through social interaction* (pp. 97–120). San Francisco: Jossey Bass.

Daiute, C., & Jones, H. (in press). Diversity discourses: Reading race and ethnicity in children's writing. In S. Greene & D. Abt-Perkins (Eds.), *Talking, reordering, writing, and race: Contribution to racial understanding by literacy research*. New York: Teachers College Press.

Daiute, C., Stern, R., & Lelutiu-Weinberger, C. (in press). Negotiating violence prevention. *Journal of Social Issues*.

Hamburg, M. A. (1998). Youth violence is a public health concern. In D. S. Elliott, B. Hamburg, & K. R. Williams (Eds.), *Violence in American schools: A new perspective* (pp. 31–54). New York: Cambridge University Press.

Hermans, H. J. M., & Hermans-Jansen, E. (1995). *Self-narratives: The construction of meaning in psychotherapy*. New York: Guilford Press.

Kliewer, W., Lepore, S. J., Oskin, D., & Johnson, P. D. (1998). The role of social and cognitive processes in children's adjustment to community violence. *Journal of Consulting and Clinical Psychology, 66*(1), 199–209.

Labov, W., & Waletzky, J. (1997). Narrative analysis: Oral versions of personal experience. *Journal of Narrative and Life History, 7*(1–4), 3–38.

Laub, J. H., & Lauritsen, J. L. (1998). The interdependence of school violence and neighborhood and family conditions. In D. S. Elliott, B. Hamburg, & K. R. Williams (Eds.), *Violence in American schools: A new perspective* (pp. 127–155). New York: Cambridge University Press.

Lepore, S. J. (1997). Expressive writing moderates the relation between intrusive thoughts and depressive symptoms. *Journal of Personality and Social Psychology, 73*, 1030–1037.

Levitt, M. Z., & Selman, R. (1996). The personal meaning of risk behavior: A developmental perspective on friendship and fighting in early adolescence. In G. G. Noam & K. W. Fischer (Eds.), *Development and vulnerability in close relationships* (pp. 201–233). Mahwah, NJ: Erlbaum.

Lightfoot, C. (1998). *The culture of adolescent risk-taking*. New York: Guilford Press.

Nelson, V. M. (1993). *Mayfield crossing*. New York: Avon.

Nystrand, M., & Wiemelt, J. (1993, February). *On the dialogic nature of discourse and learning*. Paper presented at the annual meeting of the National Council of Teacher of English Research Assembly, Pittsburgh, PA.

Pennebaker, J. W. (1997). Writing about emotional experiences as part of a therapeutic process. *Psychological Science, 8*(3), 162–166.

Pennebaker, J. W., & Beall, S. (1986). Confronting a traumatic event: Toward an understanding of inhibition and disease. *Journal of Abnormal Psychology, 95*, 274–281.

Peterson, C., & McCabe, A. (1983). *Developmental psychology: Three ways of looking at children's narratives*. New York: Plenum.

Samples, F., & Aber, L. (1998). Evaluations of school-based violence prevention programs. In D. S. Elliot, B. A. Hamburg, & K. R. Williams (Eds.), *Violence in American schools* (pp. 217–252). New York: Cambridge University Press.

Schultz, L. H., & Selman, R. L. (2000). *The meaning and measurement of social competence from a developmental perspective.* Unpublished manuscript. Cambridge, MA: Harvard Graduate School of Education.

Smyth, J. M. (1998). Written emotional expression: Effect sizes, outcome types, and moderating variables. *Journal of Consulting and Clinical Psychology, 66,* 174–184.

Stein, N. L., & Albro, E. R. (1997). Building complexity and coherence: Children's use of goal-structured knowledge in telling stories. In M. Bamberg (Ed.), *Narrative development: Six approaches* (pp. 1–44). Mahwah, NJ: Erlbaum.

Surat, M. M. (1983). *Angel child, dragon child.* New York: Scholastic.

Vygotsky, L. S. (1987). Emotions and their development in childhood. In R. W. Rieber & A. S. Carton (Eds.), *The collected works of L. S. Vygotksy: Vol. 1. Problems of general psychology* (pp. 325–338). New York: Plenum Press.

Walker, P. (1998). *Voices of love and freedom.* Logan, IA: Perfection Learning Corp.

Wertsch, J. (1991). *Voices in the mind: Toward a sociocultural theory of mediated action.* Cambridge, MA: Harvard University Press.

5

THE EFFECTS OF WRITTEN EMOTIONAL DISCLOSURE AMONG REPRESSIVE AND ALEXITHYMIC PEOPLE

MARK A. LUMLEY, TINA M. TOJEK, AND DEBRA J. MACKLEM

"Write about a traumatic experience and my deepest feelings? Well, I really don't think that I've had any stressful experiences. My life has been just fine."
—Middle-aged woman with rheumatoid arthritis

"I'm not sure what has been stressful, and I don't know what I am feeling."
—Young man who reported a high level of vague physical symptoms

Whose health and functioning is most likely to benefit from written or verbal disclosure? Who will not benefit, or even worsen? We hypothesize that the success of these techniques hinges on the ability and willingness of people to access, express, process, and ultimately resolve negative emotional memories (Pennebaker, 1997). Beneficial disclosure outcomes occur when people recognize and acknowledge personally stressful experiences, access and activate emotional memories of those experiences, identify and put into words their emotions, and eventually think differently about the experience. In this chapter, we examine whether the effects of disclosure depend on people's motivation and ability to engage in these steps. In particular, we examine theory and research on people with two types of limitations in emotional awareness and expression—people with repressive

Work on this chapter was supported in part by a grant from the Arthritis Foundation.

personalities and people with alexithymia (a deficit in emotional awareness and understanding).

DIFFERENT TYPES OF LIMITED EMOTIONAL AWARENESS, UNDERSTANDING, AND EXPRESSION

Over the years, writers have used various labels for problems in emotional awareness, understanding, and expression. Terms such as *inhibited*, *ambivalent over expression, unemotional, defended, secretive, suppressed, repressed, stoic, alexithymic, low level thinking*, and *emotionally unintelligent* have proliferated, likely confusing both researchers and clinicians who try to differentiate these constructs or apply them to particular people. Kennedy-Moore and Watson (1999) have recently provided a model that has the potential to bring order to this conceptual chaos. Their model posits a series of five steps or processes that transpire between the presentation of an emotion-eliciting stimulus and the eventual expression of emotion. Each step relates to a personality characteristic or environmental factor that may block the progression of expression. Here are the five steps in their model.

Step 1: Prereflective reaction. A potentially emotion-provoking stimulus must cross a person's psychological and biological threshold to activate a basic or primary affective state and accompanying physiological arousal. If people lack or have a limited prereflective reaction, either because of a high threshold for emotional activation or an appraisal that the stimulus is benign or irrelevant, then no emotion is generated, and hence, no expression occurs.

Step 2: Conscious perception of response. If a stimulus activates a basic affective response, then one needs conscious recognition of this experience. Some people, however, have a defensive perceptual set that impedes recognition of their own negative emotions, such as anger, fear, or sadness. Such people appear to be unconsciously motivated to disavow negative experiences, and because they do not recognize negative experiences within themselves, they usually deny negative emotions and do not express them. As discussed below, this motivated lack of awareness has been referred to as *repressive coping* or the *repressive personality*.

Step 3: Labeling and interpretation of response. If a person is able to admit to conscious awareness the experience of a negative affective state, then the third step occurs—the person attempts to identify, label, and understand the emotion. Some people, however, have difficulty recognizing, differentiating, and identifying their emotions, so that they typically show attenuated or undifferentiated emotional expression and poor emotional communication.

Step 4: Evaluation of response as acceptable. If a person is able to differentiate and process emotions, then expression hinges first on a person's idiosyncratic attitudes, values, and concerns about expression. Some people's developmental or cultural histories have taught them to suppress or inhibit the expression of certain emotions. For example, although a person might recognize that he or she is angry or sad, such emotions may be characteristically inhibited because the person has a negative attitude toward expressing that emotion.

Step 5: Perceived social context for expression. Finally, even if a person typically permits himself or herself to express specific emotions, the immediate environment may discourage such expression. Thus, because of a perceived lack of opportunity to express, a person may inhibit displaying anger or fear in certain circumstances, such as when dealing with an authority or during an emergency.

In the literature on emotional disclosure, we have noted a tendency to extend the term *inhibition* or *inhibited personality* to cover various reasons for limited emotional awareness and expression. For example, *inhibited personality* has been used to describe people who are unconsciously motivated to avoid recognizing their own negative emotions, and *inhibition* has been used to refer to people who have a deficit in their ability to identify their own feelings (Paez, Basabe, Valdoseda, Velasco, & Iraurgi, 1995; Pennebaker, 1997). We feel that the terms *inhibition* or *suppression* are best reserved to describe people who do not express certain emotions because of a negative attitude toward expression (Step 4) or a perceived lack of opportunity to express (Step 5). That is, inhibition is a conscious, volitional cause of nonexpression. In our view, and in Kennedy-Moore and Watson's (1999) model, repression and alexithymia are fundamentally different processes than inhibition. We think that these distinctions are critical when considering how written disclosure studies are typically conducted.

If you were a participant assigned to the experimental condition of the typical written disclosure study, you would be given instructions that include something like the following: "Write about your very deepest thoughts and feelings about the most traumatic experience of your entire life. In your writing, I'd like you to really let go and explore your very deepest emotions and thoughts" (Pennebaker & Seagal, 1999, p. 1244). These instructions, as well as the theory that gave rise to the written disclosure paradigm, appear to assume that participants are able to engage in the first three steps of Kennedy-Moore and Watson's (1999) model but that they need help with Steps 4 and 5. That is, the traditional disclosure technique appears to be best suited for a person who has experienced an event that triggers negative emotions (Step 1), is willing to consciously admit having a negative emotional experience (Step 2), and who is able to examine and explore his or her emotions (Step 3), but who also needs support and permission to disclose and express. The typical disclosure study —with its explicit encouragement to disclose negative emotions and the privacy it guarantees—provides a wonderful opportunity for participants to reveal negative experiences if they have not done so before or to take a fresh and honest look at previously disclosed experiences as they put them into language and change their thinking about those experiences.

However, what happens if a person is not able to consciously recognize and accept having a negative emotional experience (Step 2) or is confused about the feelings and is unable to "explore" (identify, label, understand) and communicate the emotions in language (Step 3)? We hypothesize that people whose emotional awareness and expression are truncated at these earlier steps do not demonstrate benefits from the usual disclosure technique. In this chapter, we examine the effects of disclosure among people who have a motivated avoidance of negative emotions in the self (repressive personality) and people whose emotional explorations are impaired because of deficits in emotional awareness and understanding (alexithymia).

EMOTIONAL AWARENESS, UNDERSTANDING, AND EXPRESSION AS MODERATORS OF DISCLOSURE

It is important to identify differences among people that influence their response to disclosure. From an applied perspective, knowledge of such variables can reveal *who* benefits, which can lead to more reliable prescriptions for the use of disclosure and more accurate prognoses about outcomes. From a theoretical perspective, the study of individual differences can reveal *why* there is variability in responses to disclosure, which can lead to the refinement and advancement of theory.

How do researchers test the effects of individual differences in emotional awareness and expression on people's responses to disclosure? Typically, researchers assess all participants for a given characteristic at baseline, and then, after the intervention has been conducted and follow-up data collected, these characteristics are tested to see whether they "moderate" disclosure's effects on subsequent health outcomes. When moderation is present, then the effect of the intervention on the outcome is said to depend on the level of the moderator variable. The moderator variable is associated with one outcome in the experimental group but a different outcome in the control group. Researchers in psychotherapy refer to this as an *Aptitude × Treatment interaction*, and it is demonstrated statistically by a significant interaction term between group (e.g., experimental vs. control) and the individual difference moderator variable in an analysis of variance or regression model.

Although testing interaction terms in a randomized, experimental study is the most appropriate way of assessing moderators, this approach is relatively conservative, and some types of interactions are more difficult to detect statistically than others. It appears to be quite common for researchers to use less rigorous methods to explore individual difference moderators of disclosure. For example, rather than test interactions, some researchers attempt to show only that there is a significant relationship between a personality variable and outcome within the disclosure group, but no significant relationship among controls. An even more liberal approach is to demonstrate only a significant relationship between the personality variable and outcome among the disclosure group without reference to a control group. In addition, some investigators attempt to infer for whom disclosure works by comparing the types of populations for which it has or has not been found to be successful. All of these latter approaches have substantial interpretive limitations.

In their review, Pennebaker and Keough (1999) concluded that the available literature has not revealed any consistent personality measures indicating who benefits from disclosure. At the time of their review, however, few studies of disclosure moderators had been conducted. Since then, several studies have been published, and there are unpublished studies that researchers (including ourselves) have conducted that have examined individual differences in emotional awareness and expression and how they relate to the effects of disclosure. The reader is cautioned in advance, however, that research on moderators of disclosure is in its infancy, some of these studies are as yet unpublished, and some findings are not consistent. However, we wish to be comprehensive, so we present all relevant research about the relationship of emotional awareness and expression moderators to outcomes after disclosure, and we make appropriately tentative interpretations and conclusions. We recognize that our conclusions may change as more research in this maturing area emerges.

THE REPRESSIVE PERSONALITY

Kennedy-Moore and Watson (1999) have suggested that failure at Step 2 in the sequence of events leading to emotional expression—motivated lack of awareness of negative emotions—can be due to repressive coping, or a repressive personality. Here we refer to a personality style in which negative aspects of the self, especially negative emotions and motivations, are routinely denied without apparent conscious intent or recognition. Research on the repressive personality was stimulated greatly when Weinberger, Schwartz, and Davidson (1979) operationalized the construct for assessment. These authors noted that people who report low levels of anxiety consist of two groups that can be differentiated on the basis of their responses to a measure of social desirability (e.g., the Marlowe-Crowne Social Desirability [MC] Scale; Crowne & Marlowe, 1964). People reporting low negative affect who also score low in social desirability on the MC Scale are truly experiencing low levels of negative affect. However, a minority of people who report low negative affect score relatively high on the MC Scale, and these people (termed *repressors*) differ from truly low anxious people. For example, they show behavioral and physiological signs of arousal or negative emotion and avoid experiences that might challenge their positive sense of self (Schwartz & Kline, 1995; Weinberger, 1990). Although most research on repressive coping has used the approach developed by Weinberger et al. (1979), several other approaches have also been developed, including the Weinberger Adjustment Inventory (Weinberger, 1991) and the Millon Behavioral Health Inventory (Millon, Green, & Meagher, 1982).

Repressive Personality and Responses to Disclosure Tasks

The quotes presented at the start of the chapter were from two people invited to participate in written or verbal disclosure studies. The first is from a middle-aged woman with rheumatoid arthritis who was assigned to the experimental group and asked to talk about stressful experiences. She did not complete the assigned task and some weeks later dropped out of the study, stating that her life was fine and that she did not experience stress. Her response is typical of a person with a repressive personality— denying stress and avoiding experiences that require psychological examination of negative aspects of the self.

How might repressive coping affect the process and outcome of written or verbal disclosure? It could be argued that repressive individuals benefit from disclosure. Perhaps the private, self-directed task of disclosing upsetting experiences at the pace with which one feels comfortable allows the repressive individual to lower defenses and begin the process of working through negative experiences. Repeating this over several days may succeed in circumventing defenses. Unlike psychotherapy, in which the presence and responses of the therapist may elicit stronger defensive reactions from the repressive person, it is possible that the private disclosure task is ideally suited for the repressive individual. Also, it is possible that these individuals' tendency to view themselves and their experiences positively would lead to high levels of expressed positive emotion in their disclosures, which has been associated with beneficial outcomes of the disclosure task (Pennebaker, Mayne, & Francis, 1997).

We hypothesize, however, that repressive individuals experience reduced benefit from disclosure, and they may even manifest some worsening, compared with nonrepressive individuals or with repressive individuals in a control condition. As with our example above, repressive individuals may avoid participating entirely in the disclosure task because it threatens their positive self-image. When they do participate, they would be expected to have difficulty consciously acknowledging and identifying a personal negative emotional experience. If they do report an experience, they may disclose only those experiences that are relatively common, superficial, or publicly validated, such as having a medical illness or the death of a loved one. Even then, repressive individuals would be expected to deny or minimize the expression of negative affect in their disclosures, which may limit benefits.

Our review of the literature revealed only three studies that have examined repressive coping in studies of written or verbal disclosure. Pennebaker and Beall (1986) assessed the effects of written disclosure on health, short-term physiological arousal, and mood among 46 undergraduates who wrote for 4 days about one of four topics: feelings related to a trauma, facts related to a trauma, both the facts and feelings about a trauma, or trivial topics. The MC Scale was also administered at baseline. Although writing about both the facts and emotions surrounding a traumatic event led to the best health outcomes, MC scores were not related to any of the dependent measures when all participants were analyzed as a single group. Unfortunately, however, the authors collapsed experimental and control participants together, which makes it impossible to tell whether high MC scores were related to outcomes of expressive writing alone. Also, although using the MC alone may provide an approximate measure of repressive coping, it would have been preferable to identify the repressor subgroup by crossing it with a measure of negative affect.

Esterling, Antoni, Kumar, and Schneiderman (1990) had undergraduates who were seropositive for the Epstein–Barr virus (EBV) write for one 30-minute session about a personally stressful experience and then provide blood for determining immune status—titers of the EBV capsid antigen. (Higher titers indicate poorer immune control.) Essays were rated for the percentage of emotional words used, and participants were classified into high, middle, and low discloser groups as a function of the proportion of emotional words used. Participants also were classified as repressive individuals, sensitizers (nondefensive), or neither on the basis of their responses to various scales of the Millon Behavioral Health Inventory. These researchers found an interaction between personality style and amount of disclosure in predicting EBV titers. Repressive individuals had relatively high titers of EBV capsid antigen, regardless of the level of disclosure, whereas sensitizers with the highest disclosure levels had the lowest titers. This suggests that repressive participants did not benefit from emotional writing, whereas nondefensive people (sensitizers) who disclosed the most did benefit. The effect sizes were large, allowing the relatively small sample (13 repressive individuals) to yield significant results. Although this study appears to support our hypothesis, interpretations should be made cautiously. The lack of an experimental design with random assignment to a nondisclosure control group precludes a clear conclusion that repressive individuals have a unique response to the disclosure task.

In an unpublished master's thesis, Habbal (1999) asked 53 older women (mean age = 65.5 years) who had a personal (n = 45) or family (n = 8) history of cancer to write once a week for 4 weeks about either stressful life experiences (two-thirds of the women) or a control topic (daily events). The researcher also gave the Weinberger Adjustment Inventory at baseline and measured the incidence of self-reported colds as well as mood and physical symptoms at 1 and 3 months after the start of writing. Women with a high degree of defensiveness on the Weinberger Adjustment Inventory used a lower number of negative emotion words in their essays than did low defensive women. Another finding was a trend for an interaction (p = .08) between writing group and defensiveness in the prediction of colds. Women with low defensiveness were less likely to have a cold in the month following writing, whereas those with high defensiveness were similar to controls, for whom defensiveness was not related to having a cold. This suggests that defensive participants did not experience protective benefits of written disclosure. These results, however, no longer held at the 3-month interval, and no relationship between defensiveness and other health outcomes was discerned at any point.

Summary: Repressive Coping and Disclosure

Two of the studies that we reviewed (Esterling et al., 1990; Habbal, 1999) suggest that repressive individuals show less benefit in response to a disclosure task, and one of these indicated that they use fewer negative emotion words in their disclosures. However, Esterling et al. did not include a control group, and Habbal's unpublished study had findings that were limited to one dependent variable, which only approached statistical significance. The negative finding by Pennebaker and Beall (1986) can be discounted because the analytic method precluded testing whether repression was related to less benefit among only disclosure participants. Two additional studies by Christensen and colleagues (Christensen & Smith, 1993; Christensen et al., 1996) may also shed some light on the role of repression. These authors examined trait hostility as a moderator of disclosure among male undergraduates during a single, brief (approximately 5 minutes) session of either verbal self-disclosure or nondisclosure (control). In both studies, people with high trait hostility responded to the disclosure with either altered blood pressure reactivity or increased natural killer cell cytotoxicity, whereas these changes did not occur for low hostile participants or during the control session. Because one can infer that repressive individuals would not be found among the high hostile people but would comprise some subset of the low hostile people, these studies also suggest that benefit from disclosure accrues for people who acknowledge negative emotion rather than those who deny it. In summary, we feel that there is preliminary, although tentative evidence that repression interferes with the effects of written disclosure.

THE ALEXITHYMIC PERSONALITY

Kennedy-Moore and Watson's (1999) model indicates that emotional expression can be hindered at Step 3 if a person is unable to identify and label an emotionally aroused state. The term *alexithymia*, which literally means "lacking words for feelings," was coined in the early 1970s by psychodynamically-oriented clinicians who found that many of their clients with various stress-related or psychosomatic illnesses were unable to engage productively in insight-oriented psychotherapy. Such clients show little insight into the sources of negative moods and their stressful experiences, and they seem confused about the factors that exacerbate their symptoms. When asked about their feelings regarding seemingly important relationships or other emotionally provocative situations, alexithymic people typically experience confusion and are unable to answer (e.g., "I don't know"), or their answers are vague and simple (e.g., "I felt bad"). Alternatively, their responses may reflect bodily states (e.g., "my stomach hurt") or simply describe external factors, such as the times, people, or places that are associated with emotions. Alexithymic people are often rather expressionless, stiff, and monotonous, and their conversation focuses on external and concrete experiences rather than on internal, psychological experiences (Taylor, Bagby, & Parker, 1997).

Taylor and colleagues (1997) have extensively reviewed the alexithymia literature, and they have concluded that alexithymia is neither a repressive process, nor an inhibited, suppressed condition; rather, it is a deficit or lack of ability to process and regulate emotional states through the use of cognitive mechanisms such as introspection, imagination, and fantasy. Our laboratory also has contributed to this literature, and we (Lumley, Stettner, & Wehmer, 1996) have examined how alexithymia may be a risk factor for health problems. People with alexithymia are more likely to be found among the medically and psychiatrically ill, especially among people with somatoform disorders, substance abuse problems, eating disorders, anxiety disorders, hypertension, and chronic pain. Research on alexithymia has been conducted almost exclusively with the self-report Toronto Alexithymia Scale (TAS; Taylor, Ryan, & Bagby, 1985) or its 20-item revision (TAS-20; Bagby, Parker, & Taylor, 1994). Although the TAS-20 yields a total alexithymia score, many studies have also calculated and analyzed scores from its three-factor analytically derived subscales: difficulty identifying and differentiating feelings (e.g., "I am often puzzled by sensations in my body"), difficulty describing feelings (e.g., "I find it hard to describe how I feel about people"), and an externalized cognitive style that lacks imagination and fantasy (e.g., "I prefer to just let things happen rather than to understand why they turned out that way").

Alexithymia and Responses to Disclosure Tasks

The second quote at the start of the chapter was from a young man with elevated physical symptoms who was participating in a written disclosure study. The quote is typical of an alexithymic person, reflecting confusion about feelings and uncertainty about sources of stress.

How might alexithymic participants respond to disclosure interventions? One could argue that they might benefit from written disclosure. Alexithymic people may have never been encouraged or given the opportunity to engage in the task of trying to examine their psychological lives with the goal of understanding and resolving stress. They may not have valued such a process before, and therefore, never taken the time to engage in it. In addition, their physical symptoms or relationship struggles may prompt them to try anything to improve functioning. Thus, the alexithymic person might take advantage of this new opportunity offered by the task to learn to introspect, disclose, and process stressful experiences.

Nonetheless, we hypothesized that alexithymia interferes with the process and outcome of the typical disclosure task. Alexithymic people are likely to be confused by the simple instructions to write or talk about a stressful experience, including all of their feelings. These instructions go to the heart of the alexithymic deficit—the inability to understand one's internal state and the cognitive triggers for emotions, and the inability to appropriately express one's feelings. As suggested by the observations of clinicians who have worked with alexithymic clients, such clients may be quite willing to attempt a disclosure intervention, but they may be confused, perhaps be unable to identify a stressor, have trouble differentiating and labeling negative emotions or positive emotions, and demonstrate little insight into their experiences. In theory, these deficits should hinder the emotional as well as cognitive work needed to benefit from disclosure.

In several published and unpublished studies, researchers have examined how alexithymia predicts responses to disclosure. The first study appears to contradict our hypothesis. Paez, Velasco, and Gonzalez (1999) had undergraduates conduct either intensive writing (3 days) or brief writing (1 day for 3 minutes) about traumatic events. Participants also completed the difficulty describing the feelings subscale of the TAS-20. Participants with greater difficulty describing feelings had essays that were rated as less introspective, had fewer self-references, and fewer positive (but not negative) emotional words. Regarding outcomes, the authors reported that participants with high difficulty describing feelings had a substantial reduction in negative affect (but no change in positive affect) 2 months after intensive writing compared with brief writing, whereas this pattern was not seen for those with low difficulty describing feelings. In contrast, among only those participants who wrote briefly, greater difficulty describing feelings was associated with greater negative affect after 2 months. Although the authors concluded that alexithymic individuals seemed to improve in mood after expressive writing, it is important to note that the single TAS subscale that the authors analyzed does not capture the full alexithymia construct, but appears to measure introversion and reluctance to discuss feelings interpersonally (Bagby, Taylor, & Parker, 1994) and is closely linked with shame (Suslow, Donges, Kersting, & Arolt, 2000). Thus, this study provides only preliminary evidence that more days of expressive writing may be beneficial for people who are socially or emotionally inhibited and do not routinely talk about their feelings, but the results may not apply to people who are truly alexithymic.

Smyth, Anderson, Hockemeyer, and Stone (in press) examined the relationship of alexithymia using the TAS-20 to several aspects of essays, mood changes, and health outcomes among 71 people who had either rheumatoid arthritis or asthma. Analyses revealed no significant relationships between the total TAS-20 score and judges' ratings of how personal or emotional the essays were, how much narrative structure the essays had, the degree of mood changes from before to after writing, and physician-evaluated physical health status at 4 months. These negative findings are noteworthy because the sample was relatively large, the study was carefully conducted, and clinical samples were used. There are several caveats to these negative findings for health outcomes, however. Control group participants were not included in the analysis, and it remains possible that alexithymia would be related to outcomes differently among control participants. Moreover, these authors reported a single outcome measure, so we do not know if the lack of relationship between alexithymia and outcome would apply to other outcome measures. Finally, as these authors noted, the mean alexithymia score for the sample was low (for TAS-20, M = 44.5), suggesting that there may have been a restriction of range on alexithymia, which could have contributed to the failure to find significant relationships.

In Habbal's (1999) unpublished thesis described above, the TAS was used to obtain a baseline level of alexithymia in 53 women with a history of cancer. Higher alexithymia was related to using significantly fewer negative emotion words in essays ($r = .34$, $p < .05$), and there was a marginally significant interaction ($p = .10$) between group and TAS score in the prediction of physical symptoms at 1-month follow-up. Participants who were in the disclosure group and who were low in alexithymia had reduced symptoms at follow-up; however, disclosure group participants who were high in alexithymia showed no benefits. These effects were not found at 3 months, nor was an alexithymia effect found for other measures (e.g., mood, colds).

Two studies from our laboratory also suggest that alexithymia reduces the benefits of disclosure (Lumley, Naoum, & Kelley, 2001). In one study, students with elevated physical symptoms were assigned to write for 4 days either about stressful life events (disclosure) or neutral topics (control). We administered the TAS-20 to 61 participants and obtained various health measures at baseline and again 3 months after writing. Using moderated regression, we found that the group interacted with the TAS-20 total score in predicting change in symptoms of upper respiratory illness (URI) on an 8-symptom scale, $F(1, 57) = 4.18$, $p = .045$. Figure 5.1 shows this interaction. In the disclosure group, greater alexithymia predicted a slight increase in URI symptoms over 3 months (standardized $\beta = .23$, $p = .22$), whereas among the control group, greater alexithymia predicted a decrease in URI symptoms (standardized $\beta = -.30$, $p = .10$). We also assessed change in depression symptoms, and although neither the TAS-20 total nor the first two subscales were moderators, the subscale of externally oriented thinking marginally interacted with group in predicting change in depression, $F(1, 57) = 3.61$, $p = .06$. Among disclosure participants, greater externally oriented thinking was associated with an increase in depression (standardized $\beta = .44$, $p = .014$), whereas there was no relationship between this externally oriented thinking and change in depression among control participants (standardized $\beta = -.08$, $p = .68$).

We also recently examined alexithymia (Lumley et al., 2001) using data from an earlier study of the effects of verbal disclosure among patients with rheumatoid arthritis (Kelley, Lumley, & Leisen, 1997). Patients were assigned to talk into a tape recorder privately at home for 4 days about either stressful life events or neutral topics. We assessed 68 patients at baseline and 3 months later for their health status, which included self-

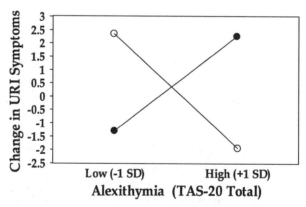

Figure 5.1. Alexithymia (from the Toronto Alexithymia Scale-20; TAS-20) moderates the relationship between disclosure group (filled circle) and changes in upper respiratory illness (URI) symptoms over 3 months (follow-up minus baseline) among physically symptomatic undergraduates. (Open circle = controls.)

reported pain and physical dysfunction on the Arthritis Impact Measurement Scales-2 (AIMS-2; Meenan, Jason, Anderson, Guccione, & Kazis, 1992), as well as their joint impairment (a composite of walking time, grip strength, and joint swelling and tenderness as assessed by a rheumatologist). We assessed alexithymia at baseline using the TAS-20. Although the full TAS-20 total did not moderate any relationships, one of the three subscales did. Using moderated regression, we found a significant interaction between group and the subscale of difficulty identifying feelings in predicting change in self-reported disability (AIMS-2) over 3 months, $F(1, 64) = 4.35$, $p = .04$. Figure 5.2 shows this interaction. Greater difficulty identifying feelings predicted increased disability among disclosure patients (standardized $\beta = .28$, $p = .12$), but greater difficulty identifying feelings predicted decreased disability among control patients (standardized $\beta = -.39$, $p = .03$). Note that disclosure did not influence disability among patients with high difficulty identifying feelings, but it did lead to improvements in disability among disclosers who were low on this alexithymia facet. We also found a marginally significant interaction in predicting change in joint impairment, $F(1, 61) = 2.97$, $p = .09$. Consistent with the finding for disability, among disclosure patients, greater difficulty identifying feelings was associated with an increase in joint impairment (standardized $\beta = .29$, $p = .11$), whereas among controls, greater difficulty identifying feelings had a weak relationship with improved joint condition (standardized $\beta = -.17$, $p = .35$).

Summary: Alexithymia and Disclosure

In two studies from our lab and the study by Habbal (1999), alexithymia or some subset of its characteristics was found to interfere with

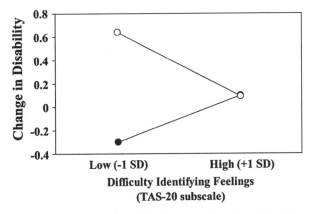

Figure 5.2. The Difficulty Identifying Feelings subscale (of the Toronto Alexithymia Scale-20) moderates the relationship between disclosure group (filled circle) and change in self-reported disability (Arthritis Impact Measurement Scales-2) over three months (follow-up minus baseline) among patients with rheumatoid arthritis. (Open circle = controls.)

health benefit among disclosure participants relative to controls. However, the unpublished status of these studies as well as the occasional marginally rather than fully significant findings limit their influence. The study by Paez et al. (1999) appears to counter the hypothesis that alexithymia interferes with the benefits of disclosure, at least at first glance. However, we think that their findings are better interpreted to mean that inhibition predicts benefits of disclosure, perhaps because of introversion or shame. The negative findings by Smyth et al. (in press) are more challenging to the hypothesis that alexithymia interferes with disclosure benefits. However, the lack of a control group analysis, the use of only a single outcome measure, and the possibility of restricted range on the alexithymia measure reduces the impact of this negative finding.

Some additional support for the hypothesis that alexithymia interferes with the benefits of disclosure comes from two studies of unique populations. Disclosure was found to have no effect on a large sample of bereaved older adults (Stroebe & Stroebe, 1996), and it was found to have deleterious effects after 5 weeks in a small sample of people with posttraumatic stress disorder (Gidron, Peri, Connolly, & Shalev, 1996). Pennebaker and Seagal (1999) suggested that these negative effects occurred because the participants had substantial anxiety or depression, which may have resulted in deficient cognitive processing and impaired ability to organize the trauma. This description is consistent with alexithymia, and many people with depression or posttraumatic stress disorder are known to have elevated levels of alexithymia (Taylor et al., 1997), suggesting that the negative effects in these studies might have been due to alexithymia. We acknowledge that this is speculation, because alexithymia was not directly assessed. In summary, we found some preliminary support for the hypothesis that alexithymia interferes with the benefits of disclosure.

CLINICAL IMPLICATIONS

For whom are disclosure techniques best suited? Several studies support our contention that people whose expression is hindered by inhibition (Steps 4 and 5 of the model) are most likely to benefit from disclosure. For example, Lepore and Greenberg (in press) studied college students who wrote about a romantic break-up and found beneficial health effects only among those who had initial high levels of intrusive thoughts, but not among those with low levels of intrusive thoughts. Earlier, Lepore (1997) found a similar effect—expressive writing about an upcoming exam improved mood only for those who had high levels of intrusive thoughts about the exam. Intrusive thinking is considered to be a sign that a person is inhibiting and attempting to avoid emotional distress, but the person still recognizes the presence of distress (Horowitz, 1986). Sullivan and

Neish (1999) examined the effects of briefly writing about dental fears among people who were to have dental hygiene treatment. Better adjustment (reduced pain, better mood) was found among disclosing participants who were pain "catastrophizers," that is, who acknowledged their worry and perceived inability to control pain. In a recent study in our laboratory, Norman, Lumley, Dooley, Schram, and Diamond (2001) found that women with chronic pelvic pain who were ambivalent about emotional expression benefited when writing about the distressing consequences of their pain problem, in comparison to ambivalent women in the control group who wrote about positive life experiences. Ambivalence about emotional expression is a clear acknowledgment of conscious emotional inhibition. Finally, Smyth's (1998) meta-analytic review suggested that men were more likely to benefit from expressive writing than women, and men are thought to be more likely than women to inhibit emotional expression. Thus, there is preliminary evidence that people who recognize having negative emotions but who are ambivalent over expressing them, who attempt to inhibit or avoid them, or who have intrusive thoughts and worry, are most likely to benefit from disclosure.

In contrast, we suspect that people with repressive coping or alexithymia may need alternative stress management approaches or a modified disclosure technique to improve adjustment. Although very little treatment literature exists on people with a repressive style, Millon (1996) has suggested that an initial focus on traditional behavioral and cognitive techniques to manage stress may be most useful. Techniques such as relaxation training, problem solving, and assertiveness training are less threatening psychologically and may be accepted more readily by repressive individuals. Some repressive people with pain or other physical problems respond to biofeedback by gradually becoming curious about why their muscles or nervous systems react when they talk about events in their lives—events that they subjectively feel are not bothersome. Such psychologically safe initial approaches may motivate some repressive people to begin the process of exploring their psychological sources of stress. Thus, it may be that disclosure and other techniques that require the capacity to introspect and disclose negative affective experiences are better used as second tier techniques with repressive individuals, after structured and less psychologically threatening cognitive–behavioral approaches have been used.

As with repressive individuals, very little research has addressed interventions with alexithymic people, although alexithymia is commonly found among patients with a range of psychiatric and psychosomatic conditions. Clinical observations suggest that alexithymic people rarely benefit from traditional insight-oriented approaches, because their external cognitive orientation and difficulty in understanding their emotions interfere with insight and emotional processing. Furthermore, the relational style of alexithymic patients is distant and unengaging, which renders interpersonal approaches to therapy difficult (Freyberger, 1977). Yet, alexithymic people in behavioral therapy are often reliable, attend sessions regularly, and attempt homework assignments (Lumley, Downey, Stettner, Wehmer, & Pomerleau, 1994). This suggests that with increased structure and guidance, alexithymic people may engage in tasks that allow them to build their skills at emotional awareness and cognitive processing. Beresnevaite (2000) has shown that alexithymic people with cardiac disease responded well to a group therapy intervention that made use of multiple, structured exercises to increase psychological awareness. These exercises led to reduced alexithymia as well as fewer subsequent cardiac problems.

Although we suspect that alexithymic people have difficulty with the disclosure task as it is usually presented, modifications of the task may prove useful. Perhaps writing for more days will gradually help those people whose emotional skills are limited. Several authors have explored the possibility of providing more instructions or guidance to the writer. For example, Cameron and Nichols (1998) found that asking individuals to write about coping strategies along with disclosure resulted in gains for people who had rated themselves as pessimists. We have recently developed and have been testing a modification of the written disclosure task that consists of four didactic modules designed to help alexithymic participants maximize the effectiveness of written disclosure over 4 days of writing. These modules are intended to help participants recognize stressful experiences, identify and label various negative emotions, understand how stressful experiences affect cognitions and relationships, and then how to change cognitions about the experience. We are testing this modified approach against the usual disclosure instructions, and we hypothesize that alexithymic people will benefit from the more structured approach.

CAVEATS AND FUTURE RESEARCH DIRECTIONS

Several aspects of the available research lead us to temper our conclusions about individual differences in emotional awareness and expression as moderators of disclosure. With respect to study design, some studies do not have a control group or do not include the control group in their analyses. Without controls, one does not know whether the effect of the moderator is unique to disclosure, or whether one has found an overall effect of a personality variable; that is, that people with some characteristic perform better or more poorly in general. Tests of moderators should include the control group and examine the Group × Moderator interactions. Second, most researchers appear to concentrate first on creating a difference between disclosure and control groups, and regard concerns about moderators as secondary. Yet, research studies that plan only for main effects, haphazardly add a handful of personality measures at baseline, and then explore moderators in a post hoc fashion typically yield either negative moderator findings or findings that do not replicate in later studies. Redressing this shortcoming means planning to test for moderators from the outset, using large enough samples to detect them, and perhaps recruiting participants who vary widely on the potential moderator.

We also have concerns about the interpretation of findings. First, findings of moderation, even within an experimental study, are by definition correlational, and, therefore, open to various interpretations about causality. One cannot conclude that repression or alexithymia (or any other moderator) alters the performance on a task, because the personality variable may be a proxy for some other variable that is the true source of the moderator effect. Second, we have treated repression and alexithymia as stable characteristics of the person, yet the stability of these variables can be questioned. For example, alexithymia appears to result from trauma (Lumley et al., 1996), as may repression. Furthermore, it is possible that either repression or alexithymia could be attenuated or reduced in response to an emotional awareness intervention, including, possibly, disclosure tasks. We have studies in progress that reassess these personality variables after disclosure to determine whether disclosure leads to changes in alexithymia and repression.

We encourage researchers to examine the topics that people with different emotional awareness and expression styles choose to write or talk about. To our knowledge, no one has yet done this with a personality variable. For example, do repressive people avoid disclosure or write more often about superficial or publicly validated problems (such as an illness) than do nonrepressive people? Do alexithymic people exhibit confusion in choice of a topic or emotions used in their writings? We also would like to see researchers link baseline individual differences to process variables and to the health outcomes, using, for example, path analytic techniques. Finally, we encourage researchers to conduct analyses of moderator variables, even when a main effect of experimental group is found. Negative findings also are important, and we encourage authors to include results of negative findings for moderator variables in their primary article.

Research on emotional processes requires better theoretical models to explain various types of emotional functioning, to guide the selection of constructs for study, and to point clinicians in appropriate directions for intervention. Although the model of Kennedy-Moore and Watson (1999) has guided our thinking in this chapter, little empirical evidence supports or refutes its tenets, including wither the five expression processes are mutually exclusive, and whether they operate in a sequential order leading to eventual expression. We do not know whether the myriad processes and labels that have been noted in the literature related to emotional awareness, understanding, and expression can be subsumed under this model, or whether alternative models are better. Several theoretical models have been proposed that should be investigated. For example, Lane and Schwartz (1987) have proposed a stage model of increasing emotional awareness and complexity, Labouvie-Vief (1999) has offered a two-dimensional model of affect valence modulation and affect complexity, and Mayer and Salovey (1997) have promulgated an emotional intelligence model and associated assessment battery. These models should be considered in future research and clinical work on emotional disclosure.

REFERENCES

Bagby, R. M., Parker, J. D. A., & Taylor, G. J. (1994). The twenty-item Toronto Alexithymia Scale–I. Item selection and cross-validation of the factor structure. *Journal of Psychosomatic Research, 38,* 23–32.

Bagby, R. M., Taylor, G. J., & Parker, J. D. A. (1994). The twenty-item Toronto Alexithymia Scale–II. Convergent, discriminant, and concurrent validity. *Journal of Psychosomatic Research, 38,* 33–40.

Beresnevaite, M. (2000). Exploring the benefits of group psychotherapy in reducing alexithymia in coronary heart disease patients: A preliminary study. *Psychotherapy and Psychosomatics, 69,* 117–122.

Cameron, L. D., & Nicholls, G. (1998). Expression of stressful experiences through writing: Effects of a self-regulation manipulation for pessimists and optimists. *Health Psychology, 17,* 84–92.

Christensen, A. J., Edwards, D. L., Wiebe, J. S., Benotsch, E. G., McKelvey, L., Andrews, M., & Lubaroff, D. M. (1996). Effect of verbal self-disclosure on natural killer cell activity: Moderating influence of cynical hostility. *Psychosomatic Medicine, 58,* 150–155.

Christensen, A. J., & Smith, T. W. (1993). Cynical hostility and cardiovascular reactivity during self-disclosure. *Psychosomatic Medicine, 55,* 193–202.

Crowne, D. P., & Marlowe, D. (1964). *The approval motive: Studies in evaluative dependence.* New York: Wiley.

Esterling, B. A., Antoni, M. H., Kumar, H., & Schneiderman, N. (1990). Emotional repression, stress disclosure responses, and Epstein–Barr viral capsid antigen titers. *Psychosomatic Medicine, 52,* 397–410.

Freyberger, H. (1977). Supportive psychotherapeutic techniques in primary and secondary alexithymia. *Psychotherapy and Psychosomatics, 28,* 337–342.

Gidron, Y., Peri, T., Connolly, J. F., & Shalev, A. Y. (1996). Written disclosure in posttraumatic stress disorder: Is it beneficial for the patient? *Journal of Nervous and Mental Disease, 184,* 505–507.

Habbal, R. (1999). *Emotional disclosure in women: The moderating effects of personality.* Unpublished master's thesis, San Diego State University.

Horowitz, M. J. (1986). *Stress response syndromes* (2nd ed.). Northvale, NJ: Jason Aronson.

Kelley, J. E., Lumley, M. A., & Leisen, J. C. C. (1997). Health effects of emotional disclosure in rheumatoid arthritis patients. *Health Psychology, 16,* 331–340.

Kennedy-Moore, E., & Watson, J. C. (1999). *Expressing emotion: Myths, realities, and therapeutic strategies.* New York: Guilford Press.

Labouvie-Vief, G. (1999). Emotions in adulthood. In V. Bengston & K. W. Schaie (Eds.), *Theories of adult development and aging* (pp. 253–267). New York: Springer.

Lane, R. D., & Schwartz, G. E. (1987). Levels of emotional awareness: A cognitive–developmental theory and its application to psychopathology. *American Journal of Psychiatry, 144,* 133–143.

Lepore, S. J. (1997). Expressive writing moderates the relationship between intrusive thoughts and depressive symptoms. *Journal of Personality and Social Psychology, 73,* 1030–1037.

Lepore, S. J., & Greenberg, M. A. (in press). Mending broken hearts: Effects of expressive writing on mood, cognitive processing, social adjustment, and health following a relationship breakup. *Psychology and Health.*

Lumley, M. A., Downey, K., Stettner, L., Wehmer, F., & Pomerleau, O. F. (1994). Alexithymia and negative affect: Relationship to cigarette smoking, and nicotine dependence, and smoking cessation. *Psychotherapy and Psychosomatics, 61,* 156–162.

Lumley, M. A., Naoum, L., & Kelley, J. (2001, March). *Alexithymia as a moderator of the effects of written and verbal emotional disclosure.* Poster presented at the annual meeting of the American Psychosomatic Society, Monterey, CA.

Lumley, M. A., Stettner, L., & Wehmer, F. (1996). How are alexithymia and physical illness linked? A review and critique of pathways. *Journal of Psychosomatic Research, 41,* 505–518.

Mayer, J. D., & Salovey, P. (1997). What is emotional intelligence? In P. Salovey & D. J. Sluyter (Eds.), *Emotional development and emotional intelligence: Educational implications* (pp. 3–31). New York: Basic Books.

Meenan, R. F., Jason, J. H., Anderson, J. J., Guccione, A. A., & Kazis, L. E. (1992). AIMS2: The content and properties of a revised and expanded Arthritis Impact Measurement Scales Health Status Questionnaire. *Arthritis and Rheumatism, 35,* 1–10.

Millon, T. (1996). *Disorders of personality: DSM–IV and beyond.* New York: Wiley.

Millon, T., Green, C. J., & Meagher, R. B. (1982). *Millon Behavioral Health Inventory.* Minneapolis, MN: Interpretive Scoring Systems.

Norman, S., Lumley, M., Dooley, J., Schram, L., & Diamond, M. (March, 2001). *Written emotional disclosure in women with chronic pelvic pain.* Poster presented at the annual meeting of the American Psychosomatic Society, Monterey, CA.

Paez, D., Basabe, N., Valdoseda, M., Velasco, C., & Iraurgi, I. (1995). Confrontation: Inhibition, alexithymia, and health. In J. W. Pennebaker (Ed.), *Emotion, disclosure, & health* (pp. 195–222). Washington, DC: American Psychological Association.

Paez, D., Velasco, C., & Gonzalez, J. L. (1999). Expressive writing and the role of alexithymia as a dispositional deficit in self-disclosure and psychological health. *Journal of Personality and Social Psychology, 77,* 630–641.

Pennebaker, J. W. (1997). *Opening up: The healing power of expressing emotions* (Rev. ed.). New York: Guilford Press.

Pennebaker, J. W., & Beall, S. K. (1986). Confronting a traumatic event: Towards an understanding of inhibition and disease. *Journal of Abnormal Psychology, 95,* 274–281.

Pennebaker, J. W., & Keough, K. A. (1999). Revealing, organizing, and reorganizing the self in response to stress and emotion. In R. J. Contrada & R. D. Ashmore (Eds.), *Self, social identity, and physical health* (pp. 101–121). New York: Oxford University Press.

Pennebaker, J. W., Mayne, T. J., & Francis, M. E. (1997). Linguistic predictors of adaptive bereavement. *Journal of Personality and Social Psychology, 72,* 863–871.

Pennebaker, J. W., & Seagal, J. D. (1999). Forming a story: The health benefits of narrative. *Journal of Clinical Psychology, 55,* 1243–1254.

Schwartz, G. E., & Kline, J. P. (1995). Repression, emotional disclosure, and health: Theoretical, empirical, and clinical considerations. In J. W. Pennebaker (Ed.), *Emotion, disclosure, & health* (pp. 177–193). Washington, DC: American Psychological Association.

Smyth, J. M. (1998). Written emotional expression: Effect sizes, outcome types, and moderating variables. *Journal of Consulting and Clinical Psychology, 66,* 174–184.

Smyth, J. M., Anderson, C. F., Hockemeyer, J. R., & Stone, A. A. (in press). Does emotional non-expressiveness or avoidance interfere with writing about stressful life events? An analysis in patients with chronic illness. *Psychology and Health.*

Stroebe, M., & Stroebe, W. (1996, July). *Writing assignments and grief.* Paper presented at The Non-Expression of Emotions and Health and Disease Conference, Tilburg, The Netherlands.

Sullivan, M. J. L., & Neish, N. (1999). The effects of disclosure on pain during dental hygiene treatment: The moderating role of catastrophizing. *Pain, 79,* 155–163.

Suslow, T., Donges, U. S., Kersting, A., & Arolt, V. (2000). 20-Item Toronto Alexithymia Scale: Do difficulties describing feelings assess proneness to shame instead of difficulties symbolizing emotions? *Scandinavian Journal of Psychology, 41,* 329–334.

Taylor, G. J., Bagby, R. M., & Parker, J. D. A. (1997). *Disorders of affect regulation: Alexithymia in medical and psychiatric illness.* New York: Cambridge University Press.

Taylor, G. J., Ryan, D., & Bagby, R. M. (1985). Toward the development of a new self-report alexithymia scale. *Psychotherapy and Psychosomatics, 44,* 191–199.

Weinberger, D. A. (1990). The construct validity of the repressive coping style.

In J. L. Singer (Ed.), *Repression and dissociation: Implications for personality theory, psychopathology, and health* (pp. 337–386). Chicago: University of Chicago Press.

Weinberger, D. A. (1991). *Social-emotional adjustment in older children and adults: Psychometric properties of the Weinberger Adjustment Inventory.* Unpublished manuscript, Case Western Reserve University, Cleveland, OH.

Weinberger, D. A., Schwartz, G. E., & Davidson, R. J. (1979). Low-anxious, high-anxious, and repressive coping styles: Psychometric patterns and behavioral and physiological responses to stress. *Journal of Abnormal Psychology, 88,* 369–380.

III

EMOTIONAL, COGNITIVE, AND BIOLOGICAL PROCESSES

6

EXPRESSIVE WRITING AND HEALTH: SELF-REGULATION OF EMOTION-RELATED EXPERIENCE, PHYSIOLOGY, AND BEHAVIOR

STEPHEN J. LEPORE, MELANIE A. GREENBERG, MICHELLE BRUNO, AND JOSHUA M. SMYTH

... the brightest spot of all is that at least I can write down all my thoughts and feelings; otherwise, I'd absolutely suffocate."
—Anne Frank (March 16, 1944)

There is mounting evidence that people who have experienced stressful life events reap physical and psychological health benefits when they engage in expressive writing (Smyth, 1998). In this chapter, we discuss how self-regulation processes might mediate the beneficial effects of expressive writing. Specifically, we suggest that expressive writing can improve regulation of emotion-related experience, physiological responses, and behaviors, which, in turn, can enhance physical and mental health outcomes (also see M. A. Greenberg & Lepore, in press).

EMOTION

More than a century ago, Darwin (1872) and James (1884) suggested that emotions are adaptive behavioral and physiological response tenden-

This work was supported in part by a grant from The City University of New York PSC-CUNY Research Award Program and National Institutes of Health Grant CA68354.

cies evoked by evolutionarily significant situations. For instance, in the primeval jungle, a sudden noise might have signaled an approaching predator. The adaptive response in such a situation would be to stop all other activities, shift attention to the noise source, and mobilize energy for fight or flight. Because such responses increase survival odds, biological factors supporting them were transmitted to future generations. Therefore, humans express strong negative emotional responses to sudden noises, even though in a modern context such responses are not necessarily adaptive. In addition to the ingrained emotional responses, humans learn novel emotional responses in the course of normal development. For instance, shame can be acquired through social interaction, and disgust can be acquired through associative learning, as is evident in persons experiencing food poisoning. For the present discussion, we assume that innate and learned emotional responses facilitate adaptation by engaging and directing responses to significant stimuli.

Emotional responses involve at least three systems: subjective–experiential, neurophysiological–biochemical, and behavioral–expressive (Lang, 1968). Each system influences a person's relation to significant stimuli. The *experiential component* refers to feeling states, which have a positive (e.g., pleasure) or negative (e.g., pain) valence. These states alert a person that something significant transpired and signal the need to approach or avoid a stimulus. The *physiological component* refers to activities in the central and autonomic nervous systems, as well as the neuroendocrine system, which modulate arousal. Arousal levels prevent action by conserving energy or support action by releasing it. Finally, the *behavioral component* refers to facial, bodily, and verbal responses. This component serves various functions, such as guiding one's own approach or avoidance to stimuli and signaling others to approach or move away.

Response tendencies in the experiential, physiological, and behavioral emotion channels are partly independent. For instance, in the presence of a snake, a person could report feeling unafraid but exhibit physiological signs of fear (Rachman & Hodgson, 1974). Particular response tendencies, such as a rapid heart rate, accompany diverse emotional states, including fear, anger, and sadness (Cacioppo, Berntson, Larsen, Poehlmann, & Ito, 2000). Subjective perceptions of stress and arousal during acute stress exposures are only weakly correlated with physiological changes (Feldman et al., 1999). These findings suggest that each emotion component has its own determinants, and any approach to regulating emotions might have differential effects on the components. As we discuss later, this might explain why expressive writing sometimes has a stronger effect on physical than on mental health. This might occur if, for instance, expressive writing modulates physiological arousal more than, or prior to, subjective emotional experience.

EMOTION REGULATION

Emotion regulation is part of the broader construct of self-regulation, or self-control. It refers specifically to control over the quality, frequency, intensity, or duration of responses in any of the three emotion channels —experience, physiology, and behavior (cf. Eisenberg, Fabes, Guthrie, & Reiser, 2000). It influences which emotions people have, in what situations they have them, and how they experience and express them. This definition emphasizes agency and, by inference, implies effortful, conscious processes; however, such processes are not always controlled, effortful, and conscious.

Emotion regulation can be viewed on a continuum with the anchors *underregulated, optimally regulated,* and *overregulated.* People at the extreme ends of this continuum have dysregulated emotions, which puts them at increased risk for physical and psychological health problems. People who are underregulated have little or no control over their responses to emotion-provoking stimuli. They experience emotions intensely, have exaggerated physiological arousal, and have little control over expressing and acting on impulse. Frequent or chronic activation of physiologic systems that respond to stressors can result in cumulative damage to these response systems, which undermines a person's ability to adapt to future stressors (McEwen, 1998). Perhaps as a result of these pathophysiological processes, chronic, exaggerated arousal during stress is a risk factor for cardiovascular disorders and infectious illnesses (Lepore, 1998). High levels of negative emotions, such as hostility, anxiety, and depression, constitute risk factors for asthma, arthritis, and coronary artery disease (Friedman & Booth-Kewley, 1987). Hostility and impulsiveness also contribute to interpersonal problems (Smith, 1992).

In contrast, people who are overregulated constrict, avoid, inhibit, or suppress emotional response tendencies. Excessive control over emotions has been implicated in cancer (Gross, 1989) and cardiovascular disorders (chapter 2, this volume). One theory is that inhibition requires physiological work that leads to unhealthy, chronic arousal (Pennebaker, 1989). For instance, people who avoid conflict might inhibit anger, which could contribute to chronic increases in autonomic arousal and, eventually, coronary heart disease. Emotion suppression has been linked to increased sympathetic activation (Gross & Levenson, 1993) and compromised immune system functioning (Petrie, Booth, & Pennebaker, 1998). People who avoid upsetting information might ignore signs and symptoms of disease, delay help seeking, and not work on problematic situations or relationships.

EXPRESSIVE WRITING AND EMOTION REGULATION

When people experience stressful life events, they need to strike a balance between emotionally overreacting and underreacting. As shown in Figure 6.1, expressive writing might help people to achieve emotional balance by facilitating emotion regulation processes, such as directing attention, facilitating habituation, and aiding in cognitive restructuring. Although we discuss these regulatory mechanisms in separate sections below, they are interrelated and mutually influential.

Attention

Attention is central to emotion regulation, because people must attend to emotional responses and antecedent stimuli before controlling

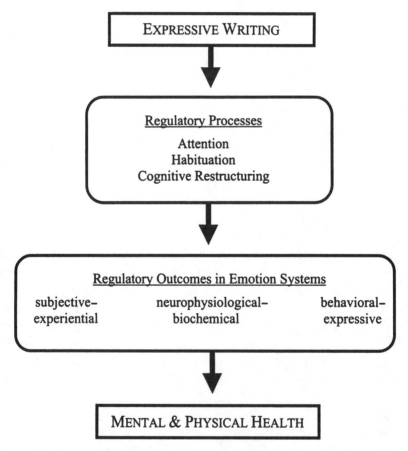

Figure 6.1. An emotion regulation model of the effects of expressive writing on health.

them. Expressive writing can direct attention to sources of stress; different aspects of stressors; and subjective, physiological, and behavioral responses. By directing attention to these components, expressive writing can facilitate other emotion regulation processes. For example, directing attention toward negative stress-related thoughts and feelings can facilitate emotional habituation (e.g., attenuated physiological and affective responses).

Writing instructions can direct attention to different aspects of a situation and one's emotional response to the situation. Early theorizing by Pennebaker (1989) emphasized directing attention to negative aspects of stressors, which tend to be avoided. It was thought that inhibition of undesirable, stress-related thoughts and feelings required physiological work that resulted in unhealthy levels of chronic arousal. The writing manipulation developed by Pennebaker instructs people to write about their deepest thoughts and feelings about stressful events. Consistent with expectations, this approach increases people's expression of emotions, particularly negative emotions; discourages avoidance, or excessive control of emotions; and increases short-term experiences of negative emotion (Smyth, 1998). This approach may also reduce arousal and improve longer term mood (Smyth & Pennebaker, 2001).

Although Pennebaker's manipulation reduces physical and emotional health problems in diverse populations, the negative focus of attention might not be necessary. Recent work suggests that directing attention to positive aspects of stressors, or to perceived benefits accrued from experiencing stressful events, can enhance health (chapters 3 and 7, this volume). This latter approach is more likely than Pennebaker's approach to elicit expression of positive affect, which might, in part, explain why it can produce health benefits. Researchers have shown that positive emotion can "undo" or attenuate residual arousal and long-term distress that may result from negative emotional responses to stressors (Bonanno, 2001; Fredrickson & Branigan, 2001). Thus, writing about positive aspects of stressors might evoke positive emotions, which act as a buffer to the negative emotions evoked by the stressor. Positive emotions also can facilitate development of new personal and social resources to deal with future stress (Frederickson & Branigan, 2001). For example, interest and excitement can motivate exploratory and skill-building behavior, whereas happiness can facilitate positive social engagements that strengthen social ties.

Although writing that directs attention to positive aspects of stressors might enhance health, Pennebaker's approach might produce stronger health benefits. Stanton and Danoff-Burg (chapter 2, this volume) randomly assigned women with breast cancer to one of three writing groups in which they were to focus on facts related to their cancer experience, their deepest thoughts and feelings about their cancer experience, or the benefits they perceived in their cancer experience. At 3-month follow-up, the group writing about their deepest thoughts and feelings reported a greater decrease in physical symptoms than the group that wrote only about cancer facts; the group writing about benefits fell in between the other two. These findings suggest that exploring a broad range of thoughts and feelings, including negative ones, is on average, more beneficial than focusing on a restricted range of positive thoughts and feelings. Nonetheless, the finding that people might enhance their health by writing on positive aspects of stressors and not confronting undesirable thoughts and feelings has important clinical implications. Some people might prefer the alternative approach, or some clinical situations might require this alternative because people cannot bear to confront the stressor directly.

An important goal for future research in this area is to consider why these vastly different writing approaches both result in positive outcomes. We posit two plausible explanations. First, different people might benefit from different approaches. For instance, people who are overregulated might benefit from confronting negative thoughts and emotions, whereas people who are underregulated might benefit from redirecting attention from negative to positive aspects of situations. Indeed, in a recent study of women with HIV, Mann (2001) found that writing about a positive future was associated with better medication adherence and decreased distress among women who were relatively pessimistic but that it had the opposite effect among women who were relatively optimistic. Second, attending to different aspects of a stressor (e.g., losses vs. benefits) or of one's response to a stressor (e.g., sadness vs. relief) might affect different health mediators. For instance, focusing on negative thoughts and emotions associated with a stressor might reduce negative emotional responses primarily through habituation processes. In contrast, focusing on positive aspects of a stressor might reduce negative emotional responses primarily through cognitive restructuring or, as suggested above, by increasing positive affect. It is even possible that increasing positive affect facilitates cognitive restructuring (e.g., Bonanno, 2001; Fredrickson & Branigan, 2001).

Habituation

Habituation is defined simply as decreased response to repeated stimulation (Groves & Thompson, 1970). Expressive writing interventions have been likened to forced exposure therapies: Through repeated exposure to stressful stimuli, expressive writing extinguishes negative emotional associations (Lepore, 1997). In considering the ways in which expressive writing could influence habituation processes, we draw on work by Watson and Marks (1972). These investigators observed that emotional habituation could be produced in phobic people by exposure to phobic-specific stimuli (e.g., exposing people with agoraphobia to scenes of crowded places) or by exposure to phobic-irrelevant, but fear-provoking stimuli (e.g., exposing people with agoraphobia to scenes of a person being eaten by a tiger).

Phobic clients exposed to either of these conditions showed decreases in anxiety and avoidance. Watson and Marks suggested that exposure to any fear-arousing stimulus promotes physiological and psychological habituation, leading to a reduction of the fear response over time. Thus, two different types of habituation were identified: stimulus-related and response-related.

Stimulus-related habituation is decreased emotional reactivity to specific fear-provoking stimuli that results from prolonged exposure to those stimuli. *Response-related habituation* is decreased emotional reactivity resulting from prolonged or intense exposure to fear responses provoked by any stimulus. While writing about stressful events, people often describe elements of the experience—the scenery, actors, and activities—and their responses, including physical sensations, emotions, and thoughts. In addition, writing evokes negative emotions, as people remember stressful experiences. Thus, expressive writing should facilitate both stimulus- and response-related habituation.

Recent writing studies provide data consistent with stimulus-related habituation. Expressive writing reduced the effects of stress-related intrusive thoughts on mental and physical health outcomes, suggesting that people became desensitized, or habituated, to the intrusive thoughts. In one study (Lepore, 1997), expressive writing attenuated the association between intrusive thoughts about an important impending examination and depressive symptoms. As shown in Figure 6.2, intrusive thoughts measured 1 month prior to the exam were positively related to depressive symptoms 3 days prior to the exam in the control-writing group but not in the expressive-writing group. In another study (Lepore & Greenberg, in press), expressive writing attenuated the association between a composite measure of intrusive–avoidant thoughts about a relationship breakup and upper respiratory illness (URI) symptoms. Specifically, a higher level of intrusive–avoidant reactions was related to short-term increases in URI symptoms in participants who wrote about a control topic, but it was unrelated to URI symptoms in participants who wrote expressively about their breakup.

Investigators also have shown habituation during writing about stressors. Smyth, Stone, Hurewitz, and Kaell (1999) examined emotional reactions in patients with asthma or rheumatoid arthritis, who wrote about their most stressful life experiences on three consecutive days. Participants rated their level of positive and negative mood immediately before and after each writing session. Mood change scores (prewriting–postwriting) were calculated for each writing day. As shown in Figure 6.3, writing produced larger increases in negative mood on the first day than on subsequent days ($p < .01$). There was a similar trend for positive affect ($p < .08$; Hockemeyer, Smyth, Anderson, & Stone, 1999). Others have examined how expressive writing relates to physiological arousal, as assessed by skin conductance levels (SCL). Pennebaker, Kiecolt-Glaser, and Glaser (1988)

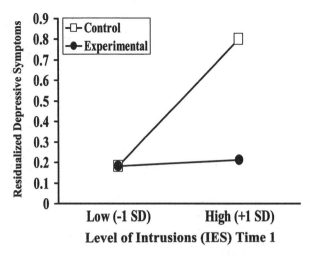

Figure 6.2. Slope of the relation between intrusive thoughts and changes in depression from Time 1 to Time 2 (residualized) as a function of writing condition. The experimental group wrote about an impending entrance examination, whereas the control group wrote about daily activities. Time 1 measurement occurred 1 month before the examination, and Time 2 measurement occurred 3 days before the examination. The writing manipulation was administered 10 days before the examination. High = +1*SD*; low = −1*SD*. IES = Impact of Events Scale (Horowitz, Wilner, & Alvarez, 1979). From "Expressive Writing Moderates the Relation Between Intrusive Thoughts and Depressive Symptoms," by S. J. Lepore, 1997, *Journal of Personality and Social Psychology, 73*, p. 1033. Copyright 1997 by the American Psychological Association. Reprinted with permission of the author.

found no effects on SCL. In contrast, Petrie, Booth, Pennebaker, Davison, and Thomas (1995) found SCL exhibited a steady decline over writing days for participants in a trauma-writing group, whereas SCL declined in the first 2 days of writing but rose again in the last 2 days in a control-writing group. Overall, these data suggest that participants become emotionally habituated to stress-related stimuli through the repeated exposures during writing.

Results from another study are consistent with response-related habituation (M. A. Greenberg, Wortman, & Stone, 1996). Participants in the study were randomly assigned to write about past personal traumas, imaginary traumas, or nonemotional events. Imaginary trauma participants were yoked to their real trauma counterparts and wrote about the same topics. As shown in Figure 6.4, both real and imaginary trauma groups visited the student health center for illness less often at 1-month follow-up relative to controls. The authors argued that participants in the imaginary group had the opportunity to accommodate themselves to negative emotions in a safe context, which might have conferred health benefits by

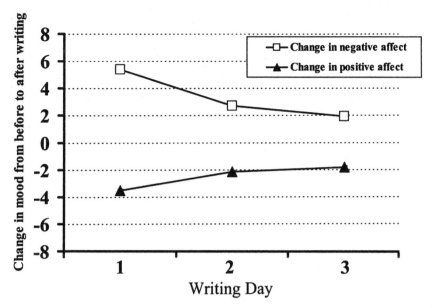

Figure 6.3. Emotional habituation across writing days as indicated by change (post–pre) in positive and negative mood. Scores represent the mean.

increasing perceived control over and tolerance of negative emotion in other areas of their lives.

Emotional engagement is important for habituation. Foa (1997) argued that for successful habituation, people should experience strong negative emotions initially, followed by gradual decreases in negative emotion within and across exposures. Results from some writing studies are consistent with the engagement hypothesis. In a secondary analysis of data from one of our studies (Lepore & Greenberg, in press), we found a significant inverse association between the proportion of negative emotion words (e.g., *sad*) expressed in writing and changes in symptoms of URI from baseline to follow-up ($r = -.26, p < .05, n = 73$). Expressing more negative emotion was prospectively associated with improvements in reported health. Unlike other studies (e.g., Pennebaker, Mayne, & Francis, 1997), we did not find an association between expression of positive emotion and health outcomes. In another study, participants with a higher proportion of emotion-focused words in their essays had lower levels of antibody to Epstein–Barr virus (EBV), indicating better immune functioning, than those who expressed less emotion (Esterling, Antoni, Fletcher, & Margulies, 1994). Finally, participants who wrote about stressful events that they rated subjectively as more severe had fewer physical symptoms at follow-up than those who wrote about less severe events (M. A. Greenberg & Stone, 1992). Writing about more severe stressors presumably would increase exposure to negative emotions.

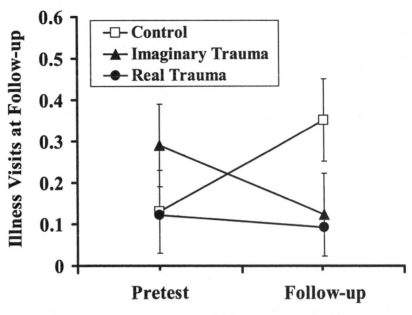

Figure 6.4. Group means for illness visits at pretest and follow-up. The real trauma group wrote about an actual past trauma, the imaginary trauma group wrote about a hypothetical trauma, the control group wrote about trivial events. Pretest was 1 month preceding, and follow-up was 1 month following essay writing. From "Emotional Expression and Physical Health: Revising Traumatic Memories or Fostering Self-Regulation?" by M. A. Greenberg, C. B. Wortman, & A. A. Stone, 1996, *Journal of Personality and Social Psychology, 71*, p. 592. Copyright 1996 by the American Psychological Association. Adapted with permission from the authors.

Cognitive Restructuring

The third mechanism of emotion regulation is cognitive restructuring. Several contributors to this volume have argued that expressive writing can result in changes in stress-related thoughts and appraisals. We propose that changes in how people view internal (e.g., memory) and external (e.g., environmental) stressor-related stimuli, or changes in how they view their emotional reactions to such stimuli, can contribute to how well they regulate their emotions.

As with habituation, cognitive restructuring is a complex construct and has been operationalized in various ways. One approach has been to analyze the content of written essays. Pennebaker and colleagues (1997) used this approach and found that people writing about stressful life experiences exhibited the greatest improvements in health outcomes when they increased their use of cognitive terms (e.g., *understand, know, realize*) over writing sessions. However, some investigators have not replicated this finding (e.g., Lepore & Greenberg, in press). Donnelly and Murray (1991) obtained ratings of the extent to which essays showed beneficial cognitive change (e.g., expressing a better understanding of the problem). Participants who wrote about stressful events evidenced more beneficial cognitive change than controls, providing some evidence that writing facilitates cognitive restructuring.

Another way investigators measure cognitive restructuring is through examining changes in the frequency of intrusive thoughts. This indirect method rests on the assumption that intrusions reflect incomplete cognitive processing of stressors (Lepore, 1997). Cognitive processing theories maintain that intrusions are a product of the mental struggle involved in cognitively assimilating information from stressful events that is incongruous with preexisting schemas. To the extent that people can cognitively integrate stressful events, they should experience a reduction and possible eradication of intrusive thoughts. Research examining the effects of expressive writing on intrusive thoughts has produced mixed results. Schoutrop reported that undergraduates who wrote about stressful life experiences exhibited declines in intrusive thoughts after the intervention, whereas control participants did not show improvement (also see chapter 8, this volume). In contrast, several investigators found that expressive writing did not affect the frequency of intrusive thoughts; instead, it attenuated the negative effects of intrusive thoughts on mood and psychological and physical symptoms (Lepore, 1997; Lepore & Greenberg, in press; Smyth, True, & Souto, 2001).

The mixed results with intrusive thoughts may be due to several factors, including differences in sampling, the type of stressors, and the time frame of measurement. Alternatively, it is possible that expressive writing alters both the frequency and emotional impact of intrusive thoughts (see Lepore, 1997; Lepore, Ragan, & Jones, 2000). Schoutrop (2000) reported that relative to a wait-list control group, participants writing about negative experiences exhibited a greater decline in intrusive thoughts and depressive symptoms. In addition, among participants writing about negative experiences, those who had a high level of intrusive thoughts at baseline showed greater declines in depressive symptoms at follow-up than those who had a relatively low level of intrusive thoughts. This latter finding is consistent with the hypothesis that expressive writing increases habituation to intrusive thoughts. However, the authors did not report the relation between intrusive thoughts and depression in the control group, so we cannot be certain that desensitization is occurring only in the experimental group. In general, these findings suggest that expressive writing can decrease both the frequency and impact of intrusive thoughts. We do not yet know the parameters or appropriate time frame for obtaining specific effects.

Another approach to examining cognitive restructuring is to assess changes in beliefs and attitudes through self-report measures. In one study, participants rated how much a writing intervention had changed their thoughts and attitudes toward the topic and their self-perceptions (e.g., feeling more positive about the topic or one's self; Donnelly & Murray, 1991). Participants who wrote about stressful events reported more positive cognitive change relative to participants who wrote about trivial topics. In the study on romantic breakups, Lepore and Greenberg (in press) measured participants' feelings and attitudes toward their ex-partner (e.g., resentment) and themselves (e.g., guilt) before and after writing. Results revealed changes in attitudes about the breakup over time, but not as a function of writing. Thus, contrary to expectations, these findings suggest that core beliefs about the self, others, and the situation were unaffected by expressive writing.

Investigators also have used experimental approaches to examine the role of cognitive organization in mediating expressive writing effects. For instance, people were randomly assigned to write about a control topic (time management), a detailed narrative about their response to a traumatic event, or a fragmented list describing their response to a trauma (Smyth et al., 2001). Participants who formed a narrative account reported fewer activity restrictions related to illness compared with both the control and fragment writing groups. This suggests it may be necessary to form a cohesive story in order to experience health benefits. However, these findings also could be the result of greater exposure and habituation to stimulus, response, or meaning elements of trauma schemas in the narrative versus fragmented writing group.

In addition to changing perceptions about a situation, expressive writing can change people's perceptions about their responses to a situation. Expressive writing can help people to feel more connected with their own selves and to experience and accept their emotional reactions. Acceptance of one's own feelings is sometimes difficult to achieve after a trauma, particularly if members of one's social network act distant, critical, or uncomfortable upon hearing about those feelings (Lepore, Silver, Wortman, & Wayment, 1996). The instructions in writing manipulations typically encourage writers to explore their deepest thoughts and feelings, implying that such feelings are valid and potentially beneficial to experience. Delving into one's own feelings without having to monitor one's self-presentation, include the perspectives of others, or make the story easier for others to hear may help people to see their feelings as an integral part of themselves, rather than as something to be pushed away. Furthermore, integrating feelings with thoughts and memories during disclosure may enhance the subjective validity of these reactions. People may begin to understand the roots of these feelings in specific past or ongoing events. Emotional disclosure manipulations, like certain psychotherapies, may therefore set the stage for "allowing into awareness an organization of one's experience previously regarded as unacceptable and accepting it" (L. S. Greenberg & Safran, 1987, p. 193).

Empirical studies provide some support for these hypotheses. In one study, some participants wrote about doubting their own feelings and trying to suppress them (M. A. Greenberg et al., 1996). In another disclosure study, participants with more alexithymic deficits—that is, those with an impaired ability to differentiate and describe their feelings—had larger reductions in negative mood than less alexithymic participants, suggesting that disclosure may enhance emotional experiencing (Paez, Velasco, & Gonzales, 1999). Swanbon (1999) found that gay men who wrote about their deepest thoughts and feelings about being gay tended to report increased clarity of gay-related feelings at follow-up, relative to controls writing about inconsequential events. The experimental group also reported decreases in avoidance of gay-related feelings, and this was associated with decreases in psychosomatic symptoms.

In addition to promoting cognitive and emotional clarity, expressive writing can provide a mastery experience in which people observe themselves tolerating and diminishing fear and other negative emotions. As a result, their self-concept might change in that they now see themselves as people who can handle negative emotions. In other words, their self-efficacy for emotional regulation should increase. In the study by Paez and colleagues (1999), people writing expressively about traumas subsequently perceived these experiences as more controllable. When people feel more control over their emotional experience, negative moods should dissipate, resulting in less chronic subjective stress. Indeed, stronger mood regulation expectancies have been linked to lower distress and physical symptoms in caregivers of Alzheimer's patients (Brashares & Catanzaro, 1994).

CONCLUSIONS

Expressive writing interventions are exciting to clinicians and researchers alike because of their relative simplicity and their robust effects on a wide range of mental and physical health outcomes. In attempting to explain the benefits of writing, we drew on theory and research on emotion and emotion regulation. Emotional response tendencies and self-regulation of emotional responses are plausible mediators of both mental and physical health outcomes. Furthermore, many of the findings in the literature could be explained from this perspective.

The links between emotion regulation and mental health outcomes are most obvious. Internalizing disorders, such as depression, and externalizing problems, such as anxiety, are practically defined as problems in regulating emotions. Behavioral problems, too, such as aggression, risk taking, and withdrawal, have also been conceptualized as problems in emotion regulation (Eisenberg et al., 2000). Links between emotion regulation and physical health are not as obvious; but here, too, we find evidence that the undercontrol or overcontrol of negative moods, behaviors, and physiological arousal can undermine physical health. In addition to highlighting the relation between emotion regulation and both physical and mental health outcomes, we sought in this chapter to outline the links between expressive writing and emotion regulation processes. We focused on three regulatory processes—attention, habituation, and cognitive restructuring—that are prominently featured in different models of emotion regulation and have been identified as mediators in the literature on emotional disclosure.

Attention is clearly a central regulator of emotion. It can mediate emotion responses in a rudimentary manner by controlling the probability and duration of exposure to stressful stimuli. By directing attention toward or away from different aspects of a stressor and one's responses, attention can directly dampen or activate responses in all three of the emotional systems—experience, physiology, and behavior. Furthermore, attention can influence activity in these emotional systems indirectly by influencing other emotion regulation processes, such as habituation and cognitive restructuring.

It is clear that expressive writing influences attention deployment, but there are still areas in need of further investigation. First, it is not yet clear why attending to either negative or positive aspects of stressors produces benefits. We have suggested that different writing approaches might be more or less beneficial depending on the writer's attention style (e.g., approach, avoid). This is an important area for future research, because it could inform clinicians about how to tailor writing interventions to maximize benefits in people with different personalities or coping styles. In addition, we need more studies on the effects of positive writing. The few studies that have been conducted are innovative, but they do not convincingly show that participants benefit from writing exclusively about positive aspects of stressors. Even when instructed to emphasize positive aspects, people inevitably write and think about negative aspects of stressful experiences. It is important to pursue this line of research, because positive writing might be more beneficial than negative writing to some people, and because it might confer health benefits without the short-term negative emotional effects that sometimes result from writing with a negative emphasis. Second, we need research on the long-term effects of writing on attention. Manipulation checks of expressive writing tasks indicate that attention is altered during writing, but we know virtually nothing about attention in the period after writing. It is possible that brief writing interventions have robust effects on adjustment because they trigger long-term changes in attention, which affect emotion systems that mediate health outcomes.

Evidence from several studies suggests that expressive writing facilitates both stimulus and response habituation. Most of the data support a model of habituation in the experiential emotion system. During writing, more frequent writing reduces the intensity of negative emotions and, to a lesser extent, positive emotions (Hockemeyer et al., 1999). After writing, there is a reduction in the positive association between intrusive thoughts about a stressor and depressive symptoms (Lepore, 1997). Moreover, after writing about imaginary trauma, people may have greater tolerance for negative emotions (M. A. Greenberg et al., 1996). We found mixed evidence of habituation in the physiological emotion system (Pennebaker et al., 1988; Petrie et al., 1995), as well as some indirect evidence: Lepore and Greenberg (in press) observed that expressive writing reduced tension and fatigue, which can be caused by sustained arousal. Overall, the evidence suggests that this is a promising area for additional research.

It is especially important to examine the relation between habituation in the experiential and physiological emotion systems. There is evidence that expressive writing has beneficial effects on physical health even in the absence of strong effects on mood (e.g., Lepore & Greenberg, in press; chapter 3, this volume). We speculate that physiological habituation may occur independently of and possibly prior to subjective habituation. One could argue that physiological responses precede subjective experience in emotion (James, 1884). Therefore, health-promoting physiological changes could occur prior to changes in mood. If a person's physiological responses to a stressor become habituated, it could result in health benefits despite ongoing feelings of distress.

Investigators have looked for evidence of cognitive restructuring during and after expressive writing using various methods, including content analysis, global ratings, self-reports about the frequency of stress-related intrusive thoughts, and self-reports about changes in thoughts and attitudes about stressful events. The results of these investigations have been mixed, with positive, null, or contradictory findings. Although there is some evidence of short-term cognitive changes related to writing, there are no compelling data that writing can produce enduring and profound changes in fundamental schemas about the world, self, and relations with others. In addition, it is not clear whether cognitive changes result in changes in the emotion systems that could mediate the health effects of writing. The study of cognitive restructuring is more complex than the study of attention and habituation processes. It is possible that the measures used to date have been too crude (e.g., word counts), unreliable (e.g., global ratings), or indirect (e.g., frequency of intrusive thoughts). It is also possible that the frequency and duration of experimental writing (generally 60–80 minutes over 1–4 weeks) has been too brief to achieve such lasting changes. Larger doses of writing intervention may be necessary to change schematic beliefs (see Lange et al., chapter 12, this volume). Until these issues are resolved, we should not rule out cognitive restructuring as a mechanism. It may be time to borrow methods from other areas, such as cognitive psychology (see Klein, chapter 8, this volume), or to apply more qualitative approaches, to get more sensitive assessments of changes in cognitive representations.

In summary, expressive writing can facilitate adjustment to stressors through emotion regulation mechanisms. Research in psychiatry, as well as clinical, health, and social psychology, supports the proposition that emotion dysregulation—either excessive or inadequate control over emotional experience, physiology, and behavior—has inimical effects on mental and physical health. Findings presented in this chapter suggest that expressive writing influences attention and habituation to stressful stimuli and to negative emotions and that it may influence restructuring of cognitions related to stressors and stress responses. Our approach extends others presented in this volume by integrating cognitive, emotional, and physiological mechanisms under the single rubric of emotion regulation. One implication of our approach is that future investigations should use multiple methods and measures to capture effects in the different emotion systems. Additionally, research designs should be developed to determine the relative importance of the different systems for mental versus physical health outcomes. Research that further delineates the relations between specific emotion regulation mechanisms (e.g., attention, habituation, cognitive restructuring) and specific emotional responses (e.g., subjective, physiological, behavioral), as well as the patterning of these relations over time, can enhance understanding of why expressive writing has robust effects on diverse mental and physical health outcomes.

REFERENCES

Bonanno, G. A. (2001). Emotion self-regulation. In T. J. Mayne & G. A. Bonanno (Eds.), *Emotions: Current issues and future directions* (pp. 251–285). New York: Guilford Press.

Brashares, H. J., & Catanzaro, S. J. (1994). Mood regulation expectancies, coping responses, depression, and sense of burden in female caregivers of Alzheimer's patients. *Journal of Nervous and Mental Disease, 182,* 437–442.

Cacioppo, J. T., Berntson, G. G., Larsen, J. T., Poehlmann, K. M., & Ito, T. A. (2000). The psychophysiology of emotion. In M. Lewis & J. M. Haviland-Jones (Eds.), *Handbook of emotions* (2nd ed., pp. 173–191). New York: Guilford Press.

Darwin, C. (1872). *The expression of the emotions in man and animals.* New York: Appleton.

Donnelly, D. A., & Murray, E. J. (1991). Cognitive and emotional changes in written essays and therapy interviews. *Journal of Social and Clinical Psychology, 10,* 334–350.

Eisenberg, N., Fabes, R. A., Guthrie, I. K., & Reiser, M. (2000). Dispositional emotionality and regulation: Their role in predicting quality of social functioning. *Journal of Personality and Social Psychology, 78*, 136–157.

Esterling, B. A., Antoni, M. H., Fletcher, M. A., & Margulies, S. (1994). Emotional disclosure through writing or speaking modulates latent Epstein–Barr virus antibody titers. *Journal of Consulting and Clinical Psychology, 62*, 130–140.

Feldman, P., Cohen, S., Lepore, S. J., Matthews, K., Kamarck, T., & Marsland, A. (1999). The impact of negative emotions on acute physiological responses to stress. *Annals of Behavioral Medicine, 21*, 211–215.

Foa, E. B. (1997). Psychological processes related to recovery from a trauma and an effective treatment for PTSD. *Annals of the New York Academy of Sciences, 821*, 410–424.

Frank, A., & Pressler, M. (Eds.). (1997). *The diary of a young girl: The definitive edition*. Bantam Books: New York.

Fredrickson, B. L., & Branigan, C. (2001). Positive emotions. In T. J. Mayne & G. A. Bonanno (Eds.), *Emotions: Current issues and future directions* (pp. 251–285). New York: Guilford Press.

Friedman, H. S., & Booth-Kewley, S. (1987). The "disease-prone" personality: A meta-analytic view of the construct. *American Psychologist, 42*, 539–555.

Greenberg, L. S., & Safran, J. D. (1987). *Emotion in psychotherapy*. New York: Guilford Press.

Greenberg, M. A., & Lepore, S. J. (in press). Theoretical mechanisms involved in disclosure: From inhibition to self regulation. In I. Nyklicek & A. J. J. M. Vingerhoets (Eds.), *The expression and non-expression of emotions in health and disease*. Amsterdam: Harwood Academic.

Greenberg, M. A., & Stone, A. A. (1992). Emotional disclosure about traumas and its relation to health: Effects of previous disclosure and trauma severity. *Journal of Personality and Social Psychology, 63*, 75–84.

Greenberg, M. A., Wortman, C. B., & Stone, A. A. (1996). Emotional expression and physical health: Revising traumatic memories or fostering self-regulation. *Journal of Personality and Social Psychology, 71*, 588–602.

Gross, J. J. (1989). Emotional expression in cancer onset and progression. *Social Sciences and Medicine, 28*, 1239–1248.

Gross, J. J., & Levenson, R. W. (1993). Emotional suppression: Physiology, self-report, and expressive behavior. *Journal of Personality and Social Psychology, 64*, 970–986.

Groves, P. M., & Thompson, R. F. (1970). Habituation: A dual-process theory. *Psychological Review, 77*, 419–450.

Hockemeyer, J., Smyth, J., Anderson, C., & Stone, A. (1999). Is it safe to write? Evaluating the short-term distress produced by writing about emotionally traumatic experiences. *Psychosomatic Medicine, 61*[Abstract].

Horowitz, M. J., Wilner, N., & Alvarez, W. (1979). Impact of Events Scale: A measure of subjective stress. *Psychosomatic Medicine, 41*, 209–218.

James, W. (1884). What is an emotion? *Mind, 9*, 188–205.

Lang, P. J. (1968). Fear reduction and fear behavior: Problems in treating a construct. In J. M. Schlien (Ed.), *Research in psychology* (Vol. 3, pp. 90–103). Washington, DC: American Psychological Association.

Lepore, S. J. (1997). Expressive writing moderates the relation between intrusive thoughts and depressive symptoms. *Journal of Personality and Social Psychology, 7*, 1030–1037.

Lepore, S. J. (1998). Problems and prospects for the social support-reactivity hypothesis. *Annals of Behavioral Medicine, 20*, 257–260.

Lepore, S. J., & Greenberg, M. A. (in press). Mending broken hearts: Effects of expressive writing on mood, cognitive processing, social adjustment, and health following a relationship breakup. *Psychology and Health.*

Lepore, S. J., Ragan, J., & Jones, S. (2000). Talking facilitates cognitive–emotional processes of adaptation to an acute stressor. *Journal of Personality and Social Psychology, 78*, 499–508.

Lepore, S. J., Silver, R. C., Wortman, C. B., & Wayment, H. A. (1996). Social constraints, intrusive thoughts, and depressive symptoms among bereaved mothers. *Journal of Personality and Social Psychology, 70*, 271–282.

Mann, T. (2001). Effects of future writing and optimism on health behaviors in HIV-infected women. *Annals of Behavioral Medicine, 23*, 33.

McEwen, B. S. (1998). Protective and damaging effects of stress mediators. *New England Journal of Medicine, 338*, 171–179.

Paez, D., Velasco, C., & Gonzalez, J. L. (1999). Expressive writing and the role of alexithymia as a dispositional deficit in self-disclosure and psychological health. *Journal of Personality and Social Psychology, 77*, 630–641.

Pennebaker, J. W. (1989). Confession, inhibition, and disease. In L. Berkowitz (Ed.), *Advances in experimental and social psychology* (Vol. 22, pp. 211–244). Orlando, FL: Academic Press.

Pennebaker, J. W., Kiecolt-Glaser, J. K., & Glaser, R. (1988). Disclosure of traumas and immune function: Health implications for psychotherapy. *Journal of Consulting and Clinical Psychology, 56*, 239–245.

Pennebaker, J. W., Mayne, T. J., & Francis, N. E. (1997). Linguistic predictors of adaptive bereavement. *Journal of Personality and Social Psychology, 72*, 863–871.

Petrie, K. J., Booth, R. J., & Pennebaker, J. W. (1998). The immunological effects of thought suppression. *Journal of Personality and Social Psychology, 75*, 1264–1272.

Petrie, K. J., Booth, R. J., & Pennebaker, J. W., Davison, K. P., & Thomas, M. G. (1995). Disclosure of trauma and immune response to a hepatitis B vaccination program. *Journal of Consulting and Clinical Psychology, 63*(5), 787–792.

Rachman, S., & Hodgson, R. (1974). Synchrony and desynchrony in fear and avoidance. *Behavior Research and Therapy, 12*, 311–318.

Schoutrop, M. (2000). *Structured writing and processing traumatic events.* Unpublished doctoral dissertation, University of Amsterdam.

Smith, T. W. (1992). Hostility and health: Current status of a psychosomatic hypothesis. *Health Psychology, 11*, 139–150.

Smyth, J. M. (1998). Written emotional expression: Effect sizes, outcome types, and moderating variables. *Journal of Consulting and Clinical Psychology, 66*, 174–178.

Smyth, J. M., & Pennebaker, J. W. (2001). What are the health effects of disclosure? In A. Baum, T. A. Revenson, & J. E. Singer (Eds.), *Handbook of health psychology* (pp. 339–348). Hillsdale, NJ: Erlbaum.

Smyth, J. M., Stone, A. A., Hurewitz, A., & Kaell, A. (1999). Effects of writing about stressful experiences on symptom reduction in patients with asthma or rheumatoid arthritis. *Journal of the American Medical Association, 281*, 1304–1329.

Smyth, J. M., True, N., & Souto, J. (2001). Effects of writing about traumatic experiences: The necessity of narrative structuring. *Journal of Social and Clinical Psychology, 20*, 161–172.

Swanbon, T. (1999). *The physical and psychological health effects of self-disclosure in homosexual males.* Unpublished doctoral dissertation, California School of Professional Psychology, San Diego.

Watson, J. P., & Marks, I. M. (1972). Relevant and irrelevant fear in flooding: A crossover study of phobic patients. *Behavior Therapy, 2*, 275–293.

7

GAIN WITHOUT PAIN? EXPRESSIVE WRITING AND SELF-REGULATION

LAURA A. KING

Two strong conclusions can be made with regard to the benefits of writing. First, expressive writing has health benefits. Second, no one really knows why. A variety of mechanisms have been posited as explanations for the myriad benefits of writing. These range from Freudian notions of catharsis and insight (Freud, 1901/1960) to the behaviorist concepts of habituation and extinction (Domjan, 1998). These explanations fit in with a view of writing as therapy and certainly have an intuitive appeal. Yet, emerging empirical research using the writing paradigm challenges these sorts of explanations. In this chapter, I briefly review the conceptual evolution of the writing studies and then highlight some newer empirical evidence that cannot be accounted for by these earlier explanations. Throughout, I try to expand on the possibility that writing benefits can be explained through the impact of writing on self-regulation. I argue that considering the act of writing about life events as incorporating these events into the life story allows us to understand why some stories may be better than others. In addition, I argue that focusing on negative life events

Preparation of this chapter as well as the research reported within was supported in part by National Institute of Mental Health Grant 54142.

has hampered our ability to understand what it is that we do when we write in a concerted fashion about anything. Finally, I suggest possible future research directions that might clarify this ubiquitous but puzzling effect.

WHAT IS EFFECTIVE SELF-REGULATION?

For the purposes of this chapter, *self-regulation* refers to the capacity of a person to effectively pursue goals, to register feedback in that pursuit, and to adjust his or her behavior accordingly. From a control theory perspective (Powers, 1973), one can think of motivation as existing in a hierarchy of feedback loops. The person pursues higher level goals by way of lower level goals, monitoring progress throughout (King, Richards, & Stemmerich, 1998). The effectiveness of this type of regulation should be increased by activities that allow for more accurate identification of goals, better monitoring of feedback, and more prolific generation of strategies for goal pursuit. One of the key features of human self-regulation is affective response. Carver and Scheier (1982) discussed how positive and negative emotions serve as mechanisms of feedback in self-regulation. We feel happy or sad, exhilarated or downtrodden, depending on how our progress toward our valued goals compares to our expected level of progress.

What happens when self-regulation increases? As individuals learn about themselves, their priorities, and the meaning of their emotional reactions, they are more able to effectively strive toward their valued goals. In addition, well-regulated individuals experience emotions contingent on their goal pursuits. Thus, their emotional reactions are more finely tuned and informative (Carver & Scheier, 1982). One might also consider why individuals who have experienced trauma might suffer in the area of self-regulation. Experiences that are traumatic might be seen as disrupting the system through which regulation occurs. These events might change central beliefs and values (e.g., Janoff-Bulman, 1992) that guide the selection of goals. The meaning of the events for the higher levels of a motivation hierarchy must be clarified. Changes at the highest level of the motivational hierarchy may cause lower level goals to be considered obsolete. Furthermore, the emotional disturbance incited by unexpected traumatic events might muddy the waters of affective feedback. Intrusive thoughts and lingering emotions from traumatic life events can, thus, be viewed in a context of self-regulatory disruption. However, it is important to note that self-regulation presents a general process that is not inextricably tied to negative or traumatic life events.

Before I address how this general view of self-regulation applies to the writing paradigm, it may be worthwhile to consider the evolution of the writing paradigm. This examination allows the review of the explanatory mechanisms that have been considered as well as some of the conventions that have been incorporated into empirical investigations of the healing power of writing.

WHY WRITING WORKS: INITIAL HYPOTHESES

The earliest candidates for explanatory mechanisms underlying the health benefits of writing were emotional catharsis and insight. These early ideas about why writing might be beneficial were rooted in a wider theoretical context of the physical health benefits of expressing emotion (King & Emmons, 1990; Pennebaker 1989). These hypotheses were based on the assumption that unexpressed emotion would lead to chronic autonomic arousal and eventual illness. Thus, one could conclude that letting emotions out—even in the isolated and controlled setting of a laboratory writing session—should be beneficial.

It is worth noting that the instructions for the typical writing study include encouraging the participant to "freely express any and all emotions or thoughts that you have about the experience" (e.g., King & Miner, 2000, p. 223). These instructions highlight the presumed role of emotional release in the process by which writing benefits physical health. Certainly, having individuals write about a traumatic life event in this way has been correlated with fewer physical illnesses over time relative to a control group writing about a nonemotional topic (Pennebaker & Beall, 1986) and to a variety of other positive outcomes like enhanced immune function (Petrie, Booth, Pennebaker, & Davison, 1995), reduced health problems (Greenberg & Stone, 1992), and better adjustment to college (Pennebaker, Colder, & Sharp, 1990).

That these results might derive from the connection between emotional expression and autonomic arousal was supported in research showing lower skin conductance levels (Pennebaker, Hughes, & O'Heeron, 1987) in individuals who completed the writing exercise. Higher skin conductance has typically been viewed as an indicator of "holding back," as in a lie detector test, and lower skin conductance has been viewed as evidence for "letting go," or disinhibiting. Furthermore, the importance of emotional release was demonstrated in research showing that participants who avoided emotional content showed no positive effects (Pennebaker & Beall, 1986). Correlational research also supported the connection between the benefits of writing and the relation between emotional expression and health. For instance, Pennebaker and O'Heeron (1984) reported that among bereaved persons, differences in health status 1 year following a loss were accounted for by the degree of confiding. Thus, early on, the benefits of writing seemed to represent a demonstration of the larger benefits of emotional expression.

The concept of active inhibition was proposed by Pennebaker (1989) to explain the effect of writing on the body. *Active inhibition* refers to the effortful holding back of impulse to disclose about a traumatic life event. It was posited that this exertion of will results in chronic autonomic arousal and eventual weakening of the immune system. The writing exercise would allow the person to release the pent-up emotion and to come to terms with the (often previously undisclosed) trauma. A vast number of studies used this active inhibition framework and demonstrated health benefits in a variety of ways. Again and again, "regular folk" (typically nonclinical samples of college undergraduates) would demonstrate physical health benefits (in the form of reduced illnesses) after participating in the writing studies. The implied portrait of humanity is a truly fascinating one: We live in a world where nearly everyone is holding back some terrible past trauma, and we can all benefit by freeing ourselves from the chains of inhibition. The writing exercise appeared to rest on the processes of catharsis and insight. Dropping the psychoanalytic bent that these terms conjure, one could likewise argue for a more behavioral view. If individuals were not talking about their past traumas because of fear of social censure, repeatedly writing about the traumatic experience without negative social consequences should extinguish this fear and reduce wear and tear on the body. Repeatedly confronting the traumatic life event might allow the individual to habituate to it and reduce the stress aroused by the memory.

It is worthwhile to consider some of the conventions that have been incorporated into the writing paradigm. Such an examination is necessary because the methods used in these studies have been enormously influential in the way we have thought about the processes underlying the positive benefits of writing. Regardless of the underlying mechanism posited, a few common features of writing studies are notable. First, most have involved writing repeatedly (three or four times) over a short period of time. Second, the topic of writing is typically in the past (though not always—a few notable exceptions include Lepore, 1997; Pennebaker et al., 1990; and a study by Cameron & Nicholls, 1998, which is discussed later in this section). Most important, however, writing has typically involved a personally significant negative event. Note that these common features have been largely a matter of convention and have not grown out of the dictates of a particular theory.

I suggest that many of these studies have started with a particular bias —that benefiting from writing must involve encountering and coping with a traumatic event. In other words, (physical) gain requires (psychological) pain. Explanations of the healing power of writing have assumed that individuals must confront traumas in a concentrated fashion often over several occasions. Typically, the topic of the writing is a negative event, and the experience of writing is an emotionally negative one.

A variety of studies have called into question the importance of some of these conventions (see chapter 6, this volume). Greenberg, Wortman, and Stone (1996) found that participants who wrote about someone else's trauma only once (for 20 minutes) showed physical health benefits relative to a group who wrote about a control topic. These findings are quite startling and speak against the role of habituation or extinction in the benefits of writing (because with a single trial these processes are much less likely to occur). In addition, these results indicate that the writing topic need not be rooted in the individual's own life for benefits to occur. Unless we assume that most or all of the participants somehow made the imagined trauma their own and symbolically wrote about something of relevance to themselves, mechanisms such as finding meaning in one's trauma would seem to be, at least partially, discounted as explanatory mechanisms. Greenberg and her colleagues postulated that the traumatic event itself was relatively unimportant in producing health benefits—rather, the simple act of confronting a negative emotion and being able to control it led to increased affective regulation, which in turn led to health benefits. In other words, through emotional writing about any trauma, individuals come to see themselves as capable of handling intense and challenging emotional experiences.

It is notable that Greenberg and colleagues still included the focus on the past that is characteristic of writing studies. In contrast, Cameron and Nicholls (1998) found health benefits for writing about one's plans for coping with coming to college—an instruction that was intended as a self-regulation task. In this study, college students wrote about the coping with a particular forthcoming trauma and showed health benefits (particularly for pessimistic individuals). Thus, writing about trauma, even one focused on the future, appears to be associated with health benefits.

It is interesting to note that, in discussing the role of self-regulation in the beneficial effects of writing about traumas, Greenberg and colleagues (1996) stated that "any stimulus that arouses a moderate degree of negative affect should be adequate to produce . . . (these effects)" (p. 589). Thus, they implied that negative emotion is required to enhance self-regulation. Yet, one implication of the health benefits of writing about imagined trauma is that any writing that facilitates self-regulation may produce health benefits, even writing that does not invite the experience of strong negative emotion.

QUESTIONING THE ROLE OF NEGATIVE EMOTION

To examine the processes underlying the "healing power of writing," Pennebaker conducted a series of fascinating analyses that challenged the central role of "letting out" negative emotion in obtaining health benefits from writing. Pennebaker and Francis (1999) conducted a content analysis using a computerized word count program (Linguistic Inquiry and Word Count) in order to examine exactly what sorts of words were associated with health benefits in the experimental groups. Analyzing the essays written by participants in the trauma group of a typical writing study, Pennebaker found that independent of emotional expression in the essays, the use of insight words, causal words, and words associated with cognitive activity was associated with health improvements. In addition, the expression of more positive emotion relative to negative tended to be characteristic of those who enjoyed greater health benefits (Pennebaker, Mayne, & Francis, 1997). Pennebaker (1997) asserted that whereas a reduction in inhibition might play a role in obtaining health benefits from writing, the cognitive changes manifested in these word-use differences as well as the use of positive emotion words more strongly predict physical health. Thus, increasing understanding and insight seem to be the key feature of benefiting from expressive writing. In addition, Smyth (1998) performed a meta-analysis of the writing paradigm and found that, although emotional writing tended to increase short-term distress, there was no relation between the intensity of that distress and later benefits of writing. Contrary to the notion of "no pain, no gain," physical health gains might accrue independently of the painful emotional work long assumed to be necessary.

The finding that the use of positive emotion terms seems to distinguish those who benefited from writing from those who did not may seem somewhat counterintuitive. Yet, this finding is corroborated by recent research on the role of positive emotional experience in coping. For instance, Folkman and Moskowitz (2000) have found that positive emotional experience is common even during very negative life events. Keltner and Bonanno (1997) found that the expression of genuine positive emotion (particularly Duchenne laughter and smiling—smiling that involves the muscles around the eyes and the appearance of "crow's feet") during bereavement was related to heightened adjustment on a variety of levels. Fredrickson and Levenson (1998) found that positive emotion may undo the effects of negative emotion on cardiovascular function. Thus, the experience of the positive in the context of traumatic or negative life events might have implications for psychological and physical well-being. The finding that distress is not an essential part of gaining the health benefits of writing sets the stage for considering other reasons why writing is beneficial. Perhaps experiencing and expressing negative emotion are less important to the benefits of writing than is constructing a sensible story of the experience, one in which there are some positive insights.

Perhaps a caveat is appropriate at this point. The finding that the experience of negative emotion during and after writing is unrelated to the health benefits of writing may seem to indicate that avoidance of negative emotion is a healthier alternative. Several considerations are worth noting. First, all of the studies included in Pennebaker's text analyses used nonclinical samples—for the most part healthy undergraduates. Second, traumatized individuals who are unable to experience and express negative emotions may be less able to identify and control these feelings. Surely, in such cases a focus on the negative emotional aspects of an experience may be important. However, I would maintain that researchers have, for the most part, insufficiently questioned the assumed role of negative emotion in the benefits of writing. Furthermore, it is notable that issues of defensiveness are only brought up with regard to the positive—is it safe to assume that if something is negative, it must be true?

Consider the writing paradigm from a narrative perspective, in order to understand the importance of incorporating the positive even in stories of the very negative. McAdams's life story approach to identity (e.g., McAdams, 1992, 1993) asserts that the stories individuals tell about their life experiences are the building blocks of identity. Integrating experiences into the self implies constructing narratives that fit into the frame of the storied self. Thus, one can think of individuals who are engaged in disclosive writing as writing their life experiences into their life narratives. Incorporating these life experiences into life stories, to make them something we are, not something that has happened to us, may be part of the way writing works, and one of the reasons positive emotion may be important to writing "good" (i.e., health promoting) stories. From a self-regulatory perspective, writing is a process of self-exploration and understanding. From a narrative perspective, writing is also a process of self-construction. Writing about important life experiences means authoring the self (cf. McAdams 1992).

To the extent that it is adaptive that we like ourselves, these stories, *that are our selves*, must be stories we can like. Thus, the rewriting of the life story to accommodate new experiences means integrating life experiences into a narrative that is coherent and manageable and that probably contains something positive. One way to incorporate positive experience into negative life events is to find positive benefits in those negative events.

FOCUSING ON THE POSITIVE ASPECTS OF NEGATIVE LIFE EVENTS

The theme of finding benefit in negative life circumstance is common in theories of coping (Affleck & Tennen, 1996; Janoff-Bulman, 1992). In addition, being able to find benefits in even severely negative life experiences is associated with better adjustment (Tennen, Affleck, & Mendola, 1991) and more effective adaptation (King, Scollon, Ramsey, & Williams, 2000; Taylor, Wood, & Lichtman, 1983). Finding something good in negative life experiences may help individuals to disengage from past traumas (Taylor & Armor, 1996). In addition, research on posttraumatic growth portrays personal growth as coming out of extreme life circumstances (e.g., Tedeschi & Calhoun, 1995). Feeling that one has grown through a life experience is one way to construct a happy ending to the story. Perhaps finding this kind of meaning in an event is associated with more easily writing it into the life story.

King and Miner (2000) performed a study in which individuals positively reframed a past trauma by constructing a happy ending to some negative life event. Participants were randomly assigned to write about a trauma or to write about only the perceived benefits of their traumas. In the perceived benefits condition, participants were asked to think about a traumatic event and then to "focus on the positive aspects of the experience . . . write about how you have changed or grown as a person as a result of the experience" (King & Miner, 2000, p. 223).

King and Miner found that individuals who wrote only about the positive aspects of their traumatic life experiences tended to use more positive emotion and insight words than those writing about trauma only. In addition, individuals who wrote only about traumas experienced less positive emotion than all other groups. It is significant that individuals in the perceived benefits group showed identical health benefits to those who wrote about trauma only. Furthermore, assignment to the perceived benefits group interacted with the number of insight words used in the essays to predict lowered illness visits, indicating that not only can individuals be coaxed into gaining insight into their negative life experiences by positively reframing these, but that successfully doing so has health benefits. Note that in this study, participants in the perceived benefits group were forbidden from "really getting into" the negative aspects of their traumas.

These results are consistent with the previous discussion of self-regulation. Writing about topics that allow individuals to understand what their emotional reactions mean may facilitate goal pursuit. Increased feelings of efficacy may emerge not only from dwelling on the negative, but also from positively reframing a negative life experience (Scheier & Carver, 1985; Taylor, 1983). One way that individuals say they have benefited from a negative life event is through a reordering of priorities. Thus, by examining negative events, we might come to understand what is really important—those goals that are most important to us.

Placing these results in the context of the life narrative, we might posit that individuals who are able to focus on the positive aspects of negative life events have authored a story they can live with, out of the randomness that life has presented. Incorporating these happy endings into the life story may, ultimately, relate to enhanced self-esteem and meaning in life.

This study calls into question the necessity of freely expressing and experiencing negative emotion, yet, like past writing studies, it included negative events as a focus on the writing instructions. A more recent study challenges the centrality of negative life events in benefiting from writing. In this study, participants wrote about a future oriented topic with no reference to personal trauma or negative events.

The goals that individuals espouse for themselves have been seen as a window into self-regulatory processes (Austin & Vancouver, 1996). Thus, it seemed that having individuals write about their life goals might be a way to enhance self-regulation without fostering negative mood. From a narrative perspective, we can think of this focus as pushing people to expand on the future chapters of the life story (McAdams, 1993). King (2001) conducted a study in which participants were randomly assigned to write (for 20 minutes a day for 4 days) about a control topic, a life trauma, their best possible future selves, or both a trauma (on the first 2 days) and their best possible future self (the last 2 days). Possible selves are personalized representations of goals (Markus & Nurius, 1986). Aspects of possible selves have been shown to relate to a variety of outcome measures including well-being. For the best possible self condition, participants were instructed to think about their lives in the future and to "imagine that everything has gone as well as it possibly could . . . Think of this as the realization of all of your life dreams . . . write about what you imagined" (King, 2001, p. 801).

Before and after each writing session, participants completed ratings of their positive and negative moods. They also rated their writing each day on how important it was, how emotional, and how upsetting. Three weeks after writing, participants completed questionnaire measures of subjective well-being and gave the experimenter access to their health center records.

With regard to emotional experience after writing, results demonstrated that, controlling for mood before writing, writing about one's best possible self was associated with a significant increase in positive mood and that those who wrote about their best possible selves were significantly happier than those who wrote about trauma only. Yet, participants found both tasks to be engaging. Participants rated writing about trauma and writing about their best possible selves as important, emotional, and challenging activities. However, as expected, such writing was significantly less upsetting than writing about trauma. With regard to subjective well-being, individuals who wrote about their best possible selves were significantly higher in psychological well-being 3 weeks after the study's completion than other participants (King, 2001).

With regard to physical illness measures, results were equally striking. These results are shown in Figure 7.1. No significant differences were present among the groups 3 months prior to writing. However, at the 5-month follow-up, the best possible self and trauma only group were both significantly lower in illness than the control groups. As can be seen in Figure 7.1, the combination group fell between these groups and the control

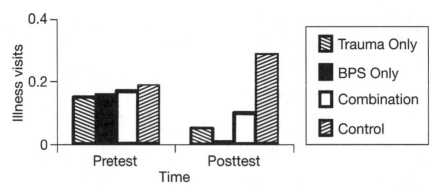

Figure 7.1. Residualized health center visits for illness as a function of writing topic. BPS = best possible self. These data were previously reported in a different format in King (2001).

group. This finding (i.e., that the "combination group" did not benefit from writing) replicates a null effect from the study by King and Miner (2000). Switching topics does not appear to be associated with the typical benefits of writing.

Results with regard to writing about life goals indicate that one can enjoy the health benefits of writing without the emotional costs associated with writing about trauma. Indeed, writing about one's life goals was associated with feeling less upset and more happy and getting sick less often. Note that the physical benefits of writing about one's best possible self were equal to or better than writing about trauma, whereas writing about a traumatic life event also entailed feeling upset and experiencing lowered mood. Thus, it may be possible to enjoy the benefits of writing without writing about trauma at all.

These data truly challenge many previous ideas about why writing works. It may be that we simply have difficulty appreciating the psychological importance of more positive aspects of our lives. These results indicate that benefiting from writing about our deepest thoughts and feeling need not mean writing about negative aspects of our lives. Casting these results against the previous discussion of self-regulation, they would seem to indicate that writing instructions that promote awareness of one's goals and priorities may be a way to gain the benefits of writing. From a narrative perspective, we can see these writing instructions as transforming life goals from something we hope to attain to something we are, a part of the life story that is the self.

To appreciate the psychological weight of positive, hopeful topics (such as life goals), it may be helpful to examine some typical examples of essays written in this study. What follows are writing samples from individuals who showed decreases in health center visits for illness.

The following is an excerpt from a participant from the trauma only group. This young woman described the loss of her father and her own coping with the loss:

> Although I dream about my dad a lot, and they are usually peaceful, they still disturb me. Especially when I have the ones where he's really alive and he says the hospital really made a mistake . . . Anyway, the loss of my father and the fear of the loss of my mother and the fact that my sister lives in Italy with her family. . . . It's better now that a couple of my friends know the whole story because I used to have to say that my father died of lung cancer—because my mom wouldn't let me tell the truth—but I decided on my own that telling would help me deal. I've even done questionnaires before about the loss of a loved one but I never told the whole truth. . . . I have to realize loss is a big part of life and I'm not the only one who experiences it. I can still be happy—even if/or when I am "alone" literally because I'll always have my sister.

In a sense, this example bears all the signs of "healthy" writing about trauma as described by Pennebaker et al. (1997). The participant is sharing a largely undisclosed trauma yet is able to incorporate some positive emotion and seems to be doing the work of finding meaning in her loss and creating a coherent story.

The next excerpt comes from a participant in the best possible self condition, who also showed health benefits:

> My happily ever after would be when I'm living in California around San Francisco, and I've got at least a medium production assistant job with a well-known film production company. I'd be married with two kids and a dog. . . . We'd also have the hobby of learning something new every couple of months, like yoga or study a foreign country and then go there. I love having future knowledge to look forward to— and that way our marriage wouldn't be too repetitive each day or each year. . . . I guess I want a pretty normal middle class life. I want just a medium-size house—no mansions even if I could afford it. . . . My main goal is to keep experiencing as much as I can even when it seems there isn't anything else, there always is. Really, I just want a good marriage, where we are both confident together and compliment each other's personalities. Once we are happy together we could be happy in lots of different situations—even if it means some sacrifice. My ideal would be for us both to love, or at least be proud of, our jobs, but also always strive for more.

The following excerpt is drawn from a participant in the best possible self condition as well. This participant also demonstrated the health benefits of writing:

> I hope my life allows me to travel. I have this passion to spend extended amounts of time in countries that are drastically different from my own. I'd love to visit India, China, Israel, Nepal, Africa again.

So— ... I want to travel. I also envision being the associate pastor of a moderately sized church in Arizona working with adult education programming and cross-cultural awareness. Hopefully somewhere along the line I will find someone that I want to commit to sharing my life with. I would like to have 3 children. I really wouldn't mind living in another country! I certainly don't want to be in the military, but I'd love to do medical missions in third world countries or something like that. I also would like to teach Religion courses at the college level someday ... Maybe I could be a religious archeologist! Then I could travel and learn amazing things all at the same time! Life is just full of possibilities. See, there is all this stuff I want to do with part of my life, but I also really do desire a home and family.

Individuals write in clearly different ways about their best possible selves and about trauma. These essays contain more fantasy and more shopping lists of things that make the writer happy. At the same time, however, there is also a process of understanding that occurs—by envisioning what will make them happy in the future, participants are forced to consider their priorities and values and to think about what they really need to make a good life. Although we tend to think of personal growth as emerging out of negative life events (e.g., Tedeschi & Calhoun, 1995), participants do seem to be able to learn about the self and to clarify priorities, even when writing about positive topics.

These examples show that there may be something useful—something to be gained—from exploring the most hopeful aspects of our lives. That such an exercise also has health benefits is all the more intriguing. The mechanisms that underlie these results are not clear; however, it might be that individuals who focus on and write about their best possible futures actually are able to more effectively pursue these goals. Research on visualization has shown that individuals who can imagine themselves accomplishing tasks are often better able to do them (e.g., Pham & Taylor, 1999; Rivkin & Taylor, 1999). Although we speak of negative life events as being integrated into the life story self, we should also consider positive events —our hopes and dreams—and how integrating these into the self may affect the person. Perhaps writing about life goals allows us to pursue our goals more effortlessly and less self-consciously. In this sense, writing about goals may increase the experience of flow (Csikzentmihalyi, 1990).

WRITING TOPICS: UNLOCKING THE POSSIBILITIES

An interesting question about the writing paradigm is this: What should people write about to enjoy the health benefits of writing? The answer depends, for the most part, on the mechanisms we think underlie the benefits of writing. If halting emotional inhibition is the key, then writing about undisclosed trauma is a good idea. If coping with negative emotion is the key, then any negative emotional writing should work. If gaining insight is important, then instructions that promote insight should be preferred. If incorporating an aspect of experience into the life story is important, then events and experiences that require such processes should be used. The results of the study by King (2001) seem to indicate that aspects of our lives that we might not think of as requiring "coping" may be usefully and beneficially explored through writing. Writing about topics that allow us to learn about our own needs and desires may be a way to harness the positive benefits of writing. These lessons about the self, I maintain, are also available through exploration of the negative aspects of our lives, but they are not located exclusively there.

Research is required that compares a variety of writing topics in order to tease apart the various topic characteristics most likely to yield benefits. One possibility would be to look at intensely positive experiences. Another might be to ask questions about individuals' most meaningful life experiences and their philosophies of life. Writing that is not emotional but that promotes awareness of one's goals, priorities, and so on might be used to foster self-regulation. Future researchers may call into question the ultimate importance of emotion per se in the healing power of writing.

One topic of concern that warrants some discussion is whether a broad and encompassing model or mechanism may account for the healing power of writing. There is certainly an appealing parsimony to uncovering a single broad mechanism, but it may be that writing about different topics shares much in terms of the method but little else. Given that writing about trauma and writing about best possible selves have different emotional correlates, it seems likely that they differ in terms of their psychophysiological correlates as well. Thus, it may be that the physiological substrates of these kinds of writing effects differ.

Future work must move beyond demonstrating that writing works. It is crucial to identify dependent measures that tap into the processes that underlie the benefits of writing. A variety of measures are necessary to make conclusions about the underpinnings of the writing effect. Cognitive measures are useful in identifying the kinds of changes that writing might foster. What happens to the self when experiences are written into it?

In conclusion, there is no question that disclosive writing has important implications for psychological and physical health. However, understanding why writing works may require us to question the concepts at the very core of our views of what is important about human life and what aspects of existence require examination. It clearly is possible to gain from writing without experiencing pain. Indeed, health benefits may also be associated with writing that incites happiness, joy, and excitement about the future.

REFERENCES

Affleck, G., & Tennen, H. (1996). Construing benefits from adversity: Adaptational significance and dispositional underpinnings. *Journal of Personality, 64,* 899–922.

Austin, J. T., & Vancouver, J. B. (1996). Goal constructs in psychology: Structure, process and content. *Psychological Bulletin, 120,* 338–375.

Cameron, L. D., & Nicholls, G. (1998). Expression of stressful experiences through writing: Effects of a self regulation manipulation for pessimists and optimists. *Health Psychology, 17,* 84–92.

Carver, C. S., & Scheier, M. F. (1982). Control theory: A useful conceptual framework for personality–social, clinical, and health psychology. *Psychological Bulletin, 92,* 111–135.

Csikzentmihalyi, M. (1990). *Flow.* New York: Harper & Row.

Domjan, M. (1998). *The principles of learning and behavior, 4th ed.* Pacific Grove, CA: Brooks/Cole.

Folkman, S., & Moskowitz, J. T. (2000). Stress, positive emotion, and coping. *Current Directions in Psychological Science, 9,* 115–118.

Fredrickson, B. L., & Levenson, R. W. (1998). Positive emotions speed recovery from the cardiovascular sequelae of negative emotions. *Cognition and Emotion, 12,* 191–220.

Freud, S. (1901/1960). *Introductory lectures on psych-analysis.* In Standard edition, Vols. 15 and 16. London: Hogarth Press.

Greenberg, M. A., & Stone, A. A. (1992). Emotional disclosure about traumas and its relation to health: Effects of previous disclosure and trauma severity. *Journal of Personality and Social Psychology, 63,* 75–84.

Greenberg, M. A., Wortman, C. B., & Stone, A. A. (1996). Emotional expression and physical health: Revising traumatic memories or fostering self-regulation? *Journal of Personality and Social Psychology, 71,* 588–602.

Janoff-Bulman, R. (1992). *Shattered assumptions: Towards a new psychology of trauma.* New York: The Free Press.

Keltner, D., & Bonanno, G. A. (1997). A study of laughter and dissociation: Distinct correlates of laughter and smiling during bereavement. *Journal of Personality and Social Psychology, 73,* 687–702.

King, L. A. (2001). The health benefits of writing about life goals. *Personality and Social Psychology Bulletin, 27,* 798–807.

King, L. A., & Emmons, R. A. (1990). Conflict over emotional expression: Psychological and physical correlates. *Journal of Personality and Social Psychology, 58,* 864–877.

King, L. A., & Miner, K. N. (2000). Writing about the perceived benefits of traumatic events: Implications for physical health. *Personality and Social Psychology Bulletin, 26,* 220–230.

King, L. A., Richards, J., & Stemmerich, E. D. (1998). Daily goals, life goals, and worst fears: Means, ends, and subjective well-being. *Journal of Personality, 66,* 713–744.

King, L. A., Scollon, C. K., Ramsey, C. M., & Williams, T. (2000). Stories of life transition: Happy endings, subjective well-being, and ego development in parents of children with Down Syndrome. *Journal of Research in Personality, 34,* 509–536.

Lepore, S. J. (1997). Expressive writing moderates the relation between intrusive thoughts and depressive symptoms. *Journal of Personality and Social Psychology, 73,* 1030–1037.

Markus, H., & Nurius, P. (1986). Possible selves. *American Psychologist, 41,* 954–969.

Markus, H., & Ruvolo, A. (1989). Possible selves: Personalized representations of goals. In L. A. Pervin (Ed.), *Goal concepts in personality and social psychology* (pp. 211–242). Hillsdale, NJ: Erlbaum.

McAdams, D. P. (1992). Unity and purpose in human lives: The emergence of identity as life story. In R. A. Zucker, A. I. Rabin, J. Aronoff, & S. Frank (Eds.), *Personality structure in the life course* (pp. 323–376). New York: Springer.

McAdams, D. P. (1993). *The stories we live by: Personal myths and the making of the self.* New York: Morrow.

Pennebaker, J. W. (1989). Confession, inhibition, and disease. In L. Berkowitz (Ed.), *Advances in experimental social psychology* (Vol. 22, pp. 211–244). New York: Springer-Verlag.

Pennebaker, J. W. (1993). Putting stress into words: Health, linguistic, and therapeutic implications. *Behavior Research and Therapy, 31,* 539–548.

Pennebaker, J. W. (1997). Writing about emotional experiences as a therapeutic process. *Psychological Science, 8,* 162–166.

Pennebaker, J. W., & Beall, S. (1986). Confronting a traumatic event: Toward an understanding of inhibition and disease. *Journal of Abnormal Psychology, 95,* 274–281.

Pennebaker, J. W., Colder, M., & Sharp, L. K. (1990). Accelerating the coping process. *Journal of Personality and Social Psychology, 58,* 528–537.

Pennebaker, J. W., & Francis, M. E. (1999). *Linguistic Inquiry and Word Count: LIWC.* Mahwah, NJ: Erlbaum.

Pennebaker, J. W., Hughes, C. F., & O'Heeron, R. (1987). The psychophysiology of confession: Linking inhibitory and psychosomatic processes. *Journal of Personality and Social Psychology, 52,* 781–793.

Pennebaker, J. W., Mayne, T. J., & Francis, M. (1997). Linguistic predictors of adaptive bereavement. *Journal of Personality and Social Psychology, 72,* 863–871.

Pennebaker, J. W., & O'Heeron, R. C. (1984). Confiding in others and illness rate among spouses of suicide and accidental-death victims. *Journal of Abnormal Psychology, 93,* 473–476.

Petrie, K. J., Booth, R. J., Pennebaker, J. W., & Davison, K. P. (1995). Disclosure of trauma and immune response to a hepatitis B vaccination program. *Journal of Consulting and Clinical Psychology, 63,* 787–792.

Pham, L. B., & Taylor, S. E. (1999). From thought to action: Effects of process-versus outcome-based mental simulations on performance. *Personality and Social Psychology Bulletin, 25,* 250–260.

Powers, W. T. (1973). *Behavior: The control of perception.* Chicago: Aldine.

Rivkin, I. D., & Taylor, S. E. (1999). The effects of mental simulation on coping with controllable stressful events. *Personality and Social Psychology Bulletin, 25,* 1451–1462.

Scheier, M., & Carver, C. S. (1985). Optimism, coping and health: Assessment and implications of generalized outcome expectancies. *Health Psychology, 4,* 219–247.

Smyth, J. M. (1998). Written emotional expression: Effect sizes, outcome types, and moderating variables. *Journal of Consulting and Clinical Psychology, 66,* 174–184.

Taylor, S. E. (1983). Adjustment to threatening events: A theory of cognitive adaptation. *American Psychologist, 38,* 1161–1173.

Taylor, S. E., & Armor, D. A. (1996). Positive illusions and coping with adversity. *Journal of Personality, 64,* 873–898.

Taylor, S. E., Wood, J. V., & Lichtman, R. R. (1983). It could be worse: Selective evaluations as a response to victimization. *Journal of Social Issues, 39,* 81–102.

Tedeschi, R. G., & Calhoun, L. G. (1995). *Trauma and transformation: Growing in the aftermath of suffering.* Thousand Oaks, CA: Sage.

Tennen, H., Affleck, G., & Mendola, R. (1991). Coping with smell and taste disorders. In T. Gechell, R. Doty, L. Bartoshuk, & J. Snow (Eds.), *Smell and taste in health and disease* (pp. 787–801). New York: Raven.

8

STRESS, EXPRESSIVE WRITING, AND WORKING MEMORY

KITTY KLEIN

As the chapters in this volume document, there is an enormous amount of evidence that expressive writing about stressful experiences produces remarkable physical and psychological benefits. My purpose in this chapter is to integrate theory and data from social, cognitive, and clinical psychological perspectives to propose that writing has sizable effects on fundamental cognitive processes, in addition to its effects on health outcomes. I further discuss the importance of such processes for behavior and speculate on how these cognitive changes may ultimately be tied to some of the widely observed health effects of expressive writing.

EFFECTS OF LIFE STRESS ON COGNITIVE PROCESSES

An enormous amount of work has been devoted to the effects of environmental stressors such as noise, heat, cold, and pharmacological agents on memory function and problem solving. Fewer studies have investigated the relationship between cognitive functions and aversive and sometimes traumatic life events, such as getting divorced, being fired from a job, or the death of someone we love. My own work in this area began with a straightforward test of the hypothesis that people undergoing high levels of life stress would be poorer problem solvers compared to people reporting fewer stressful experiences, particularly if they were sensitive to their own somatic sensations (Baradell & Klein, 1993). The bases for these predictions were first, that life event stress should be reflected in autonomic somatic reactions that draw attention from task demands; and second, that people who are highly aware of such reactions would experience even more competition for scarce attentional resources (Mandler, 1993).

To test these hypotheses, Baradell and I (1993) measured participants' life stress using the Life Experiences Scale (LES; Sarason, Johnson, & Siegel, 1978). They used the Private Body Consciousness Test (PBC; Miller, Murphy & Buss, 1981), a 5-item measure of awareness of bodily sensations, to measure somatic sensitivity. The problem-solving task required participants to select from six alternatives the response that best completed a verbal analogy problem. For example: "Son is to father, as mother is to: (a) wife, (b) great grandmother, (c) daughter, (d) grandmother, (e) father, (f) sister." Compared with persons reporting fewer stressful experiences, persons with high levels of life stress solved fewer analogy problems and used less efficient problem-solving strategies. These deficits were not apparent on easier analogies tasks (Klein & Barnes, 1994) and were particularly striking in individuals with high somatic sensitivity.

In another analogies study (Klein, 1995), I tested the explanation that task-irrelevant thoughts were the link between life stress and problem solving. Using Sarason's Cognitive Interference Questionnaire (CIQ; Sarason, Sarason, Keefe, Hayes, & Shearin, 1986), participants reported how frequently they thought about task-irrelevant issues while working on the analogies problems. Again, highly stressed participants with more somatic awareness performed the worst. They also reported more off-task thinking, and the poorer their performance, the more off-task thinking they reported. However, a mediation test did not support the prediction that highly stressed participants solved fewer problems because they experienced higher levels of off-task thoughts. Both life stress and off-task thinking contributed independently to problem-solving deficits. In retrospect, it seems likely that the self-reports of off-task thinking may have been subject to demand characteristics. Participants who believed they had done poorly on the analogies problems may have been handicapping themselves by claiming higher levels of off-task thinking.

The analogies used in these experiments involve a number of complex mental operations, any one of which could be affected by stressful life events. To work toward a better understanding of the cognitive functions impaired by life stress, I turned to working memory (WM), a core component of analogical reasoning and of problem solving generally. WM capacity is "the capacity for controlled, sustained attention in the face of interference or distraction" (Engle, Kane, & Tuholski, 1999, p. 104). According to Hasher, Zacks, and May (1999), this controlled attention determines the content of consciousness. Controlled attention is required to keep goal-relevant information active and to inhibit extraneous goal-irrelevant information. Because attentional resources are not infinite, they must be allocated between the demands of ongoing tasks and irrelevant off-task thoughts. Goal-relevant information is pertinent to doing well on the task at hand, be it performing well during a job interview or flying an airplane. Goal-irrelevant cognitions are not pertinent to the task and include intentional (Conway & Pleydell-Pearce, 2000) and unintentional (Brewin, Dalgleish, & Joseph, 1996) thoughts about our own experiences. Such thoughts can arise from cues that are internal (e.g., symptoms of fatigue) or external (e.g., being reminded of an old friend upon meeting someone similar in appearance). Whatever their source, cognitions about ongoing or unresolved stressful events are among the irrelevant demands that compete for WM resources. Given a task of sufficient difficulty, devoting attention to such thoughts or trying to suppress them results in performance impairments on the primary task.

LIFE STRESS AND WORKING MEMORY

In a series of three experiments designed to examine the link between life stress and WM capacity, I (Klein and Boals, 2001b) measured WM with the Operation Span task (OSPAN; Turner & Engle, 1989). OSPAN is a standard, highly reliable and stable (Klein & Fiss, 1999) test that requires the switching of attention between reading and solving equations and retaining words for later recall. The OSPAN is a series of simple arithmetic operations, in which each operation is followed by a one-syllable word (e.g., $(7 \times 6) + 3 = 47$ bird). These stimuli are presented one at a time on a computer screen. Participants indicate verbally whether the answer given to the operation is true or false, and then they verbalize the word. After sets of 2–7 equation–word pairs, participants are prompted to write down as many of the words as possible from the previous set. A person's OSPAN score is the number of words recalled that were paired with correctly answered equations.

In the first study of this series, compared to participants with less stress, people reporting high levels of life event stress performed more poorly on the OSPAN, particularly at higher levels of task load (the six- and seven-item sets). In the second study, participants with higher levels of stress incorrectly recalled more words from earlier trials on the task, an indication of poor inhibitory control (Hasher et al., 1999). In the third study, people described both an extremely positive and an extremely negative personal experience and then used the Impact of Events Scale (IES;

Horowitz, Wilner, & Alvarez, 1979) to assess the extent of their intrusive and avoidant thinking about these events. Two weeks later, they took the OSPAN task. Unwanted thoughts about the negative, but not the positive, experience correlated with OSPAN performance. Participants who had high IES scores tended to show increasing WM deficits as operation set size increased.

EFFECTS OF EXPRESSIVE WRITING ON WORKING MEMORY

Given our findings that stress was related to WM, the next step was to test whether reducing stress would increase WM. Because of its demonstrated ability to mitigate the effects of stressful experiences, Pennebaker's (1997) writing paradigm appeared to be an ideal manipulation. In two recent experiments (Klein & Boals, 2001a) expressive writing indeed did produce improvements in WM capacity.

The first writing experiment compared changes in WM performance for two groups of first semester college students: One group was assigned to write three times about their deepest thoughts and feelings about coming to college, and a control group was assigned to write about how they had spent the day. The experiment used Pennebaker, Colder, and Sharp's (1990) writing instructions and procedure. WM was assessed using the OSPAN before the writing sessions, 1 week after the last writing session, and again 7 weeks later. OSPAN scores did not change between the pretest and 1 week after writing. Seven weeks later, participants who had been assigned to write about their thoughts and feelings exhibited a 6% improvement in their OSPAN scores compared to the control group whose WM increased 3%. Additionally, writers who had the greatest WM gains used more cause and insight words than other writers, and these linguistic characteristics were associated with narrative coherence (Pennebaker, Mayne, & Francis, 1997). The greater the improvement in OSPAN scores, the higher the students' academic grade point averages (GPA's) for both the experimental semester and the following spring semester.

Although the WM gain in the expressive writing group was statistically greater than that obtained in the control group, the two samples did not differ significantly on the final measure of WM. It is possible that the manipulations were more effective for some writers than for others, because college is not equally stressful for all freshmen. To address this concern, a second writing experiment was conducted in which students first described briefly (20 words or less) a personally important negative experience and an important positive experience from their lives. Students' negative experiences were both discrete (e.g., death of a grandparent) and chronic (e.g., father's drinking problem). Similarly, positive experiences were sometimes discrete events (e.g., winning an athletic contest) and sometimes continuous (e.g., having an adult mentor). After providing the descriptions, the participants took the IES (Horowitz et al., 1979) to assess how often they thought about each event and how often they tried to avoid thinking about each. Two weeks later, participants were randomly assigned to write expressively about either the negative or positive life experience they had described or to describe how they spent their time. As in the first writing experiment, they measured WM (OSPAN results) before, after, and almost 2 months after the writing sessions. They administered the IES again at the final session.

As shown in Figure 8.1, at the final session OSPAN scores of participants who had written about a negative event were significantly greater than those of participants who had written about a positive event and of the control group participants, who did not differ from each other. Control group participants showed an average increase of 3% from prewriting to the posttest, WM scores of participants who wrote about positive events increased 4%, and the WM scores of participants who wrote about negative events increased 11%, an increase that was significantly greater than the other two groups.

To examine the effects of expressive writing on unwanted thoughts, the intrusive and avoidant subscale scores were combined to calculate a total IES score for each event. Over the course of the experiment, unwanted thoughts about positive events decreased, regardless of writing topic. However, unwanted thoughts about the negative event decreased at a greater rate and decreased significantly more for students assigned to write

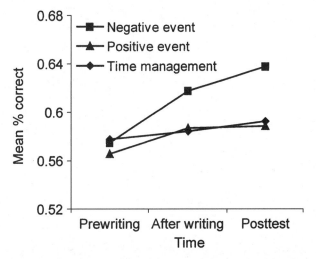

Figure 8.1. Effects of writing condition on percentage of correctly recalled words. From "Expressive Writing Can Increase Working Memory Capacity," by K. Klein and A. Boals, 2001, *Journal of Experimental Psychology: General*, *130*, p. 565. Copyright 2001 by the American Psychological Association. Reprinted with permission.

about that event. Further analysis using a mediation test indicated that the likely pathway from expressive writing to improved WM performance was through the decrease in intrusive and avoidant thinking.

Again, there was a link between increases in linguistic indices of cohesion and changes in WM. Among students assigned to write about negative events, an increase in the use of causal words across essays was related to WM improvements. As was the case in the first experiment, WM improvements were predictive of improvements in GPAs. The more intrusive and avoidant thinking about the negative event reported at the final session, the poorer the participant's grades. Reported thoughts about positive events were unrelated to GPA.

HOW EXPRESSIVE WRITING INCREASES WORKING MEMORY CAPACITY

In addition to demonstrating the effect of expressive writing on an important cognitive process, the results of these two experiments provide some ideas about how this might have occurred. The clues of particular interest are the absence of any effects of the prompt to write about a positive experience, the association between the use of certain linguistic categories and WM, and the decline in unwanted thoughts that coincided with the expressive writers' WM improvements. Using the data discussed here and the research and theories from a variety of psychological traditions, I propose a model that links the benefits of expressive writing to its ability to transform poorly organized cognitive representations of stressful experiences into more coherent memory structures that impose fewer claims on attentional resources. A summary of the model is presented in Figure 8.2.

The model has four primary assumptions; I present and justify each in turn.

1. Memories of Stressful Experiences Initially Have Different Memorial Representations Than Memories of Nonstressful Experiences

According to Conway and Pleydell-Pearce (2000), autobiographical memories are constructed from event-specific knowledge stored in memory. The content of these dynamic constructions depends in part on the goals of the working self-memory system. Memories have the potential to bring back the emotions of an experience and if these emotions are intense enough, they may disrupt other cognitive processes. To protect against such disruption, the self-memory system tries to retrieve only selected portions of the event-specific knowledge base in order to minimize the reexperience

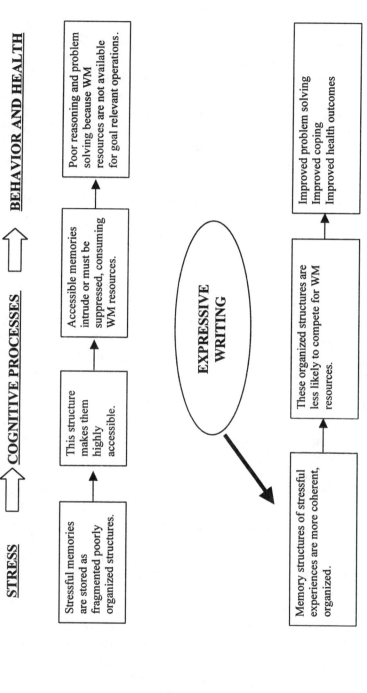

Figure 8.2. A model for the effects of expressive writing on cognitive processes and behavior. WM = working memory.

of the painful emotions. Brewin et al. (1996) likewise propose that trauma memories often do not incorporate the emotional aspects of an experience.

The present model adopts the position that, at least initially, memory reconstructions of stressful experiences are fragmented and poorly organized (Foa & Kozak, 1986; Foa, Steketee, & Rothbaum, 1989). Integrating these fragments of knowledge and associated emotions is difficult because there are rarely generic knowledge structures or schema to guide this integration (Creamer, Burgess, & Pattison, 1992; Janoff-Bulman, 1992). Even when members of a culture share scripts for the events preceding and following a loss, such as for the impending death of a loved one, bereaved partners often experience overwhelming sadness because the script did not prepare them for their own reactions to their loss (Stein, Liwag, & Wade, 1996). Stressful experiences that cannot be integrated with other experiences or with the self schema perpetuate the fragmentary and disorganized representations of the experience (Fivush, 1998). In contrast, memories of less stressful events can be more readily integrated into preexisting generic knowledge structures that let people understand what has occurred so far, predict what may happen next, and determine appropriate responses to the event (Barsalou, 1988).

I have recently conducted a pilot study designed to shed some light on how people experiencing higher and lower levels of stress cognitively represent the same experience. The experience selected was "college," whose stressfulness varies among the student population. In this preliminary work, I assumed that among students, there is some consensus regarding the "college" schema, which can be taken as the standard or prevailing view of this domain. Students whose cognitive structures for "college" differ from this normative view should report higher levels of stress compared to students who have more typical views. The rationale for this prediction was that if the first assumption of the model is correct, people who are experiencing high levels of stress in a particular domain have not constructed a coherent memory representation of the domain.

In the present study, the method used to assess the mental representation of "college" was multidimensional scaling analysis (MDS; Torgerson, 1952). MDS is a statistical algorithm; it produces a group n-dimensional space that Klirs and Revelle (1986) called the *common world*. Events that are perceived similarly cluster closer together in this space; events that are regarded as dissimilar are located farther away from each other. The stimuli in this study were 10 events representative of the college domain (e.g., "studying in the library," "conducting a laboratory experiment," "eating in the dining hall"). A variant of MDS, INDSCAL (Carroll & Chang, 1970), was used to derive Young and Harris's (1997) Weirdness Index for each participant. The weirdness index is a coefficient that "indicates how unusual or weird each subject's weights are relative to the weights of the typical subject being analyzed" (p. 165). The weirdness index can range from 0 to 1.0; the lower the index, the more proportional the individual's weights to the mean weights of the group performing the ratings. One could argue that individuals with atypical weights have more fragmented, less coherent, cognitive representations of the domain, compared to individuals whose dimensionality conforms more closely to the group space. Thus, the model suggests that individuals with atypical weights will report greater college-related stress.

As predicted, students experiencing higher levels of college-related stress did have higher weirdness indices. Of additional interest was the finding that students with lower WM capacity also had more aberrant cognitive representations of the college experience.

2. Stressful Memories Are Highly Accessible

The second assumption of the model is that because of their weak organization, activation of these stressful memories requires little, if any, attention or effort even though attempts to suppress them require effortful processing (Wegner, 1994). Brewin (2001; Brewin et al., 1996) proposed that the sensory features of stressful experiences are actually represented in a separate knowledge system that is accessed automatically in response to external or internal stimuli that are similar to the experience. When the self-memory system cannot suppress these highly accessible memories, they erupt into consciousness as unwanted and involuntary thoughts. Involuntary memories of both stressful and nonstressful events have been of particular interest to clinical psychologists because of their presence in many psychiatric disorders (Brewin, 1998). Continuing involuntary memories are usually associated with more severe and long-lasting symptoms (Greenberg, 1995), but this relationship is not always found in nonclinical participants (Lepore, 1997). Among people exposed to stressful events, intrusive memories begin to decline 2 weeks after the events (Harber & Pennebaker, 1992).

Horowitz (1975) has proposed that memories associated with past stressful events continue to intrude until they can be integrated with pre-existing schematized knowledge. Depending on the severity of the stressful event, such integration may require many years (Creamer et al., 1992). In some cases, people may never come to terms with traumatic experiences (Tait & Silver, 1989), particularly if they attempt to inhibit or avoid such thoughts (Kuyken & Brewin, 1999).

Wegner's (1994) ironic processing theory provides the theoretical rationale for this assumption of the model. Wegner and Smart (1997) have proposed that individuals try to keep unwanted painful thoughts in a state of deep cognitive activation, beyond the reach of consciousness. Unfortunately, cognitions maintained in this state, although unavailable for controlled processing, are highly accessible and have a propensity to intrude into consciousness. To avoid these intrusions people try to suppress these thoughts, denying them access to consciousness. In Wegner's model, suppression attempts involve an automatic process in which a search is made for unwanted thoughts and a controlled intentional process that is used to identify appropriate distracting thoughts when an unwanted thought is detected. When cognitive resources are inadequate to fuel the intentional process, attempts at suppression have the unintended effect of increasing the accessibility of these stressful memories.

Under normal circumstances, most people have the resources needed to suppress their unwanted thoughts (Kelly & Kahn, 1994). In studies with nonclinical samples, a high percentage of involuntary memories are not products of stressful events. In fact, the hallmark of these involuntary memories appears to be the extent to which they deviate from everyday scripts, whereas their repetitiveness is linked to their emotionality, regardless of valence (Bernsten, 1996). These data are not surprising if the automatic search process attuned to detect unwanted thoughts is functioning effectively.

Suppressing unwanted thoughts not only consumes mental resources, it has the untoward effect of perpetuating the fragmented nature of these thoughts. Wegner, Quillian, & Houston (1996) proposed that when an individual is trying to inhibit the memory of a painful event, the automatic monitoring process often discerns fragments of the memory that can be suppressed before the entire thought is retrieved. However, each detection produces a new distracting thought generated in an attempt to suppress the fragment. Consequently, numerous linkages between the fragments of the unwanted memory and other cognitions are forged, resulting in even greater demands on attentional resources to prevent the memory's intruding into consciousness. The increased accessibility of isolated fragments can disrupt memory for order, delay the integration of the memories, and prolong their intrusiveness. Thus, memories of emotional experiences remain difficult to access in their entirety.

3. Stressful Memories Consume Attentional Resources

The third proposition of the model is that stressful memories compete for limited attentional resources through either intrusion or suppression mechanisms. In addition to the work already discussed, there is evidence that concurrent or prior experimental manipulations of stress can impair WM capacity. Sorg and Whitney (1992) found that participants high in trait anxiety who were exposed to a competitive version of a video game subsequently performed more poorly on a WM task. Darke (1988) found that when a WM task was administered under ego-threatening conditions, highly trait anxious individuals did more poorly. Although these experiments assumed that participants' anxious thoughts about failure interfered with performance on the WM task, participants themselves may not have been consciously aware of these thoughts.

Theory and data suggest that the suppression of unwanted thoughts may be quite common. People are motivated to avoid thinking about unpleasant events (Petrie, Booth, & Pennebaker, 1998; Wegner & Smart, 1997) and go to some lengths to do so. Cuing studies consistently produce a bias against the retrieval of intense negative memories, suggesting that retrieving these memories could have a disruptive effect on other cognitive operations (Conway & Pleydell-Pearce, 2000).

Intrusion seems more likely to occur in some situations than others. Obviously, some experiences, such as the September 11 terrorist attack on the World Trade Center and the Pentagon, produce thoughts of such urgency that attempts to devote full attention to their suppression do not succeed; these memories derail all other cognitive activities. There are also individuals, particularly those with depression, who are habitually plagued by interfering thoughts (Nolen-Hoeksema, Parker, & Larson, 1994). Intrusive thoughts may also be likely when task requirements are minimal, such as when one is not engaged in other mentally demanding or distracting activities. In information-sparse settings, such as during a long automobile trip, unwanted thoughts might actually be very likely to intrude because distracting thoughts are more difficult to come by in such a setting. Finally, intrusive thoughts may rebound after suppression attempts in other settings. Regardless of whether thoughts about stressful events are suppressed or intrude into conscious thought, they consume WM resources to the detriment of other goal-relevant processing.

4. Developing a Coherent Narrative About a Stressful Experience Loosens Its Claim on Scarce Attentional Resources

The fourth claim of the model is that creating a narrative transforms the organization and content of stressful memory constructions (Pennebaker & Seagal, 1999). In particular, Pennebaker and Seagal have focused on the importance of narrative development as a necessary element in the curative powers of expressive writing. Narrative creation alters the original memory so that it can be "summarized, stored and forgotten more efficiently" (p. 1248). In this section, I explore some of the mechanisms by which this transformation might occur.

It is now widely accepted that memory is never an exact reproduction of experience (Stein & Liwag, 1997). For people trying to make sense of stressful experiences, constructing a narrative is as important as what is reported to have actually happened (Bruner, 1994). Following stressful events, narratives can be induced (Amir, Stafford, Freshman, & Foa, 1998), or they can occur spontaneously (Harvey, Orbuch, Chwalisz, & Garwood, 1991; van der Kolk & Fisler, 1995). Whatever the impetus, being able to compose a story about a stressful experience reduces the size and complexity of the original experience into a smaller unit that "lets memory work less hard" and "provides a constancy of lessons to be learned that does not need to be constantly reexamined" (Schank & Abelson, 1995, p. 42). Schank and Abelson have argued further that in the course of narrative creation, memories of negative events become embedded in the story, weakening the accessibility of these bad experiences and lessening the likelihood that internal or external stimuli will activate them. Memories that are not activated do not require cognitive resources either for further processing or suppression. Echoing Pennebaker and Seagal, this line of thought suggests that narrative development "repackages" the fragmented memories of stressful events so that their accessibility is diminished and their recall becomes more a matter of deliberate retrieval. The effects of this narrative creation take some time to develop. In several studies (Pennebaker, 1997), the moods of experimental writers became depressed shortly after writing, and in my own work, the improvements in WM were small 1 week after writing, becoming practically and statistically significant 7 weeks later.

If one believes that the narrative produced by expressive writing alters memory representations, identifying and quantifying these changes becomes an important challenge. There are at least three ways to assess the cognitive changes induced by expressive writing. One is to examine the writers' self-reports about how often unwanted thoughts intrude into consciousness. Another is to analyze linguistic changes in the essays, and the third is to observe changes in other cognitive processes. All of these techniques involve the inference that observable differences reflect differences arising from the underlying processes of interest. The self-report technique assumes that cognitive events are represented in the contents of consciousness and can be reported. Analysis of the words used in the essays assumes that changes across essays mirror changes in the mental representation of the stressful experience. Finally, assessing change through the measurement of other cognitive processes assumes that these are produced by alterations in the mental representation of fundamental interest.

Self-Reports of Intrusive Thinking

Asking people to report directly on how often they think about (or try not to think about) an upsetting experience is one means of tracking cognitive change induced by narrative creation. Abundant clinical data and theory suggest that integrating a stressful experience into a coherent account ends or diminishes the intrusive thinking that often follows traumatic events (Creamer, 1995; Greenberg, 1995).

Not surprisingly, a number of investigators have examined the effects of expressive writing on reports of unwanted thoughts. Páez, Velasco, and

González (1999) found no differences in intrusive or avoidant thinking following writing about disclosed or undisclosed traumatic events. In some studies (Klein & Boals, 2001a; Segal, Bogaards, & Chatman, 1998; Segal & Murray, 1994), expressive writing or talking reduced the intrusiveness of thoughts about stressful events. In other experiments (Lepore, 1997; Lepore & Greenberg, in press; Lutgendorf, Antoni, Kumar, & Schneiderman, 1994), writing appears to break the link between intrusiveness and negative outcomes but does not reduce the frequency of intrusions. Among the reasons for these differences may be the time courses of the stressors studied (whether the event is anticipated or has already occurred), the chronicity or duration of the stressor, and whether the essay topic is assigned to or selected by the writer. Additional explanations of contradictory findings may be the methodological differences in the number of writing sessions, the length of time intervening between writing and measuring intrusive thinking, and possible floor effects in studies in which very low levels of intrusive thinking are reported.

Linguistic Changes in Essays

In an attempt to understand how essay content might be related to health improvements, Pennebaker and Francis (1999) developed a linguistic analysis program, the Linguistic Analysis and Word Count (LIWC). A LIWC analysis of an essay provides a count of words in particular categories. The categories receiving the greatest attention are two cognitive categories, words denoting cause and insight, and two emotion categories, positive and negative emotion words. In an analysis of essays from several experiments, Pennebaker et al. (1997) found that writers who increased their use of positive emotion words and used a moderate number of negative emotion words experienced the greatest health benefits. It was an increase in cognitive word use, however, that was most predictive of improved health and behavior outcomes. Furthermore, increases in cognitive words were associated with the judges' ratings of the essays' narrative coherence.

Changes in Other Cognitive Processes

When one examines how writing affects other cognitive processes, the assumption is that writing produces changes in the cognitive representation of the stressful event that are responsible for observable changes on other variables. One approach, used by Pennebaker and Francis (1996), rests on the assumption that expressive writing affects the accessibility of constructs related to the topic of the essays. In an experiment in which students wrote about coming to college, Pennebaker and Francis used two tasks to measure the construct accessibility of "college." Their first task required the classification of exemplars. First-semester students, who had written about coming to college or had been in a control group, indicated as quickly as possible whether a stimulus word was associated with the category "coming to college." Stimulus words were relevant, irrelevant, or descriptive of an emotion. Pennebaker and Francis hypothesized that expressive writing should increase the construct accessibility of "college," with the result that participants assigned to the experimental condition would require less time to classify college-related stimuli. Writing condition had no effect on any of the reaction times, but expressive writers who had faster reaction times earned higher grades the subsequent semester. Pennebaker and Francis also used a thought-generation task to assess construct accessibility. Participants wrote down as many thoughts as they could to the prompt "coming to college." Again, there were no effects of the experimental manipulation on how many thoughts were generated.

A second method that can be used to track the effects of expressive writing on cognitive processes is the WM procedure detailed in this chapter. As noted, expressive writing about negative events does appear to improve WM capacity, and these improvements are linked to linguistic changes in the essays.

The memory processes targeted and the assumptions underlying the Pennebaker and Francis tasks and the OSPAN measure of WM capacity are different. First, in the OSPAN measure of WM, only the procedures necessary to solve the arithmetic equations must be retrieved from long-term memory. On the OSPAN, the emphasis is on the control of attentional shifts between processing the equations and remembering the words. In contrast, the classification of exemplars and thought generation tasks used by Pennebaker and Francis involves primarily the retrieval of long-term memory traces from secondary memory. Although WM processes are certainly involved in these tasks, their involvement is limited in most retrieval operations (A. R. A. Conway & Engle, 1994).

The underlying assumption in the Pennebaker and Francis methodology also differs from the model presented here. The reaction time and thought generation tasks were based on the hypothesis that writing would increase the accessibility of related constructs. In the present model, the assumption is that writing should decrease the accessibility of stress-related cognitions through its ability to transform the mental representation of the event. To use Wegner and Smart's terminology (1997), the present model suggests that writing can move unwanted cognitions from an unstable state of deep cognitive activation, where their hyperaccessibility means they must be continually monitored, to a state of no activation at all, where their unwanted eruption into consciousness is less likely. This decreased accessibility frees WM resources previously used to suppress these unwanted thoughts.

Problem Solving and Decision Making

To many readers, the finding that emotional disclosure can lead to improvements in WM capacity may seem rather arcane, but the importance of WM to higher order cognitive processes should not be lightly dismissed. Cantor and Engle (1993) noted that "there is now substantial evidence that WM differs among people and that this difference is manifest in a wide range of ecologically important cognitive tasks" (p. 1102). There is abundant evidence indicating correlations of .4 to .6 between WM and numerous outcomes, among them Verbal Scholastic Aptitude Scores (VSAT; Daneman & Carpenter, 1980), reading comprehension (Daneman & Carpenter, 1980), following directions (Engle, Carullo, & Collins, 1991), and academic performance (Klein & Boals, 2001a), suggesting that on average, 25% of the variance in these measures is attributable to WM differences. Using Engle, Tuholski, Laughlin, and Conway's (1999) .49 correlation between OSPAN scores and VSAT scores, the 11% improvement in WM capacity in expressive writers in our second study would correspond to a 28-point improvement in VSAT scores. WM deficits have been implicated in aircraft pilots' problems with allocation of attention, contributing to safety incidents and accidents (Morrow & Leirer, 1997) and in dangerous maneuvers by automobile drivers (Guerrier, Manivannan, & Nair, 1999). Thus, the finding that expressive writing can increase WM capacity has practical as well as theoretical implications.

Physical and Psychological Health

In the absence of health data, the model and findings presented here cannot speak to the issue of whether WM improvements produced by expressive writing mediate the writing–health relationship. The data from the WM experiments do support Smythe's (1998) contention that if writing influences health by evoking changes in cognitive processes, changes in measures of cognitive functioning should be closely tied to writing and to the cognitive effects of writing.

The relationship of WM to problem solving and fluid intelligence does suggest that WM could affect health. People who are using WM capacity to avoid stressful thoughts have less attention available for solving problems posed by stressful life events and may respond less effectively to threat and loss. The WM and problem-solving deficits experienced by highly stressed people could be one factor that contributes to the perpetuation of high levels of stress in their lives. Given that stress does have direct effects on immune function and illness development and progress, people with impaired WM capacity who experience higher levels of stress may subsequently experience poorer health.

The WM improvements produced by expressive writing might increase a person's ability to focus attention on the problem solving, planning, and proactive coping necessary to mitigate or avoid many stressful events. For example, older adults with higher WM capacity have greater recall of medication instructions (Gould & Dixon, 1997) and scheduled health appointments (Morrow, Leirer, Carver, Tanke, & McNally, 1999). This recall advantage might protect people from the adverse effects of taking too much or too little medication or missing a doctor's appointment. Better health outcomes could also result from an increased ability to engage in more appropriate coping behaviors in the wake of exposure to stressful events. Whether the WM increases observed in these experiments are of sufficient magnitude or duration to support more effective problem solving and attendant improvements in health outcomes requires further study.

It is also possible that the reductions in intrusive thinking that follow expressive writing about negative experiences may have independent effects on WM and health. There is evidence that higher cortisol levels are associated with more intrusive thinking (Lutgendorf, Reimer, Schlechte, & Rubenstein, 2001). Because stress-related cortisol elevations are linked to immune system responses, particularly secondary antibody production (Cohen, Miller, & Rabin, 2001), writing-produced reductions in intrusive thoughts could have a positive impact on immune function and subsequent health.

In summary, data indicate that (a) problem solving and WM capacity are diminished in people undergoing stressful life events, (b) expressive writing can improve WM capacity, and (c) the linguistic variables associated with WM improvements have similar relationships with health outcomes. I would argue further that the attentional resources claimed by intrusive thoughts and attempts to suppress them can impair problem solving to the extent that proactive coping and appropriate responses to subsequent stressors become unlikely. As a consequence, more stress is produced that could produce decrements in psychological and physical health. Writing about stressful experiences may interrupt this cycle through its effects on WM function.

REFERENCES

Amir, N., Stafford, J., Freshman, M. S., & Foa, E. B. (1998). Relationship between trauma narratives and trauma pathology. *Journal of Traumatic Stress, 11,* 385–392.

Baradell, J. G., & Klein, K. (1993). The relationship of life stress and body consciousness to hypervigilant decision making. *Journal of Personality and Social Psychology, 64,* 267–273.

Barsalou, L. W. (1988). The content and organization of autobiographical memories. In U. Neisser & E. Winograd (Eds.), *Remembering reconsidered: Ecological and traditional approaches to the study of memory* (Emory Symposia in Cognition, Vol. 2, pp. 193–243). New York: Cambridge University Press.

Bernsten, D. (1996). Involuntary autobiographical memories. *Applied Cognitive Psychology, 10,* 435–454.

Brewin, C. R. (1998). Intrusive autobiographical memories in depression and posttraumatic stress disorder. *Applied Cognitive Psychology, 12,* 359–370.

Brewin, C. R. (2001). A cognitive neuroscience account of posttraumatic stress disorder and its treatment. *Behaviour Research and Therapy, 39,* 373–393.

Brewin, C. R., Dalgleish, T., & Joseph, S. (1996). A dual representation theory of posttraumatic stress disorder. *Psychological Review, 103,* 670–686.

Bruner, J. (1994). The remembered self. In U. Neisser & R. Fivush (Eds.), *The remembering self: Construction and accuracy in the self-narrative* (pp. 41–54). New York: Cambridge University Press.

Cantor, J., & Engle, R. W. (1993). Working memory capacity as long-term memory activation: An individual differences approach. *Journal of Experimental Psychology: Learning, Memory, and Cognition, 19,* 1101–1114.

Carroll, J. D., & Chang, J. (1970). Analysis of individual differences in multidimensional scaling via an N-way generalization of Eckart–Young decomposition. *Psychometrika, 35,* 283–319.

Cohen, S., Miller, G. E., & Rabin, B. S. (2001). Psychological stress and antibody response to immunization: A critical review of the human literature. *Psychosomatic Medicine, 63,* 7–18.

Conway, A. R. A., & Engle, R. W. (1994). Working memory and retrieval: A resource-dependent inhibition model. *Journal of Experimental Psychology: General, 123,* 354–373.

Conway, M. A., & Pleydell-Pearce, C. W. (2000). The construction of autobiographical memories in the self-memory system. *Psychological Review, 107,* 261–288.

Creamer, M. (1995). A cognitive processing formulation of posttrauma reactions. In R. J. Kleber, C. R. Figley, & B. P. R. Gersons (Eds.), *Beyond trauma: Cultural and societal dynamics* (pp. 55–74). New York: Plenum Press.

Creamer, M., Burgess, P., & Pattison, P. (1992). Reaction to trauma: A cognitive processing model. *Journal of Abnormal Psychology, 101,* 452–459.

Daneman, M., & Carpenter, P. A. (1980). Individual differences in working memory and reading. *Journal of Verbal Learning and Verbal Behavior, 19,* 450–466.

Darke, S. (1988). Anxiety and working memory capacity. *Cognition and Emotion, 2,* 145–154.

Engle, R., Carullo, J., & Collins, K. (1991). Individual differences in working memory for comprehension and following directions. *Journal of Educational Research, 84,* 253–262.

Engle, R., Kane, M. J., & Tuholski, S. W. (1999). Individual differences in working memory capacity and what they tell us about controlled attention, general fluid intelligence and functions of the prefrontal cortex. In A. Miyake & P. Shah (Eds.), *Models of working memory: Mechanisms of active maintenance and executive control* (pp. 102–131). Cambridge, England: Cambridge University Press.

Engle, R. W., Tuholski, S. W., Laughlin, J. E., & Conway, A. R. A. (1999). Working memory, short-term memory, and general fluid intelligence: A latent-variable approach. *Journal of Experimental Psychology: General, 128,* 309–331.

Fivush, R. (1998). Children's recollections of traumatic and non-traumatic events. *Development and Psychopathology, 10,* 699–716.

Foa, E. B., & Kozak, M. J. (1986). Emotional processing of fear: Exposure to corrective information. *Psychological Bulletin, 99,* 20–35.

Foa, E. B., Steketee, G., & Rothbaum, B. O. (1989). Behavioral/cognitive conceptualizations of post-traumatic stress disorder. *Behavior Therapy, 20,* 155–176.

Gould, O. N., & Dixon, R. A. (1997). Recall of medication instructions by young and elderly adult women: Is overaccommodative speech helpful? *Journal of Language and Social Psychology, 16,* 50–69.

Greenberg, M. A. (1995). Cognitive processing of traumas: The role of intrusive thoughts and reappraisals. *Journal of Applied Social Psychology, 25,* 1262–1296.

Guerrier, J. H., Manivannan, P., & Nair, S. N. (1999). The role of working memory, field dependence, visual search and reaction time in the left turn performance of older drivers. *Applied Ergonomics, 30,* 109–119.

Harber, K. D., & Pennebaker, J. W. (1992). Overcoming traumatic memories. In S. A. Christianson (Ed.), *The handbook of emotion and memory* (pp. 359–385). Hillsdale, NJ: Erlbaum.

Harvey, J. H., Orbuch, T. L., Chwalisz, K. D., & Garwood, G. (1991). Coping with sexual assault: The roles of account-making and confiding. *Journal of Traumatic Stress, 4,* 515–531.

Hasher, L., Zacks, R. T., & May, C. P. (1999). Inhibitory control, circadian arousal, and age. In D. Gopher, D. Daniel, & A. Koriat (Eds.), *Attention and performance XVII: Cognitive regulation of performance: Interaction of theory and application* (pp. 653–675). Cambridge, MA: MIT Press.

Horowitz, M. J. (1975). Intrusive and repetitive thoughts after experimental stress: A summary. *Archives of General Psychiatry, 32,* 1457–1463.

Horowitz, M. J., Wilner, N., & Alvarez, W. (1979). Impact of Events Scale: A measure of subjective stress. *Psychosomatic Medicine, 41,* 209–218.

Janoff-Bulman, R. (1992). *Shattered assumptions.* New York: Free Press.

Kelly, A. E., & Kahn, J. H. (1994). Effects of suppression of personal intrusive thoughts. *Journal of Personality and Social Psychology, 66,* 998–1006.

Klein, K. (1995). Life stress and performance impairment: The role of off-task thinking. *Proceedings of the Human Factors and Ergonomics Society, 2,* 873–877.

Klein, K., & Barnes, D. (1994). The relationship of life stress to problem solving: Task complexity and individual differences. *Social Cognition, 12,* 187–204.

Klein, K., & Boals, A. (2001a). Expressive writing can increase working memory capacity. *Journal of Experimental Psychology: General, 130,* 520–533.

Klein, K., & Boals, A. (2001b). The relationship of life event stress and working memory capacity. *Applied Cognitive Psychology, 15,* 565–579.

Klein, K., & Fiss, W. H. (1999). The reliability and stability of the Turner and Engle working memory task. *Behavior Research Methods, Instruments and Computers, 31,* 429–432.

Klirs, E. G., & Revelle, W. (1986). Predicting variability from perceived situational similarity. *Journal of Research in Personality, 20,* 34–50.

Kuyken, W., & Brewin, C. R. (1999). The relation of early abuse to cognition and coping in depression. *Cognitive Therapy and Research, 23,* 665–677.

Lepore, S. J. (1997). Expressive writing moderates the relation between intrusive thoughts and depressive symptoms. *Journal of Personality and Social Psychology, 73,* 1030–1037.

Lepore, S. J., & Greenberg, M. A. (in press). Mending broken hearts: Effects of expressive writing on mood, cognitive processing, social adjustment and health following a relationship breakup. *Psychology and Health.*

Lutgendorf, S. K., Antoni, M. H., Kumar, M., & Schneiderman, N. (1994). Changes in cognitive coping strategies predict EBV-antibody titre change following a stressor disclosure induction. *Journal of Psychosomatic Research, 38,* 63–78.

Lutgendorf, S. K., Reimer, T. T., Schlechte, J., & Rubenstein, L. M. (2001). Illness episodes and cortisol in healthy older adults during a life transition. *Annals of Behavioral Medicine, 23,* 166–176.

Mandler, G. (1993). Thought, memory, and learning: Effects of emotional stress. In L. Goldberger & S. Breznitz (Eds.), *Handbook of stress: Theoretical and clinical aspects* (2nd ed., pp. 40–55). New York: Free Press.

Miller, L., Murphy, R., & Buss, A. (1981). Consciousness of body: Private and public. *Journal of Personality and Social Psychology, 41,* 397–406.

Morrow, D. G., & Leirer, V. O. (1997). Aging, pilot performance and expertise. In A. D. Fisk & W. A. Rogers (Eds.), *Handbook of human factors and the older adult* (pp. 199–230). New York: Academic Press.

Morrow, D. G., Leirer, V. O., Carver, L. M., Tanke, E. D., & McNally, A. D. (1999). Effects of aging, message repetition, and note-taking on memory for health information. *Journals of Gerontology: Series B: Psychological Sciences and Social Sciences, 54,* 369–379.

Nolen-Hoeksema, S., Parker, L. E., & Larson, J. (1994). Ruminative coping with depressed mood following loss. *Journal of Personality and Social Psychology, 67,* 92–104.

Páez, D., Velasco, C., & González, J. L. (1999). Expressive writing and the role of alexithymia as a dispositional deficit in self-disclosure and psychological health. *Journal of Personality and Social Psychology, 77,* 630–641.

Pennebaker, J. W. (1997). Writing about emotional experiences as a therapeutic process. *Psychological Science, 8,* 162–166.

Pennebaker, J. W., Colder, M., & Sharp, L. K. (1990). Accelerating the coping process. *Journal of Personality and Social Psychology, 58,* 528–537.

Pennebaker, J. W., & Francis, M. E. (1996). Cognitive, emotional and language processes in disclosure. *Cognition and Emotion, 10,* 621–626.

Pennebaker, J. W., & Francis, M. (1999). *Linguistic inquiry and word count: LIWC.* Mahwah, NJ: Erlbaum.

Pennebaker, J. W., Mayne, T. J., & Francis, M. E. (1997). Linguistic predictors of adaptive bereavement. *Journal of Personality and Social Psychology, 72,* 863–871.

Pennebaker, J. W., & Seagal, J. D. (1999). Forming a story: The health benefits of narrative. *Journal of Clinical Psychology, 55,* 1243–1254.

Petrie, K. J., Booth, R. J., & Pennebaker, J. W. (1998). The immunological effects of thought suppression. *Journal of Personality and Social Psychology, 75,* 1264–1272.

Sarason, I. G., Johnson, J. H., & Siegel, J. M. (1978). Assessing the impact of life changes: Development of the life experiences survey. *Journal of Consulting and Clinical Psychology, 46,* 932–946.

Sarason, I. G., Sarason, B. R., Keefe, D. E., Hayes, B. E., & Shearin, E. N. (1986). Cognitive interference: Situational determinants and traitlike characteristics. *Journal of Personality and Social Psychology, 51,* 215–226.

Schank, R. C., & Abelson, R. P. (1995). Knowledge and memory: The real story. In R. S. Wyer (Ed.), *Advances in Social Cognition, 8,* 1–85.

Segal, D. L., Bogaards, J. A., & Chatman, C. (1998, August). *Emotional expression improves adjustment to spousal loss in the elderly.* Poster session presented at the 106th annual meeting of the American Psychological Association, San Francisco, CA.

Segal, D. L., & Murray, E. J. (1994). Emotional processing in cognitive therapy and vocal expression of feeling. *Journal of Social and Clinical Psychology, 13,* 189–206.

Smythe, J. M. (1998). Written emotional expression: Effect sizes, outcome types and moderating variables. *Journal of Consulting and Clinical Psychology, 66,* 174–184.

Sorg, B. A., & Whitney, P. (1992). The effect of trait anxiety and situational stress on working memory capacity. *Journal of Research in Personality, 26,* 235–241.

Stein, N. L., & Liwag, M. D. (1997). Children's understanding, evaluation and memory for emotional events. In P. W. Van den Broek, P. J. Bauer, & T. Bourg (Eds.), *Developmental spans in event comprehension and representation: Bridging fictional and actual events* (pp. 199–235). Mahwah, NJ: Erlbaum.

Stein, N. L., Liwag, M. D., & Wade E. (1996). A goal-based approach to memory for emotional events: Implications for theories of understanding and socialization. In R. D. Kavanaugh & B. Zimmerberg (Eds.), *Emotion: Interdisciplinary perspectives* (pp. 91–118). Mahwah, NJ: Erlbaum.

Tait, R., & Silver, R. C. (1989). Coming to terms with major negative life events. In J. S. Uleman & J. A. Bargh (Eds.), *Unintended thought* (pp. 351–382). New York: Guilford Press.

Turner, M. L., & Engle, R. W. (1989). Is working memory capacity task dependent? *Journal of Memory and Language, 28,* 127–154.

van der Kolk, B. A., & Fisler, R. (1995). Dissociation and the fragmentary nature of traumatic memories: Review and experimental confirmation. *Journal of Traumatic Stress, 8,* 505–525.

Wegner, D. (1994). Ironic processes of mental control. *Psychological Review, 101,* 34–52.

Wegner, D. M., Quillian, F., & Houston, C. E. (1996). Memories out of order: Thought suppression and the disturbance of sequence memory. *Journal of Personality and Social Psychology, 71,* 680–691.

Wegner, D., & Smart, L. (1997). Deep cognitive activation: A new approach to the unconscious. *Journal of Consulting and Clinical Psychology, 65,* 984–995.

Young, F., & Harris, D. F. (1997). Multidimensional scaling examples. In M. J. Norusis (Ed.), *SPSS: SPSS Professional Statistics 7.5* (pp. 113–170). Chicago: SPSS.

9

EMOTIONAL EXPRESSION AND HEALTH CHANGES: CAN WE IDENTIFY BIOLOGICAL PATHWAYS?

ROGER J. BOOTH AND KEITH J. PETRIE

To discuss the biological pathways through which emotional expression affects health, we must appreciate the manner in which humans operate as self-generating systems in biological and psychological contexts. We begin this chapter with a brief outline of the salient features of human biology and how it relates to our psychosocial existence. This leads to a discussion of the relationship between emotions and the operation of our bodies, particularly the immune system, and some of the consequences of expressing and suppressing emotions and the factors that modulate these consequences. Finally, we consider the effects of emotional disclosure on health and discuss a model of how we might make sense of these effects in terms of human psychobiology. In doing this we focus on the fact that humans not only generate a "self" in the psychosocial sense but simultaneously maintain a biological "self" through the distinctions made by the immune and nervous systems in the biophysical domain. Although each of these selves is generated in a different domain, both reside in the same person and mutually influence one another's constitution and operation in a discernible manner. Such interaction forms the centerpiece of our explanations of the health effects of emotional disclosure.

HUMANS AS LIVING PSYCHOBIOLOGICAL SYSTEMS

The physical structure of living organisms determines how their environments affect them and how they are able to act in concert with those environments. Organisms have different physical structures and thus interact with the environment in various ways. For example, a set of macromolecules and other biochemicals comprise the vehicles through which many bacteria coordinate their activities with the components of their environments. Through biological evolution, many species have developed in such a way that cooperative interactions with other members of the species are necessary to sustain life. These "social" organisms share an environment and a history of living together such that their lives become inextricably intertwined. Social life exists as a network of mutually supportive interactions that foster the survival of the individuals that compose it.

Homo sapiens comprise such a social species. We coordinate our living together through meaningful gestures that we call *language*. As we interact through language, our structure changes to retain congruence with that linguistic environment. Conversely, as our linguistic environment changes our structure also changes. For example, as we develop as children, the structure of our facial muscles, respiratory system, and nervous system alter in ways that allow us to coordinate with others through particular forms of gesturing, speaking, observing, and listening. Such bodily changes enable us to maintain an adequate relationship with the social environments in which we live.

WHAT ARE EMOTIONS?

At every moment of our lives we are disposed to a certain set of actions by the structure of our bodies at that moment. When we talk about our own emotions, we are describing that which moves us to think, feel, and act in the particular way we are doing at that time. *E-motion* is about meaningful actions (literally leading to motion; also see chapter 6, this volume). When we attribute emotions to other people, we are commenting on our observations of their demeanor, their physical characteristics, and their behavior, and we are drawing conclusions on the basis of the relationship among these features and their resonance with our own experience. This means that emotions lie in the domains of experiences and descriptions of shared experiences.

Emotions are therefore features of social living and require a shared history among individuals in order to be experienced, described, or expressed. As we live and grow with other people, we develop consensual manners of coordinating our lives together that involve complex choreography of gestures and sounds and odors. As a species, we humans have developed to live immersed in conversations within social communities, and so it is no surprise that the structures of our bodies have evolved to facilitate such meaningful exchanges. Ekman has written widely about the importance of facial expressions in emotion and the cross-cultural similarities of basic emotions as reflected in facial expressions (Wegner, Shortt, Blake, & Page, 1990). These "basic" emotions are a consequence of the way in which human anatomical, physiological, and biochemical features have evolved to conserve the linguistic necessities of human societies.

EMOTIONS AND PHYSIOLOGY

When our emotions change, the structure of our bodies changes and we experience our lives differently. Those changes involve a broad range of attributes, from what we sense in the world and how we perceive that sensory information, through the tone and responsiveness of our voluntary and involuntary muscles, the activity of our cardio-respiratory systems, the manner in which our blood cells circulate, the performance of our digestive and excretory processes, to the operation of our reproductive systems. All these physiological changes happen in a coordinated manner through the operation of three interconnected processes that we call the *central nervous system*, *neuroendocrine system*, and *immune system*. In this regard, the nervous, neuroendocrine, and immune systems form a multi-directional communication network in which the immune system operates as a diffuse sense organ, informing the brain about molecular shape changes in the body (Blalock, 1984).

Conversely, when the structure of our bodies is altered, our emotions also follow suit. For example, after a meal, digestive processes alter blood composition, autonomic activity, and neuroendocrine operation and we feel contentment, lethargy, or some other emotion appropriate to our postprandial state. In a similar way, when our physiology is altered by an infection, the changes occurring in neuroendocrine, autonomic, and immune pathways as our bodies deal with the infectious agent evoke changes in our emotional disposition that are characteristic of what Dantzer and colleagues have termed *sickness behaviors* (Dantzer, Bluthe, & Kelley, 1991; Kent, Bluthe, Kelley, & Dantzer, 1992). Many of the features of sickness behaviors (e.g., appetite impairment, weight loss, poor concentration, increased sleep, fever, hyperalgesia, reduced social interest) can be induced in humans and other animals by injecting cytokines (hormones that modulate immune and inflammatory responses; Aubert, 1999; Walker et al., 1997), accentuating the importance of bi-directional interactions between the immune system and the central nervous system (Dantzer, 1997) in modulating physiological processes that affect behaviors and perceptions.

EXPRESSING AND SUPPRESSING EMOTIONS

As self-reflective beings, we humans are able to observe our own participation in living processes. This means that we can evaluate our own actions and behaviors from the perspective of an observer simultaneously as we experience and participate in them. Expressing emotions therefore involves acting in a way that is consistent with how we are feeling in relation to someone or some thing or some event. Conversely, suppressing emotions is constituted by actions that we regard as incongruous with our prevailing living experience. In this case our being in the world is at odds with what we feel to be an appropriate expression of our physical disposition. Given that emotions and physiology are tied to one another, we would expect there to be different physiological changes accompanying expression and suppression of emotions. This has been born out by laboratory research.

For instance, people asked to watch a short disgust-eliciting film about the treatment of burns and arm amputation, displayed physiological and behavioral differences depending on whether they were asked to suppress their emotions. Although suppression had no impact on subjective experience of emotion, it reduced observable expressive behavior and produced a mixed physiological state characterized by decreased somatic activity and decreased heart rate, along with increased blinking and indications of increased sympathetic nervous system activity (Gross & Levenson, 1993). In another study, people were asked to write about traumatic issues in an emotionally expressive way and then either to sit and relax or to deliberately try and suppress thoughts about what they had been writing. Thought suppression resulted in changes in the immune system, characterized by a significant decrease in the number of circulating T lymphocytes (Petrie, Booth, & Pennebaker, 1998).

Contorting facial features to display a particular emotion evokes the experience of the emotion in us (Levenson, Ekman, Heider, & Friesen, 1992). Conversely, deliberately modifying our emotional relationship to an event alters our physiological response to it. Gross's (1998) work exemplifies this. He asked people to watch a disgust-eliciting film and either (a) to think about the film in such a way that they would feel nothing (antecedent-focused emotion regulation through reappraisal), (b) to behave in such a way that someone watching them would not know they were feeling anything (response-focused emotion regulation through suppression), or (c) simply to watch the film (a control condition). Compared with the control condition, both reappraisal and suppression were effective in reducing emotionally expressive behavior, but reappraisal decreased disgust experience, whereas suppression increased sympathetic nervous system activation. Wegner et al. (1990) have also identified that the suppression of exciting thoughts, specifically thoughts about sex, resulted in short-term increases in levels of sympathetic system arousal as measured by skin conductance.

Suppression therefore appears to require ongoing psychological "work" in order to accommodate the disparity between what one is feeling and what one is expressing. This work, reflected in increased sympathetic nervous system activity, may have unhealthy consequences if it becomes habitual. There is evidence that suppression often has unwanted cognitive effects (a "rebound effect") where the suppressed thought increases in frequency following the suppression period (Clark, Ball, & Pape, 1991; Wegner, Schneider, Carter, & White, 1987; Zeitlin, Netten, & Hodder, 1995). This process may intensify the cognitive and immunological effects of suppression. Paradoxically, suppression can also be a feature of expressed emotions, whether written or verbal. This is because asking someone to write or talk about a traumatic or upsetting event initiates a selective process that, depending on the background and context of the request, may lead to particular events or situations being recalled but deliberately not discussed and the emotions associated with them actively suppressed because they are judged to be too sensitive or inappropriate in that context.

Because emotions, emotional expression, and suppression arise in the social domain of interpersonal relations, it is important to realize that although written emotional expression can be done alone, it still arises in a social domain. This is because self-aware individuals writing about their emotions are themselves observers of their own process and, as such, bring to the situation the socioculturally determined evaluations, judgments, and strictures that contribute to their unique personalities.

MODULATING FACTORS

The diversity of environmental conditions and social contexts in which we can find ourselves necessitates substantial plasticity in both our physiological and psychological make-up. There is a degree of elasticity in this such that emotional and physiological changes wrought by many events in our lives are often relatively transient, and our adaptive capacity quickly returns us to a more habitual manner of living. Some events, however, precipitate more lasting physiological and psychological changes. When a previously transient emotional state becomes a more enduring feature of a person's existence, we often do not label it an emotion anymore. For example, we might identify a transient episode of depression precipitated by separation from a social group as an emotion but consider it as something other if it becomes a dispositional trait, although we can observe some physiological similarities, such as elevated cortisol production, in both situations (Post et al., 1998). This is pertinent because expression of emotion is generally something that we associate with a particular event or relationship. Thus, when asked to talk or write about feelings and emotions we are asking people to recall specific situations. However, our ability to recall and the manner in which we recall events and situations is highly affected by our disposition at the time of recall, such that any emotional expression evoked in such a way is as much a reflection of dispositional factors as it is situational ones. Moreover, given encouragement to express emotions, many people may well choose situations and events as conveyors for those emotions that are most coherent with or support their dispositional traits.

Clearly the impact of events on our psychology, physiology, and health depends on a variety of factors including the nature and context of the events, our physiological state at the time, our dispositional traits, and our social background and characteristics. It is becoming apparent from recent research that certain psychosocial dispositional factors modulate the manner in which potentially adverse events affect human physiology and health. Here are some examples. Emotional stability, as assessed by a neuroticism scale, was reported to act in concert with state anxiety to modulate the effects of student examination stress on natural killer (NK) cells, the part of the immune system that is important in the early events of dealing with infections (Borella et al., 1999). Optimism and pessimism differentially affect immune system changes (NK cell activity and subsets of T lymphocytes that are central to the regulation of immune processes and some aspects of recovery from infection) associated with acute and chronic stresses. An optimistic perspective buffered the association between acute stress and subsequent immune parameters, but when stress persisted at high levels, optimists showed more subsequent immune decrements than pessimists (Cohen et al., 1999). Finally, people who worry habitually by anticipating potential future negative events displayed changes in autonomic nervous system and immune activity in response to a transient phobic stimulus that were different from those of nonworriers. Persistent patterns of change in the worriers suggested that phobic fear had disrupted a normal circadian rhythm in NK cells, possibly related to adrenergic and hypothalamus–pituitary–adrenal mechanisms (i.e., autonomic nervous system and neuroendocrine functions; Segerstrom, Glover, Craske, & Fahey, 1999).

The manner in which people express themselves and act in relation to potentially adverse situations is often referred to as their *style of coping*. Different coping styles are associated with different domains of emotion and therefore different constellations of physiological patterns. Coping styles have consistent behavioral and neuroendocrine characteristics. As such, they have the capacity to modulate the effect of situations and events on health. Animal studies indicate that proactive (or active) as opposed to reactive (or passive, avoidant) coping styles are associated with vulnerability to hypertension and atherosclerosis caused by elevated sympathetic reactivity (Koolhaas, 1994; Koolhaas et al., 1999). Other recent findings in humans are consistent with the hypothesis that dysregulation of endogenous opioid system (part of the autonomic nervous system) mediates the associations between repressive and defensive coping styles, enhanced stress responsivity, and reduced immunocompetence (Jamner & Leigh, 1999).

EMOTIONAL DISCLOSURE AND HEALTH

Since the publication of Pennebaker's pioneering work in 1989, it has become widely accepted that disclosing emotions by putting upsetting experiences into words can be healthy. Recent reviews have elaborated on the diversity and extent of research findings in this area (Esterling, L'Abate, Murray, & Pennebaker, 1999; Pennebaker, 1999). Given the intimate relationship between emotions and physiology, especially the neuroimmune network, it is pertinent to ask whether some of the health effects of emotional disclosure might be mediated through effects on immune function. Evidence is accumulating that emotional disclosure does affect immune variables and although, as yet, there is little direct evidence linking these immune effects to health benefits, extrapolation from other findings relating emotional and immune change strongly suggests that it is forthcoming.

The first evidence of a direct effect of emotional disclosure on immune variables came from studies that compared blood lymphocytes from students following four consecutive days of 30 minutes of writing about emotionally upsetting events with blood lymphocytes from individuals who wrote descriptively about mundane topics. There were small but significant differences in mitogen-induced T-lymphocyte responses between the two groups (Pennebaker, Kiecolt-Glaser, & Glaser, 1988; T-lymphocyte proliferation is necessary for many immune responses and mitogen-induced T-lymphocyte proliferation is a relatively simple way of measuring this capacity in blood cell cultures). Although the emotional disclosure group had a significantly higher level of T-lymphocyte proliferation stimulated by mitogen in culture, this cannot be taken as an indication that emotional disclosure "improves" immune function but rather as evidence that it affects immune behaviors. This is because mitogen responsiveness of blood lymphocytes is just one of many possible immune measures, and small changes in this measure do not necessarily indicate changes in the immune system as a whole.

Nevertheless, on the basis of this result, Esterling, Antoni, Kumar, and Schneiderman (1990) hypothesized that individuals who abstain from disclosing emotional material would have poorer control of latent Epstein–Barr virus (EBV) than those who express emtions, and that repressive interpersonal styles would correlate with the poorest control. They tested this by measuring anti-EBV antibody titers in blood taken from undergraduate volunteers immediately after 30 minutes of emotional writing. Emotional "repressors" who were either high or low disclosers had high levels of antibodies against EBV (indicating impaired control of latent EBV), whereas only those emotional "sensitizers" who did not disclose had high anti-EBV antibody titers (Esterling et al., 1990). Subsequently, these researchers compared written and spoken emotional expression with writing about superficial topics. Individuals in both oral and written emotional expression groups had significantly lower anti-EBV antibody titers after the intervention than those in the control group. Although there were some differences between written and oral groups in positive and negative emotional word use, content analysis indicated that the oral disclosure group achieved the greatest improvements in cognitive change, self-esteem, and adaptive coping strategies (Esterling, Antoni, Fletcher, Margulies, & Schneiderman, 1994). Moreover, individual differences in people's ability to involve themselves in the disclosure process and abandon their avoidance of the stressful topic during the course of the study were predictive of better immune control of EBV (as indicated by lower antibody levels), and these associations were more pronounced for individuals who disclosed older and more troublesome events (Lutgendorf, Antoni, Kumar, & Schneiderman, 1994).

Other research has focused on NK cell activity, an immune variable regularly found to be affected by emotions and stressful situations. People who verbally disclosed personal information regarding a traumatic or stressful experience displayed short-term increases in NK cell activity compared with nondisclosure controls. Furthermore, the effect of self-disclosure on NK cell activity was moderated by the individual's level of hostility, with high-hostility people exhibiting significantly greater NK cell activity increases than low-hostility people (Christensen et al., 1996). In view of the relationship between NK cell activity and adrenal arousal leading to epinephrine production (Benschop, Rodriguez Feuerhahn, & Schedlowski, 1996; Malarkey, Kiecolt-Glaser, Pearl, & Glaser, 1994), it is conceivable that the enhancement in NK cell activity observed for hostile people was a function of the more pronounced acute arousal response elicited by the self-disclosure task in these people. As discussed earlier, immune function is not unidimensional and so single immune variables should not be taken as indicators of overall immune function in living individuals. Furthermore, many human immune variables are measured from blood samples, and the lymphocyte components of blood comprise less than 10% of the total lymphoid pool in the human body and cannot necessarily be considered a representative sample of immune cellular activity in lymphoid organs. Nevertheless the accumulating data revealing that a variety of immune variables alter as a consequence of emotional disclosure make it more likely that health effects of the disclosure process are mediated, at least in part, through effects on the immune system.

We have investigated whether the health benefits of emotional disclosure would extend to effects on the immune response to an administered viral vaccine. Forty medical students who tested negative for hepatitis B antibodies were randomly assigned to write emotionally about personal traumatic events or to write descriptively about mundane topics during four consecutive daily sessions. On the day after the writing, all students were immunized with hepatitis B vaccine and monitored for specific antibody development over the following 6 months (Petrie, Booth, Pennebaker, Davison, & Thomas, 1995). Compared with the control group, participants in the emotional expression group developed significantly higher antibody levels against hepatitis B antigens (Figure 9.1). There were reproducible significant between-group differences in circulating T cell (CD4 and CD8) numbers and total circulating lymphocyte numbers (Booth, Petrie, &

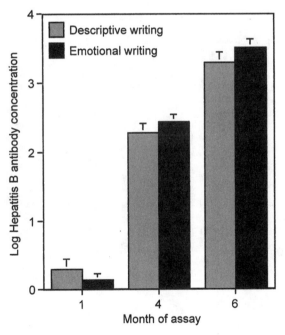

Figure 9.1. Mean and SEM log hepatitis B antibody concentrations in experiment participants immunized the day after 4 days of emotional or descriptive writing. From "Disclosure of Trauma and Immune Response to a Hepatitis B Vaccination Program," by K. J. Petrie, R. J. Booth, J. W. Pennebaker, K. P. Davison, and M. G. Thomas, 1995, *Journal of Consulting and Clinical Psychology, 63,* p. 787. Copyright 1995 by the American Psychological Association. Adapted by permission of the publisher and author.

Pennebaker, 1997). Interestingly, circulating lymphocyte numbers in the nonemotional writing group fluctuated over the course of these studies but stayed relatively constant in the emotional writing group (Figure 9.2). This suggests the possibility that buffering of temporal immune variation might be influential in the health-promoting effects of emotional disclosure. For example, these studies were conducted during the winter months when mild upper respiratory infections such as colds or flulike illnesses are rife. Preliminary data (Booth & Hurley, 2001) indicate that temporal fluctuations in the ability of blood lymphocyte populations to produce certain cytokines is associated with increased reports of upper respiratory tract symptoms during the winter months. Therefore, it would be worth investigating further whether the fluctuations in the lymphocyte populations of the control group reflect an immune susceptibility to such infections whereas the relative stability of those populations in the emotional disclosure group indicate a degree of protection. It also is conceivable (although less likely) that the immune differences between the two writing groups

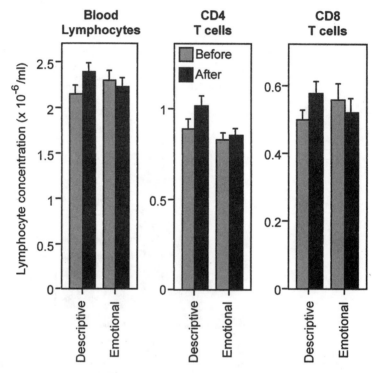

Figure 9.2. Mean and SEM CD4 (helper), CD8 (cytotoxic) and total lymphocytes in the blood of experiment participants before and after 4 days of emotional or descriptive writing. From "Changes in Circulating Lymphocyte Numbers Following Emotional Disclosure: Evidence of Buffering?" by R. J. Booth, K. K. Petrie, and J. W. Pennebaker, 1997, *Stress Medicine*, *13*(1), p. 23. Copyright 1997 by John Wiley and Sons Ltd. Adapted by permission of the publisher and author.

were not due to a beneficial effect in the emotional disclosure group but rather to an adverse effect in the control group, perhaps because they were demoralized by not being randomly assigned to the expressive writing condition.

These findings offer compelling evidence that the health benefits of emotional disclosure might result, at least in part, from effects on immune function. If so, the course of chronic illnesses with significant immune components should be beneficially affected by emotional disclosure. Smyth and colleagues (Smyth, Stone, Hurewitz, & Kaell, 1999) tested this possibility using two groups of patients with illnesses that fall into this category—asthma and rheumatoid arthritis—using quantitative disease outcome measures. Volunteer patients with asthma or rheumatoid arthritis were assigned to write either about the most stressful event of their lives or about emotionally neutral topics. Asthma patients were evaluated with spirometry, and a rheumatologist clinically examined rheumatoid arthritis patients. Four months after the writing, asthma patients in the experimental group showed improvements in lung function, whereas control group patients showed no change. Similarly rheumatoid arthritis patients in the experimental group showed improvements in overall disease activity, but control group patients did not. These effects were beyond those attributable to the standard medical care that all participants were receiving. No direct immune measure was done in this study, but it is tantalizing to suppose that improvements in disease-associated immune variables might have been present.

HOW DOES EMOTIONAL DISCLOSURE WORK?

We can draw three important conclusions from a recent meta-analysis of disclosure studies (Smyth, 1998). Men appear to benefit more from writing than women. Emotional disclosure through writing reliably brings about improvements in self-reported health, objective markers of health (e.g., physician visits), and immune changes compared with people who write about nonemotional topics. Emotional disclosure does not bring about health changes as a result of changes in health-related behaviors (e.g., changes in exercise, smoking, or diet). From our preceding discussion of the relationship between emotions and physiology, it should be apparent that we would not be able to explain the power of emotional disclosure purely in terms of neuroendocrine or immune mechanisms for two reasons. First, both the neuroendocrine and immune systems are multifactorial dynamic networks that cannot be understood in terms of concentrations of individual components. Second, emotions are an expression of interpersonal relations, and as such, they can be understood only in the domain in which people and their relationships arise—the psychosocial domain.

To expect to make sense of emotional disclosure in terms of the activities of physiological components is like expecting to understand a game of rugby by concentrating solely on the thigh muscles of New Zealand's rugby superstar, Jonah Lomu.

It may be possible, however, to identify the types of immune changes expected to be associated with health benefits of emotional disclosure by considering how the immune system conserves adaptation in the context of an individual's psychosocial milieu. To address this possibility, let us first consider what psychosocial factors might promote the salutary effects of emotional disclosure. The sorts of topics one chooses to write about are clearly important, as are the personal characteristics of the writers (see chapter 5, this volume). Greenberg and Stone (1992) found that health benefits occurred when severe traumas were disclosed, regardless of whether previous disclosure had occurred. People low in emotional inhibition were more likely to benefit from writing about personal traumatic experiences (Francis & Pennebaker, 1992), whereas a study by Cameron and Nicholls (1998) revealed differences between optimists and pessimists. This research compared students participating in three tasks: a self-regulation task (expressing thoughts and feelings about entering college and then formulating coping plans), a disclosure task (expressing thoughts and feelings only), or a control task (writing about trivial topics) for 3 weekly writing sessions. Among optimists, both the self-regulation task and the disclosure task reduced illness-related clinic visits during the following month, whereas among pessimists only the self-regulation task reduced clinic visits. Moreover, the self-regulation task beneficially affected mood state and college adjustment, whereas the disclosure task increased grade point averages.

Lutgendorf and colleagues (1997) explored the effects of emotional disclosure in relation to notification of HIV status in men at risk of AIDS. Their results highlight the importance of cognitively processing stressful or emotional material for immune functioning in HIV-positive individuals (see chapter 10, this volume). In the weeks following notification of HIV seropositive status, increased avoidance significantly predicted poorer mitogen-induced T-cell proliferative responses as well as trends toward a lower proportion of circulating CD4 (helper) T lymphocytes.

It seems that a very powerful aspect of emotional disclosure is its potential to assist people to integrate upsetting events into the flow of their lives. When people write to express emotions about traumatic or stressful events in their lives over the course of a number of days, they often change the manner in which they write. Analysis of such changes led Pennebaker (1993) to the conclusion that constructing a coherent story works in concert with the expression of negative emotions work in therapeutic writing. Antonovsky (1993) sought to address this aspect of psychobiology in his Sense of Coherence Scale. In this regard, two recent studies are illuminating. The first investigated HIV-seropositive men who had recently experienced an AIDS-related bereavement. Those who engaged in cognitive processing were more likely to find meaning from the loss. Furthermore, men who found meaning showed less rapid declines in CD4 T-cell levels and lower rates of AIDS-related mortality (Bower, Kemeny, Taylor, & Fahey, 1998). The second explored whether a sense of coherence (as assessed by Antonovsky's Sense of Coherence Scale, 1993) would buffer the effects of housing relocation on NK cell activity in a group of elderly adults. Compared with a control group, the relocation group showed decreased positive mood and NK activity and elevated thought intrusion. Positive mood mediated the relationship of moving with NK activity, whereas those who scored low on the Sense of Coherence Scale had the poorest NK activity (Lutgendorf, Vitaliano, Tripp-Reimer, Harvey, & Lubaroff, 1999).

A sense of coherence and the ability to find meaning in the events of life appear therefore to be linked to positive immune and health outcomes. It is likely that the salutogenic virtues of emotional disclosure are found in the same arena. In other words, some of the benefits lie in the process of accepting and making sense of the events in terms of the narratives we construct to explain ourselves to ourselves and to discover meaning in negative events (Booth, 1999).

Can we conceive of mechanisms by which the immune system is involved in such a process? It is difficult to do so if we think of the immune system in the traditional sense of that which has the role of defending us against the outside world. However, it becomes more feasible if we view the immune system in a broader aspect as a system that acts to conserve an appropriate relationship between our bodies and our environments—a system that maintains our physical "self–nonself" adaptation to be coherent with the living processes of our psychosocial self (Booth & Ashbridge, 1992, 1993). Thus, when there are traumatic aspects of our existence that we cannot accept or assimilate as legitimate facets of ourselves, they are not coherent with our self constructs, we are not at peace with them, and so we have to battle psychologically to keep them at bay. Perhaps this process is mirrored in a neuroimmune network that is constantly battling to maintain an incoherent "physiological self," maybe even to the extent that it is unable effectively to discriminate adequately between some self and nonself components and therefore either responds poorly or inappropriately to some nonself components resulting in susceptibility to infection or attempts to reject some normal self components resulting in autoimmune disease. By contrast, effective expressive writing about traumatic events leads to an altered relationship to those events such that they become assimilated as legitimate facets of ourselves and no longer need to be held at bay as threats to our psychosocial coherence. Under these conditions, the physiological correlates manifest a neuroimmune network that also maintains a more coherent relationship between physical self and nonself.

In Figure 9.3 we have attempted to represent these psychophysiolog-

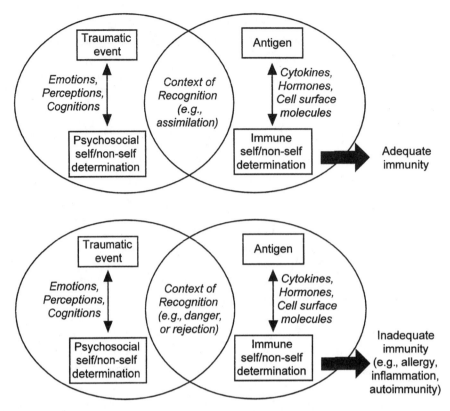

Figure 9.3. A model of the biological pathways through which emotionally expressive writing might affect immune function.

ical relationships and putative pathways in diagrammatic form as a means of providing a novel theoretical framework upon which further research into the immune effects of emotional writing might be based. The model is based on the fact that human psychosocial and biophysical domains each contain a self that is part of the person as a whole. This means not only that psychosocial and biophysical selves mutually influence one another's constitution, but also that they do so in a manner that is coherent with the overall self-identity of the individual. Thus, the context in which events are sensed (biologically) or perceived (psychosocially) in relation to that self modulate the effect of those events on the individual.

With this sort of guiding model, what might we expect to find happening in the immune systems of individuals as a consequence of emotionally expressive writing? Evaluation and response to self and nonself by the immune system involves recognition of molecular shapes (antigens) within particular contexts. Those contexts comprise a variety of modulatory components from the profile of cell surface molecules on antigen-presenting cells, through the constellation of regulatory cytokine hormones produced by helper T lymphocytes and other cells, to the pattern of neuroendocrine hormones and neuropeptides. This means that the same shape recognized in different contexts can provoke differences in the degree and type of immune responses generated. For example, when the context of antigen recognition includes a preponderance of certain cytokines (e.g., a type 1 cytokine profile), the response to that antigen is dominated by cytotoxic and inflammatory mediators. On the other hand, if the cytokine environment resembles a type 2-cytokine profile, antibody responses predominate. Another way of viewing the importance of context in antigen recognition and response is the concept of "danger" signals (Matzinger, 1994). Antigens recognized by the immune system in the presence of a set of factors that comprise danger signals are dealt with aggressively, whereas those recognized in the absence of danger signals are ignored or tolerated. This means, for example, that self-components may be ignored in one context and responded against (generating autoimmunity) in other contexts. Similarly, innocuous substances such as grass pollens or dust components may be ignored in one context and responded against (generating allergies) in other contexts.

In a sense, the molecular and cellular contexts of immune recognition could be construed as the "emotions" of the immune system—guiding, constraining, modulating, and moderating the cognitive and perceptual behavior of the immune network. Perhaps, then, the biological pathways of emotional disclosure act through coherence between psychosocial and neuroimmune "emotional" changes. A traumatic event that has not been adequately assimilated by an individual may condition the cognitive, perceptual, and emotional flow of his or her life such that the neuroimmune network provides a context in which innocuous antigens are more likely recognized inappropriately (e.g., self antigens recognized as a threat). Following a change in the psychosocial context of the traumatic event as a result of emotionally expressive writing, we might then expect to see changes in the way antigens are recognized by the immune system such that previously inappropriate or damaging patterns of immune response now become more appropriate and health-promoting.

REFERENCES

Antonovsky, A. (1993). The structure and properties of the Sense of Coherence Scale. *Social Science & Medicine, 36,* 725–733.

Aubert, A. (1999). Sickness and behaviour in animals: A motivational perspective. *Neuroscience & Biobehavioral Reviews, 23*(7), 1029–1036.

Benschop, R. J., Rodriguez Feuerhahn, M., & Schedlowski, M. (1996). Catecholamine-induced leukocytosis: Early observations, current research, and future directions. *Brain, Behavior, & Immunity, 10*(2), 77–91.

Blalock, J. E. (1984). The immune system as a sensory organ. *Journal of Immunology, 132,* 1067–1070.

Booth, R. J. (1999). Language, self, meaning and health. *Advances in Mind–Body Medicine, 15*(3), 171–175.

Booth, R. J., & Ashbridge, K. R. (1992). Teleological coherence: Exploring the dimensions of the immune system. *Scandinavian Journal of Immunology, 36,* 751–759.

Booth, R. J., & Ashbridge, K. R. (1993). A fresh look at the relationship between the psyche and immune system: Teleological coherence and harmony of purpose. *Advances in Mind–Body Medicine, 9*(2), 4–23.

Booth, R. J., & Hurley, D. G. (2001). Stress, Infection and Type 1 and Type 2 Cytokines. Unpublished observations.

Booth, R. J., Petrie, K. J., & Pennebaker, J. W. (1997). Changes in circulating lymphocyte numbers following emotional disclosure: Evidence of buffering? *Stress Medicine, 13*(1), 23–29.

Borella, P., Bargellini, A., Rovesti, S., Pinelli, M., Vivoli, R., Solfrini, V., & Vivoli, G. (1999). Emotional stability, anxiety, and natural killer activity under examination stress. *Psychoneuroendocrinology, 24,* 613–627.

Bower, J. E., Kemeny, M. E., Taylor, S. E., & Fahey, J. L. (1998). Cognitive processing, discovery of meaning, CD4 decline, and AIDS-related mortality among bereaved HIV-seropositive men. *Journal of Consulting and Clinical Psychology, 66,* 979–986.

Cameron, L. D., & Nicholls, G. (1998). Expression of stressful experiences through writing: Effects of a self-regulation manipulation for pessimists and optimists. *Health Psychology, 17,* 84–92.

Christensen, A. J., Edwards, D. L., Wiebe, J. S., Benotsch, E. G., McKelvey, L., Andrews, M., & Lubaroff, D. M. (1996). Effect of verbal self-disclosure on natural killer cell activity—moderating influence of cynical hostility. *Psychosomatic Medicine, 58*(2), 150–155.

Clark, D. M., Ball, S., & Pape, D. (1991). An experimental investigation of thought suppression. *Behavioral Research Therapy, 29*(3), 253–257.

Cohen, F., Kearney, K. A., Zegans, L. S., Kemeny, M. E., Neuhaus, J. M., & Stites, D. P. (1999). Differential immune system changes with acute and persistent stress for optimists vs pessimists. *Brain, Behavior, & Immunity, 13*(2), 155–174.

Dantzer, R. (1997). Stress and immunity: what have we learned from psychoneuroimmunology? *Acta Physiologica Scandinavica. Supplementum, 640,* 43–46.

Dantzer, R., Bluthe, R. M., & Kelley, K. W. (1991). Androgen-dependent vasopressinergic neurotransmission attenuates interleukin-1-induced sickness behavior. *Brain Research, 557*(1–2), 115–120.

Esterling, B. A., Antoni, M. H., Fletcher, M. A., Margulies, S., & Schneiderman, N. (1994). Emotional disclosure through writing or speaking modulates latent Epstein–Barr virus antibody titers. *Journal of Consulting and Clinical Psychology, 62,* 130–140.

Esterling, B. A., Antoni, M. H., Kumar, M., & Schneiderman, N. (1990). Emotional repression, stress disclosure responses, and Epstein–Barr viral capsid antigen titers. *Psychosomatic Medicine, 52*, 397–410.

Esterling, B. A., L'Abate, L., Murray, E. J., & Pennebaker, J. W. (1999). Empirical foundations for writing in prevention and psychotherapy: Mental and physical health outcomes. *Clinical Psychology Reviews, 19*(1), 79–96.

Francis, M. E., & Pennebaker, J. W. (1992). Putting stress into words: The impact of writing on physiological, absentee, and self-reported emotional well-being measures. *American Journal of Health Promotion, 6*(4), 280–287.

Greenberg, M. A., & Stone, A. A. (1992). Emotional disclosure about traumas and its relation to health: Effects of previous disclosure and trauma severity. *Journal of Personality and Social Psychology, 63*, 75–84.

Gross, J. J. (1998). Antecedent- and response-focused emotion regulation—divergent consequences for experience, expression, and physiology. *Journal of Personality and Social Psychology, 74*(1), 224–237.

Gross, J. J., & Levenson, R. W. (1993). Emotional suppression: Physiology, self-report, and expressive behavior. *Journal of Personality and Social Psychology, 64*, 970–986.

Jamner, L. D., & Leigh, H. (1999). Repressive/defensive coping, endogenous opioids and health: How a life so perfect can make you sick. *Psychiatry Research, 85*(1), 17–31.

Kent, S., Bluthe, R. M., Kelley, K. W., & Dantzer, R. (1992). Sickness behavior as a new target for drug development. *Trends in Pharmacological Science, 13*(1), 24–28.

Koolhaas, J. M. (1994). Individual coping strategies and vulnerability to stress pathology. *Homeostasis in Health & Disease, 35*(1–2), 24–27.

Koolhaas, J. M., Korte, S. M., De Boer, S. F., Van Der Vegt, B. J., Van Reenen, C. G., Hopster, H., De Jong, I. C., Ruis, M. A. W., & Blokhuis, H. J. (1999). Coping styles in animals: Current status in behavior and stress-physiology. *Neuroscience & Biobehavioral Reviews, 23*, 925–935.

Levenson, R. W., Ekman, P., Heider, K., & Friesen, W. V. (1992). Emotion and autonomic nervous system activity in the Minangkabau of west Sumatra. *Journal of Personality and Social Psychology, 62*, 972–988.

Lutgendorf, S. K., Antoni, M. H., Ironson, G., Klimas, N., Fletcher, M. A., & Schneiderman, N. (1997). Cognitive processing style, mood, and immune function following HIV seropositivity notification. *Cognitive Therapy & Research, 21*(2), 157–184.

Lutgendorf, S. K., Antoni, M. H., Kumar, M., & Schneiderman, N. (1994). Changes in cognitive coping strategies predict EBV-antibody titer change following a stressor disclosure induction. *Journal of Psychosomatic Research, 38*(1), 63–78.

Lutgendorf, S. K., Vitaliano, P. P., Tripp-Reimer, T., Harvey, J. H., & Lubaroff, D. M. (1999). Sense of coherence moderates the relationship between life stress and natural killer cell activity in healthy older adults. *Psychology and Aging, 14*, 552–563.

Malarkey, W. S., Kiecolt-Glaser, J. K., Pearl, D., & Glaser, R. (1994). Hostile behavior during marital conflict alters pituitary and adrenal hormones. *Psychosomatic Medicine, 56*(1), 41–51.

Matzinger, P. (1994). Tolerance, danger, and the extended family. *Annual Reviews in Immunology, 12*, 991–1045.

Pennebaker, J. W. (1989). Confession, inhibition, and disease. *Advances in Experimental & Social Psychology, 22*, 211–244.

Pennebaker, J. W. (1993). Putting stress into words: Health, linguistic, and therapeutic implications. *Behavioral Research & Therapy, 31*, 539–548.

Pennebaker, J. W. (1999). Disclosure and health: An interview with James W. Pennebaker. *Advances in Mind–Body Medicine, 15*(3), 161–163, 166–171; discussion 193–165.

Pennebaker, J. W., Kiecolt-Glaser, J. K., & Glaser, R. (1988). Disclosure of traumas and immune function: Health implications for psychotherapy. *Journal of Consulting and Clinical Psychology, 56*, 239–245.

Petrie, K. J., Booth, R. J., & Pennebaker, J. W. (1998). The immunological effects of thought suppression. *Journal of Personality and Social Psychology, 75*, 1264–1272.

Petrie, K. J., Booth, R. J., Pennebaker, J. W., Davison, K. P., & Thomas, M. G. (1995). Disclosure of trauma and immune response to a hepatitis B vaccination program. *Journal of Consulting and Clinical Psychology, 63*, 787–792.

Post, R. M., Weiss, S. R. B., Li, H., Smith, M. A., Zhang, L. X., Xing, G., Osuch, E. A., & McCann, U. D. (1998). Neural plasticity and emotional memory. *Development & Psychopathology, 10*, 829–855.

Segerstrom, S. C., Glover, D. A., Craske, M. G., & Fahey, J. L. (1999). Worry affects the immune response to phobic fear. *Brain, Behavior, & Immunity, 13*(2), 80–92.

Smyth, J. M. (1998). Written emotional expression: Effect sizes, outcome types, and moderating variables. *Journal of Consulting and Clinical Psychology, 66*, 174–184.

Smyth, J. M., Stone, A. A., Hurewitz, A., & Kaell, A. (1999). Effects of writing about stressful experiences on symptom reduction in patients with asthma or rheumatoid arthritis: A randomized trial. *Journal of the American Medical Association, 281*, 1304–1309.

Walker, L. G., Walker, M. B., Heys, S. D., Lolley, J., Wesnes, K., & Eremin, O. (1997). The psychological and psychiatric effects of rIL-2 therapy: A controlled clinical trial. *Psycho Oncology, 6*(4), 290–301.

Wegner, D. M., Schneider, D. J., Carter, S. R., & White, T. L. (1987). Paradoxical effects of thought suppression. *Journal of Personality and Social Psychology, 53,* 5–13.

Wegner, D. M., Shortt, J. W., Blake, A. W., & Page, M. S. (1990). The suppression of exciting thoughts. *Journal of Personality and Social Psychology, 58,* 409–418.

Zeitlin, S. B., Netten, K. A., & Hodder, S. L. (1995). Thought suppression: An experimental investigation of spider phobics. *Behavioral Research Therapy, 33*(4), 407–413.

10

COGNITIVE PROCESSING, DISCLOSURE, AND HEALTH: PSYCHOLOGICAL AND PHYSIOLOGICAL MECHANISMS

SUSAN K. LUTGENDORF AND PHILIP ULLRICH

We carry with us every story we have ever heard and every story we have ever lived, filed away at some deep place in our memory. We carry most of those stories unread, as it were, until we have grown the capacity or the readiness to read them. When that happens they may come back to us filled with a previously unsuspected meaning.
—Rachel Naomi Remen, MD, *Kitchen Table Wisdom* (1996)

The mechanisms by which writing or talking about stressful or traumatic events influence immunity and health have attracted a great deal of interest. Key questions involve the role of cognitive and emotional processing, whether insight and resolution are necessary, and whether the mere act of submitting an upsetting event to a linguistic context is the critical element in facilitating integration and assimilation. An additional challenge involves understanding the interactions of psychological processes and physiological change. For example, what aspects of psychological processing are necessary for physiological changes to be observed? We explore these questions by drawing from the literature on written and verbal disclosure, and we examine psychological processing particularly as it relates to immune outcomes.

EXPERIENTIAL MODEL OF DISCLOSURE

We begin the chapter with a discussion of the experiential model of psychological processing that guides our work. According to this model, schemas, or templates, direct the processing of stressful or traumatic events. Schemas include cognitive representations, affective responses, and specific patterns of autonomic arousal that relate to these events (Greenberg & Safran, 1987; Lang, Levin, Miller, & Kozak, 1983). "Unfinished" feelings, such as resentment, anger, fear, or grief, that derive from stressful or traumatic events, are held in part as bodily states of tension of which a person may be unaware (Gendlin, 1984, 1996; Greenberg & Safran, 1987). Alternately, a particular issue may be associated with feelings of heaviness in the chest, a sinking in the abdomen, or a knot in the stomach. Coming to terms with such events involves processing on cognitive, emotional, and physical levels.

The experiential model posits that directly experiencing facets of an emotion-laden memory, including its physiological and affective components, along with associated thoughts and images, enables a person to re-access the affective and cognitive schemas involved in that memory. This re-experiencing, which can be performed in gradual doses, is the key to its resolution. This process allows for examination of different facets of the experience that the person may have otherwise blocked from awareness (Rice, 1974). In reprocessing a past stressor more slowly and completely, the person may become aware of dimensions of the experience not previously realized and come to see it in a different way (Rice & Greenberg, 1984). A central feature of this process is cognitive reorganization, which might be facilitated when schema activation is accompanied by new information that is incompatible with previously existing cognitive–affective structures (Safran & Greenberg, 1991). This process can lead to insight or a change in perspective (reorganization of the schema), decreased distress (Gendlin, 1984; Greenberg & Safran, 1987; Rice & Greenberg, 1984), and decreased bodily tension (Wexler, 1974). The release of bodily tension associated with a problematic issue is a key element of the experiential model (Gendlin, 1984) and is specifically relevant to the physiological effects of disclosure.

The experiential model predicts that to the extent that disclosure results in affective arousal and processing of new facets of the experience, including schema-discrepant information, psychological change (resolution and integration) and release of tension will ensue. Thus, affective arousal and depth of both cognitive and affective processing may be key process variables underlying the effects of disclosure on mental and physical health. This model contrasts with cathartic explanations for the effects of disclosure in which the positive effects of disclosure are thought to ensue from the release of previously repressed or inhibited emotion (Freud 1904/1954; Pennebaker & Hoover, 1986; Pennebaker & Susman, 1988). Disclosure is thought to work like catharsis by facilitating the release of tension accumulated from lack of emotional expression. In contrast, the experiential model posits that catharsis alone is insufficient and that it must be accompanied by cognitive processing, which provides a new cognitive structure for the event. This process then results in associated changes in physiological patterns.

The experiential model also goes beyond a linguistic explanation of disclosure, which maintains that the effects of disclosure result from making stressful or traumatic events more understandable by forcing them to be submitted to language (Pennebaker, 1993). Because communicating experiences through language facilitates production of a coherent message (Clark, 1993), the linguistic expression involved in disclosure requires individuals to place a cognitive structure on their experiences and emotions. This structuring process may facilitate understanding of an experience and the emergence of a new perspective, and it may thus change the meaning of the experience. Although the linguistic model shares features with the experiential model with respect to the importance of emergence of new cognitive perspectives, the experiential model goes further by emphasizing the integration of changes in the cognitive, emotional, and physiological patterns associated with the stressor.

Theories proposed for the psychological reprocessing of traumatic events are consistent with the experiential model. Effectively overwhelming experiences, such as those accompanying very stressful and traumatic events, are thought to interfere with the cognitive integration of such events with existing cognitive schema. Additionally, memory storage of such events may include somatic, affective, and linguistic subcomponents that are not integrated into a coherent mental framework (e.g., van der Kolk & van der Hart, 1991). Thus, a person may remember a smell or a physical feeling associated with a trauma without being able to access a visual memory. Psychological reprocessing of traumatic events involves activation of the relevant schemas associated with the trauma. Controlled activation of the relevant schemas is believed to allow some of the affective intensity to dissipate, which then allows for the integration of the relevant schemas (Foa & Kozak, 1986). Because of the intensity of affect surrounding the trauma, accessing of the relevant cognitive–emotional–somatic schemas must be modulated to a certain extent to avoid resensitization to the traumatic emotions. For example, controlled exposure therapy has had some success with trauma cases (Foa & Kozak, 1986). Writing may serve as a form of controlled exposure to a traumatic memory, allowing for the integration of the disparate components of memory (see also chapter 6, this volume).

Although a posttraumatic stress disorder (PTSD) model has been used to explain the mechanisms involved in disclosure (e.g., Smyth, 1998), an examination of disclosure studies that enumerate types of events disclosed suggests that the majority of events described in disclosure studies may not be of the severity and intensity to produce consequences as severe as PTSD (Esterling, Antoni, Fletcher, Margulies, & Schneiderman, 1994; Lutgendorf, Antoni, Kumar, & Schneiderman, 1994; Petrie, Booth, Pennebaker, Davison, & Thomas, 1995; Ullrich & Lutgendorf, in press). Thus, an explanation drawing on the PTSD model may overestimate the effects of events discussed in typical disclosure studies, and effects may be more aptly described in terms of the chronic, stressful effects of unresolved painful issues. Although we address the psychology and physiology of PTSD-related stress in this chapter, we believe that non-PTSD models are more applicable to disclosure.

PSYCHOLOGICAL MECHANISMS INVOLVED IN DISCLOSURE: RESEARCH FINDINGS

Process research in psychotherapy has shown that the mere presence of disclosure in therapy is not necessarily related to positive outcomes, even though it is an essential ingredient in psychotherapeutic change (Stiles, 1987). We (Lutgendorf & Antoni, 1999) have found that submitting a traumatic event to linguistic processing per se in a disclosure paradigm is not sufficient to produce affective change. Rather, the level of "experiencing" or involvement in the disclosure was a critical factor in outcomes. In this study, students verbally disclosed their deepest thoughts and feelings about a traumatic event weekly for 3 weeks. Disclosures were recorded and transcripts were rated for total quantity of expression during the disclosure sessions (word count), emotional arousal during the disclosures (increase in reported negative affect), and experiential involvement. *Experiential involvement* is not synonymous with *expressiveness* or *emotionality*; rather, it addresses the manner in which feelings are experienced and the quality of a person's attention to inner experience and working engagement in therapy (Klein, Mathieu-Coglan, & Kiesler, 1986). Level of experiential involvement in the disclosure was rated by two raters using the well-validated Experiencing Scale (Klein, Mathieu, Gendlin, & Kiesler, 1969; 1 = *very detached* at one extreme, to 7 = *deeply involved in an intensely personal way with emerging insights* at the other). At the lower levels of the scale, the speaker remained distant from their emotional experience, avoiding feelings or conflicts. At higher levels of the scale, the speaker demonstrates progressive ownership of feelings up to a point where feelings and personal meanings are experienced with immediacy, often leading to new levels of understanding and release of tension (see Exhibit 10.1).

We found that the level of involvement during disclosure increased from Session 1 to Session 3, suggesting that participants gradually deepened their experiential involvement over time. Individuals who were more involved in the disclosure reported greater reduction in negative mood by the end of the disclosure compared to a nondisclosure control group. Intrusion of trauma-related ideation decreased in the disclosure group over

EXHIBIT 10.1
Ratings Used in the Experiencing Scale

Stage 1: Individual is remote from feelings. Reported experiences have an impersonal quality. Feelings are avoided and personal involvement is not present in communication.

Stage 2: Individual does not directly refer to feelings but a personal perspective emerges to some extent. References to the self indicate an intellectual interest but only a general and superficial involvement.

Stage 3: Individual refers to feelings with ownership but does not describe personal aspects or deeper ramifications of feelings.

Stage 4: Individual begins to draw directly from his experiencing to describe feelings and personal reactions.

Stage 5: Individual elaborates and explores own feelings, using an inner referent.

Stage 6: Individual explores feelings and finds a step of resolution. Feelings and personal meanings are immediately available as clear referents for action or self-awareness.

Stage 7: Individual has an emerging understanding and integration of present issues in a new way, and these have meaning for other areas in a person's life.

From Klein, M. H., Mathieu, P. L., Gendlin, E. T., & Kiesler, D. J. (1969). *The Experiencing Scale; a research and training manual I & II*. Madison: University of Wisconsin, Extension Bureau of Audiovisual Instruction. Reprinted with permission.

the course of the study as compared to controls. We examined a model that assessed the relative contribution of process variables to changes suggestive of resolution achieved in the disclosure. We conceptualized resolution as somewhat akin to the psychodynamic concept of "working through" an issue (Horowitz, 1997). Resolution implies coming to terms with the event in a way that allows integration or assimilation of the stressful material. Greater involvement in the disclosure and greater evocation of negative mood during the first disclosure session contributed to greater insight by the end of the intervention. In contrast, individuals using a higher number of words reported higher levels of negative mood and greater thought intrusion at the end of the study, suggesting a lack of resolution (see chapter 6, this volume; Lutgendorf & Antoni, 1999).

These findings also indicate that the quantity of disclosure, as measured in number of words by itself, was not sufficient to produce beneficial cognitive and affective change. In fact, continued high word counts by the third disclosure session suggested a lack of resolution. It may be possible to be very expressive about the same distressing material over and over again without changing the cognitive schema or affective distress related to the event. Emotional arousal during disclosure was not a strong predictor of resolution, suggesting that emotional arousal without cognitive processing might not contribute to a better understanding of an event. Rather, experiential involvement accompanied by some affective arousal may be key elements in disclosure leading to trauma resolution. These findings are consistent with the possibility that quantity of expression and depth of therapeutic involvement may be independent constructs. These findings suggest that disclosure must attain a certain level of depth to produce change, that a combination of emotional evocation and cognitive effort is important for resolution, and that a moderate level of evoked emotion is most useful in producing change.

It is difficult to assess the level of "experiencing" in written disclosure, but there is evidence to support a joint role of cognitive processing and emotional expression in positive disclosure outcomes. For example, Pennebaker and Beall (1986) asked students to write about a traumatic event, focusing on either the facts surrounding the trauma, the emotions, or both facts and emotions; a control group wrote about superficial topics. The factual group showed no postdisclosure differences from the control group, whereas the emotion-focused group and the facts and emotions group demonstrated health benefits. Not only did the facts plus emotions group report a significant reduction in health problems, but it also was the only group that did not show an increase in health center visits during the course of the study. These findings support the interaction of factual and emotional elements of disclosure in producing health benefits.

We have seen similar results in a study of the effects of intensive journaling about stressful events (Ullrich & Lutgendorf, in press). Undergraduates were instructed to write about (a) their deepest emotions about an unresolved stressful or traumatic event, (b) their thoughts and emotions about a stressful or traumatic event, or (c) the facts about a news item involving trauma. Unresolved events were selected as the focus of journaling to sustain interest in an intensive journaling procedure and to allow for the possibility of cognitive change and resolution while writing. Students were asked to write at least twice a week for at least 10 minutes over the course of a month. Journal topics included death of a family member (25%), romantic relationship (24%), family conflict (15%), academic difficulties (9%), and serious family illness (8%). Participants in the cognitions and emotions group reported more positive growth from the trauma than the other two groups. In addition, members of the emotions alone condition reported more illness after 1 month of journaling than those in the other two conditions, who did not differ from each other.

These findings suggest that dwelling on emotions alone during 1 month of writing may be counterproductive in terms of health outcomes and that emotional expression alone does not enable persons to find meaning in a stressful event. It is possible that the effects of emotion-focused journaling are similar to the effects of uncontrolled exposure to a traumatic event. Specifically, writers may be able to relive the physiological and emotional activation of the trauma during its recall, but because they are focused on the affective experience, they may not be able to work through the trauma to reach a state of resolution from which they have a different perspective (Foa & Kozak, 1986; Frueh, Turner, & Beidel, 1995). The repeated evocation of an unresolved stressor may result in repeated activation of the autonomic nervous system and of the hypothalamic–adrenal–pituitary axis, with ensuing neuroendocrine effects that may be pathogenic (Baum, 1990). Findings from this study suggest that the combination of cognitive and emotional processing results in greater psychological adaptation to a stressful or traumatic event than emotional processing alone.

The importance of both cognitive and affective processes also emerges from studies analyzing the content of written disclosure essays. Pennebaker, Mayne, and Francis (1997) analyzed the correlation between essay content and health outcomes from six written disclosure experiments. They found that increased essay content indicative of cognitive processing (e.g., insightful and causal words) was linked to physical health benefits but not to emotional benefits. They also found a curvilinear relationship between negative emotion word use and illness change, such that individuals writing with moderate levels of negative emotion showed more health benefits than individuals using either very high or very low numbers of negative emotional words. These findings suggest that moderate levels of emotional arousal combined with cognitive processing appear to be closely related to the physical health benefits of disclosure. These findings are consistent with the experiential notion that superficial emotional processing does not result in cognitive change because it tends to leave some of the most relevant schemas unactivated and therefore not amenable to change (Safran & Greenberg, 1991). Thus, attempts at modifying schemas that do not evoke emotions are thought to be less successful in producing change. However, high levels of emotional arousal may not be desired in disclosure, because this may produce so much emotion that the trauma cannot be processed in a new way (Foa & Kozak, 1986). These findings support the joint contribution of evoked emotion and cognitive processing to the effects of disclosure, particularly where health outcomes are concerned.

COGNITIVE PROCESSING, EMOTIONAL EXPRESSION, AND IMMUNE REGULATION

Although modulation of a variety of immune markers following disclosure interventions has been demonstrated (e.g., Esterling, Antoni, et al., 1994; Esterling, Kiecolt-Glaser, Bodnar, & Glaser, 1994; Lutgendorf et al., 1994; Pennebaker, Kiecolt-Glaser, & Glaser, 1988; Petrie et al., 1995), the manner by which psychological processes interact with physiological processes in disclosure is still not well understood. The work that does exist has largely been interpreted within the framework of an inhibition model (see below). Very little attention has been paid to physiological correlates of the psychological process components of disclosure. In this section, we address the cognitive and emotional processes involved in disclosure and their relationships to immune function. We also examine immune effects of traumatic and nontraumatic stress and the relevance of these patterns to disclosure.

According to the experiential model, the integration of previously nonintegrated thoughts, feelings, and somatic processes regarding a stressor or traumatic event results in release of physiological tension. We propose that this release of tension allows the body to normalize immune and neuroendocrine processes, thus contributing to the positive physiological effects of disclosure.

Pennebaker initially proposed that the beneficial health effects of disclosure were due to release of the physical tension that accompanied inhibition of traumatic memories from emerging into consciousness (e.g., Pennebaker & Hoover, 1986; Pennebaker & Susman, 1988). Several of his studies have shown a direct relation between inhibition and autonomic arousal and conversely, between disclosure and autonomic normalization. Pennebaker and colleagues (Pennebaker & Chew, 1985; Pennebaker & Susman, 1988) also found that written disclosure produced immune benefits (as indicated by increased T-cell response to stimulation by foreign antigens called *mitogens*) and fewer health center visits. Although changes in immune response were not directly correlated with autonomic changes or with health outcomes, the authors maintained that the presence of autonomic decreases and immune enhancement in the disclosure group were consistent with the hypothesis that the physiological findings were due to disclosure-induced release of inhibition. An alternate interpretation of these findings also is possible. These same findings could be interpreted as consistent with an experiential model wherein both cognitive and affective aspects of the writing enable resolution of the issues discussed. Thus, the decreased autonomic activation and positive immune changes could have been related to problem resolution accompanied by a decrease of tension.

The work of Esterling and colleagues (1994) more clearly supports the mechanism of problem resolution as opposed to release of inhibition. In one of the few studies investigating the relationship between psychological mechanisms and immunity in written disclosure, Esterling and colleagues asked students to write or speak into a tape recorder about personally stressful or traumatic events that they had not previously disclosed to other people, or to write about a trivial topic once weekly for 4 weeks. Predisclosure and postdisclosure blood measurements were taken to measure antibody titers to Epstein–Barr virus viral capsid antigen (EBV-VCA). Epstein Barr virus, the virus responsible for mononucleosis, is widespread in the population and persists in the host indefinitely after initial infection, setting up what is called a *state of latency*. Efficient regulation of EBV in this latent state is probably maintained by the cellular immune system, particularly by T lymphocytes (Tosato, 1987). Impairments in T-cell control over EBV are thought to be reflected in higher levels of circulating antibodies specific to EBV (Glaser et al., 1991; Tosato, 1987). Such impairments in immune control of EBV can be stress related. For example, under stressful conditions, EBV can reactivate and replicate, and higher levels of antibody specific to EBV are observed (Glaser et al., 1991). Esterling, Antoni, and colleagues (1994) found that 4 weeks of written or verbal disclosure of stressors or traumas produced lower EBV-VCA antibody titers than the trivial writing condition. In addition, they found that cognitive change (as reflected in increased levels of understanding and insight) was associated with decreases in EBV-VCA antibody titers, suggesting increased control of this latent virus by the cellular immune system (Esterling, Antoni, et al., 1994). These findings support a role for written or verbal disclosure in effecting a more adequate immune response in a healthy population. Secondly, these findings support a role for cognitive change in the physiological effects of disclosure. These findings are consistent with both an experiential model and a linguistic model for the effects of disclosure.

Lutgendorf and colleagues (1994) used a design similar to that of Esterling and colleagues (1994), but with a verbal disclosure task, to examine process elements of disclosure in relation to EBV-VCA antibody titers over the course of a month. We examined blood samples for EBV-VCA antibody titers prior to the first disclosure and a week following the last of three disclosure sessions. In this study, participation in three weekly sessions of verbal disclosure did not in itself produce lower EBV-VCA titers. However, important differences in EBV-VCA were found with respect to the level of psychological processing in the disclosure sessions. Those individuals showing greater "experiencing" in the disclosure showed a greater drop in EBV-VCA titers over the course of the study, which suggests that the extent of experiential involvement in disclosure is critical for immune change. In addition, individuals who became more able to face their traumas, as indicated by decreased avoidance of traumatic material over the course of the disclosure, also demonstrated decreased EBV-VCA antibody titers. This suggests that cognitive change may be an important factor that contributes to improving immune control over this virus. We propose that in our study and Esterling et al.'s study the cognitive change and emotional involvement in the disclosure may have brought about a greater state of resolution or integration of stressful material. We hypothesize that "resolution" is associated with specific physiological consequences, including reduction of physiological tension or burden associated with stressful material, decreased neuroendocrine stress-responses, and more normalized immune responses. Possible mechanisms underlying these changes are discussed below.

Pennebaker and colleagues (1988) have proposed that individuals who do not confront a trauma live with it in a chronically unresolved manner. When past stressful or traumatic events are unresolved, unbidden thoughts and emotions related to these events frequently intrude into awareness. Baum (1990) has proposed that these repeated episodes of thought intrusion from unresolved traumatic past events are accompanied by repeated autonomic activation, which ultimately leads to chronic stress as expressed in elevated stress hormones and general decrements in the immune responses. For example, in our verbal disclosure-immune study discussed above (Lutgendorf et al., 1994; Lutgendorf & Antoni, 1999), even though some of the events had occurred a number of years previously, very few participants reported that the events were completely resolved, and most reported that the events were still occupying some part of their thoughts. This is consistent with the notion of the unresolved event as a chronic stressor.

Chronic stress has been associated with various alterations in neuroendocrine and immune functioning. These include elevations in basal levels of stress hormones such as cortisol and catecholamines (Chrousos, 1992), decreases in natural killer (NK) cell activity (Kiecolt-Glaser, Dura, Speicher, Trask, & Glaser, 1991), increased reactiviation of herpes viruses as reflected in elevated antibody titers (Glaser et al., 1993), decreased ability of T-cells to proliferate in response to foreign antigens (Herbert & Cohen, 1993), decreased ability of the body to produce immune regulatory factors called *cytokines* necessary for wound healing and other functions (Glaser et al., 1999), and decreased ability to produce an adequate antibody response to vaccines (Kiecolt-Glaser, Glaser, Gravenstein, Malarkey, & Sheridan, 1996). These effects are believed to be mediated in part by stress hormones (Gatti et al., 1987; Hellstrand, Hermodsson, & Strannegard, 1985). Chronic production of stress hormones also has suppressive effects on cell-mediated immune functions, which have many roles, including protection against viral infections (McEwen, 1998).

We propose that resolution of a trauma or stressor through disclosure may diminish tonic catecholamine or cortisol elevations accompanying a chronic, unresolved stressor and thus permit more efficient immune functioning to occur. Although the effects of writing on neuroendocrine mechanisms have not been tested directly, recent findings indicate that a cognitive–behavioral stress management program successfully reduces both catecholamine and cortisol levels in men with symptomatic HIV (Antoni, Cruess, Cruess, Lutgendorf, et al., 2000; Antoni, Cruess, Cruess, Kumar, et al., 2000) and normalizes various aspects of immune function (Cruess et al., 2000). The active ingredients associated with these changes appear to include decreased depression or anxiety (Antoni, Cruess, Cruess, Lutgendorf, et al., 2000; Antoni, Cruess, Cruess, Kumar, et al., 2000; Lutgendorf et al., 1997) and cognitive change (Lutgendorf et al., 1998). To the extent that disclosure decreases levels of stress, depression, or anxiety and promotes cognitive change, it may act by similar psychological mechanisms. These effects would likely result in decreased levels of cortisol and catecholamines. Because cortisol is largely immunosuppressive, a disclosure intervention that decreases levels of cortisol may allow for more efficient immune functioning. The findings discussed above (Esterling, Antoni, et al., 1994; Lutgendorf et al., 1994) are consistent with this model. The findings of the hepatitis B study of Petrie and colleagues (1995) also are consistent with this model.

Perhaps the most clinically relevant immunologic findings in a written disclosure paradigm come from a study by Petrie and colleagues (1995), who examined the effects of written disclosure on the immunologic response to hepatitis B vaccination (see also chapter 9, this volume). Greater life stress was previously associated with poorer ability of the body to develop antibodies against the hepatitis B vaccine during the course of immunization (Glaser, Kiecolt-Glaser, Bonneau, Malarkey, & Hughes, 1992). Hepatitis B negative medical students were randomly assigned to write about personal traumatic events or trivial control topics for four consecutive days. Following completion of the last essay, participants were given the first in a series of three hepatitis B vaccinations. Booster injections were given at 1 and 3 months following the writing intervention. At 4- and 5-month follow-ups, the written disclosure group showed significantly higher antibody levels against hepatitis B than the control group. Specific information was not provided on relationships of antibody levels to psychological variables such as cognitions, affect, or insight. In the absence of such information it is difficult to ascertain what process variables may have been most important for the immune outcomes seen. However, these findings are consistent with the possibility that if writing enabled participants to reduce chronic stress, anxiety, or depression accompanying an unresolved trauma, decreased tonic levels of catecholamines or cortisol may have allowed disclosers to mount a more adequate immune response to the hepatitis vaccine.

Trauma and Immune Function

For traumatic stressors, particularly if they produce PTSD-type symptoms, other physiological pathways may operate. Because research on trauma has been used to understand the psychological effects of disclosure, an understanding of the neuroendocrine and immune effects of PTSD also may shed light on the physiological effects of disclosure. PTSD produces changes in cognitive and neural processing of information (van der Kolk, Burbridge, & Suzuki, 1997), neuroendocrine changes (Yehuda, Giller, Southwick, Lowy, & Mason, 1991), and immune changes (Boscarino & Chang, 1999). In contrast to the glucocorticoid elevations produced by chronic stress, PTSD generally has been associated with *decreased* tonic levels of cortisol, a *decreased* cortisol response to stress, and increased numbers of glucocorticoid receptors on lymphocytes (white blood cells; Yehuda et al., 1991). Although cortisol is normally associated with suppressive effects on the immune response, chronically low levels of cortisol may leave the organism vulnerable to development of inflammatory and autoimmune disorders, because there is too little cortisol or negative feedback to turn off overactive immune and inflammatory responses (Chrousos, 1992; Heim, Ehlert, & Hellhammer, 2000). It has been proposed that the disproportionately high levels of autoimmune disease in patients with histories of sexual abuse may be related to the possibility that the levels of cortisol in individuals with PTSD may be inadequate to properly regulate the immune response (Heim et al., 2000; van der Kolk, 1997).

Immune activation generally has been observed in patients with PTSD (Wilson, van der Kolk, Burbridge, Fisler, & Kradin, 1999). This means that the cellular immune system is overprepared to mount a response and may attack cells of the person's own body or overreact to foreign antigens. Abnormally high responsiveness of cell-mediated immune functions has been reported in veterans with PTSD as compared to controls (Watson, Muller, Jones, & Bradley, 1993). PTSD-positive veterans have abnormally high levels of total white blood cells, lymphocytes, total T cells, T-helper (CD4+) cells, and T-cytotoxic (CD8+) cells (Boscarino & Chang, 1999). Such findings may be clinically significant as excess proliferation and stimulation of white blood cells would tend to predispose individuals to a number of autoimmune diseases. With one exception (Ironson et al., 1997), elevations in NK cell activity have been reported with PTSD (Laudenslager et al., 1998; Mosniam et al., 1993), and these cells are involved in the body's defense against viral infections and tumors.

In general, PTSD appears to be accompanied by low levels of cortisol, blunted cortisol responses to stress, acoompanied by immune overactivation, which may put individuals with PTSD at risk for autoimmune and inflammatory diseases. If writing operates by allowing individuals to integrate traumatic content, as proposed here, it could conceivably result in normalization of some of the neuroendocrine dysregulation seen in PTSD. Such changes could result in decreased immune activation and symptom improvement. Although speculative, such physiological effects may underlie the positive effects of writing about traumas observed among patients with asthma and rheumatoid arthritis (Smyth, Stone, Hurewitz, & Kaell, 1999), both of which involve overactivation of the immune system (Sternberg, 1992).

Model of Disclosure Effects on Immunity and Health

Thus, we propose that disclosure allows individuals to psychologically integrate various aspects of a trauma or chronically unresolved stressor, thereby releasing tension and promoting normalization of bodily processes. This can occur in several ways. If the immune system is deficient, as is the case with chronic stress, normalization allows it to become stronger. If the immune system is overactive, as in PTSD, normalization helps restore the integrity of the neuroendocrine feedback system and will likely decrease immune activation. These predictions are based on inferences from the available literature and provide hypotheses to be tested in future research (see Figure 10.1).

We propose that the experiential model summarized in Figure 10.1 provides a useful framework for understanding the physiological effects of disclosure through expressive writing. With respect to psychological processes involved in disclosure, we have argued that there is strong support for the proposition that psychological resolution results from a combination of cognitive processing, moderate evocation of emotion, and experiential involvement in the disclosure process. Resolution is thought to act by decreasing tension and alleviating the chronic stress response and thereby may affect chronic neuroendocrine alterations. This process would allow for enhanced functioning of various components of the immune system and ultimately improved health. Thus, the disclosure process may have particular positive health benefits for conditions that are mediated through neuroendocrine or immunological processes. For traumatic stress resulting in PTSD, normalization may involve improved neuroendocrine regulation and decreases in the overactivation of the immune response, leading to positive health results.

FUTURE RESEARCH DIRECTIONS

This analysis of the effects of disclosure prompts a number of questions for further research. There is a paucity of information on the effects of psychological process variables on physiological parameters, including neuroendocrine and immune responses. Focusing on this area would seem to be a fundamental next step in understanding the effects of disclosure on health-related variables. Examining long-term as well as acute changes in physiological measures in tandem with changes in psychological process variables during disclosure will allow us to understand more minutely the interactions of psychological and physiological mechanisms in disclosure. For example, as neuroendocrine factors are hypothesized to mediate many of the effects of writing on the immune response and on health, it would be important to examine changes in tonic levels of urinary cortisol and catecholamines over the course of disclosure interventions (e.g., several weeks). In addition, examination of salivary cortisol before and after individual disclosure sessions would yield information on acute changes in cortisol levels during the disclosure process and enable more specific tracking of daily effects of disclosure on mood and neuroendocrine parameters.

Findings to date provide strong support for the ability of a writing

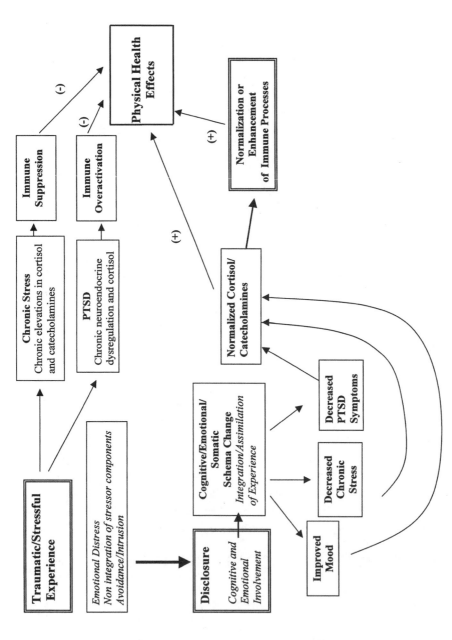

Figure 10.1. Model of psychological and physiological effects of disclosure. In the upper portion of the model, unprocessed traumatic or stressful experiences lead to chronic stress or posttraumatic stress disorder (PTSD), immune suppression or overactivation, and negative physical health effects. Alternatively, through processes such as disclosure, which may enable the integration or assimilation of traumatic and stressful experiences, chronic stress and PTSD symptoms can be decreased and mood can be improved, thereby normalizing neuroendocrine function, normalizing or enhancing immunity, and thereby promoting positive health effects. The minus (−) signs refer to proposed negative health effects and plus (+) signs refer to proposed positive health effects.

intervention to alter immune function. Petrie and colleagues' (1995) hepatitis B study provides strong evidence that the magnitude and type of immune change can be clinically relevant. In addition, the work of Smyth and colleagues (1999) with rheumatoid arthritis and asthma patients has shown clinically relevant changes in illness symptoms. However, the model that we have proposed above, linking disclosure to health outcomes via changes in immunity, has not yet been researched in its entirety. For example, does writing lead to greater resolution, which in turn leads to immune modulation, which in turn leads to improved health? This complete model must be tested in future research in a clinical population. Examination of immune and neuroendocrine effects of disclosure in clinical populations with medical conditions involving the immune system, such as rheumatoid arthritis, asthma, multiple sclerosis, or HIV, would provide further insight into physiological mechanisms underlying disclosure effects. From the research reviewed in this chapter, we would expect writing to have great health relevance for individuals with such conditions or for populations such as stressed older adults, who are vulnerable because of the interaction of life stress and age-related immune decrements.

At this point it is not clear whether disclosure interventions would be beneficial for all medical patients or only for those who have experienced highly stressful or traumatic life events. We suggest that even in the absence of other life traumas, a disclosure intervention that allows for emotional unburdening and meaning making may be expected to relieve patients' distress, increase patients' ability to cope, and reduce stress associated with the illness, thus contributing to normalization of physiological processes. However, additional life stress in the context of a disease may contribute to more profound physiological abnormalities. For example, Drossman et al. (2000) found that higher cumulative stressful life events contributed to faster progression to AIDS in a cohort of men infected with HIV. Lutgendorf et al. (1995) found that severe life stress associated with a natural disaster was followed by symptom exacerbations in chronic fatigue syndrome. Furthermore, Leserman et al. (2000) found that a history of traumatic events has been related to poorer physical status in women with a variety of gastrointestinal diseases. To the extent that stressful or traumatic life events are involved in the etiology or exacerbation of a particular physical condition, one would expect the effects of an intervention such as disclosure to be even more profound in contributing to physiological normalization and health. Future research is needed to examine the relative effects of disclosure in medical populations with and without trauma and to examine effects of psychological process elements in disclosure on physiological responses. Examination of cognitive, emotional, and experiential process factors along with physiological factors provides a useful model for understanding mechanisms underlying the effects of disclosure on health.

REFERENCES

Antoni, M. H., Creuss, D. G., Cruess, S., Lutgendorf, S., Kumar, M., Ironson, G., Klimas, N., Fletcher, M. A., & Schneiderman, N. (2000). Cognitive–behavioral stress management intervention effects on anxiety, 24-hr urinary norepinephrine output, and T-cytotoxic/suppressor cells over time among symptomatic HIV-infected gay men. *Journal of Consulting and Clinical Psychology, 68*, 31–45.

Antoni, M. H., Cruess, S., Cruess, D., Kumar, M., Lutgendorf, S., Ironson, G., Dettmer, E., Williams, J., Klimas, N., Fletcher, M. A., & Schneiderman, N. (2000). Cognitive behavioral stress management reduces distress and 24-hour urinary free cortisol among symptomatic HIV-infected gay men. *Annals of Behavioral Medicine, 22*, 29–37.

Baum, A. (1990). Stress, intrusive imagery, and chronic distress. *Health Psychology, 9*, 653–675.

Boscarino, J. A., & Chang, J. (1999). Higher abnormal leukocyte and lymphocyte counts 20 years after exposure to severe stress: Research and clinical implications. *Psychosomatic Medicine, 61*, 378–386.

Chrousos, G. P. (1992). The concepts of stress and stress system disorders. *Journal of the American Medical Association, 267*, 1244–1252.

Clark, L. (1993). Stress and the cognitive-conversational benefits of social interaction. *Journal of Social and Clinical Psychology, 12*, 25–55.

Cruess, S., Antoni, M. H., Cruess, D., Fletcher, M. A., Ironson, G., Kumar, M., Lutgendorf, S., Hayes, A., Klimas, N., & Schneiderman, N. (2000). Effects of cognitive behavioral stress management on relaxation skills, social support, neuroendocrine functioning and HSV-2 antibody titers in HIV+ gay men. *Psychosomatic Medicine, 62*, 828–837.

Drossman, D. A., Leserman, J., Li, Z., Keefe, F., Hu, Y. J., & Toomey, T. C. (2000). Effects of coping on health outcome among women with gastrointestinal disorders. *Psychosomatic Medicine, 62*, 309–317.

Esterling, B. A., Antoni, M. H., Fletcher, M. A., Margulies, S., & Schneiderman, N. (1994). Emotional disclosure through writing or speaking modulates latent Epstein–Barr virus antibody titers. *Journal of Consulting and Clinical Psychology, 62*, 130–140.

Esterling, B., Kiecolt-Glaser, J., Bodnar, J., & Glaser, R. (1994). Chronic stress, social support, and persistent alterations in the natural killer cell response to cytokines in older adults. *Health Psychology, 13*, 291–298.

Foa, E. B., & Kozak, M. J. (1986). Emotional processing of fear: Exposure to corrective information. *Psychological Bulletin, 99*, 20–35.

Freud, S. (1954). *The origins of psychoanalysis.* New York: Basic Books. (Original work published 1904)

Frueh, B. C., Turner, S. M., & Beidel, D. C. (1995). Exposure therapy for combat-related PTSD: A critical review. *Clinical Psychology Review, 15*, 799–817.

Gatti, G., Cavallo, R., Sartori, M. L., Delponte, D., Masera, R. G., Salvadori, A.,

Carignola, R., & Angelil, A. (1987). Inhibition of human natural killer cell activity by cortisol. *Journal of Steroid Biochemistry, 265,* 29–58.

Gendlin, E. T. (1984). The client's client: The edge of awareness. In R. F. Levant & J. M. Schlein (Eds.), *Client-centered therapy and the person centered approach* (pp. 76–108). New York: Praeger.

Gendlin, E. T. (1996). *Focusing-oriented psychotherapy.* New York: Guilford Press.

Glaser, R., Kiecolt-Glaser, J. K., Bonneau, R. H., Malarkey, W. S., & Hughes, J. (1992). Stress induced modulation of the immune response to recombinant hepatitis B vaccine. *Psychosomatic Medicine, 54,* 22–29.

Glaser, R., Kiecolt-Glaser, J. K., Marucha, P. T., MacCallum, R. C., Laskowski, B. F., & Malarkey, W. B. (1999). Stress-related changes in proinflammatory cytokine production in wounds. *Archives of General Psychiatry, 56,* 450–460.

Glaser, R., Pearson, G. R., Bonneau, R. H., Esterling, B. A., Atkinson, C., & Kiecolt-Glaser, J. K. (1993). Stress and the memory T-cell response to the Epstein-Barr virus in healthy medical students. *Health Psychology, 12,* 435–442.

Glaser, R., Pearson, G. R., Jones, J. F., Hillhouse, J., Kennedy, S., Mao, H.-Y., & Kiecolt-Glaser, J. (1991). Stress related activation of Epstein–Barr virus. *Brain Behavior, and Immunity, 5,* 219–232.

Greenberg, L. S., & Safran, J. D. (1987). *Emotion in psychotherapy.* New York: Guilford Press.

Heim, C., Ehlert, U., & Hellhammer, D. H. (2000). The potential role of hypocortisolism in the pathophysiology of stress-related bodily disorders. *Psychoneuroendocrinology, 25,* 1–35.

Hellstrand, K., Hermodsson, S., & Strannegard, O. (1985). Evidence for B-adrenoceptor mediated regulation of human natural killer cells. *Journal of Immunology, 134,* 4095–4099.

Herbert, T. B., & Cohen, S. (1993). Stress and immunity in humans: A meta-analytic review. *Psychosomatic Medicine, 55,* 364–379.

Horowitz, M. J. (1997). *Stress-response syndromes: PTSD, grief, and adjustment disorders* (3rd ed.). Northvale, NJ: Jason Aronson.

Ironson, G., Wynings, C., Schneiderman, N., Baum, A., Greenwood, D., Benight, C., Antoni, M., Klimas, N., & Fletcher, M. A. (1997). Posttraumatic stress symptoms, intrusive thoughts, loss, immune function after Hurricane Andrew. *Psychosomatic Medicine, 59,* 128–141.

Kiecolt-Glaser, J. K., Dura, J. R., Speicher, C. E., Trask, O. J., & Glaser, R. (1991). Spousal caregivers of dementia victims: Longitudinal changes in immunity and health. *Psychosomatic Medicine, 53,* 345–362.

Kiecolt-Glaser, J. K., Glaser, R., Gravenstein, S., Malarkey, W. S., & Sheridan, J. (1996). Chronic stress alters the immune response to influenza virus vaccine in older adults. *Proceedings of the National Academy of Sciences, 93,* 3043–3047.

Klein, M. H., Mathieu-Coglan, P. L., & Kiesler, D. J. (1986). The Experiencing

Scale. In L. S. Greenberg & W. M. Pinsof (Eds.), *The psychotherapeutic process: A research handbook* (pp. 21–71). New York: Guilford Press.

Klein, M. H., Mathieu, P. L., Gendlin, E. T., & Kiesler, D. J. (1969). *The Experiencing Scale; a research and training manual I & II.* Madison: University of Wisconsin, Extension Bureau of Audiovisual Instruction.

Lang, P. J., Levin, D. N., Miller, G. A., & Kozak, M. J. (1983). Fear imagery and the psychophysiology of emotion: The problem of affective response integration. *Journal of Abnormal Psychology, 92,* 276–306.

Laudenslager, M. L., Aasal, R., Adler, L., Berger, C. L., Montgomery, P. T., Sandberg, E., Wahlberg, L. J., Wilkins, R. T., Zweig, L., & Reite, M. L. (1998). Elevated cytotoxicity in combat veterans with long-term post-traumatic stress disorder: Preliminary observations. *Brain, Behavior, & Immunity, 12,* 74–79.

Leserman, J., Petitto, J. M., Golden, R. N., Gaynes, B. N., Gu, H., Perkins, D. O., Silva, S. G., Folds, J. D., & Evans, D. L. (2000). Impact of stressful life events, depression, social support, coping, and cortisol on progression to AIDS. *American Journal of Psychiatry, 157,* 1221–1228.

Lutgendorf, S. K., & Antoni, M. H. (1999). Emotional and cognitive processing in a disclosure paradigm. *Cognitive Therapy and Research, 23,* 423–440.

Lutgendorf, S. K., Antoni, M. H., Ironson, G., Fletcher, M. A., Penedo, F., Baum, A., Schneiderman, N., & Klimas, N. (1995). Physical symptoms of chronic fatigue syndrome are exacerbated by the stress of Hurricane Andrew. *Psychosomatic Medicine, 57,* 310–323.

Lutgendorf, S. K., Antoni, M. H., Ironson, G., Klimas, N., Kumar, M., Starr, K., McCabe, P., Cleven, K., Fletcher, M. A., & Schneiderman, N. (1997). Cognitive–behavioral stress management decreases dysphoric mood and herpes simplex virus-type 2 antibody titers in symptomatic HIV-seropositive gay men. *Journal of Consulting and Clinical Psychology, 65,* 31–43.

Lutgendorf, S. K., Antoni, M. H., Ironson, G., Starr, K., Costello, N., Zuckerman, M., Klimas, N., Fletcher, M. A., & Schneiderman, N. (1998). Changes in cognitive coping skills and social support during cognitive behavioral stress management intervention and distress outcomes in symptomatic human immunodeficiency virus (HIV)-seropositive gay men. *Psychosomatic Medicine, 60,* 204–214.

Lutgendorf, S. K., Antoni, M. H., Kumar, M., & Schneiderman, N. (1994). Changes in coping strategies predict EBV antibody titers following a stressor disclosure induction. *Journal of Psychosomatic Research, 38,* 63–78.

McEwen, B. (1998). Protective and damaging effects of stress mediators. *New England Journal of Medicine, 338,* 171–179.

Mosniam, A. D., Wolf, M. E., Maturana, P., Mosniam, G., Puente, J., Kucuk, O., & Gilman-Sachs, A. (1993). In vitro studies of natural killer cell activity in post traumatic stress disorder patients. Response to methionine-enkephalin challenge. *Immunopharmacology, 25,* 107–116.

Pennebaker, J. W. (1993). Putting stress into words: Health, linguistic, and therapeutic implications. *Behaviour Research and Therapy, 31,* 539–548.

Pennebaker, J. W., & Beall, S. K. (1986). Confronting a traumatic event: Toward an understanding of inhibition and disease. *Journal of Abnormal Psychology, 95*, 274–281.

Pennebaker, J. W., & Chew, C. H. (1985). Behavioral inhibition and electrodermal activity during deception. *Journal of Personality and Social Psychology, 49*, 1427–1433.

Pennebaker, J. W., & Hoover, C. (1986). Inhibition and cognition: Toward an understanding of trauma and disease. In R. J. Davidson, D. E. Schwartz, & D. Shapiro (Eds.), *Consciousness and self-regulation* (Vol. 4, pp. 107–136). New York: Plenum.

Pennebaker, J. W., Kiecolt-Glaser, J. K., & Glaser, R. (1988). Disclosure of traumas and immune function: Health implications for psychotherapy. *Journal of Consulting and Clinical Psychology, 56*, 239–245.

Pennebaker, J. W., Mayne, T. J., & Francis, M. E. (1997). Linguistic predictors of adaptive bereavement. *Journal of Personality and Social Psychology, 72*, 863–871.

Pennebaker, J. W., & Susman, J. R. (1988). Disclosure of traumas and psychosomatic processes. *Social Science and Medicine, 26*, 327–332.

Petrie, K. J., Booth, R. J., Pennebaker, J. W., Davison, K. P., & Thomas, M. G. (1995). Disclosure of trauma and immune response to a hepatitis B vaccination program. *Journal of Consulting and Clinical Psychology, 63*, 787–792.

Remen, R. N. (1996). *Kitchen table wisdom: Stories that heal.* New York: Riverhead Press.

Rice, L. N. (1974). The evocative function of the therapist. In D. A. Wexler & L. N. Rice (Eds.), *Innovations in client-centered therapy* (pp. 289–312). New York: Wiley.

Rice, L. N., & Greenberg, L. S. (1984). *Patterns of change.* New York: Guilford Press.

Safran, J. D., & Greenberg, L. S. (1991). Affective change processes: A synthesis and critical analysis. In J. D. Safran & L. S. Greenberg (Eds.), *Emotion, psychotherapy & change* (pp. 339–362). New York: Guilford Press.

Smyth, J. M. (1998). Written emotional expression: Effect sizes, outcome types, and moderating variables. *Journal of Consulting and Clinical Psychology, 66*, 174–184.

Smyth, J., Stone, A., Hurewitz, A., & Kaell, A. (1999). Writing about stressful events produces symptom reduction in asthmatics and rheumatoid arthritics: A randomized clinical trial. *Journal of the American Medical Association, 281*, 1304–1309.

Sternberg, A. M. (1992). The stress response and the regulation of inflammatory disease. *Annals of Internal Medicine, 117*, 854–866.

Stiles, W. B. (1987). "I have to talk to somebody." A fever model of disclosure. In V. J. Derlega & J. H. Berg (Eds.), *Self-disclosure: Theory, research, and therapy* (pp. 257–282). New York: Plenum Press.

Tosato, G. (1987). The Epstein–Barr virus and the immune system. *Advances in Cancer Research, 49,* 77–125.

Ullrich, P. M., & Lutgendorf, S. K. (in press). Journaling about stressful events: Effects of cognitive processing and emotional expression. *Annals of Behavioral Medicine.*

van der Kolk, B. A. (1997). The psychobiology of posttraumatic stress disorder. *Journal of Clinical Psychiatry, 58*(Suppl. 9), 16–24.

van der Kolk, B. A., Burbridge, J. A., & Suzuki, J. (1997). The psychobiology of traumatic memory. Clinical implications of neuroimaging studies. *Annals of the New York Academy of Sciences, 821,* 99–113.

van der Kolk, B. A., & van der Hart, O. (1991). The intrusive past: The flexibility of memory and the engraving of trauma. *American Imago, 48,* 425–454.

Watson, P. B., Muller, H. K., Jones, I. H., & Bradley, A. J. (1993). Cell-mediated immunity in combat veterans with post-traumatic stress disorder. *The Medical Journal of Australia, 159,* 513–516.

Wexler, D. A. (1974). A cognitive theory of experiencing, self-actualization, and therapeutic process. In D. A. Wexler & L. N. Rice (Eds.), *Innovations in client-centered therapy* (pp. 49–116). New York: Wiley.

Wilson, S. N., van der Kolk, B., Burbridge, J., Fisler, R., & Kradin, R. (1999). Phenotype of blood lymphocytes in PTSD suggests chronic immune activation. *Psychosomatics, 40,* 222–225.

Yehuda, R., Giller, E. L., Southwick, S. M., Lowy, M. T., & Mason, J. W. (1991). Hypothalamic–pituitary–adrenal dysfunction in posttraumatic stress disorder. *Biological Psychiatry, 30,* 1031–1048.

IV

NEW DIRECTIONS IN CLINICAL APPLICATIONS OF EXPRESSIVE WRITING

11

TRANSLATING RESEARCH INTO PRACTICE: POTENTIAL OF EXPRESSIVE WRITING IN THE FIELD

JOSHUA M. SMYTH AND DELWYN CATLEY

> "Research for the Real World: Big money is being pumped into effectiveness research. Will it change practice?"
>
> —APA Monitor, July/August 2000

The quote cited above, a headline taken from an *APA Monitor* article, reflects the new emphasis of the National Institutes of Health on the value of moving beyond establishing treatment efficacy to demonstrating its effectiveness in clinical practice. Recent work has demonstrated that, in the context of a controlled, clinical trial, focused expressive writing about stressful life events can lead to a variety of health improvements in both healthy and ill individuals (Smyth, 1998; Smyth & Pennebaker, 1999). In this chapter, we examine the goal of translating the writing intervention, previously shown to be efficacious, into an effective supplemental treatment in the context of medical or psychological care.

One major obstacle is the difference between controlled, experimental research (efficacy) and the reality of clinical application (effectiveness). Although efficacy studies are necessary to establish causal links and specific treatment benefits, they often do so at the cost of external validity (the ability to infer that a presumed causal relationship can be generalized to different types of persons and settings). For example, in a trial of a written disclosure intervention, certain characteristics of the participants included may be limited (e.g., restricted age or disease severity). It remains likely, then, that intervention—although effective in randomized trial—will not work as successfully for diverse practitioners operating under the constraints of clinical practice with diverse populations. The demonstration that treatment results generalize to a clinical population must be reexamined. This step of translating scientific findings to practical clinical applications is imperative if new treatments are to be implemented on a wide ' scale. In this chapter we discuss the process, obstacles, and guidelines for translating this written disclosure task into supplemental treatment.

EFFICACY AND EFFECTIVENESS

We use the term *efficacy* in the context of evaluating the effects of a novel treatment. In most cases, the designation of a treatment as efficacious follows a regulatory model based on the requirements of the Food and Drug Administration's guidelines to approve a drug or a medical device (Norquist, Lebowitz, & Hyman, 2000). Under this model, a treatment is efficacious if it is demonstrated in the context of a randomized controlled trial (RCT) to have specific beneficial effects that cannot be explained by alternative causal explanations, such as the passage of time, the effects of psychological assessment, or the presence of different types of clients in the various treatment conditions (Chambless & Hollon, 1998). The construct of treatment efficacy, then, is conceptually close to the construct of internal validity (our confidence that an observed relationship between two variables is causal; Cook & Campbell, 1979). The higher the internal validity of an RCT demonstrating treatment effects, the greater our confidence in the efficacy of the treatment (American Psychological Association [APA] Task Force, 1995). Several types of RCTs have been used to support clinical efficacy; some are designed to demonstrate that a novel treatment is superior to no treatment, nonspecific therapy, or alternative therapy (Chambless & Hollon, 1998).

In contrast to this demonstration of clinical efficacy through high standards of internal validity, the question of effectiveness must be evaluated by different means. The question is this: Is the treatment effective when administered under real world constraints? The evaluation of treatment effectiveness is based on issues of generalizability, that is, the degree to which efficacy observed in the "laboratory" (RCT) generalizes to the clinical setting. This issue of generalizability is perhaps best captured by the concept of external validity (e.g., Cook & Campbell, 1979) and can be represented by issues such as the treatment generalizing to new patients and new contexts, treatment feasibility in terms of implementation and acceptance, and evaluation of costs and benefits (APA Task Force, 1995). There are reasons to believe that, at least under some circumstances, results observed in RCTs may not be applicable to actual clinical work. (These issues are explored in some depth below.) There is also another concern, namely, that RCTs may not adequately represent the actual variability observed in clinical practice or may include participants who, in the absence of recruitment efforts, would not have been referred to treatment or even sought treatment. In addition, specific controls inherent to RCTs (e.g., randomization) may not reflect the reality of clinical contact (Seligman, 1995). For these and other reasons it can be argued that treatment effectiveness may be judged using methods other than RCTs. Specifically, quasi-experimental and nonexperimental designs may provide insight into the degree to which treatment effects generalize across patients, treatment modalities, clinic settings, and so forth (Cook & Campbell, 1979).

GENERALIZATION FROM THE LABORATORY TO THE FIELD

As noted above, the results from RCTs may not generalize to the actual practice of clinical care. Care must be taken, however, that we do not assume that the dimensions of efficacy and effectiveness, or internal and external validity, are inexorably at odds with one another. Some RCTs are conducted with high external validity and some non-experimental or quasi-experimental studies with low external (and internal) validity. The point to be made is merely that, with adequate care taken in experimental design, experimentally rigorous research may be undertaken without sacrificing external validity (Chambless & Hollon, 1998). Often, however, much more attention is paid to ensuring adequate internal validity than to maximizing external validity within the constraints of the research paradigm. As a result, the research produces a very strong test of treatment efficacy with more limited external validity. A variety of issues relevant to the evaluation of treatment effectiveness (external validity) were raised by the APA Task Force (1995) and included issues of generalizability, feasibility, and cost–benefit analysis. These are discussed below. (The interested reader is referred to Chambless and Hollon, 1998, for a discussion of defining empirically supported therapies and concerns over effectiveness. They provide an excellent discussion of the issues raised in this chapter and offer instances where RCTs have overcome many of the limitations described herein.)

TREATMENT GENERALIZABILITY

Patient Characteristics

One important issue of treatment generalizability revolves around the selection of experimental participants. Characteristics of patients in the context of a randomized trial may differ from those of patients seen in clinical care settings. One reason for this difference is that, to the degree that RCTs use strict participant inclusion criteria, a highly homogenous sample that differs from the rich variety of patients seen in the clinic can result (although there are strong arguments for the utility of such practices; Kendall & Lipman, 1991). If the patients enrolled in RCTs are highly dissimilar from those seen in clinical care, treatment may not be as effective when implemented in the clinic. For example, an RCT may demonstrate efficacy in research participants who are selected to be highly similar on one dimension (e.g., hostility) but are limited as to the presence of co-morbid psychological (e.g., depression) or medical conditions (e.g., cardiovascular disease) and are often excluded if receiving other treatments (e.g., cognitive behavior therapy). Patient characteristics may also be limited as a result of the selection process (e.g., student subject pool at a university, community volunteers recruited through advertisements), the location and extent of the recruitment area (e.g., geographic area, cultural and racial diversity), and numerous other factors specific to a particular research endeavor. Patients seen in the clinic, however, are often not limited on these dimensions; they commonly have comorbid conditions; they frequently are already receiving other treatments (either "formally" or attempts at self management through supplemental or alternative means); and they are heterogeneous in terms of factors such as age, culture, and gender. In contrast, clinic patients may be more homogeneous in other factors, such as socioeconomic status, treatment options, and treatment preference.

Despite the growing body of research supporting the efficacy of structured writing assignments, it is important to evaluate whether such efficacy support is based on fairly homogenous samples of participants that would lessen our confidence in the generalizability (external validity) of extant results. Previous studies have certainly differed on the nature of participants they have enrolled. Although many studies have included exclusively student participants (e.g., Greenberg & Stone, 1992; Pennebaker & Beall, 1986), a great many have used nonstudent samples. Francis and Pennebaker (1992) found a reduction in absentee rates relative to controls for university employees writing about upsetting experiences. Spera, Buhrfeind, and Pennebaker (1994) found that recently unemployed professionals assigned to write about their job loss were reemployed more quickly than those who wrote about nontraumatic topics. Richards, Beal, Segal, and Pennebaker (2000) found that among maximum security prison inmates, those assigned to write about past traumas showed a drop in illness visits after writing compared to those assigned to write about neutral topics. Smyth, Stone, Hurewitz, and Kaell (1999) examined patients with one of two chronic physical illnesses, asthma or rheumatoid arthritis, and found improved health after writing, relative to participants with chronic illness writing about neutral topics.

Writing about stressful events has also been shown to be efficacious in groups of varying education, in several languages, and in several countries and cultures. As noted above, structured writing about stressful events has produced similar benefits for senior professionals with advanced educational degrees, university students, and maximum-security prisoners with little formal education. Differences among college students' ethnicity or native language have not been related to outcomes. Additionally, writing interventions have consistently produced positive results among French-speaking Belgians (Rimé, 1995), Spanish-speaking residents of Mexico City (Dominguez et al., 1995), multiple samples of adults and students in The Netherlands (Schoutrop, Lange, Brosschot, & Everaerd, 1996), and medical students in New Zealand (Petrie, Booth, Pennebaker, Davison, & Thomas, 1995). The generalizability of writing does not seem to be related to participant characteristics such as age, culture, or education. However, other features common to nearly all research participants may limit the generalizability of research findings to actual clinical practice.

By way of example, we can review our recent study examining the efficacy of focused expressive writing in patients with chronic physical illness (asthma or rheumatoid arthritis; Smyth et al., 1999). Patients were selected on the basis of their illness and a willingness to participate as well as a variety of exclusion criteria (e.g., the absence of psychiatric disorders). In this sample, writing was shown to be efficacious in reducing physician assessed disease severity (Smyth et al., 1999).

There are several factors that may limit the external validity of this, and nearly all, efficacy studies. Perhaps most important is the self-selection of participants into the study. To the best of our knowledge, all participants in all published studies themselves elected to participate in the research both in response to some advertisement (e.g., a class announcement for students, a newspaper advertisement for community studies) and after completing an informed consent form. Although it is not possible to know exactly the characteristics of individuals who elect not to participate, it is not unreasonable to assume that, for one or more reasons, they are less interested or amenable to the processes involved in the structured writing task. Such factors include, but are not limited to, less interest in research, less confidence that psychological intervention may be helpful for them, less comfort or interest in a process that involves the expression of thoughts and feelings, and less time or energy to participate in a fairly demanding protocol (that typically includes visits to offices or laboratories over several consecutive days). It is, unfortunately, not possible to know the extent to which the "opportunity costs" of such factors skew the results. That is, we simply do not know how many people never respond to our recruitment strategies at all, although it is possible that the numbers are high.

We have examined the related issue of participant loss in our study of asthma and rheumatoid arthritis patients (Smyth et al., 1999). These data suggest that, even after we have "lost" an unspecified number of potential participants, 20–30% of eligible participants do not participate after receiving more information about the process and requirements of the study. In the Smyth and colleagues (1999) study, this concern was mitigated somewhat because individuals who were not eligible or not interested did not differ statistically from participants on any demographic measures assessed (age, gender, number of children, education, employment status, income). Nonetheless, we cannot predict confidently that the nonparticipants—if provided the opportunity to complete the focused expressive writing task—would benefit similarly to those who elected to participate in our study.

Care must be taken, however, not to extend this concern too far. In theory, this argument can be made against any treatment (psychological or otherwise), and many of the factors that lead people to decline participation in a study offering a certain treatment are likely to lead people to decline that treatment in the "real world." Moreover, although there may be reduced treatment effectiveness if the treatment were "prescribed" in a relatively widespread fashion (such that it included those patients who would not normally elect to have the treatment), the value of such interventions should be evaluated from a more public health or preventive model (a point we return to when discussing the costs and benefits of structured writing exercises).

In addition to the unspecified number of people electing not to participate in our research, we exclude a number based on (often study-specific) criteria designed to increase internal validity. Smyth and colleagues used three conditions to exclude interested participants: (a) an ongoing defined psychiatric disorder or ongoing psychotherapy, (b) certain prescription drugs (such as mood altering medication), and (c) inability to comply with the protocol, including being unable to write for 20 minutes or being unable to attend the required writing sessions in our offices. We have already touched on the issue of comorbidity and concurrent treatment and merely note here that such requirements make our participant sample different from those individuals who might be in nonstudy settings (e.g., those in a clinic already receiving individual or group therapy). This also distinguishes the results obtained in this trial (and many other efficacy trials using a similar criterion) from the potential effectiveness of writing exercises as a supplemental treatment to ongoing therapy or other treatments. A further point is that, for the most part, efficacy studies have not been conducted on individuals selected for extreme trauma, based either on objective parameters (e.g., verified abuse history) or on subjective parameters (e.g., posttraumatic symptoms). Although some existing work suggests that, in fact, severely traumatized individuals can benefit from structured writing tasks (e.g., chapter 12, this volume), this important issue bears further research consideration.

In the interest of internal validity, Smyth and colleagues excluded interested individuals who were on mood-altering medication. As discussed throughout this volume, the specific mechanisms of change underlying the health benefits of writing are still the focus of debate. It seems clear, however, that all of these theories involve emotion and cognition to a degree. If characteristics of participants limited their ability to experience, express, or process emotions and cognitions, such factors might limit the generalizability of results. In addition to the use of mood-altering medications, such factors might include affective or cognitive psychopathology, certain coping strategies (e.g., denial or disengagement), or alexithymia, just to name a few. (For a more complete discussion of this issue, see chapter 5, this volume.) If structured writing exercises were evaluated in a broader context without these requirements, as would be the case in effectiveness trials, it is possible that individuals with affective and cognitive deficiencies or those on affective or cognitive medication would be included. (This dovetails with the issue of comorbidity raised above, e.g., in the case of an individual with major depression on antidepressant medication.) To the degree that such factors impeded the underlying mechanism (e.g., emotional and cognitive processing, self-regulation), the effectiveness of the structured writing tasks would be lower than previously shown in the efficacy studies. Although plausible, it should be noted that these outcomes are still speculative and will no doubt be evaluated in future research. In addition, it is also possible that stronger treatment effects could be obtained by including some of the participants who have been excluded. For example, those on mood-altering medications may be more likely to have histories of trauma and may receive particular benefit from the writing treatment, or writing may positively (synergistically) interact with other treatments (psychological, pharmacological, or others; see chapter 14, this volume).

In efficacy studies, researchers often apply a broader exclusion category, one that is based on the ability to complete all experimental tasks. Although this requirement also is designed to maximize internal validity (and minimize compliance concerns and missing data), it may further homogenize participants in several important ways. One factor, perhaps already encompassed in the self-selection processes discussed above, is having the available time and resources necessary for participation. In most studies, individuals must be able to travel to research offices or laboratory space and write for 20–30 minutes, often for several days. This requirement may disallow the participation of an otherwise interested and eligible individual. For example, someone who has certain professional or social obligations that make the time required prohibitive (e.g., full-time employment, caregiving responsibilities), or someone who does not have transportation options (which may in turn co-vary with other factors such as income). Another, sometimes implicit, requirement is that the participants should be literate. Certainly one cannot participate in a writing task if one is unable to read or write (and probably would not be meaningfully exposed to recruitment efforts in the first place). This may place a boundary condition on the effectiveness of structured writing as an intervention if applied to individuals who are illiterate or barely literate in English. Some options for overcoming this limitation are available. Certainly it is possible to have individuals speak if they cannot write (perhaps into a tape recorder; Kelley, Lumley, & Liesen, 1997), or to have participants who are literate in another language write in their native tongue. This raises concerns, open to future investigation, about the continued efficacy of treatments evaluated in one modality (writing) being administered in another (e.g., speaking). Another interesting direction for future work would be to examine the relative benefit of writing tasks conducted in participants' native language versus writing in a second tongue. For those individuals for whom expressing themselves in language (written, spoken, or otherwise) is not possible, this intervention might never be appropriate or effective.

Characteristics of the Therapist and Therapy Setting

It has been argued (e.g., Chambless & Hollon, 1998) that RCTs of psychological treatments may produce more robust results and provide evidence for treatment efficacy, in part because therapists who conduct trials receive extensive training. Such training is typically not available to (or desired by) therapists outside of the RCT. A further argument is made that the degree of control (i.e., lack of flexibility or responsiveness to individual client presentation) in the provision of treatment in RCTs may make treatment more or less effective (although it has been noted that the effect of such control on treatment effectiveness is unclear; Chambless & Hollon, 1998). Furthermore, the highly formalized and legitimate context in which most RCTs are conducted (e.g., university or hospital setting, highly trained research staff, professionally prepared materials) may differ from therapy provided in a more typical therapy environment or conducted in individuals' natural environments (e.g., self-administered manuals completed in the home).

The relatively unique nature of the focused expressive writing task makes evaluation of these concerns quite different from discussions of other psychological treatments. For instance, therapists do not directly administer the structured writing exercises, rendering questions about therapist expertise less relevant (however, see chapters 12 and 13, this volume). The concept of control also is somewhat different in this context. Although the majority of efficacy studies on focused expressive writing exercises have been conducted using a fairly standard set of instructions (and thus a standard, i.e., highly controlled, intervention), recent work has begun to explore the efficacy of alternative instructions (and thus, a variant intervention; see chapters 3, 7, and 14, this volume; Smyth, True, & Souto, 2001). However, to our knowledge no research has examined giving the investigator–clinician the opportunity to alter the instruction set given to participants–clients in reaction to individual response to writing. Lange and colleagues (chapter 12, this volume), however, are exploring the process of providing individualized feedback to study participants writing over the Internet. This and other exciting avenues of study are critical to evaluating the parameters of treatment effectiveness. We are not aware of any published work that explicitly allows the individual to alter the instructions over the course of writing. Clearly, the volume of the writing output, the content, and the nature and style of the writing differ dramatically among research participants. This suggests that, in addition to reflecting a variety of individual differences, some degree of tailoring of the writing intervention may be taking place.

One final issue for this section is the nature of the setting in which the writing takes place. The great majority of efficacy trials, particularly those with robust effects (see Smyth, 1998), take place in the highly formalized research settings of universities or medical centers, although some studies are reporting success in locations such as the home (Lepore & Greenberg, in press) and over the Internet (chapter 12, this volume). Nevertheless, some aspects of the environment may have (perhaps unintended) consequences on research participants. For example, the "legitimate authority" engendered by the research environment (and potentially the researcher as well) may alter the research participants' behavior (cf. Milgram, 1965). Such alterations may include (among others) careful attention to instructions, improved compliance, and an increased sense of value in the structured writing exercises. Although the random assignment of participants to experimental conditions rules out a pure (main) effect of environment or location, we cannot confidently rule out an interaction between experimental condition (i.e., writing about stressful or traumatic events) and environment (research–medical setting). In the next section we discuss the consequences of having individuals complete writing exercises on their own, perhaps in their own homes.

FEASIBILITY

Feasibility refers to the degree or extent to which a treatment can actually be delivered to patients. This encompasses issues such as the location of treatment (e.g., home or clinic), patient willingness to engage in treatment (acceptability), compliance with treatment, and ease of the administration and dissemination of the treatment (APA Task Force, 1995).

Patient Acceptability and Compliance

Patients may not desire a particular treatment, even if it has been shown to be efficacious, for a variety of reasons—cost or inconvenience, fear of adverse reactions to the treatment, and social stigma or other repercussions. In general, across the many published studies available, participants are willing to engage in structured writing exercises and report the experience to be valuable. As we have previously discussed, however, such studies are based on a group who chose to participate in research studies. Furthermore, research participants often are given incentives to participate, in addition to the potential benefit of the writing intervention. For instance, student participants typically receive course extra credit whereas community participants often receive financial remuneration (e.g., $50 for completion of study; Smyth et al., 1999).

It is difficult to predict the response of nonparticipants exposed to this potential treatment. The compensation usually given to research participants may provide an incentive that, if not present, would greatly reduce the acceptability of the treatment to the patient. On the other hand, patients in clinics or primary care facilities may have greater dysfunction at baseline, increasing the allure of potential treatment. This issue is further complicated by the location and logistic requirements of the treatment. Namely, if (as is commonly the case in research studies) patients had to come to a central location (e.g., clinic) on several consecutive days to write, they probably would find the treatment less acceptable. The more convenient alternative, writing on one's own (e.g., using structured manuals, over the Internet), raises the aforementioned issues that the treatment may not prove as effective outside of the "legitimate" environment of a research or medical facility.

A second issue revolves around concerns for side effects or adverse reactions to treatment. It is completely understandable that patients may not want to "open up a can of worms" by writing about past stressful or traumatic events. Such concerns are supported by data suggesting that the (typical) instructions to write about a stressful or traumatic event do, in fact, reliably produce increases in distress (Smyth, 1998). However, such concerns can be overcome. First, the short-term distress evoked by writing does not appear to persist for any length of time (e.g., Stone, Smyth, Kaell, & Hurewitz, 2000). In fact, such distress may dissipate over a matter of hours (Hockemeyer, Smyth, Anderson, & Stone, 1999). Second, recent alterations of the standard instructions have yielded promising results that health and well-being benefits might be achieved without the short-term distress typically observed (see, e.g., chapter 7, this volume). These two lines of evidence suggest that structured writing exercises may readily be adapted for use without extreme concern for patient distress. Of course, when dealing with individuals in great distress (e.g., severely depressed or suicidal), the appropriateness of the intervention should be carefully considered and, as with any intervention, the individual should be carefully monitored. One final issue is the potential for social stigma or other social repercussions. Available data suggest that many people who may desire to discuss traumatic events with others experience social constraints that force them not to disclose (which in turn places them at greater risk of adverse outcomes; e.g., Lepore, Silver, Wortman, & Wayment, 1996; Pennebaker & Harber, 1993). Structured writing exercises may, in circumstances where interpersonal expression is not feasible, provide an avenue of expression that removes the risk of negative social responses. Additionally, if the exercise is presented in a format that can take place outside of the traditional treatment facilities (e.g., psychological clinic), the risk of social stigma (e.g., being labeled as having a psychological problem) is greatly reduced. Although there is currently very little data to evaluate these issues, some preliminary data presented in the chapter by Lange and colleagues (chapter 12, this volume) suggest that structured writing may be well received by patients. Lange and colleagues report that the majority of their research participants preferred anonymous writing exercises conducted over the Internet to face-to-face therapy. In summary, considerable evidence indicates that writing would be an acceptable, and perhaps desirable, mode of treatment when considering social repercussions.

Dissemination

Concerns about ease of dissemination typically revolve around a number of issues (APA Task Force, 1995) that, for the most part, are not relevant to the structured writing intervention. This is particularly true if developed and administered in self-guided formats, such as over the Internet or in a manual. Such concerns include the number of competent clinicians–practitioners, requirements for training, and the opportunities for training. Other issues are more relevant but, generally speaking, are assets to effective dissemination of structured writing exercises as an intervention. (We return to some of these when discussing the costs and benefits of structured writing exercises.) There are no requirements for costly equipment or technology, and the need for additional support personnel is minimal. In fact, structured writing tasks could easily be integrated as a supplemental treatment into existing care settings (psychological or medical), with little additional burden on the human resource infrastructure. In general, there appear to be few barriers to easy dissemination of structured writing exercises as a supplemental treatment.

COSTS AND BENEFITS

Rising health care costs in the United States have prompted a search for ways to reduce costs. Recommendations can be divided into two broad categories: those that address the supply of health care such as improving the efficiency of treatment and services and those that address the demand for services. Expressive writing interventions may offer opportunities in both categories. With regard to reducing the demand for services, Friedman, Sobel, Myers, Caudill, and Benson (1995) have pointed out that various psychosocial factors influence the medical utilization costs. For example, psychological stress can exacerbate or be involved in the etiology of illness, whereas lack of recognition of underlying psychological problems can lead to recurrent ineffective treatment. Although there is often a need to demonstrate that psychological treatments can offset costs for physical health care, expressive writing studies have been focused on health-care utilization reductions as the primary outcome. The wealth of efficacy data clearly indicates the potential value of this treatment for reducing the demand for services.

With regard to efficiency, it is imperative that the treatment be delivered without the cost of delivery outweighing the benefits in reduced health-care utilization. Expressive writing can be implemented in a variety of ways, with different cost-benefit implications. For example, in the traditional psychotherapy model writing could be a component of treatment delivered by professionals who guide patients with a history of trauma in its implementation; in the public health prevention model, writing could be implemented at the community level to as broad a population as possible.

Although focused expressive writing does not require the involvement of expert therapists, there are advantages to individualized therapy approaches, including the ability to tailor treatment to individual needs, monitor compliance, and address implementation problems. In clinical settings where patients are more likely to present with comorbid and severe psychiatric conditions, these may be important considerations. Nevertheless, it is clear that such an approach is relatively cost inefficient in that face-to-face provision of treatment dramatically limits the number of individuals that can receive treatment from a given source (e.g., a psychologist, a physician; see chapter 13, this volume).

Although other modes of delivery may be more efficient, the use of expressive writing in traditional clinical settings as a supplement to existing treatment could yield cost savings in a variety of areas. An efficient intervention is one that can produce the same results at lesser costs. Given interventions that produce the same results, the intervention that requires a fewer number of sessions, uses para-professionals over professionals, or can take place on an outpatient basis is more efficient. Using expressive writing, it may be possible to treat greater numbers of individuals with fewer sessions and on an outpatient basis (L'Abate, 1999). Expressive writing may also be especially suitable for group therapy, which is more cost-effective than individual therapy.

The greatest cost efficiencies, however, should be realized by moving beyond individual level interventions to community level interventions.

Community level interventions can have a greater impact through a greater reach. Cost savings are realized by efficiencies obtained through reaching a higher number of people relative to the number of health professionals required (Jeffery, Folsom, Leupker, Jacobs, Gillum, Taylor, et al., 1984; Sallis, Flora, Fortmann, Taylor, & Maccoby, 1985). These advantages have to be weighed against a potential loss of intensity of the intervention when implemented on a wide scale (Puska, Wijo, McAlister, Koskela, Smolander, Pekkola, et al., 1985). Because the expressive writing intervention can be self-administered at virtually no cost, it lends itself to a community level implementation. The simplicity and demonstrated efficacy of the intervention with large nonclinical cohorts (e.g., students) also suggest that efficacy loss may be limited when it is implemented at a community level.

FUTURE DIRECTIONS

Effectiveness Studies

We have noted several features of the writing intervention that may limit its generalizability to clinical settings. Future work clearly must examine structured writing in the context of effectiveness studies—most obviously conducting research in clinical settings with fully representative samples of patients. Comorbid conditions, age, drug use, and other patient characteristics—rather than excluding participants from the research—are specifically evaluated for their impact on treatment efficacy. A number of challenges, however, must be addressed when conducting quality effectiveness studies. For instance, it is a considerable challenge to maximize internal validity while expanding outcome research designs to include effectiveness issues (Clarke, 1995). Evaluation of effectiveness may have to be conducted at multiple levels and require consideration of organizational factors as well (Klein & Smith, 1999). For example, the results of a single, well-conducted effectiveness study may themselves not generalize (e.g., results from an urban clinic may not generalize to a rural one; Klein & Smith, 1999), requiring multisite effectiveness trials. Despite such challenges, however, effectiveness research in the near future has tremendous potential.

Community-Level Interventions

Efficacy studies have demonstrated the viability of the intervention with university students and community volunteers. More research, however, is needed to address ways in which the intervention could be disseminated and implemented outside the context of compensation for participation in research studies. Public health frameworks and models such as diffusion of innovations, social marketing, and communication theory may be valuable in the development of community level interventions (e.g., Glanz, Lewis, & Rimer, 1997; Winett, 1995). Appropriate points of intervention (e.g., work sites, schools) and effective modes of reaching people and delivering the intervention (e.g., through media programs, self-help materials, Web sites) must be identified.

SUMMARY

The issues reviewed in this chapter suggest that, although the efficacy of structured writing exercises has been substantiated, there remain areas of concern about generalization to treatment effectiveness. Such concerns can be remedied by thoughtful examination of existing research and through carefully designed effectiveness studies. Evidence exists that structured writing exercises can readily be adapted to an effective supplemental treatment. In particular, approaches to deliver structured writing exercises that adopt a public-health and preventive orientation, particularly when informed by future effectiveness studies, have tremendous potential to promote health, prevent or reduce disease, and improve psychological well-being.

REFERENCES

American Psychological Association Task Force on Psychological Intervention Guidelines. (1995). *Template for developing guidelines: Interventions for mental disorders and psychological aspects of physical disorders*. Washington, DC: American Psychological Association.

Chambless, D., & Hollon, S. (1998). Defining empirically supported therapies. *Journal of Consulting and Clinical Psychology, 66,* 7–18.

Clarke, G. (1995). Improving the transition from basic efficacy research to effectiveness studies: Methodological issues and procedures. *Journal of Consulting and Clinical Psychology, 63,* 718–725.

Cook, T., & Campbell, D. (1979). *Quasi-experimentation: Design and analysis issues for field settings*. Boston: Houghton Mifflin.

Dominguez, B., Valderrama, P., Meza, M. A., Perez, S. L., Silva, A., Martinez, G., Mendez, V. M., & Olvera, Y. (1995). The roles of emotional reversal and disclosure in clinical practice. In J. W. Pennebaker (Ed.), *Emotion, disclosure, and health* (pp. 255–270). Washington, DC: American Psychological Association.

Francis, M. E., & Pennebaker, J. W. (1992). Putting stress into words: Writing about personal upheavals and health. *American Journal of Health Promotion, 6,* 280–287.

Friedman, R., Sobel, D., Myers, P., Caudill, M., & Benson, H. (1995). Behavioral medicine, clinical health psychology, and cost offset. *Health Psychology, 14,* 509–518.

Glanz, K., Lewis, F. M., & Rimer, B. K. (1997). *Health behavior and health education: Theory, research, and practice* (2nd ed.). San Francisco: Jossey-Bass.

Greenberg, M. A., & Stone, A. A. (1992). Emotional disclosure about traumas and its relation to health: Effects of previous disclosure and trauma severity. *Journal of Personality and Social Psychology, 63,* 75–84.

Hockemeyer, J., Smyth, J., Anderson, C., & Stone, A. (1999). Is it safe to write? Evaluating the short-term distress produced by writing about emotionally traumatic experiences [Abstract]. *Psychosomatic Medicine, 61,* 99.

Jeffery, R. W., Folsom, A. R., Leupker, R.V., Jacobs, D. R., Jr., Gillum, R. F., Taylor, H. L., et al. (1984). Prevalence of overweight and weight loss behavior in a metropolitan adult population: The Minnesota Heart Survey experience. *American Journal of Public Health, 74,* 349–357.

Kelley, J. E., Lumley, M. A., & Leisen, J. C. (1997). Health effects of emotional disclosure in rheumatoid arthritis patients. *Health Psychology, 16,* 331–340.

Kendall, P., & Lipman, A. (1991). Psychological and pharmacological therapy: Methods and modes for comparative outcome research. *Journal of Consulting and Clinical Psychology, 59,* 78–87.

Klein, D., & Smith, L. (1999). Organization requirements for effective clinical effectiveness studies. *Prevention and Treatment, 2,* Article 0002a. Retrieved August, 5, 2001, from http://journals.apa.org/prevention.

L'Abate, L. (1999). Taking the bull by the horns: Beyond words in psychological interventions. *The Family Journal: Counseling and Therapy With Couples and Families, 7,* 6–20.

Lepore, S. J., & Greenberg, M. A. (in press). Mending broken hearts: Effects of expressive writing on mood, cognitive processing, social adjustment, and health following a relationship breakup. *Psychology and Health.*

Lepore, S. J., Silver, R. C., Wortman, C. B., & Wayment, H. A. (1996). Social constraints, intrusive thoughts, and depressive symptoms among bereaved mothers. *Journal of Personality and Social Psychology, 70,* 271–282.

Milgram, S. (1965). Some conditions of obedience and disobedience to authority. *Human Relations, 18,* 57–76.

Norquist, G., Lebowitz, B., & Hyman, S. (2000). Expanding the frontier of treatment research. *Prevention and Treatment, 2,* Article 0001a. Retrieved August, 5, 2001, from http://journals.apa.org/prevention.

Pennebaker, J. W., & Beall, S. K. (1986). Confronting a traumatic event: Toward an understanding of inhibition and disease. *Journal of Abnormal Psychology, 95,* 274–281.

Pennebaker, J. W., & Harber, K. (1993). A social stage model of collective coping: The Loma Prieta earthquake and the Persian Gulf War. *Journal of Social Issues, 49*(4), 125–146.

Petrie, K. J., Booth, R., Pennebaker, J. W., Davison, K. P., & Thomas, M. (1995).

Disclosure of trauma and immune response to Hepatitis B vaccination program. *Journal of Consulting and Clinical Psychology, 63,* 787–792.

Puska, P., Wijo, J., McAlister, A., Koskela, K., Smolander, A., Pekkola, J., et al. (1985). Planned use of mass media in national health promotion: The "Keys to Health" TV program in 1982 in Finland. *Canadian Journal of Public Health, 76,* 336–342.

Richards, J. M., Beal, W. E., Seagal, J., & Pennebaker, J. W. (2000). The effects of disclosure of traumatic events on illness behavior among psychiatric prison inmates. *Journal of Abnormal Psychology, 109,* 156–160.

Rimé, B. (1995). Mental rumination, social sharing, and the recovery from emotional exposure. In J. W. Pennebaker (Ed.), *Emotion, disclosure, and health* (pp. 271–292). Washington, DC: American Psychological Association.

Sallis, J. F., Flora, J. A., Fortmann, S. P., Taylor, C. B., & Maccoby, N. (1985). Mediated smoking cessation programs in the Stanford Five-City Project. *Addictive Behaviors, 10,* 441–443.

Schoutrop, M., Lange, A., Brosschot, J., & Everaerd, W. (1996, June). *The effects of writing assignments on reprocessing traumatic events: Three experimental studies.* Paper presented at The (Non) Expression of Emotions and Health and Disease Conference, Tilburg, The Netherlands.

Seligman, M. (1995). The effectiveness of psychotherapy: The *Consumer Reports* study. *American Psychologist, 50,* 965–974.

Smyth, J. (1998). Written emotional expression: Effect size, outcome types, and moderating variables. *Journal of Consulting and Clinical Psychology, 66,* 174–184.

Smyth, J., & Pennebaker, J. (1999). Sharing one's story: Translating emotional experiences into words as a coping tool. In C. R. Snyder (Ed.), *Coping: The psychology of what works* (pp. 70–89). New York: Oxford University Press.

Smyth, J., Stone, A., Hurewitz, A., & Kaell, A. (1999). Writing about stressful events produces symptom reduction in asthmatics and rheumatoid arthritics: A randomized trial. *Journal of the American Medical Association, 281,* 1304–1309.

Smyth, J., True, N., & Souto, J. (2001). Effects of writing about traumatic experiences: The necessity for narrative structure. *Journal of Social and Clinical Psychology, 20,* 161–172.

Spera, S., Buhrfeind, E., & Pennebaker, J. (1994). Expressive writing and coping with job loss. *Academy of Management Journal, 37,* 722–733.

Stone, A., Smyth, J., Kaell, A., & Hurewitz, A. (2000). Structured writing about stressful events: Exploring potential psychological mediators of positive health effects. *Health Psychology, 19,* 619–624.

Winett, R. A. (1995). A framework for health promotion and disease prevention programs. *American Psychologist, 50,* 341–350.

12

INTERAPY: A MODEL FOR THERAPEUTIC WRITING THROUGH THE INTERNET

ALFRED LANGE, MIRJAM SCHOUTROP, BART SCHRIEKEN, AND
JEAN-PIERRE VAN DE VEN

Two mechanisms are most widely considered to be crucial in overcoming traumatic events: (a) habituation to the frightening stimuli that occurs after exposure through self-confrontation to the traumatic memories and avoided stimuli (Foa & Riggs, 1995; chapter 6, this volume; Vaughan & Tarrier, 1992) and (b) cognitive reappraisal of the traumatic experiences (chapters 6 and 10, this volume; Resick & Schnicke, 1992). These mechanisms lead to two main ingredients in the cognitive–behavioral treatment of posttraumatic stress disorder (PTSD) and pathological grief: Imaginary exposure is used to help patients to confront the sensory perceptions, emotions, and thoughts they usually avoid. Cognitive reappraisal implies challenging dysfunctional automatic thoughts and stimulating reinterpretation of misattributions about the traumatic event, in order to accommodate a new symbolic meaning about the experience. The effectiveness of treatment by self-confrontation is well-established (Jaycox & Foa, 1996). There is also evidence for the effectiveness of cognitive therapy for patients with PTSD and pathological grief (Shalev, Bonne, & Eth, 1996).

Structured writing assignments provide an alternative to imaginary confrontations during sessions with a therapist. The method combines self-confrontation and cognitive reappraisal, and it results in a product that facilitates the process of sharing. Several case studies have demonstrated the usefulness of structured writing assignments in the treatment of pathological grief and posttraumatic stress (L'Abate, 1991; Lange, 1994, 1996). Patients receive precise instructions about the content of the writing, manner of writing, frequency, amount of time spent, and location. In face-to-face sessions, the therapist guides the process of writing, through feedback and adjustment of the instructions to the results of the writing.

The effects of structured writing assignments on health and well-being have been investigated in many experiments (Smyth, 1998), typically using a brief writing intervention developed by Pennebaker (Pennebaker & Beall, 1986). Participants write about assigned topics for three to five consecutive days, 15 to 45 minutes each day. Experimental participants write about their deepest thoughts and feelings, whereas controls are asked to write about trivial topics. In a meta-analysis, Smyth (1998) showed that the average effect size of structured writing in this type of experimental study was .47, which is comparable to the effects of other psychological interventions. This is a promising statistic because the protocols used in these trials are less stringent than those used in clinical practice.

The first part of this chapter presents an overview of our approach to using structured writing assignments in clinical practice. The second part describes experiments that evaluate the outcome of writing assignments for PTSD patients and the role of habituation versus cognitive reappraisal in the process of overcoming trauma and grief. One study permitted us to investigate the importance of social sharing. The third part describes how we translated the face-to-face protocol into an interactive format for writing therapy through the Internet.

OVERVIEW OF THE CLINICAL MODEL

Below we describe the proceedings in structured writing in clinical practice. The model comprises three phases.

Phase 1: Self-confrontation. The patient informs the therapist about the traumatic experiences. The therapist helps the patient by asking questions and providing psychoeducation and explains the importance of self-confrontation in general and of the use of writing assignments in particular. The therapist checks whether the patient is stable enough to meet the demands of self-confrontation and provides a supportive environment. If therapist and patient agree, a treatment contract is established. The therapist then helps the patient to focus on the most painful images and thoughts and encourages the patient to talk about them. When the most painful elements become more or less clear, the therapist gives the first writing instructions. The patient may simply write an essay about the events or address the writing to a person who was involved or even caused the trauma or grief or to a significant other person. Exhibit 12.1 gives an overview of the instructions the therapist provides at the start of the writing process.

Phase 2: Cognitive reappraisal. When the patient reports that the emotions had become less strong and that focusing on the writing is becoming difficult, it is time to change the content of writing. The patient is then instructed to challenge negative dysfunctional thinking (e.g., shame about being left behind, guilt after being raped). The therapist might suggest that the patient imagine giving advice to a good friend who had been victimized in the same way. For instance, what would the patient tell that friend? In this phase, the format of writing (place, time, etc.) is not changed and the patient should not be worried about style, mistakes, and so forth. The writing is still uncensored.

Phase 3: The dignified letter and taking leave of the past. When the patient has completed the writing assignment, he or she is instructed to write his last letter or essay. This should be a dignified, immaculate piece of work. It should express the patient's feelings in such a way that it can be sent to the designated person. The therapist reads the writing and might

EXHIBIT 12.1
Instructions in Writing Assignments

- Writing occurs at a fixed place, at fixed times, and for a fixed duration.
- Patient concentrates on the most painful elements and writes about them.
- When time is up, the patient stops. At the next session, he starts with reading the past writing before writing.
- Patient is alone in the room, if possible, and the telephone is turned off to reduce distractions.
- Writing in the first phase is uncensored. Only the therapist is going to read it. Spelling and grammar are unimportant; the essay or letter does not have to be written in a correct or "nice" way. Emphasis is on expression of feelings, and this expression should not be obstructed by demands of quality in writing or loyalty to the person(s) to whom the essay is addressed.
- Late at night before sleeping is not a good time to carry out the writing assignment. The patient should schedule some relaxing activities after the writing, such as reading, listening to music, taking a walk. The exact nature of these may differ from patient to patient.
- At each session, the therapist and patient discuss the impact. If permitted, the therapist reads the written material. This helps the therapist to establish whether or not the patient has avoided the real painful elements. If necessary, he may help the patient to address these elements more forcefully.
- The amount of time between sessions depends on the nature of the traumatic experiences and the resources of the patient.

give suggestions to improve the style and content. If the patient does not actually mail the letter, he or she may send it in a symbolic, ritual way (e.g., by burying it or placing it in a special box).

THE AMSTERDAM WRITING PROJECT

We discuss the effectiveness of two clinical trials of the above-described method of structured writing at the University of Amsterdam. The experiments were based on three pilot studies with students. The first pilot study demonstrated that social workers of the Dutch Postal Services could be trained to apply the writing protocol in the clinical treatment of their clients who had suffered from severe traumas (e.g., sexual abuse, hold-ups). In the second pilot study, an experimental protocol of four writing sessions was developed and administered to 32 undergraduates who had suffered from traumatic events. Participants improved significantly in mood and depressive symptoms (Schoutrop, 2000). In addition, a third pilot study was carried out among 48 traumatized students. Participants in the expressive writing condition reported significant reductions in avoidance and intrusions, as measured by the Impact of Event Scale (IES; Horowitz, Wilner, & Alvarez, 1979), and significant improvements in psychological functioning, as measured by the Symptom Checklist–90 (SCL–90; Derogatis, 1977). The waiting list control group did not show improvement. Analyses revealed that the effects were moderate to large (Schoutrop, 2000).

The three studies described below included premeasurement, post-measurement, a 6-week follow-up, and a longer term follow-up. In both experiments the emphasis was on the reduction in the degree of trauma-related symptoms, measured by the Dutch adaptation of the IES. Exploratory analyses were carried out on general psychological functioning, which was measured by the Dutch adaptation of the SCL–90. Both instruments had been adapted and validated for the Dutch population, and normative scores are available for the general and the psychiatric population (Arrindell & Ettema, 1986; Brom, Kleber, & Hofman, 1993).

Study 1: Habituation Vs. Cognitive Reappraisal Vs. Trivial Writing Vs. Waiting List

As we noted above, a controversy exists over the mechanisms of adjustment to traumatic events. Habituation and cognitive reappraisal are widely seen as the most important elements. Study 1 was set up to investigate the impact of writing assignments and gather insight into the role of these mechanisms.

Experimental Design

The protocol followed the clinical steps described above. The SCL–90 and IES were used. Pretreatment measurement took place 1 week before intervention and on the day the intervention started. The average of these two premeasures was used as the indication of the baseline situation. Further measures were administered immediately after the intervention, 6 weeks later, and 2 years later. The intervention consisted of one introductory session and four 45-minute writing sessions spread over a 2-week period. Participants were randomly assigned to one of the five experimental conditions described below (for more detail, see Schoutrop, 2000).

Five participant groups were used. Participants in the self confrontation condition were instructed to concentrate on a trauma and describe the most painful and threatening memories, images, and emotions it evoked. They were instructed to refrain from writing about their thoughts and coping strategies. This writing instruction was designed to stimulate habituation, which is analogous to the primary goal of behavior therapy for PTSD (Shalev, Bonne, & Eth, 1996).

The cognitive reappraisal instruction was designed to stimulate a process of cognitive reappraisal that corresponds with the aim of cognitive therapy. The text in the cognitive reappraisal instruction was derived from Ellis, Gordon, Neenan, and Palmer (1997).

Participants in the combination condition received the self confrontation and the cognitive reappraisal instructions without the instruction to refrain from writing about thoughts and coping as given in the self-confrontation condition.

Participants in the trivial control condition wrote about their plans and activities of that day without affective content. The waiting list control group completed the questionnaires before treatment, right after, and six weeks later (first follow-up). Participants in this condition and in the trivial writing condition received actual treatment after the follow-up measurement of the participants in the three experimental conditions.

Participants

Local physicians and victim assistance agencies referred their patients with posttraumatic stress symptoms or pathological grief. Potential participants were screened using the computerized Depression Interview Schedule (Alem et al., 1991). A structured interview was used to assess the specific trauma-related events and symptoms. Participants were excluded if (a) they did not experience trauma-related symptoms; (b) the traumatic events took place less than 3 months prior to the study; (c) they were addicted to drugs or alcohol; (d) they met criteria for bipolar depression, psychotic disorder, or organic disorder; (e) they reported the use of psychopharmacological medication; or (f) they were currently involved in other psychologically oriented treatment. One hundred and twenty-two participants were eligible for the study (82 women and 40 men). The average age was 51 years ($SD = 11.0$, range = 23–66), and the majority of participants (73%) had experienced a traumatic event longer than 6 months before entering the study. Nineteen participants dropped out of the experiment, leaving 103 to complete the study. Attrition appeared to be random. Prior to the intervention, the mean level of trauma-related distress (IES) was 34.3 ($SD = 15.3$), which is above the cut-off score of 28 that indicates PTSD (Harrison & Kinner, 1998). The posttraumatic stress symptoms they were suffering from were caused by physical or sexual abuse, violence in the family, loss of significant others, loss of health, and loss of jobs.

Measures and Manipulation Check

Primary outcome measures were the IES and the SCL–90. Content analysis was performed on the essays to test whether participants complied with the instructions. Two trained clinical psychologists who were blind to experimental condition and degree of improvement independently rated each essay. They rated the extent to which the essays expressed painful emotions and cognitive restructuring on a scale from 1 (*not at all*) to 7 (*very much*). Pearson correlation coefficients between the raters ranged from .68 to .76.

Results

As expected, the participants in the cognitive reappraisal condition wrote significantly more about cognitive aspects of the traumatic experience and more about future coping strategies than participants in the other conditions. Participants in the self-confrontation condition expressed more emotions about the traumatic event and showed less avoidance of painful facts and emotions. The essays of participants in the combination condition showed elements of both writing instructions (for details, see Schoutrop, 2000, chapter 5, this volume).

Table 12.1 shows the reduction in avoidance and intrusions from baseline, posttest, 6 weeks later, and 2 years later. Inspection of Table 12.1 suggests that writing with the emphasis on cognitive reappraisal alone or in combination with self-confrontation resulted in improvement from pretreatment to posttreatment and first follow-up (i.e., 6 weeks after completion of the writing assignment). The highest improvement (lower scores on the IES) occurred during the 6-week follow-up period. Participants in the self-confrontation condition showed less improvement than participants in the cognitive restructuring condition. Participants in the trivial condition and the waiting list condition demonstrated no progress at all on any measure immediately after the intervention and 6 weeks later.

TABLE 12.1
Avoidance and Intrusion Scores for the Experimental and Control Conditions in Study 1 at Four Points in Time

Condition	Baseline		Posttest		Follow-up I		Follow-up II	
	M	SD	M	SD	M	SD	M	SD
Self-confrontation								
Avoidance	14.2	7.6	11.2	8.9	12.4	8.9	8.7	8.6
Intrusions	18.7	7.5	16.5	8.5	15.4	8.3	13.4	9.2
Cognitive reappraisal								
Avoidance	16.4	8.5	14.7	8.1	10.1	8.6	6.7	6.4
Intrusions	17.1	6.6	14.5	9.0	11.3	7.5	7.5	6.7
Combination								
Avoidance	12.3	9.0	11.1	8.7	8.4	8.6	3.3	6.9
Intrusions	15.6	8.8	14.4	9.1	9.7	9.1	4.6	5.0
Trivial writing								
Avoidance	17.5	8.2	13.2	9.5	15.9	8.4		
Intrusions	17.8	8.6	17.4	10.0	16.3	10.2		
Waiting list								
Avoidance	13.2	7.1	14.0	9.8	12.3	9.6		
Intrusions	17.1	7.9	16.2	8.0	15.8	9.3		

Note. These data are from Schoutrop (2000).

The statistical significance of the effects of the writing on the dependent variables was first analyzed by two multivariate analyses of variance (MANOVAs) for repeated measures for intrusions and avoidance. If an overall condition effect or an overall condition by time effect was found, analyses of variance (ANOVAs) for repeated measures on each of the separate subscales separately were carried out, followed by planned comparisons analyses (for details, see Schoutrop, 2000; chapter 5, this volume). There was significant improvement (decrease) in avoidance and intrusions in the experimental conditions versus no improvement in the control conditions. Effect sizes (Cohen, 1977) were medium to large (*ds* = .5 for avoidance and .7 for intrusions). The improvements were maintained during the long-term follow-up. There were significantly more reductions in symptoms among participants in the cognitive reappraisal condition as compared to those in the self-confrontation condition. These differences were found at posttest, after the first follow-up, and at the 2-year follow-up. No differences were found between the two control conditions. The cut-off criteria by Harrison and Kinner (1998) were used to establish how many of the participants did change in a clinically relevant degree. Six weeks after termination of the intervention, 64% of the participants in the cognitive reappraisal condition and 53% of those in the combination treatment condition appeared to have experienced significant improvements. Only 24% of the participants in the self-confrontation condition changed to that degree. At the 2-year follow-up, these changes remained.

Exploratory analyses on the SCL–90 data showed that participants in all experimental conditions improved significantly in psychological well-being as compared to the two control groups.

Study 2: Habituation, Cognitive Reappraisal, and Social Sharing

In Study 2, we partly replicated Study 1 and extended it by transforming the last essay into a polished letter that could be sent to a significant other person. Our decision to include this new element was based on several studies (which we discussed in the introduction) that demonstrate the beneficial effects of sharing traumatic events with significant other people (Lange et al., 1999; Rimé, 1995). It also corresponds with our clinical experiences as laid out in the first part of this chapter. In this experiment, social sharing was manipulated by the instruction to write the last essay in a dignified style and send it to a significant other person. However, we cautioned the participants that if they did not know any person that they would trust with the material, they should simply write the letter in polished form but not mail it.

There were five experimental conditions: (a) self-confrontation (habituation) followed by social sharing, (b) habituation (self-confrontation) without social sharing, (c) cognitive reappraisal followed by social sharing, (d) cognitive reappraisal without social sharing, and (e) a waiting-list control condition. Participants were recruited in the same manner as in Study 1, using the same selection criteria. Ninety-five participants (75 women and 20 men) were randomly assigned to one of the five conditions. The average age of this group was 49 years (SD = 14.4). Nearly half of the participants (47%) had suffered from the traumatic events for 5 years or more. The same instruments as in Study 1 were used to measure the results. All tests were based on MANOVAs and planned comparisons (for details, see Schoutrop, 2000; chapter 7, this volume).

As in Study 1, the manipulation of the writing instruction was checked by two trained judges with high interrater reliabilities (rs = .81 to .90). The ratings showed the expected differences in writing between the self-confrontation and cognitive reappraisal conditions.

After termination of the intervention and 6 weeks later, the four experimental conditions showed significantly greater reductions in trauma symptoms than the control group, $F(2, 182)$ = 3.59, p < .05, and the average effect size was small to medium (.3; Cohen, 1977). The differences in outcome between self-confrontation and cognitive reappraisal conditions, as found in Study 1, were not replicated. Furthermore, after the intervention and 6 weeks later, no significant differences could be established between the participants who were instructed to send the letter off and those who were not. However, a follow-up 12 months later revealed the expected differences. Participants in the social sharing conditions (the vast majority of whom had sent the letter) showed significantly more reduction in avoidance and intrusions than the participants who had not received the instruction to send their letters, $F(3, 117) = 3.90$, $p < .01$, and $F(1, 42) = 3.44$, $p < .07$, respectively. A similar pattern was found with regard to somatic complaints (on the SCL–90).

In summary, the experiments described above demonstrate that a short and simple writing intervention yields positive effects, with moderate to large effect sizes, on trauma symptoms and general psychological well-being in severely traumatized participants. Our data also show that the effects of writing hold for relatively long periods and, possibly, strengthen with time. The data of Study 1 suggest that cognitive reappraisal is relatively more important than habituation in the process of overcoming the consequences of traumatic events. However, the results of Study 2 do not confirm the data of Study 1 in that matter.

INTERAPY: STRUCTURED WRITING THROUGH THE INTERNET

To date, computers have been used in psychological practice mainly as a tool for assessment and complex behavior observation programs. Furthermore, some self-help programs offering computer-mediated therapies have been developed. In these therapies the patient works independently without contact with a therapist. Studies have shown that some computer-mediated therapies are more effective than no therapy and as effective as the face-to-face treatment with which they have been compared (Marks, 2000).

The Internet increases the therapeutic possibilities of computers. It enables patients who engage in computer-mediated therapy to interact with therapists, without face-to-face contact. Many persons prefer to reveal their innermost thoughts and feelings to a computer screen rather than to a real person (Erdman, Klein, & Greist, 1985). Administering therapy through the Internet also has other advantages (see chapter 13, this volume), including reducing barriers to care. For instance, persons with physical disabilities or persons who are afraid to seek face-to-face therapy because they are anxious or fear stigmatization can be treated at home. For persons who live in remote areas, a choice of treatment options becomes available.

Treatment through the Internet also might have disadvantages (see chapter 13, this volume). The medium does not allow therapists and patients to establish a deep relationship. Hence, the Internet will probably be suited exclusively for administering well-established treatment protocols for clearly defined disorders. We report here on the results of such a protocol-based treatment through the Internet, for patients who suffer from PTSD and pathological grief. The protocol is based on our ongoing research and is founded on the principles of self-confrontation, cognitive reappraisal, and social sharing through structured writing assignments. The protocols of the face-to-face experiments above were short (only four sessions of writing) with little feedback provided to participants. The protocol we devised for the Internet therapy (Interapy) comes closer to clinical practice. Below we describe the site and the treatment protocol.

The Internet Site (http://Interapy.nl)

To establish a computer-mediated communication between participants and therapists, we developed an interactive Web site. Participants and therapists may use a normal Internet browser to follow the complete therapeutic procedure, which includes completing questionnaires, writing essays, and reading instructions for the next stage. Any recent version of Netscape Navigator or Internet Explorer is sufficient. The Interapy program was built to be platform-independent (i.e., it can be read by all systems, including Unix, Windows, or Macintosh).

Interapy is set up as a client-server system (for details, see Lange, van de Ven, Schrieken, Bredeweg, & Emmelkamp, 2000).[1] Briefly, the client side (the interfaces of participants and therapists) is provided by a set of dynamically generated Web pages, wherein the information and functionality presented depend on the data that are available on the server side. The server side is the part of the system where all information is gathered, processed, and stored. A special computer, the Web server, examines every action performed by participants and therapists, stores the necessary information in another special computer (the relational database server, Butler), and finally returns adequate feedback. The Web server provides the security of all information that is sent over the network connection. Several steps ensure the privacy of clients. First, clients use a login combination known only to them. Second, all communication between clients and therapists is encrypted using the standard https (i.e., hypertext transfer protocol secure), thus preventing data from being intercepted during transmission over the Internet. Therapists use a group login account in addition to their personal account to enter the site. Recently, Interapy was re-implemented on a Linux system, with additional security safeguards.

Procedures

When potential clients contact the Interapy home page, their first step in the treatment process includes browsing the Interapy information pages. These pages comprise psychoeducation about PTSD and pathological grief and the main features of treatment, with emphasis on structured writing assignments. These pages also provide information about the su-

---

[1]The start of Interapy was made possible by two grants from the Dutch Society for Mental Health.

pervisors and therapists of Interapy, how to apply for treatment, institutions where they may apply for treatment if they decide not to continue with Interapy or if they are excluded, and references for further reading.

After applying for treatment, participants enter the screening procedure during which they complete questionnaires and indicate the type and dosage of any psychotropic medication they currently use. The Interapy system automatically examines the answers of the participants, computes scale scores, and compares these to the inclusion cut-off scores. Participants may proceed to the next pages only if they have answered all questions on the present page. (This applies for the measures of the effects as well.) The system immediately informs the participants whether they fit the inclusion criteria. Therapists check only the questions about quantity and type of medication to decide whether the pharmacological status of the participant allows inclusion. Participants who do not meet the inclusion criteria receive information about other institutions where they may seek help.

Participants who are admitted complete the pretest. Subsequently, they describe the traumatic experiences. The system then randomly assigns each participant to one of the therapists, ensuring that each therapist receives the same number of clients. Treatment starts when the therapist has received the Informed Consent form with a written signature from his client. This is the only interaction between therapists and clients that does not take place through the Web site.

Screening: Exclusion Criteria

Individuals can participate in Interapy if they are over 18 years old and have experienced a traumatic event at least 3 months before they apply for therapy. They are excluded from Interapy if they meet one of the following criteria:

1. Extreme depression. Applicants are excluded from participation if they have extremely high scores on the Depression subscale of the SCL-90 (above the cut-off score of the highly depressed group in the norm tables for the psychiatric population; Arrindell & Ettema, 1986). For these applicants it might be inappropriate to follow a therapy protocol that stimulates self-confrontation unless they are able to adjust the protocol and add other elements, including medication.
2. Inclination to psychological dissociation. Because the Interapy protocol is a demanding therapy we do consider it safe to include applicants who have a tendency to dissociate. This is measured by The Somatoform Dissociation Questionnaire (*SDQ-5*; Nijenhuis, Spinhoven, van Dyck, van der Hart, & Vanderlinden, 1997). Applicants are excluded if their scores are above the cut-off score of the SDQ-5.

3. Risk of psychosis. Because all writing occurs at home, and the writing task may cause considerable emotional upheaval, the risk for decompensation is high. Risk of psychosis is measured by the Dutch Screening Device for Psychotic Disorder (*SDPD*; Lange, Schrieken, Blankers, van de Ven, & Slot, 2000). Applicants are excluded from participation if they score above the cut-off score of the Dutch norm group.
4. Medication. Applicants are excluded from participation if they use neuroleptic medication.
5. Ongoing therapy. Applicants who are receiving other psychological treatment are excluded from participation.

Measures

We used the IES and SCL–90 as the primary outcomes. For exploratory reasons, we also included a biographical information questionnaire (e.g., demographics, computer and Internet experience, level of typing skills) and a questionnaire consisting of precoded questions about the evaluation by the participants of online psychoeducation, the amount of time to complete questionnaires on-screen, and experiences with online contact with the therapists.

The Therapists and the Treatment

Eighteen graduate students in clinical psychology (4 men, 14 women) were the therapists in the three trials described below. They had completed coursework in cognitive–behavioral therapy. Before entering the Interapy program as therapists, they received special training in the application of structured writing in the treatment of PTSD and pathological grief. The emphasis in this training was on learning to interpret written material and to provide feedback to patients within the boundaries of the protocol.

Figure 12.1 shows an overview of the treatment process. Treatment takes place over a period of 5 weeks during which participants write 10 times. Each writing session takes 45 minutes. Participants write two essays a week. They are required to make a schedule, which is registered in the system at the beginning of each of three treatment phases. In the middle of each phase, the therapists provide the participants with feedback about their writing and give instructions on how to proceed. The participants receive the feedback within two working days after they send their essays. If the content of an essay signals that Interapy treatment might not be appropriate (e.g., the client seems psychologically endangered or the topic is not appropriate for writing assignments), the therapist consults with a supervisor. This may result in an e-mail to the client, sometimes followed by a telephone call to discuss another way of treatment. The treatment protocol consists of the following three phases:

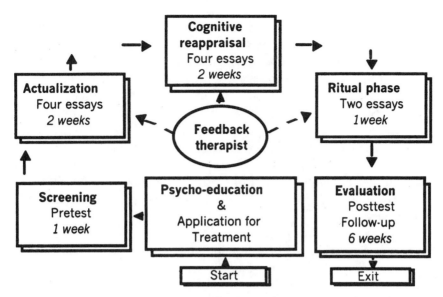

Figure 12.1. Overview of the Interapy treatment procedure.
Note. From "INTERAPY. Treatment of Posttraumatic Stress Through the Internet: A Controlled Trial," by A. Lange, J.-P. van de Ven, B. Schrieken, and P. Emmelkamp, 2001, *Behavioral Research and Experimental Psychiatry, 32,* p. 21. Copyright 2001 by Elsevier Science. Reprinted with permission.

1. *Phase 1: Self-confrontation.* At the start of treatment the participants receive on-line psycho-education about the rationale of self-confrontation (habituation). The therapists instruct the participants to describe their traumatic event in detail and to write about their intimate fears and thoughts concerning the traumatic event. This is the theme of the first four writing sessions. To stimulate self-confrontation and habituation, participants are to write in the first person and in the present tense, describing as precisely as possible the sensory perceptions they experienced at the time of the traumatic event, including olfactory, visual, and auditory stimuli. Participants are instructed to write freely and to ignore style, spelling, grammar, and chronology.

2. *Phase 2: Cognitive reappraisal.* Participants receive psycho-education about the principles of cognitive reappraisal. The main goal in this phase is to develop new views on the traumatic event and to regain a sense of control. This is achieved by instructing participants to write encouraging advice for a hypothetical friend who has experienced the same traumatic event. The advice should deal with issues such as the positive influence of the event on this person's life and what could be learned from it.

3. *Phase 3: Sharing and farewell ritual.* Participants receive psycho-education about the positive effects of sharing. Subsequently, they take symbolic leave of the traumatic experience by writing a letter to themselves, a significant other person, or a person who has been involved in the traumatic event. If necessary, the therapist advises them not to send the letter.

Interapy 1: Controlled Trial With Traumatized Students

An uncontrolled (no control group) pilot study with 20 traumatized students had shown a strong decrease in trauma symptoms and improvement in psychological functioning, which lasted for up to 18 months after termination of treatment (Lange, Schrieken, van de Ven, et al., 2000; Roemer & Skøgerbø, 2000). The pilot study was followed by a controlled study including 41 traumatized undergraduate students who applied for treatment in an Interapy study that had a 2 (between conditions) × 3 (within, repeated measures) design. Eleven of the applicants did not pass the screening. Participants were assigned at random to treatment or to the waiting-list control condition (five participants in the latter condition dropped out of the study). The participants in the control condition received the Interapy treatment after the experimental group had terminated treatment. The participants had suffered from traumatic events such as loss of a significant other, sexual abuse, family violence, loss of health, accidents, robbery, or violent crime. On average, the traumatic episodes had taken place more than 5 years previously. There were no systematic differences between the treatment and waiting-list control condition.

Decrease in Trauma-Related Symptoms

At posttreatment assessment, participants in the treatment group showed a strong reduction in intrusion and avoidance. Improvements were sustained during the 6-week follow-up period, with a further decrease in avoidance and intrusions. T tests revealed significance levels of $< .001$, with large effect sizes (1.50 on avoidance measures and 1.99 on intrusion measures). Participants in the control condition also showed a small reduction in symptoms. However, a MANOVA proved the improvement in the treated group to be significantly larger than that of the control group, $F(2, 22) = 5.14$, $p < .015$. A detailed account of these tests and the ones discussed in the next section can be found in Lange, van de Ven, Schrieken, and Emmelkamp (2001).

Decrease in General Psychopathology

Participants in the treatment condition showed a strong decrease in anxiety, depression, and somatization, which was sustained during the follow-up. T tests showed the differences between pretreatment and posttreatment to be significant (all $ps < .05$; effect sizes for anxiety, depression, and somatization were 1.23, 1.28, and 1.25, respectively). In the control condition no changes were found. The difference in change between treatment and control group, tested by MANOVAs, showed the expected interaction effect to be significant, $F(3, 21) = 3.69$, $p < .03$ (improvement in the treatment group and no improvement in the control group).

Clinical Relevance

For all participants in the treatment and control groups, we calculated whether they changed from above the cut-off score for each variable to below the cut-off score, according to the method described by Jacobson and Truax (1995). According to these criteria, 86% of the participants in the treatment condition showed a clinically relevant change in avoidance symptoms, whereas 29% in the control group changed to a relevant degree. On intrusions, 82% of the treated participants and 56% of the control group showed marked improvements. All of the treated participants showed clinically significant changes in anxiety and somatization (in the control group, 58% and 20%, respectively). Eighty-eight percent of the participants showed clinically significant changes in depression (50% in the control group).

Interapy 2: Controlled Trial With Highly Traumatized Participants

After the pilot and the controlled study, the site was opened for participants all over the world who were able to read and write in the Dutch language. In The Netherlands, Interapy had received much publicity from TV, radio, and leading journals. Screening, time schedules, measures, and procedure were identical to those used in the previous experiment. The trial started when 28 out of 50 applicants had passed the screening. The ages of the participants who passed the screening ranged from 22 to 55 years with an average age of 38 ($SD = 9.9$). They were randomly assigned to the treatment or control condition. Two of the 17 participants who had started treatment did not complete the postmeasurements. Fifteen participants in the treatment group fully completed Interapy. Thirteen persons participated in the waiting-list control group. Most participants lived in The Netherlands, but some lived in the Dutch Caribbean and Flemish-speaking part of Belgium. On average, the traumatic events had taken place more than 6 years before. In nearly half of the participants, the trauma was related to the death of loved ones. Other traumas included rape, robbery, and loss of health. Before treatment, the trauma symptoms (as measured by the IES) were high compared to the Dutch PTSD norm group. There were no differences in trauma symptoms between participants assigned to the treatment and waiting-list control conditions (for details, see van Asselt & Peetoom, 2000).

Decrease in Trauma-Related Symptoms

Figure 12.2 shows dramatic declines in avoidance and intrusions before and after treatment in participants in the treatment group, whereas the control group showed no changes. ANOVAs demonstrated the difference in improvement between treated and nontreated participants to be highly significant: $F(1, 26) = 18.56$, $p < .001$, in avoidance and $F(1, 26) = 5.72$, $p < .05$, in intrusions. Compared to Cohen's (1977) norms, the effect sizes are very large (1.66 and .95, respectively).

Decrease in General Psychopathology

The pattern of the changes in general psychopathology (anxiety, depression, and somatization) in the experimental and control condition follow the same pattern as in Figure 12.2. A strong decrease was found in participants in the treatment condition in anxiety, depression, and somatization as measured before and after treatment. Participants in the control condition did not improve. The differences between control and experimental condition were highly significant, with $F(1, 26)$ ranging from 5.96 ($p < .05$) to 11.70 ($p < .001$). Effect sizes were large (ranging from .96 for anxiety to 1.35 for somatization). The follow-up showed no relapse.

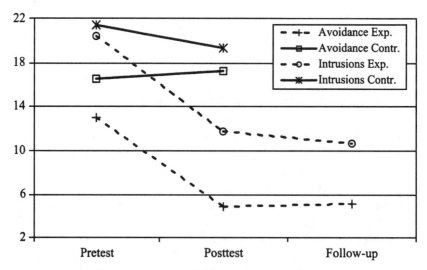

Figure 12.2. Interapy 2: Changes in avoidance and intrusions for treatment experimental (exp.) and control (contr.) conditions.

Clinical Relevance

The method described by Jacobson and Truax (1995) was used to calculate the percentages of clinically improved and deteriorated participants on each variable. As Table 12.2 demonstrates, in almost all variables most of the treated participants evidenced clinical improvements and none deteriorated. Only in intrusions, less than half of the treated participants had benefited in a clinically significant manner. The control group was different, with only few improvements and some deterioration.

Explorations in Interapy: For Whom Does It Work?

In the three studies described above, we explored variables that might predict which participants profit most from Interapy. Here we briefly summarize the combined findings.

- Experience with the Internet. The improvement levels of participants with little or no experience with the Internet were comparable with the improvement of participants who had extensive experience on the Internet.
- Biographical data. None of the studies reveal differences in improvement between participants differing in any demographic variable, such as gender or age.
- Preference for face-to-face treatment. In the general population (Study 2) none of the participants preferred face-to-face contacts. This probably is the reason these participants chose to be treated through the Internet. The students (Study 1) had not made a conscious choice for treatment through the Internet. To them, participation in a research project was an incentive in addition to getting treatment. Nearly half of the student participants indicated that they would have preferred face-to-face treatment. Yet, these participants did not im-

TABLE 12.2
Clinically Relevant Changes in Interapy 2 for Treated and Control Group (in Percentages)

Variable	Treatment group		Control group	
	Improved	Deteriorated	Improved	Deteriorated
Avoidance	72	0	0	0
Intrusions	46	0	10	0
Anxiety	88	0	0	15
Depression	80	0	15	15
Somatization	67	0	7	7

Note. These data are based on an internal report by van Asselt and Peetoom (2000).

prove less than those participants who preferred treatment through the Internet.

To investigate the psychological predictors of the effectiveness of Interapy, we added data from Interapy in the general population after termination of Study 2. This made it possible to conduct stepwise regression analyses on the data of 69 participants. Variables that had seemed to predict the effects of Interapy in previous univariate analyses were now tested in a multivariate design. The independent variables were age, gender, time passed since the trauma, disclosure versus nondisclosure before Interapy, and general psychological functioning (as reflected by SCL–90 scores). Kuut and Jager (2000) described the analysis and results in detail. Two of the six independent variables emerged as significant predictors of treatment success, as measured by the total IES score.

- Disclosure. Participants who had indicated that they had not spoken about their traumatic experiences before Interapy showed the most reduction in IES scores at posttreatment. This variable explained 24% of the variance of the IES scores at posttreatment, after the pretreatment scores had been included in the regression equations. Pretreatment IES scores accounted for only 11% of the posttreatment scores. These findings support the emphasis on sharing as expressed by Rimé (1995).
- Age. This variable accounted for 31% of the posttreatment IES scores after controlling for pretreatment scores. The younger the participants, the more they benefited from Interapy.

In these multivariate analyses we investigated the contribution of each variable while controlling for the others. Accordingly, the importance of disclosure cannot be explained by age or elapsed time since the trauma, nor can the importance of age be explained by elapsed time since the trauma or disclosure.

Interapy: First Conclusions

The results of Interapy were even better than we had hoped, with effect sizes two to three times as high as the effect sizes found in our face-to-face experiments and reported in Smyth's meta-analysis (1998). The improvements also held up for at least 18 months (Roemer & Skøgerbø, 2000). The positive outcome might be due to a very effective protocol with its 10 sessions of writing with very specific and tightly controlled instructions, in a specific order that is based on an established theoretical model. The protocol in the face-to-face experiments was simpler, with fewer writing sessions, less order in the writing, and less precise feedback. In this respect, Interapy treatment is probably also more complex than the protocols of the studies analyzed by Smyth (1998). Furthermore, most of the participants preferred to share their inner feelings through the Internet rather than face-to-face with a therapist. However, they did feel and appreciate the existence of the Interapy therapist on the other side of the line. There was a positive therapist–client relationship. The positiveness of this relationship is probably enhanced by the fact that the therapists do not have to react immediately, which decreases the likelihood that they give less appropriate feedback. Whenever one of the therapists felt unsure, she showed the participants' written material and her previous feedback to a colleague or supervisor. The inability to see and evaluate nonverbal messages of the clients did not seem to have handicapped therapists from providing proper feedback. In fact, our therapists may have been more effective because they were not distracted from the core elements of treatment: self-confrontation and cognitive reappraisal.

The transparency of the entire process is not only beneficial for the client–therapist relationship and the quality of the interventions, it is also important for the research designs, ensuring treatment integrity and the possibility of checking treatment integrity. For researchers it is a blessing to have complete sets of data with all items and all questionnaires fully completed. The Interapy program automatically ensures that a participant cannot proceed to the next question or questionnaire if a previous one is not completed. However, participants in our study were sometimes unable to log in and complete their essays, and some participants simply forgot to complete the follow-up questionnaires. (These participants were considered as dropouts.) We expect that these practical problems will decrease as the technical equipment and Internet technology further improves. We have also planned to create an adequate help function on the Interapy site and a good help-desk service to reduce the percentage of dropouts, which is now about 20%. Finally, in clinical practice we plan to use e-mail contacts if necessary to guide participants through Interapy.

In the first controlled study with student participants we found some clinically relevant improvements in a considerable number of participants in the control group waiting for therapy. This might have been due to the Interapy format, providing psycho-education to applicants before they applied for treatment and before they were randomly assigned to the treatment or control conditions. Furthermore, the participants in the control condition knew that they would receive the Interapy treatment within a short time. These positive effects of the Interapy format were not found in Interapy 2, with nonstudent participants who were more severely traumatized. These data correspond with those of Sithartan, Kavanagh, and

Sayer (1996), who found positive results from mere written psycho-education in a sample of individuals with mild forms of alcoholism.

The positive impact of the Interapy psycho-education is of practical value, making it less awkward when applicants cannot be treated right away but have to wait for some weeks or months. In future research, it will be interesting to directly compare the effects of Interapy not only with the present type of waiting list, but also with a control group that receives no psycho-education before treatment or with placebo treatments and similar but face-to-face treatments.

Although Interapy excludes only those patients with high risk for psychosis, dissociation, and severe major depression, it has not been not used with "light cases," either. On the contrary, it was most beneficial for the participants who were highly depressed and traumatized for a long period.

So far, Interapy is a Dutch phenomenon, only open to Dutch-speaking clients. In the near future we will adapt Interapy into English and other languages, providing cross-cultural help and research.

General Discussion

The writing model we advocate, whether face-to-face or through the Internet, is based on clinical research and practice. Several of the details are important, including the fixed amount of time and the precise schedule. Because structured expressive writing may be hard for clients (they have to confront themselves), it is important that therapists offer unconditional support, even with clients who avoid painful topics. The Interapy studies prove that it is possible to give support and commitment through the Internet, probably better than in the face-to-face experiments with limited feedback possibilities.

Study 2 of the face-to-face studies demonstrates the long-term positive effects of writing a polished letter at the end of the process of writing. This might be due to the extra effort made by the participant in creating a meaningful document and the symbolic power this exerts. That the letter is shared with a significant other might also explain the positive effects. We have no hard data on this, but reports from clinical practice (Lange, 1996) and studies such as Rimé's (1995) support this notion. Support may also be derived from the predictor study in Interapy, showing that participants who had not spoken about the trauma before Interapy benefited more than participants who had.

It would be interesting to inquire in follow-up studies on writing assignments whether participants have sent their letters off and whether it helped them to share their traumatic events. Subsequently, improvement of those who did send the letters off and those who did not might be compared. Preliminary data of the follow-up studies in Interapy support the importance of sending the letter.

In the face-to-face experiments we tried to find conclusive data as to the relative importance of habituation (self-confrontation), cognitive reappraisal, and social sharing. Study 1 seemed to favor cognitive reappraisal above habituation as the main element. This is consistent with Van den Hout and Merckelbach (1993), who suggested that self-confrontation in people with agoraphobia is only effective because it leads to cognitive reappraisal. However, the data of Study 2 do not fully support the data of Study 1 in this respect. Furthermore, Van Zuuren, Schoutrop, Lange, Louis, and Slegers (1999) found in a qualitative study that self-confrontation and cognitive reappraisal are both crucial in overcoming the traumatic events. There seems to be a chronological order: self-confrontation (habituation) to the painful elements is necessary in the beginning of the process, followed by cognitive reappraisal. Social sharing may help to strengthen what is achieved in therapy and to build a support system to maintain the changes. These findings have theoretical and practical implications for the treatment protocols in clinical practice.

Most of the clinical researchers in outpatient settings use validated self-report measures to test the effectiveness of experimental treatments. Especially in our Internet studies, where participants are anonymous, there is not much reason to expect bias in their reporting. Nevertheless, it would be advisable to try and find other criteria for assessing the impact of these treatments. In our studies, structured writing seems to be effective for the following problem areas: PTSD after violence, robbery, pathological grief after loss of beloved ones through death or divorce, loss of jobs, and loss of health. Structured writing has clinically been shown to be effective in cases where rancor or fears with regard to the family of origin play an important role. This ties in with the theoretical framework of cognitive therapy and of intergenerational family therapy (Bedrosian & Bozicas, 1994; Lange, 1996).

REFERENCES

Alem, V. van, Bosma, D., Corven, J. van, Dingemans, P. M. A. J., Geerlings, P. J., Limbeek, J. van, Linszen, D. H., Smeets, R. M. W., & Wouters, L. F. J. M. (1991). *The Diagnostic Interview Schema (DIS) version III*. Amsterdam: University of Amsterdam.

Arrindell, W. A., & Ettema, J. H. M. (1986). *SCL-90: Handleiding bij een multidimensionele psychopathologie-indicator* [SCL-90: Manual for a multidimensional indicator of psychopathology]. Amsterdam/Lisse: Swets & Zeitlinger.

Bedrosian, R. C., & Bozicas, G. D. (1994). *Treating family of origin problems: A cognitive approach*. New York: Guilford Press.

Brom, D., Kleber, R. J., & Hofman, M. C. (1993). Victims of traffic accidents: Incidence and prevention of post-traumatic stress disorder. *Journal of Clinical Psychology, 49*, 131–140.

Cohen, J. (1977). *Statistical power analysis for the behavioral sciences* (Rev. ed.). New York: Academic Press.

Derogatis, L. R. (1977). *SCL–90 (R): Administration, scoring and procedures manual–I for the revised version of other instruments of the Psychopathology Rating Scale series.* Baltimore: Clinical Psychometrics Research Unit, Johns Hopkins University of Medicine.

Ellis, A. J., Gordon, J., Neenan, M., & Palmer, S. (1997). *Stress counseling. A rational emotive approach.* London: Cassell.

Erdman, H. P., Klein, M. H., & Greist, J. H. (1985). Direct patient computer interviewing. *Journal of Consulting and Clinical Psychology, 53*, 760–773.

Foa, E. B., & Riggs, D. S. (1995). Posttraumatic stress disorder following assault: Theoretical considerations and empirical findings. *Current Directions in Psychological Science, 4*(2), 61–65.

Harrison, C. A., & Kinner, S. A. (1998). Correlates of psychological distress following armed robbery. *Journal of Traumatic Stress, 11*, 787–798.

Horowitz, M., Wilner, N., & Alvarez, W. (1979). Impact of Event Scale: A measure of subjective distress. *Psychosomatic Medicine, 41*, 209–218.

Jacobson, N. S., & Truax, P. (1995). Clinical significance: A statistical approach to meaningful change in psychotherapy research. In A. E. Kazdin (Ed.), *Methodological issues & strategies in clinical research* (pp. 631–650). Washington, DC: American Psychological Association.

Jaycox, L. H., & Foa, E. B. (1996). Obstacles in implementing exposure therapy for PTSD: Case discussions and practical solutions. *Clinical Psychology and Psychotherapy, 3*(3), 176–184.

Kuut, T., & Jager, J. (2000). *Interapy: predictie analyses* [Interapy: prediction analysis]. Unpublished doctoral dissertation, University of Amsterdam, Department of Psychology.

L'Abate, L. (1991). The use of writing in psychotherapy. *American Journal of Psychotherapy, 45*, 87–98.

Lange, A. (1994). Writing assignments in the treatment of grief and traumas from the past. In J. Zeig (Ed.), *Ericksonian approaches, the essence of the story* (pp. 377–392). New York: Brunner/Mazel.

Lange, A. (1996). Using writing assignments with families managing legacies of extreme traumas. *Journal of Family Therapy, 18*, 375–388.

Lange, A., de Beurs, E., Dolan, C., Lachnit, T., Sjollema, S., & Hanewald, G. (1999). Long-term effects of childhood sexual abuse: Objective and subjective characteristics of the abuse and psychopathology in later life. *Journal of Nervous and Mental Disease, 187*(3), 150–158.

Lange, A., Schrieken, B., Blankers, M., van de Ven, J.-P., & Slot, M. (2000). Constructie en validatie van de Gewaarwordingenlijst (GL): een hulpmiddel bij het signaleren van een verhoogde kans op psychosen [Construction and validation of the Sensory Perception Inventory: A tool to detect risk of psychosis]. *Directieve Therapie, 20*(2), 162–173.

Lange, A., Schrieken, B., van de Ven, J.-P., Bredeweg, B., Emmelkamp, P. M. G., van der Kolk, J., Lydsdottir, L., Massaro, M., & Reuvers, A. (2000). "INTERAPY": The effects of a short protocolled treatment of post-traumatic stress and pathological grief through the Internet. *Behavioural and Cognitive Psychotherapy, 28*(2), 103–120.

Lange, A., van de Ven, J.-P., Schrieken, B., Bredeweg, B., & Emmelkamp, P. M. G. (2000). Internet-mediated, protocol driven treatment of psychological dysfunction. *Journal of Telemedicine and Telecare, 6*(1), 15–21.

Lange, A., van de Ven, J.-P., Schrieken, B., & Emmelkamp, P. (2001). INTERAPY. Treatment of posttraumatic stress through the Internet: A controlled trial. *Behavioral Research and Experimental Psychiatry, 32*, 73–90.

Marks, I. (2000). Forty years of psychosocial treatment. *Behavioural and Cognitive Psychotherapy, 28*, 323–334.

Nijenhuis, E. R. S., Spinhoven, P., van Dyck, R., van der Hart, O., & Vanderlinden, J. (1997). The development of the somatoform dissociation questionnaire (SDQ–5) as a screening instrument for dissociative disorders. *Acta Psychiatrica Scandinavica, 96*, 311–318.

Pennebaker, J. W., & Beall, S. (1986). Confronting a traumatic event: Toward an understanding of inhibition and disease. *Journal of Abnormal Psychology, 95*, 274–281.

Resick, P. A., & Schnicke, M. K. (1992). Cognitive processing therapy for sexual assault victims. *Journal of Consulting and Clinical Psychology, 60*, 748–756.

Rimé, B. (1995). Mental rumination, social sharing, and the recovery from emotional exposure. In J. W. Pennebaker (Ed.), *Emotion, disclosure and health* (pp. 271–291). Washington, DC: American Psychological Association.

Roemer, M., & Skøgerbø, A. (2000). *Long-term effects of a protocolled writing treatment of grief and PTSD through the Internet.* Amsterdam: University of Amsterdam, Department of Clinical Psychology.

Schoutrop, M. (2000). *Structured writing in processing traumatic events.* Unpublished doctoral dissertation, University of Amsterdam.

Shalev, A. Y., Bonne, O., & Eth, S. (1996). Treatment of posttraumatic stress disorder: A review. *Psychosomatic Medicine, 58*(2), 165–182.

Sithartan, T., Kavanagh, D. J., & Sayer, G. (1996). Moderating drinking by correspondence: An evaluation of a new method of intervention. *Addiction, 91*, 345–355.

Smyth, J. M. (1998). Written emotional expression: Effect sizes, outcome types, and moderating effects. *Journal of Consulting and Clinical Psychology, 66*, 174–184.

Van den Hout, M., & Merckelbach, H. (1993). Over exposure. *Directieve Therapie, 13*(3), 192–203.

van Asselt, I., & Peetoom, T. (2000). *Gestructureerd schrijven via Internet door een klinische populatie: vergelijking experimentele en controlegroep* [Structured writing via Internet by outpatients: Comparison of treatment and control]. Amsterdam: University of Amsterdam, Department of Clinical Psychology.

Van Zuuren, F. J., Schoutrop, M. J. A., Lange, A., Louis, C. M., & Slegers, J. E. M. (1999). Effective and ineffective ways of writing about traumatic experiences: A qualitative study. *Psychotherapy Research, 9,* 363–380.

Vaughan, K., & Tarrier, N. (1992). The use of habituation training with posttraumatic stress disorders. *British Journal of Psychiatry, 161,* 658–664.

13

WORKBOOKS: TOOLS FOR THE EXPRESSIVE WRITING PARADIGM

LUCIANO L'ABATE AND ROY KERN

"... we need to consider other directions for the worlds of both research and practice." (Bickman, 1999, p. 966)

The "writing cure" is a discontinuous (and one hopes forward) step beyond traditional talk-based, face-to-face psychotherapy. It implies a completely different set of assumptions about human nature and how and when to intervene. It requires a serious shift in how psychological interventions are delivered at a distance to respondents. Distance writing (DW) is another way to overcome the current status quo in psychotherapy. DW might make psychological interventions more efficient, cost-effective, specific, and explicit than face-to-face talk-based psychotherapy. This discontinuity will be even more pronounced in programmed DW, as exemplified by workbooks (Esterling, L'Abate, Murray, & Pennebaker, 1999; L'Abate, 1986, 1990, 1992, 1999a, 1999b, 1999c, 1999d, 1999e, 2000, 2001b, 2001c, 2002, in press). Thus far, DW is not yet part of mainstream, established psychotherapeutic interventions. It is not mentioned in leading and recent texts in this field (Hubble, Duncan, & Miller, 1999; Snyder & Ingram, 2000) or among empirically based interventions (Dobson & Craig, 1998; Nathan & Gorman, 1998), perhaps because much of the research to date on DW is based on undergraduate rather than on clinical (i.e., patient) populations.

In comparing talk with writing, some differences between these two media merit highlighting. For instance, talk is learned earlier in life than writing, and, therefore, it is easier to learn than writing. Talk is automatic, whereas writing must be taught systematically. Consequently, it takes less effort to speak than to write. Talk is spontaneous and dependent on the immediate social context, whereas writing is deliberate and more autonomous; thus, it takes less time and planning to speak than to write. Furthermore, there are more ideas in speaking per unit of time, whereas there are more ideas per number of words in writing. Usually there is no permanent record in speech unless it is tape-recorded. However, it takes time and money to transcribe audiotapes into a written format. Writing is itself a permanent record. Speech is syntactically less complex and more concrete than writing. Because of these differences there is more retention in reading and writing than there is in speaking. As a result, more issues can be confronted in writing than can be done verbally per unit of therapist time (L'Abate, 1990, 1992, 1994, 1997, 1999a, 1999b, 1999e). Finally, it could be argued that talking and writing originate from different hemispheric specializations—talking being mostly right, frontal lobe and writing being mostly left, frontal lobe. Of course, there are additional physiological functions involved. The following is a sketchy summary of possible hemispheric and cerebral differences already considered elsewhere (L'Abate, 2002; Reed, McMahan, & L'Abate, 2001).

The following differences between psychotherapy and DW also merit highlighting. For some therapists, reliance on style or personal presence is more important than method. In DW, reliance on method is more important than style or personal presence. Style varies from one therapist to another, whereas in DW there is less variance and greater uniformity of approach. Style in the latter is either secondary or irrelevant. The process of face-to-face, personal contact, talk-based psychotherapy is claimed to be idiographic (i.e., strictly and specifically individually oriented), whereas DW can be both idiographic and nomothetic, in the sense that it can be delivered to groups or even masses of people. As shown in Exhibit 13.1, however, workbooks, which are among the most programmed of various degrees of structure in DW, can be made to be extremely idiographic, especially if instructions allow respondents to rank items defining a given subject (e.g., anxiety, depression) according to their individual preferences. In psychotherapy, the content is dynamic and flexible within and between sessions. In DW, on the other hand, content can be varied or fixed, within somewhat restricted limits. As Seligman (1998) concluded, psychotherapy is too vague to be specific, whereas DW, especially workbooks, can be very specific and explicit, making them replicable from one professional to another and from one clinical setting to another. The result of inadequate specificity makes psychotherapy a rather inefficient and costly pursuit, whereas costs for DW are relatively low, especially if one considers the

EXHIBIT 13.1
Possible Functions of Workbooks

1. Workbooks can serve as structured interviews or scripts for professionals and students who are not familiar with the viewpoint or research underlying a particular workbook. For instance, many workbooks are based on viewpoints that are not immediately available to the traditional clinical repertoires of many professional helpers. Thus, workbooks do increase the possible choices that are available to both professionals and respondents.
2. Workbooks can increase the awareness and critical evaluation of set beliefs, cognitions, and behavioral patterns.
3. Workbooks can save time in clinical practice by maximizing cost-effectiveness of interventions and by helping respondents who cannot afford weekly, face-to-face interventions.
4. By maintaining a continuum of care between sessions, especially when professional helpers are on vacation or unavailable, workbooks are designed to manage care requirements of accountability and cost-effectiveness.
5. Workbooks can teach respondents coping and problem-solving strategies, without the direct presence or influence of professionals.
6. On the basis of tentative and preliminary evidence (Smyth & L'Abate, 2001), workbooks could provide a synergistic process when coupled with face-to-face talk-based therapy sessions.
7. Workbooks could enhance the intake phase of therapy with checks prior to face-to-face, verbal interventions. For example, homework assignments could be designed to teach respondents how best to benefit from therapy and the importance of completing assignments after each therapy session.
8. Workbooks could provide a method of assessing readiness for change and the degree to which respondents are willing to take on responsibility for change.
9. Workbooks can serve as tools after a face-to-face, verbal intervention session. Some former psychotherapy patients could profit by completing homework assignments in writing (L'Abate, 2000).
10. Workbooks can train beginning graduate students to deal with a variety of mental health issues with individuals, couples, and families by initially using them as scripts for structured interviews and as guidelines for interventions (Jordan, 2001), thereby reducing guesswork in treatment planning.
11. By following diagnosis-specific treatment plans based on leading mental health assessment tools or referral questions, workbooks can provide uniform treatment and convenient protocols for either verbal face-to-face or tape-recorded interventions.
12. Workbooks can serve as software for computer-mediated-interventions, mental health training, prevention, psychotherapy, and rehabilitation.
13. Using workbooks, researchers can conduct inexpensive and easily controlled studies, thus minimizing the need for elaborate record keeping, coding, and classification and enabling them to reach many more respondents in the same amount of time.

mass-production of printed matter (L'Abate, 2001c). Consequently, under conditions that have yet to be specified, DW may be more cost-effective than talk (L'Abate, 1999e), because it costs the paper it is printed on and accounts for what respondents did without having to record their utterances, as in face-to-face talk. The latter is a very expensive enterprise left in the hands of few, grant-supported researchers.

Finally, to understand this relatively new "cure," a classification of writing is necessary. Writing can range from expressive, creative, and spontaneous (contextual, constructive stories) to instructive and contrived (vocabulary, spelling, style, grammar, logic, sentence construction) to a combination of the two. Also, different but overlapping writing interventions can range from "unstructured and unrestricted" to "structured and restricted." For instance, as far as structure is concerned, open-ended writing, as in journals or diaries, represents the least structured or unrestricted extreme of this dimension. Focused writing on one topic, as in autobiographies or Pennebaker's (1997) expressive format, illustrates a more structured, restricted level. Guided writing, as in questions about already written compositions asked in writing, represents another level in the structure (restriction) dimension. Programmed writing, as in workbooks, represents the most restricted (structured) extreme, a technology proposed in this chapter and other works. Additional dimensions of goals (cathartic vs. prescriptive), specificity (high vs. low), content (traumatic vs. trivial, general vs. specific), and level of abstraction (high vs. low) complete a classification of DW (L'Abate, 1992, 2002).

Given these contextual premises, we propose that programmed DW, as represented by mental health workbooks, coupled with existing Internet technology, may well constitute an evolutionary step, if not a revolutionary paradigmatic shift, in the delivery of mental health services (L'Abate, 2001c, in press). With computers, workbooks may also be viewed as software modules or packets that can be implemented through the Internet, e-mail, and facsimile. Within this technology, workbooks can be viewed as alternatives, supplements, adjuncts, or replacements for more traditional, unstructured, either face-to-face or even Internet-conducted, unstructured interventions that mimic face-to-face, verbal psychotherapy. Consequently, workbooks can be of benefit in primary, secondary, and tertiary prevention practices (L'Abate, 1990, 1992, 1999c, 1999d, 1999e, in press; McMahan & L'Abate, 2001; Reed et al., 2001; Smyth & L'Abate, 2001). The results of meta-analyses by Kazantzis (2000) and his co-workers (Kazantzis, Deane, & Ronan, 2000) support the usefulness of homework assignments in psychotherapy. Their results support the administration of systematically written homework assignments, or workbooks, either in face-to-face psychotherapy or at a distance from respondents, though the mail, facsimile, or Internet.

STRUCTURE AND CLASSIFICATION OF WORKBOOKS

Workbooks consist of a sequential series of programmed, written homework assignments involving questions, tasks, and exercises that systematically address specific topics. Contents of workbooks can be designed to focus on a variety of clinical to nonclinical referral questions, to address such topics as anger, procrastination, depression, sibling rivalry, temper tantrums, and self-esteem (L'Abate, 1996, 2001a). Workbooks have been created from several assessment instruments. The Beck Depression Inventory (BDI; Beck, 1976) and Minnesota Multiphasic Personality Inventory–2 (MMPI–2; Greene & Clopton, 1999) are two examples of workbooks for individuals, couples, and families, which have been developed from test instruments. Other published workbooks (L'Abate, 1996, 2001a, 2002) cover most mental health issues, problems, and symptoms ranging from clinical to nonclinical, criminal to normative populations. DW, workbooks, and structured computer-assisted interventions may be useful in the treatment of character disorders, as well as criminal and acting-out behaviors.

Workbooks are classified according to the following overlapping dimensions: (a) stages in the life-cycle (children, adolescents, adults, couples, and families); (b) referral questions (e.g., anxiety, depression, couple conflict), single score test (BDI and others), or multiple score test profiles (MMPI–2 and others); (c) specificity for individuals by normalization, personality disorders of internalization (anxiety, depression, fear), externalization (anger, aggression, hostility, and impulsivity), and severe psychopathology; (d) straightforward, linear versus circular style; (e) nomothetic versus idiographic format; (f) theory-derived versus theory-independent; and (g) content, by title of intended target population (e.g., addictions, affective disorders, acting out, intimacy, family relationships).

We acknowledge that workbooks are definitely an unabashedly mechanistic, completely American, technology based on a catalog of "solutions" —in other words, given a psychological condition, clinical, nonclinical, criminal, or chronic, there is (or there will be) a workbook to deal with it, matching problem or diagnosis with intervention. It remains to be seen, however, whether the intervention is in fact a solution. Workbooks are designed to address the tailoring of treatment to match the presented concern as well the "diagnosis" of a specific condition. For instance, there are at least seven workbooks for the treatment of depression (L'Abate, 2001a). The issue is to effectively match the workbook with the type or level of depression. This approach, therefore, parallels the medical model. For every physical symptom or disease there is a limited number of optimal replicable medications or operations. If one medication does not work well, one searches for the medication that best fits the patient's needs. This approach is specific to the administration of workbooks and in no way denies a humanistic model based on compassionate, unconditional regard, empathy, and warmth. One could argue that the medical model (L'Abate, 2001c) is actually the most human model by being based on evidence rather than on wishful thinking, as in the case of many psychological interventions. Workbooks, therefore, are to psychological interventions what medications are to psychiatry and medicine (L'Abate, in press). There is wide choice of workbooks to deal with the same condition, and each workbook has a predetermined "dosage," or length of treatment in terms of the number of assignments required to complete the workbook. This analogy breaks down when one considers that medications are sometimes administered for life, whereas a workbook is usually not administered repeatedly.

Workbooks also represent a systematic distillation and applied encapsulation of existing knowledge that would remain inert or unused otherwise (L'Abate, 2001c, in press). For instance, workbooks have been derived from existing single-score tests, like the BDI, or multidimensional ones, like the MMPI–2 (L'Abate, 1996). As stated earlier, workbooks were derived to link evaluation with intervention much more directly and explicitly than can be achieved verbally. Other workbooks were developed on the basis of (a) clinical experience, (b) existing theories or theoretical models, (c) factor analyses, (d) research, and (e) even self-help, popular literature. An example of what is meant by assignment is shown in the first, introductory workbook developed to facilitate emotional expression (Exhibit 13.1). As one can glimpse from this example, workbooks represent a level of specificity and explicitness that is either impossible or very difficult and expensive to achieve through talk. How many sessions of face-to-face, talk-based psychotherapy would it take to deliver the same information and then make sure that respondents obtain and retain it?

The addition of DW, as a possibly cost-effective, mass-distributed innovation, would produce a continuum of care—primary, secondary, and tertiary—composed of successive steps, sequential increments or sieves, in the delivery of mental health services, ranging from the least to the most expensive (L'Abate, 2002). However, like any newly proposed delivery model for mental health services, it is important to consider the empirical bases of this approach. De Giacomo and De Nigris (2001) as well as Gould (2001) have shown how some patients prefer using computers rather than face-to-face psychotherapy. In some cases, computer-assisted workbooks were precursors to family or group therapy. They produced the motivation for entering into a face-to-face verbal contact with a professional.

SUPPORTING RESEARCH

L'Abate (2001c) summarized 12 studies about homework assignments performed in his laboratory over a 25-year span with undergraduate populations. Two of these studies have been published in their entirety (McMahan & L'Abate, 2001; Reed et al., 2001). Effect size estimates among these studies were extremely varied and not always in the expected direction. L'Abate (2001c), therefore, concluded that there were at least three major shortcomings with the research efforts he summarized: (a) They were conducted by the author of the workbooks and his collaborators, introducing an evident experimenter bias that raises questions about the validity of these results, (b) they appeared in secondary works published by the author or in low-impact journals with little if any refereed feedback, and (c) at least three unpublished studies produced paradoxically negative results (i.e., control groups did better than experimental groups). These negative results confirm Pennebaker's (2001) findings that expressive, focused DW about one's traumas have disruptive effects on respondents. Another hypothesis for the relative success of control groups is compensatory rivalry. Compensatory rivalry refers to the awareness of control participants that they are being compared with participants from an experimental group. Whether these effects are long term or stronger with some individuals than with others are questions that remain unanswered.

Unexpected and paradoxical results—in a study involving MMPI–2 workbooks in which the control group obtained significantly greater mean change scores than the experimental group, in a study with outpatients (Bird, 1992), and in McMahan and L'Abate's study (2001) with seminarian couples—suggest that the use of workbooks to treat psychological disorders requires more extensive study. Some workbooks may elicit in respondents pent-up anxieties or reactions to past toxic events that were avoided, denied, repressed, or suppressed. The undeniable fact that in at least three studies control groups obtained higher gain scores than experimental groups suggests that this is an important area to investigate in the future. What is the nature of these lowered scores? Are they temporary or long lasting? Are lowered gain scores indications of an antitherapeutic workbook effect? Research is required to compare workbooks developed from different empirical and theoretical sources to answer a related question: "Which workbook is effective with what problems and which populations?"

To address some of the foregoing issues, Smyth and L'Abate (2001) conducted a meta-analysis of 18 workbook studies. The goal was to determine to what degree workbooks lead to improvements in mental and physical health. Meta-analytical methods provide an alternative, and in many ways preferable, approach to evaluating research literature than a narrative or "box-score" approach. There are, however, some unique difficulties posed by the literature on workbooks. Vast differences exist between studies in overall design and quality of methods and statistics used. There are, however, a relatively small number of studies that contrast workbooks to a control condition (often a delayed treatment condition). All studies included in the analysis used workbooks in conjunction with or as the sole form of therapy. Studies also were required to contain some outcome measure of health. Such health outcomes could be in the domain of either mental or physical health, or more general measures of performance (e.g., student grades, cognitive performance). Studies also had to contain statistical information necessary to calculate an effect size. Magnitude and significance of the overall mean weighted effect size was computed for all outcomes and all 18 studies. One effect size was computed for each study by averaging the individual effect sizes for each outcome in the study. These study effect sizes were then cumulated across all studies (corrected for bias) for an overall effect size of workbooks.

The overall effect size across all outcomes and all studies was .30 (r = .15; 95% CI 0.21–0.39, $p < .0001$). There was considerable variability in effect sizes between studies, ranging from −.22 to 1.16. Effect size for workbooks alone was .36 (r = .15; 95% CI 0.22–0.50), whereas the effect size for workbooks used in conjunction with other treatment was .26 (r = .13; 95% CI 0.15–0.37). The difference between these two effect sizes was not significant. Overall effect size for mental health outcomes was .44 (r = .21; 95% CI 0.29–0.59). Overall effect size of workbooks on physical health outcomes was .25 (r = .12; 95% CI 0.14–0.35). Unlike mental health outcomes, the test for homogeneity of effect sizes was significant, $Qw(5) = 10.79$, $p = .05$.

Results of this analysis, as well as conclusions presented above, suggest that workbooks may produce a medium effect size in mental health and a somewhat lower effect size for physical health. This effect size is similar to the one obtained from average minimal treatment (placebo) effect size (.42) obtained from a recent review of meta-analyses of psychological treatment (Asay & Lambert, 1999). This analysis provides partial support for the use of workbooks as additions or as alternatives to preventive, psychotherapeutic, and rehabilitative practices, making them ancillary as well as independent methods of intervention.

Benefits of Workbooks

The use of workbooks as a cost-effective, mass-produced, easily repeatable, and explicitly specific intervention has the potential to improve behavior by bringing individuals, groups, couples, and families together to work on issues that are relevant to their functioning and well-being. Workbook interventions, with a focus on specific mental health topics, as administered through a computer-assisted modality, can provide respondents with some of the functions listed in Exhibit 13.2. Whether these suggested functions are advantageous to respondents or therapists remains to be seen. Functions represent a service, whereas advantages represent possible benefits that can accrue from using these services. A function may have disadvantages as well.

Ultimately, workbooks can serve as a dynamic test of theory. Instead of applying the at times sterile and unproductive testing of theories or models through psychometric instruments, workbooks, which are created from different empirical bases or theoretical viewpoints, can become the applied ground for comparative evaluation of different or opposing viewpoints. For instance, if a workbook on depression is developed from a

EXHIBIT 13.2
Possible Advantages from Workbook Administration

1. Workbooks provide treatment plans that are more specific and detailed than verbally administered treatment plans.
2. The use of workbooks creates a link between mental health professionals and laypersons by demystifying mental health jargon. Workbooks and programmed assignments push the professional to operationalize many of the technical terms used in the mental health delivery systems (L'Abate, 2002).
3. The use of workbooks may be a more efficient method of increasing the generalization effect of learning and behaviors for respondents in homes, schools, and work settings.
4. When workbooks are developed from existing tests, like the MMPI–2, it is possible to link evaluation specifically with treatment. This specific link has been and continues to be difficult and expensive to achieve as long as psychological treatments are based on talk rather than on the written medium (Bickman, 1999; L'Abate, 1999e, 2002).
5. Workbooks provide respondents with concrete, direct, and explicit suggestions on how to deal with presenting concerns by requiring homework assignments that extend the typical 50-minute face-to-face psychotherapy or counseling session.
6. Workbooks are a possible tool for enriching and deepening understanding of issues discussed in therapy sessions.
7. Workbooks help respondents to segment and break down presenting concerns, problems, or symptoms into smaller and more manageable units or modules.
8. Workbooks permit respondents to take on more responsibility in their change and growth processes, thereby conserving the efforts and time of paid professionals.
9. Workbooks are a technology for reaching underserved populations, such as the home-bound and the handicapped, military personnel, Peace Corps volunteers, missionary families abroad, and incarcerated felons and juveniles.
10. Workbooks present a paradigm to conduct more rigorous research as a result of the specificity of the repeatable treatment inherent in workbook methodology. This process would be unimpeded and unobstructed by extraneous and sometimes interfering variables like voice and nonverbal behaviors. These variables can be measured and observed online in more controlled ways than in face-to-face, verbal contacts (L'Abate, 2001c).

cognitive–behavioral viewpoint, it could be compared with another workbook developed on the basis of an interpersonal viewpoint.

Advantages

The advantages of using workbooks as described in Exhibit 13.3 may outweigh their potential, as yet unknown, disadvantages. These suggested advantages require additional scrutiny and discussion through professional and scientific inquiry. Anyone planning to use a workbook approach should also use at least a short test battery and obtain a signed informed consent form.

The most distinct advantage of workbooks, in addition to providing a direct link between evaluation and intervention, lies in dealing with

EXHIBIT 13.3
Possible Disadvantages and Dangers of Workbook Administration

1. The workbook chosen may not be an appropriate solution for the problem (as a result of inadequate diagnosis and incorrect workbook administration).
2. Therapeutic contract may be improper (e.g., nonadministration of an informed consent form and more information related to before and after evaluation criteria).
3. The administrators may not track and match completed evaluation instruments and assignments with respondents involved in completing workbook assignments.
4. It is difficult to verify that the respondents who were evaluated and who signed the informed consent form are the same ones who completed homework assignments. This danger is especially relevant with acting-out, impulsive, and criminal populations.
5. Some of the restrictions listed in the informed consent form limiting and excluding the use of workbooks with special populations may be violated.
6. Administrators may not provide adequate, positive, and supportive feedback throughout the process.
7. Only a few workbooks have been validated (L'Abate, 1992, 2001c, 2002; L'Abate, Boyce, Fraizer, & Russ, 1992). Very few of those available on the market (L'Abate, 2001a) have been validated at all. Hence, it behooves professionals to use as many precautions and controls when using workbooks that have not been specifically validated.
8. Compliance problems are present in any administration out of the immediate control of the professions, and workbooks and homework assignments are no exception. Treatment, however, can be provided or withheld when homework assignments are not completed.

comorbid conditions. For instance, if an individual is treated medically for a bipolar disorder and refuses psychotherapy, an appropriate, all-purpose workbook could be used as an alternative or as preparation for face-to-face psychotherapy (De Giacomo & De Nigris, 2001; Gould, 2001). It would be possible to have one partner in couple therapy being treated for depression, with either medication or psychotherapy, while the other partner is being treated for some other specific mental health issue. Both individuals could benefit by completing a workbook on arguing and fighting or intimacy. In family therapy with a child who is acting out in school, family members could benefit from a workbook related to interpersonal conflict and intimacy issues, parent–child conflicts, sibling rivalry, lying, time-out, and binging, among others (L'Abate, 1996, 1999c, 1999d, 1999e, 2001c, 2002).

Another advantage of using workbooks is their potential for revisions and improvements on the basis of research and professional experience. By contrast, it is almost impossible to "revise" therapists. When therapists begin practicing what they learned during their training, evaluation of improved effectiveness is either difficult or unlikely (Bickman, 1999). Workbooks, on the other hand, can be revised with less effort and expense. Additional advantages of the use of workbooks include a possible decrease in unproductive sessions, decrease in expense to respondents, and a way of enhancing accountability and cost-effectiveness strategies as they relate to managed mental health care.

Critical Issues and Potential Disadvantages and Dangers

Possible disadvantages and dangers of workbook use are summarized in Exhibit 13.4 (L'Abate, 2001c). In addition to these limitations, one must identify the interplay of individual differences related to preference and capacity for verbal versus written expression. McMahan and L'Abate (2001) conducted research with seminarian couples in two experimental groups using two different workbooks and found significantly lower mean change scores than a no-workbook control group. These paradoxical results parallel those obtained by comparing participants using MMPI–2 workbooks with participants in a control group who wrote about trivial topics. These results suggest that respondents are not immune to strong emotions elicited by certain workbooks, as in the case of Pennebaker's work (Esterling et al., 1999; Esterling & Pennebaker, 2001; Pennebaker, 2001). Unfortunately, we do not yet know whether these decreases are temporary, transient, or long lasting. This, as well as the issue of liability and responsibility for a professional administering workbooks at a distance, require further study (L'Abate, 2002).

Self-diagnosis, self-administration, and the administration of workbooks through the Internet could cause additional problems. We are certain that other, as yet unknown disadvantages and even dangers may also be present (see also chapter 12, this volume). However, the usefulness of this approach will remain unknown unless it is applied with functional and dysfunctional populations.

A SAMPLE OF THE PRODUCT

We conclude this chapter with a summary of two other workbooks: one that uses a fixed format for the development of an "emotional competence" and one that uses a more flexible format to encourage "emotional expression."

Emotional Competence Workbook

The writing assignment illustrated in Exhibit 13.4 is based on the workbook developed, in part, by Saarni (1999) within the context of other treatises on emotionality (L'Abate, 2002), as well as from L'Abate's (1994, 1997) stress on "hurt feelings," a catch-all term used as somewhat equivalent to Pennebaker's (1997) "traumas." The focus of the emotional com-

EXHIBIT 13.4
Development of Emotional Competence Workbook

ASSIGNMENT NO. 1: THE IMPORTANCE OF OUR FEELINGS AND EMOTIONS

The purpose of this workbook is to help improve your emotional competence. The purpose of this first assignment is to find how important feelings and emotions (yes, there is a difference between these two!) for your survival and even your enjoyment of life. Many people do not know how to deal with their feelings and emotions because they have not paid attention to them, have avoided them altogether, or did not have adequate models for emotional regulation in their families of origin. Hence, it is important to find out what feelings and emotions mean to you.

1. To begin with, on a scale of 1 to 10, with 1 meaning complete, absolute control and delay over your feelings and emotions and 10 meaning complete, free, and unabashed explosion and discharge of feelings and emotions, regardless of the consequences, underline where you fit most of the time:

     Delay   1   2   3   4   5   6   7   8   9   10   Discharge

2. Please check which of these applies to you. For you (and no one else), feelings and emotions are:

    a. _____ Completely unimportant   d. _____ Important

    b. _____ Unimportant   e. _____ Very important

    c. _____ Neutral or indifferent   f. _____ Extremely important

3. Explain how you arrived at this view of feelings and emotions:

4. List as many feelings and emotions as you are aware of:

5. From this list of feelings and emotions which do you use most often?

6. Why do you use these particular feelings and emotions?

7. How do you deal with your feelings in most situations?

8. How are these feelings and emotions related to you as a person?

EXHIBIT 13.4 (*Continued*)

9. How were feelings and emotions dealt with in your family of origin? Explain in detail and even give particular instances of how feelings and emotions were dealt with in your family:

10. In what situations did you experience extreme feelings and how did you express them? Write about three situations where you experienced extreme feelings. Write: a) what happened to you, b) how you did react, and c) what happened to you or others afterwards:

Situation 1.

Situation 2.

Situation 3.

Homework: During the coming week, keep a list of all the feelings or emotional situations that faced *you on a daily basis*. It is very important for you to keep this daily list if you really want to go on with this workbook and understand and improve your emotional competence.

petence workbook, instead, is to teach individuals to cope with feelings and emotions in more constructive ways than was heretofore possible.

Assignments of this workbook are composed of topics ranging from (a) importance of feelings and emotions, (b) awareness of feelings and emotions, (c) experience of feelings and their expression, (d) awareness of others' feelings and emotions, (e) use of the vocabulary of emotional experience and expression, (f) capacity for empathic involvement, (g) ability to cope with painful feelings and distressful situations, (h) awareness of emotional communication in relationships, (i) capacity for emotional self-effectiveness, and (j) emotional incompetence and abnormality. There is a follow-up assignment to foster and record feedback about the whole process of workbook administration and completion. Ideally, objective criteria would be used to assess change in respondents' emotional competence. This workbook could be used in tandem with or as supplement to the workbook described below.

Emotional Expression Workbook

The concept of an emotional expression workbook is based on Bonanno and Keltner (1997), as well as on the work of many other emotion theorists (see L'Abate, 2002). A relevant feature of this workbook is the inclusion of the respondent's partner or family members in the process of dealing with feelings. It includes three assignments:

1. The introductory, diagnostic, and prescriptive assignment related to becoming aware of feelings requires respondents to define and provide examples for 11 feeling words listed at the beginning of the assignment, with room for three additional feeling words provided by either professionals or respondents. After definitions and examples are completed, the list of feelings is rank-ordered according to relevance for each respondent. Subsequent assignments of the workbook are administered on the basis of the initial (idiographic) rank ordering. The same process is repeated either by a partner or members of the family of origin.

2. A standard format assignment includes questions about origin, development, frequency, duration, intensity, and intrapersonal and interpersonal outcomes of each feeling. Each assignment is specifically devoted to one specific feeling, a process that would be difficult if not impossible to undertake verbally.

3. A concluding feedback assignment includes questions about the usefulness of the workbook, rank-order of feelings and emotions that were part of each assignment, and respondents' feelings about each assignment and the whole workbook.

This approach (definitions, rank order, and administration of assignments on the basis of the prescriptive rank order) is followed in many other workbooks developed by L'Abate (1996). Hence, even though workbooks may be conceived as representing a nomothetic approach, the same workbook for all respondents, individual rank-orders of any list of items, contained in the first diagnostic–prescriptive assignment, allows assignment administration to follow an idiographic sequence that is unique to one individual or couple.

CONCLUSION

Workbooks to help distressed individuals, couples, and families and those with ordinary developmental concerns have the potential to fulfill many preventive, psychotherapeutic, and rehabilitative functions. Research on their range of preventive and paratherapeutic applications is still in its infancy. Much more evidence is required before this approach is adapted to clinical populations.

The challenge of the future, then, is to create a personal link in the delivery of mental health services with the existing and ever-expanding technology of the Internet. We believe that programmed workbooks coupled with computer-assisted interventions, an approach proposed here, has promise. This proposal is a possible solution for the shortcomings of verbal, face-to-face psychotherapy (Bickman, 1999; L'Abate, 1999a, 2002). Evaluation of this approach must be undertaken by researchers who have not been involved in its development.

REFERENCES

Asay, T. P., & Lambert, M. J. (1999). The empirical case for the common factors in therapy: Quantitative findings. In M. A. Hubble, B. L. Duncan, & S. D. Miller (Eds.), *The heart and soul of change: What works in therapy* (pp. 23–55). Washington, DC: American Psychological Association.

Beck, A. (1976). *Cognitive therapy and the emotional disorders*. New York: Meridian Press.

Bickman, L. (1999). Practice makes perfect and other myths about mental health services. *American Psychologist, 54*, 965–978.

Bird, G. (1992). *Programmed writing as a method for increasing self-esteem, self-disclosure, and coping skills* [Unpublished Doctoral Dissertation]. Department of Counseling and Psychological Services, Georgia State University, Atlanta.

Bonanno, G. A., & Keltner, D. (1997). Facial expression of emotion and the course of conjugal bereavement. *Journal of Abnormal Psychology, 106*, 126–137.

De Giacomo, P., & De Nigris, S. (2001). Computer workbooks in psychotherapy with psychiatric patients. In L. L'Abate (Ed.), *Distance writing and computer-assisted interventions in psychiatry and mental health* (pp. 113–133). Stamford, CT: Ablex.

Dobson, K. S., & Craig, K. D. (Eds.). (1998). *Empirically supported therapies: Best practice in professional psychology*. Thousand Oaks, CA: Sage.

Esterling, B. A., L'Abate, L., Murray, E., & Pennebaker, J. M. (1999). Empirical foundations for writing in prevention and psychotherapy: Mental and physical outcomes. *Clinical Psychology Review, 19*, 79–96.

Esterling, B. A., & Pennebaker, J. W. (2001). Focused expressive writing, immune functions, and physical illness. In L. L'Abate (Ed.), *Distance writing and computer-assisted interventions in psychiatry and mental health* (pp. 47–60). Westport, CT: Ablex.

Gould, R. (2001). A feedback-driven computer program for outpatient training.

In L. L'Abate (Ed.), *Distance writing and computer-assisted interventions in psychiatry and mental health* (pp. 93–111). Stamford, CT: Ablex.

Green, R. L., & Clopton, J. R. (1999). Minnesota Multiphasic Personality Inventory-2 (MMPI-2). In M. E. Maruish (Ed.), *The use of psychological testing for treatment planning and outcomes assessment* (pp. 1023–1049). Mahwah, NJ: Erlbaum.

Hubble, M. A., Duncan, B. L., & Miller, S. D. (Eds.). (1999). *The heart & soul of change: What works in therapy.* Washington, DC: American Psychological Association.

Jordan, K. B. (2001). Teaching psychotherapy through workbooks. In L. L'Abate (Ed.), *Distance writing and computer-assisted interventions in psychiatry and mental health* (pp. 171–190). Westport, CT: Ablex.

Kazantzis, N. (2000). Power to detect homework effects in psychotherapy outcome research. *Journal of Consulting and Clinical Psychology, 68,* 166–170.

Kazantzis, N., Deane, F. P., & Ronan, K. R. (2000). Homework assignments in cognitive and behavioral theory: A meta-analysis. *Clinical Psychology: Science and Practice, 7,* 189–202.

L'Abate, L. (1986). *Systematic family therapy.* New York: Brunner/Mazel.

L'Abate, L. (1990). *Building family competence: Primary and secondary prevention strategies.* Thousand Oaks, CA: Sage.

L'Abate, L. (1992). *Programmed writing: A self-administered approach for interventions with individuals, couples, and families.* Pacific Grove, CA: Brooks/Cole.

L'Abate, L. (1994). *A theory of personality development.* New York: Wiley.

L'Abate, L. (1996). Workbooks for better living. Retrieved from http://www.mental-healthhelp.com

L'Abate, L. (1997). *The self in the family: A classification of personality, criminality, and psychopathology.* New York: Wiley.

L'Abate, L. (1999a). Decisions we (mental health professionals) need to make (whether we like them or not): A reply to Cummings and Hoyt. *The Family Journal: Therapy and Counseling for Couples and Families, 7,* 227–230.

L'Abate, L. (1999b). Increasing intimacy in couples through distance writing and face-to-face approaches. In J. Carlson & L. Sperry (Eds.), *The intimate couple* (pp. 328–344). Philadelphia: Taylor & Francis.

L'Abate, L. (1999c). Programmed distance writing in therapy with acting-out adolescents. In C. Schaefer (Ed.), *Innovative psychotherapy techniques in child and adolescent therapy* (pp. 108–157). New York: Wiley.

L'Abate, L. (1999d). Structured enrichment and distance writing for couples. In R. Berger & T. Hannah (Eds.), *Preventive approaches in couples therapy* (pp. 106–124). Philadelphia: Taylor & Francis.

L'Abate, L. (1999e). Taking the bull by the horns: Beyond talk in psychological interventions. *The Family Journal: Therapy and Counseling for Couples and Families, 7,* 206–220.

L'Abate, L. (2000). Psychoeducational strategies. In J. Carlson & L. Sperry (Eds.),

Brief therapy strategies with individuals and couples (pp. 396–436). Phoenix, AZ: Zeig/Tucker.

L'Abate, L. (2001a). *An annotated bibliography of selected self-help mental health workbooks in print.* Manuscript submitted for publication.

L'Abate, L. (2001b). Distance writing and computer-assisted interventions in the delivery of mental health services. In L. L'Abate (Ed.), *Distance writing and computer-assisted interventions in psychiatry and mental health* (pp. 215–226). Westport, CT: Ablex.

L'Abate, L. (2001c). Systematically written, systematic homework assignments: The case for homework-based treatment. In N. Kazantzis, F. P. Doane, K. R. Ronan, & L. L'Abate (Eds.), *The use of homework assignments in cognitive–behavioral therapy.* Manuscript submitted for publication.

L'Abate, L. (2002). *Beyond psychotherapy: Programmed writing and structured computer-assisted interventions.* Westport, CT: Ablex.

L'Abate, L. (Ed.). (in press). *Workbooks in mental health: A practical resource for clinicians.* Binghamton, NY: Haworth.

L'Abate, L., Boyce, J., Fraizer, L., & Russ, D. (1992). Programmed writing: Research in progress. *Comprehensive Mental Health Care, 2,* 45–62.

McMahan, O., & L'Abate, L. (2001). Programmed distance writing with seminarian couples. In L. L'Abate (Ed.), *Distance writing and computer-assisted interventions in psychiatry and mental health* (pp. 135–156). Stamford, CT: Ablex.

Nathan, P. E., & Gorman, J. M. (Eds.). (1998). *A guide to treatments that work.* New York: Oxford University Press.

Pennebaker, J. M. (1997). *Opening up: The healing power of expressing emotions.* New York: Guilford Press.

Pennebaker, J. M. (2001). Explorations into the health benefits of disclosure: Inhibitory, cognitive, and social processes. In L. L'Abate (Ed.), *Distance writing and computer-assisted interventions in psychiatry and mental health* (pp. 33–44). Westport, CT: Ablex.

Reed, R., McMahan, O., & L'Abate, L. (2001). Workbooks and psychotherapy with incarcerated felons. In L. L'Abate (Ed.), *Distance writing and computer-assisted interventions in psychiatry and mental health* (pp. 157–167). Westport, CT: Ablex.

Saarni, C. (1999). *The development of emotional competence.* New York: Guilford.

Seligman, M. E. P. (1998, December). Why therapy works. *Psychological Monitor,* p. 2.

Smyth, J., & L'Abate, L. (2001). A meta-analytic evaluation of work-book effectiveness in physical and mental health. In L. L'Abate (Ed.), *Distance writing and computer-assisted interventions in psychiatry and mental health* (pp. 77–90). Westport, CT: Ablex.

Snyder, C. R., & Ingram, R. E. (Eds.). (2000). *Handbook of psychological change: Psychotherapy processes & practices for the 21st century.* New York: Wiley.

14

TO EVERYTHING THERE IS A SEASON: A WRITTEN EXPRESSION INTERVENTION FOR CLOSURE AT THE END OF LIFE

CAROLYN E. SCHWARTZ AND ELIZABETH DAVID

To everything there is a season, and a time to every purpose under the heaven.

—Ecclesiastes (3:1)

The diagnosis of cancer has often been described as a traumatic event in the life of a cancer patient (Butler, Koopman, Classen, & Spiegel, 1999; Lepore, 2001; Stuber, Kazak, Meeske, & Barakat, 1998), because it is inevitably a watershed experience. Although the growth in psychosocial oncology over the past two decades has led to a plethora of supportive interventions for patients soon after diagnosis or over the course of their quest for a cure, there is a relative paucity of psychosocial interventions aimed at helping patients to face their mortality and achieve closure on the emotional and existential issues that are relevant to them at the end of their life.

Our personal and professional experience with numerous people who

We would like to acknowledge Hester Hill for her support and assistance in recruiting participants for this work; Yungsheng Ma and George Reed for their data analytic assistance; Anne Pratt for data entry services provided; and Amin Vidal for setting up the database. We would also like to express our gratitude to Stephen Lepore for his helpful comments on earlier drafts of this manuscript.

257

have died of cancer has been that the last year of life is usually spent in a continued quest for a cure, in which patients use increasingly invasive medical interventions despite low odds of success. Current services available to patients do not address the existential concerns of facing one's imminent mortality. Consequently, patients lack outlets to discuss and assimilate their thoughts and feelings during this significant time. Clinicians have noted that patients do not discuss their dying unless they are given a context in which to do so (Kubler-Ross, 1969) and that when patients are given opportunities to shift their focus to inner life concerns—existential and relational concerns—then a sense of preparedness for coping with mortality may enhance emotional well-being during this poignant period (Byock, 1997; Groopman, 1997).

When cancer patients focus on the medical at the exclusion of other facets of their lives, we believe that they miss critical opportunities to address the emotional and existential issues that would lead to intimacy with loved ones and closure. These issues are critical to improving quality of life at the end of life and in fact have recently been documented as being core attributes to a "good death" experience for 81–90% of patients (Steinhauser et al., 2000). In the spirit of facilitating this process, we have developed a written expression intervention that seeks to provide patients with a vehicle for processing the emotional and existential issues that arise in the face of the later stages of a terminal illness. The purpose of this chapter is to describe this intervention and to present preliminary data on its putative impact. These data were collected in a series of pilot groups and are intended to provide estimates of expected effect sizes on measured outcomes to facilitate planning a randomized controlled trial of the intervention.

WRITTEN EXPRESSION INTERVENTION

Background

Entitled "Seasons of Life," this intervention is based on the idea that acknowledging a "season" for thinking about the legacy one leaves behind after death helps people to address emotionally salient and poignant topics. We believe that providing this service at a time when people have more physical and emotional resources is preferable to providing it later, such as closer to the active dying phase of life, when their physical, cognitive, and affective resources are increasingly restricted. The intervention builds on a Jungian tradition (see Jung, 1964) in which artistic and written expression is a means of accessing emotional processes that may not be fully acknowledged in the individual's day-to-day encounters and activities. In the Jungian tradition, techniques such as visualization, drawing, and written expression have been increasingly applied to chronically and terminally ill patient populations (Kelley, Lumley, & Leisen, 1997; Richardson et al., 1997; Simonton & Sherman, 1998).

Each writing exercise is preceded by a relaxation induction. This structure is based on the belief that the resulting reduction in arousal enhances and possibly deepens participants' cognitive and emotional processing. Furthermore, the relaxation may help to attenuate defenses (e.g., avoidance, suppression), thereby allowing more unconscious content to surface (Jung, 1927). In this way, individuals might be able to sort through both their thoughts and their feelings related to death. Fully comprehending that death is imminent can be anxiety provoking. In some cases, the anxiety might not be disadvantageous, however, if it induces a person into taking positive steps in other areas of one's life (e.g., enhancing relationships, finishing projects). In other cases, individuals may be able to habituate to the negative thoughts and emotions they have by engaging in them fully. Relaxation may thus allow them to experience and not avoid negative thoughts and emotions. This immersion in negative thoughts and emotions can help them to habituate to negative thoughts and emotions (Greenberg & Lepore, in press; chapter 6, this volume). In the short run this could be painful, but in the long run it might reduce negative emotional, physiological, and cognitive outcomes when individuals are reminded of impending death.

Any expressive therapy is seen as a "vehicle" for accessing emotional processes, and the particular mode may be implemented in an open-ended, nondirective fashion. In the Seasons of Life intervention, we aimed to help people expand their repertoire for their personal journal-writing by demonstrating or suggesting different types of writing exercises and topics upon which they might expand on their own. In the initial group sessions, we selected writing exercises that were more open-ended and then used more pointed and poignant exercises in the later sessions. This structure builds on the increasing group cohesion that develops naturally over time (Korchin, 1976)

General Format

The intervention was designed to take place in six bi-weekly sessions. We chose this format because we felt that it would be more feasible for the relatively sick patients in the group to attend a meeting every other week rather than every week. We also hoped that it would facilitate their integrating a writing habit into their routine. Co-led by an expressive therapist (Elizabeth David) and a behavioral scientist (Carolyn E. Schwartz), each session lasts 1½ hours and begins with a quieting relaxation exercise (e.g., guided progressive muscle relaxation). Two writing exercises then follow, each initiated by a visualization exercise that is designed to relax the individual and to stimulate the imagination regarding the image or concept of the writing exercise. A period of writing then takes place, followed by an opportunity to process the experience in the group. The processing might involve sharing emotional reactions to the exercise, sharing portions of what one wrote, or passing (i.e., choosing not to participate). There was no explicit pressure to participate in the processing discussion, although group members seemed to prefer to contribute. Although participants were invited to share their writing during the group's processing of the writing exercises, we did not require participants to give us their journaling notebooks. (Exhibit 14.1 is from someone who voluntarily shared her writing.) We felt that allowing them to keep their writing private would facilitate a deeper, more personal process.

After the two writing exercises were completed, a brief check-out exercise was done to provide participants with an opportunity to share a broad assessment of their current emotional state. Homework exercises were then assigned, with an eye toward inviting participants to continue

---

EXHIBIT 14.1
Participant's Response to the Light Exercise (Session 1)

LIMELIGHT

Riding my bicycle in the wee hours along dark and silent suburban streets, I feel that the whole world is asleep: no sounds of passing cars, no children playing in the streets, no clouds in the sky. The silence and darkness envelope me, except when I pass beneath a street lamp: I see ahead of me a circle of light cast on the pavement—I draw nearer, and as I pass directly under the lamp, a small dark shadow appears beneath me. As I ride on, the shadow lengthens and grows dimmer until it merges with, disappears, is absorbed once again by the dark night. Riding on, I see ahead of me a much larger circle of light illuminating the dome of the Bahai Temple . . . The whiteness of the dome is radiant against the black sky. As I contemplate the dome, a flock of swallows flies into the circle of light, the undersides of their vigorously-flapping wings illuminated briefly as they pass through the circle of light, then disappear into the dark night. Though visible to me for only the briefest instant, I know that the birds' journey began long before and continues long after their brief apparition-like appearance in the circle of light surrounding the dome.

*　　*　　*　　*

Child: Why do people have to die?

Mother: If everyone who had ever been born were alive right now, there wouldn't be enough room for all of them on the earth. In order for new people to be born, everyone has to die.

Child: Is it like taking turns?

Mother: Yes, that's a good way to think of it.

Child: It's our turn now, right?

Mother: Yes, . . . it's our turn now.

Note. From "Limelight," by Carol Farley. Copyright © 1998 by Carol Farley. Reprinted with permission.

the writing exercises of that particular session over the intervening 2 weeks until the next session. Thus, each session's homework simply suggested that participants revisit the written expression exercises done in that session. In general, compliance was high, with most people setting aside some time between group sessions for continuing the writing exercises begun in the group. The specific exercises involved in the six sessions are described in more detail below. (See the Appendix for specific visualization texts for the writing exercises.)

Sessions 1 and 2

The first two sessions set the context by using written expression exercises that are relatively open-ended and aimed at suggesting new avenues for telling one's story. The first session begins with a review of the "rules of conduct": (a) What is said during group sessions is confidential, (b) patients can pass during postwriting exercise discussions, (c) groups begin and end on time, and (d) patients commit to attending all six sessions but must call in advance if they are unable to make a session. We then proceed with the more open-ended writing exercises: "Light" and "I Remember" in the first session and "Silence" and "Sound" in the second. These exercises were adapted from Goldberg (1986).

Session 3

In the third session one more relatively open-ended exercise is completed, and then work at a more intimate level begins. The open-ended exercise, "Touch," asks participants to think about how their experience of (physical) touching and being touched by others has changed over the course of the cancer experience. This exercise is intended to be relatively brief, so that there is adequate time for the more intimate exercise, the "Life Review" exercise, adapted from Shachter-Shalomi and Miller (1995). In this latter exercise, participants are encouraged to think about specified chronological periods in their life (e.g., childhood, adolescence, midlife) and to write about the most poignant (positive or negative) memories from each. The exercise format is different than previous formats in that participants are asked to jot down a few words to cue key memories from a period during the course of the visualization. After the visualization, participants are then invited to fill out the images or stories that came to mind when prompted by the written cues.

Session 4

Building on the foundation provided by the Life Review exercise, the fourth session involves two Life Repair exercises (Shachter-Shalomi & Miller, 1995), where participants are encouraged to consider two different painful or distressing experiences and to write about them as a movement toward letting go of the pain and forgiving. This session can aid participants in identifying relationships that they wish to work on or to facilitate insight on long-standing issues in current relationships. For example, one woman in the group found the Life Repair exercise a catalyst for recognizing a competitive relationship with her mother that prevented her from being herself around this important parental figure. She reported feeling that this acknowledgment was a first step in freeing herself of this unfortunate dynamic.

Session 5

The fifth session helps participants to write an Ethical Will (Shachter-Shalomi & Miller, 1995). Borrowed from the Jewish tradition, this document is intended for loved ones to read after the patient has died. It is a document that one might write and revise numerous times over a lifetime and can be useful for crystalizing one's essential beliefs and values. It is thus intended to be a written expression of the legacy one hopes to leave for one's family and friends. Because the document is intended to be read after one's death, adhering to guidelines can be important for maximizing its positive impact (see Exhibit 14.2). Writing an Ethical Will does not restrict one from sharing its contents either verbally or in written form prior to one's death. It can, in fact, provide a context for patients to have important discussions with their loved ones before they die. The format of

EXHIBIT 14.2
Guidelines For Writing An Ethical Will

1. Are there specific things you wish to say to specific people?
2. What are the important teachings, messages, etc. you would like to leave as your legacy?
3. What qualities in the people you are writing to have given you pride or pleasure? What do you want to affirm about them?
4. If you have a life partner would you want to give him or her permission to re-couple?
5. What acts of charity would you like survivors to do in your memory? Do you want money donated? To a specific cause?

DO'S AND DON'TS

1. Do include your favorite jokes and memories of the good times you've shared.
2. Don't scold, criticize or use this as a guilt trip to punish people.
3. Don't make funeral requests too firm. Funerals are for survivors. (Of course your funeral may be over when this is read. Better to discuss funeral plans while you're still alive.)
4. Do inform loved ones, in advance of your death, where you have stored your Ethical Will.
5. Do update periodically.
6. Do consider writing the document in long-hand in addition to using a word processor. This personal touch can enhance the document for the recipient.

this session is similar to that of the third session: Participants are asked to jot down a few words to cue recipients of the Ethical Wills they wish to develop during the visualization. They then flesh out the letters during the writing period in the session.

Session 6

The final session is reserved for closure and discussion about thoughts, feelings, and reactions to the group process. Two writing exercises are done in this session. The first, "The Closest You Ever Felt to God and Nature," invites participants to recall an experience in which they encountered their "higher power," a secular term used to describe a sense of a positive force greater than themselves that is related to their best and essential self. In the second exercise, "Leaving," participants are invited to contemplate the feelings and thoughts that arise as they acknowledge that this is the last session of the writing group. These exercises are intended to facilitate closure with the group, so that they can continue to write on their own after the group sessions end. They are also provided with a list of lay references that address writing in general, writing one's autobiography, or journal writing specifically. The idea is to encourage them to keep writing and to continue to allow time for their inner life.

PRELIMINARY ESTIMATES OF THE INTERVENTION IMPACT ON QUALITY OF LIFE OUTCOMES

Participants

The work was done with patients who responded to brochures left in a community-based support service agency (The Wellness Community) or who were referred by the chief of oncology social work at the Beth Israel Deaconess Medical Center in Boston, Massachusetts. Interested participants met with the project director (Carolyn E. Schwartz) for an initial intake interview, at which time the focus of the intervention was explained ("to facilitate processing the emotional and existential issues of advanced cancer") and written informed consent was obtained.

Procedure

The written expression intervention was developed and tested in three pilot groups. Although our emphasis was to provide this intervention to people for whom death was relatively imminent, the initial pilot group included people who were at an earlier stage of cancer. We did not deny them the opportunity to participate because they felt a need to face the existential issues of cancer and sought out this group intervention. The second and third groups were restricted, however, to cancer patients with recurrent or metastatic cancer who were up and about at least 50% of their waking hours. Eighteen patients participated in intake interviews and signed informed consent, and 17 of them participated in a pilot group. These patients were all women and included 9 women with breast cancer, 3 with ovarian cancer, 2 with Hodgkin's disease, and 1 each with melanoma, small intestine cancer, and endometrial cancer. Five people dropped out of the group because of discomfort with the planned content or the format of the exercises (one prior to the first session, two after the first session, two after the second session). One patient died in the course of the group. This left 12 patients with complete data.

Outcomes Measured

A quality of life (QOL) questionnaire packet was completed by the participants and returned by mail at two points in time: prior to the first group session and after the last group session. The questionnaire included reliable and validated measures of QOL in five areas: perceived functional status, mood, existential well-being, reframing coping, and modes by which participants maintained a sense of control. Patient's self-reported functional status was measured using the European Organization for Research and Treatment of Cancer cancer specific version of the QOL Questionnaire-C30 (version 3.0; Aaronson et al., 1993), which incorporates subscales for cognitive function, role function, social function, and emotional function. Mood was assessed using the Bradburn Positive Affect Scale (Bradburn, 1969), which asks respondents to indicate how often in the past week they have experienced various positive emotional states. Existential well-being was measured by the Ryff Happiness Scale—Short Form (Ryff, 1989), which includes scales measuring purpose in life, personal growth, autonomy, environmental mastery, social relatedness, and self-acceptance. In the present study, only a global composite score was computed. Fear of Death was measured by the Collette–Lester Fear of Death Scale (Lester, 1974), which has scales for anxiety about one's own death, one's own dying, others' death, and others' dying. Reframing coping was measured by the Post-Traumatic Growth Inventory (Tedeschi & Calhoun, 1996). This measure assesses positive outcomes reported by people who have experienced traumatic events and includes New Possibilities, Relating to Others, Personal Strength, Spiritual Change, and Appreciation of Life subscales (Tedeschi & Calhoun, 1996). Sense of Control was measured using the modes of control subscales of the Shapiro Control Inventory (Shapiro, 1994). The control subscales yield four scores that quantify whether one gains or cedes control by positive means (i.e., positive assertive or positive yielding) or negative means (i.e., negative assertive, negative yielding). Maintaining a balance of positive assertive (i.e., active, altering) and positive yielding (i.e., trusting, accepting) modes of gaining or relinquishing control has been shown to predict better QOL outcomes in cancer patients (Astin et al., 1999; Schwartz, Feinberg, Jilinskaia, & Applegate, 1999). The Collette–Lester Fear of Death Scale and the Shapiro Control Inventory were added to the QOL packet after the first pilot group, so data are available on only nine patients.

Statistical Analysis

Effect size for each QOL outcome was estimated using Cohen's (1988) formula: $(\mu_1 - \mu_2)/\sigma$. This approach yields estimates of the magnitude of change over time in units of standard deviations, where an effect size of 0.2 to 0.4 is considered small, 0.41 to 0.79 is considered medium, and greater than 0.80 is considered large. We computed two different effect sizes. A clinical effect size estimates clinically significant change and is computed by dividing the mean change score by the average standard deviation of the baseline and posttest measurements. A statistical effect size is useful for power calculations in planning a future clinical trial and is computed by dividing the mean change score by the standard deviation of the change score.

Results

We found that the written expression intervention yielded significant clinical and statistical effect sizes on more than half of the outcomes measured but not always in the desired direction (see Figure 14.1 for magnitude of the effects). The group was associated with positive (i.e., desirable) effects on enhancing role, cognitive, social, and emotional functioning; existential well-being, one aspect of posttraumatic growth (i.e., Relating to Others); and use of a positive yielding mode of control. It was associated with negative (i.e., undesirable) effects on death anxiety and use of a negative assertive mode of control. There were no detectable effects on positive affect, most of the Post-Traumatic Growth Inventory subscales, positive assertive mode of control, or negative yielding mode of control. Statistical effect sizes tended to be larger than the clinical effect sizes, suggesting that the correlation of the measures within subjects is greater than 0.50.

Discussion

The data presented here are intended to be a Phase I/II trial (Schwartz, Chesney, Irwin, & Keefe, 1997) for this written expression intervention. Accordingly, the study is intended to develop and pretest the

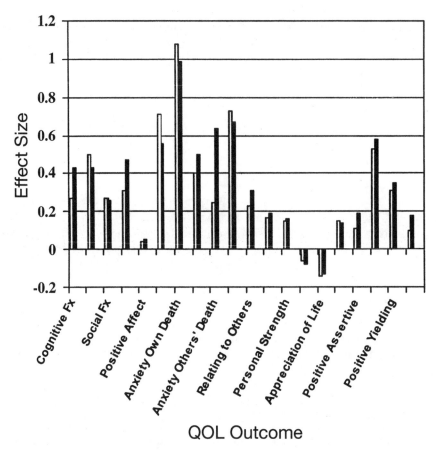

Figure 14.1. Clinical and statistical effect sizes (ES) for quality of life (QOL) outcomes measured.
Note. An ES of .2 to .39 is considered small, an ES of .4 to .79 is considered moderate, and an ES greater than or equal to .8 is considered large. Filled bars denote results with statistical ES; open bars denote clinical ES.

intervention (Phase I), as well as to begin to define relevant outcomes and to begin to determine the appropriate frequency, duration, and intensity of the treatment (Phase II). At this early stage, a control group is unwarranted because so many of the intervention parameters are in development. Rather, it is more important to identify the benefits and costs of participation, a process that is linked to pretesting various outcome measures to determine whether they are sensitive to the types of changes engendered by the intervention. These preliminary data suggest that there are indeed benefits and costs. Specifically, participants reported experiencing enhanced functional status, existential well-being, and ability to engage in one aspect of reframing coping, namely, feeling enhanced social connection as a result of their cancer. In contrast, participants appeared to suffer from increased death anxiety over the 2 months of the intervention. A similar paradox was found regarding use of modes of control. Participants increased their use of adaptive passive modes of control (e.g., as described by adjectives such as *gentle, calm, accepting,* and *listening*), but also appeared to increase their use of less adaptive assertive modes of control (e.g., as described by adjectives such as *impatient, aggressive, selfish,* and *overcontrolling*).

These somewhat paradoxical experiences may support a reconceptualization of Kubler-Ross's model of death and dying along the lines of current thinking that individuals accommodate diverse stages of development at the same time (Bibace, Dillon, & Sagarin, 1999; Bibace, Sagarin, & Dyl, 1998). Accordingly, several of Kubler-Ross's (1969) stages (i.e., denial and isolation; anger; bargaining; depression; acceptance) may coexist. For example, people with a terminal illness may experience anger (e.g., negative assertive mode of control), depression, or their consequences (e.g., death anxiety), at the same time as they experience a growing acceptance of death (e.g., positive yielding mode of control, existential well-being).

Although people who are in the denial and isolation stage may not have opted to participate or to continue to participate in the written expression intervention, those who remained in the group were seeking guidance in facing and getting closure on the existential issues of the end of life. By helping patients discover alternative methods of self-expression and by encouraging them to make time in their daily lives for developing their inner lives, the intervention appeared to influence participants' QOL in measurable ways. We have attempted to provide enough information about our written expression intervention to facilitate the next step in developing this line of investigation, that is, implementing a randomized controlled trial, in which the written expression intervention would be compared to a standard treatment control group (e.g., cancer patient support group).[1] Because most of the outcomes we assessed were associated with small to medium effect sizes, it would be best to power a potential trial adequately to detect such expected effect sizes. A conservative estimate of the requisite sample size would be 64 participants per study arm for a moderate effect size and up to 400 participants per study arm to detect a small effect size (Cohen, 1992). However, a randomized trial would include a control group, so the statistical power of the trial depends on how the control group fares relative to the experimental group. For instance, if the control group gets

---

[1]Isolating the effects of the written expression intervention from the group process might seem like a worthwhile goal for a subsequent randomized trial, but it would require three rather than two study arms (i.e., group intervention without writing, writing alone, combined writing and group intervention). We do not recommend such a design. First, our experience suggests that participant accrual is difficult, so increasing the required sample size by 50% would risk the feasibility of the trial. Second, the nature of the intervention is more focused on the individual's inner experience rather than on the group's cohesion. It is not a support group, and participants are informed of this at the intake interview. We thus do not believe that it is worthwhile to expend the resources to implement the three-arm study.

worse as death approaches whereas the experimental group improves, the statistical power to detect a difference increases. If, however, both groups get worse but at different rates, power is decreased. Thus, the clinical and statistical effects for all of the examined outcomes as shown in Figure 14.1 represent a conservative estimate of the expected effect sizes for which one might plan a study.

Other issues that a future clinical trial should attend to include using data collection procedures that minimize demand characteristics and any potential bias of experimenter expectancies. For example, well-implemented studies by mail (e.g., Dillman, 1978) or by the Internet may be preferable for some outcomes (e.g., mental health). If deeper, more qualitative information about the participant's experience is preferred, then it would be worthwhile to have neutral parties implementing the interviews. A future trial would also be enhanced if normative data were available on all of the selected outcome measures. In the present work, normative data were not available for all of the measures, but the standardized pretest and posttest scores shown in Table 14.1 would suggest a ceiling effect on several of the subscales, which, if present, might have limited our ability to detect change.

In reflecting on our experience in the couple of years spent developing and pretesting this intervention, a few issues seem worthy of mentioning. First, the intervention seems not only to be palatable but actually welcome to those patients who chose to participate. Given the pointed and poignant nature of some of the exercises, this impression is particularly striking. In general, the patients who chose to participate in the pilot groups expressed a need to "go beyond a support group," in which the *modus operandi* was maintaining a positive attitude, a fighting spirit, and search for a cure. They sought a context in which they could think and talk about the more frightening existential implications of cancer.

A second recurring experience was that people were struck by the unexpected nature of what they wrote about. Open-ended exercises elicited cancer-specific memories or musings about mortality (see Exhibit 14.1), and the more pointed exercises seemed to yield surprising or unexpected memories and realizations. Some participants expressed the experience in terms of having encountered an "inner guide" or "a little person on my shoulder" who prompted them in ways they would not have expected. We believe that preceding the writing exercises with a relaxation and visualization portion renders participants more susceptible to precognitive processes than they might otherwise be. This idea is consistent with the Jungian concept of the *unconscious*, which Jung (1927) defined as

> everything of which I know, but of which I am not at the moment thinking; everything of which I was once conscious but have now forgotten; everything perceived by my senses, but not noted by my conscious mind; everything which, involuntarily and without paying

attention to it, I feel, think, remember, want, and do; all the future things that are taking shape in me and will sometime come to consciousness: all this is the content of the unconscious. (p. 185)

Because the concept of the unconscious is not popular in the current research climate, documentation of similar effects in other written expression interventions is unlikely. It is thus difficult to know how similar our experience is to that of other investigators. We believe that qualitative research on the participants' experience could reveal more information about these experiences and would be worthwhile. It would be useful to ascertain, for example, the impact of accessing such precognitive resources for the processes involved in closure at the end of life.

A third salient issue in this work is a consistent difficulty we en-

TABLE 14.1
Pretest and Posttest Scores for QOL Outcomes*

Construct (*scale*)	n	Pretest scores		Posttest scores	
		Mean	SD	Mean	SD
Functional Status (*EORTC*)					
Cognitive Function	12	77.78	21.71	83.33	20.10
Role Function	12	73.61	18.06	81.94	15.01
Social Function	12	70.83	18.97	76.39	22.98
Emotional Function	12	73.61	16.60	78.47	14.42
Mood					
(*Bradburn Positive Affect Scale*)	12	73.61	12.18	74.17	14.29
Existential Well-Being					
(*Ryff Happiness Scale*)	12	63.35	7.02	68.00	5.82
Death Anxiety					
(*Collette–Lester Fear of Death Scale*)					
Anxiety Own Death	9	56.60	13.11	71.53	14.53
Anxiety Own Dying	9	42.01	18.50	50.00	21.48
Anxiety Others' Death	9	40.51	19.64	48.96	13.80
Anxiety Others' Dying	9	42.16	26.15	59.03	20.28
Reframing Coping					
(*Post-Traumatic Growth Inventory*)					
Relating to Others	12	65.95	11.13	70.71	9.68
New Possibility	12	57.67	20.71	61.33	22.46
Personal Strength	12	69.17	12.03	71.25	15.97
Spiritual Change	12	53.33	27.41	51.67	30.70
Appreciation of Life	12	84.44	9.98	82.78	13.17
Modes of Control					
(*Shapiro Control Inventory*)					
Positive Assertive	9	53.24	17.83	55.32	20.71
Negative Assertive	9	78.98	11.27	84.13	8.07
Positive Yielding	9	56.37	14.20	61.01	16.06
Negative Yielding	9	85.19	11.92	86.67	16.67

*Scores were standardized to range in magnitude from zero to 100.

countered over the past 2 years in recruiting participants. We have attempted to recruit participants from two teaching hospitals as well as several community-based facilities that provide support group services to people with cancer and newspaper ads. We found that oncologists rarely referred patients to the pilot study. This low referral rate may have reflected their lack of interest in the work, their discomfort acknowledging that they could no longer cure the patient, or their lack of time for unremunerated research activities because of the financial crises faced by all teaching hospitals at this time. Our primary sources of patients were a community-based support service agency and an oncology social worker who provided support groups to advanced cancer patients at a major teaching hospital. Not one referral was made by the patients' treating oncologists.

In addition to the possible reticence of health care providers to refer patients, we noted that the resulting group of participants who presented themselves for our pilot groups tended to be relatively homogeneous. They tended to be female, Caucasian, well-educated, and relatively affluent. It is not possible to determine whether the written expression intervention would yield benefits for patients of different socioeconomic status, gender, or ethnic background. We did find that patients who dropped out of the group after the first couple of sessions (2 out of a total of 17 enrolled) reported that their reasons included not feeling that they had enough in common with the other participants (e.g., not perceiving that their disease was as advanced) and feeling uncomfortable with the visualization exercises or with writing as self-expression. We believe that furthering this line of investigation would help determine which patients choose to participate (cf. Schwartz & Fox, 1995) and ascertain whether it is possible to modify the recruitment strategies to access a more heterogeneous patient population.

Despite the difficulties in recruiting participants for the pilot groups described herein, we feel that this approach to a written expression intervention holds promise for the burgeoning field of research on using writing to influence health outcomes. If this work were to be extended to a larger clinical trial setting, then it would be possible to examine whether the intervention has an impact on factors relevant to clinical care. For example, do participants in the intervention shift their focus from curative to palliative treatments earlier than control group patients? What is the impact on health care expenditures? Do these patients enjoy more quality-adjusted time than control group patients, that is, by choosing treatments aimed at comfort rather than aggressive treatment when cure is not likely? Such testable questions would be relevant to ascertaining whether the intervention leads to both individual-level and societal gains. With the growing interest in end of life care, we believe that it is appropriate and increasingly necessary to apply psychosocial interventions aimed at improving QOL at the end of life.

REFERENCES

Aaronson, N. K., Ahmedzai, S., Bergman, B., Bullinger, M., Cull, A., Duez, N. J., Filiberti, A., Flechtner, S., Fleishman, S. B., de Haes, J. C. J. M., Kaasa, S., Klee, M., Osoba, D., Razavi, D., Rofe, P. B., Schraub, S., Sneeuw, K., Sullivan, M., & Takeda, F. (1993). The European Organization for Research and Treatment of Cancer QLQ-C30: A quality-of-life instrument for use in international clinical trials in oncology. *Journal of National Cancer Institute, 85,* 365–376.

Astin, J., Anton-Culver, H., Schwartz, C. E., Shapiro, D. H., McQuade, J., Breuer, A. M., Taylor, T., Kurosaki, T., & Lee, H. (1999). A longitudinal study of sense of control and quality of life among women with breast cancer. *Behavioral Medicine, 25,* 101–109.

Bibace, R., Dillon, J. J., & Sagarin, J. D. (1999). Toward a coexistence concept of causal reasoning about illness in children and adults. In R. Bibace, J. J. Dillon, & B. N. Dowds (Eds.), *Partnerships in research, clinical and educational settings* (pp. 27–36). Stamford, CT: Ablex.

Bibace, R., Sagarin, J. D., & Dyl, J. (1998). The heuristic value of Werner's coexistence concept of development. *Journal of Applied Developmental Psychology, 19,* 153–163.

Bradburn, N. M. (1969). *The structure of psychological well-being.* Chicago: Aldine.

Butler, L. D., Koopman, C., Classen, C., & Speigel, D. (1999). Traumatic stress, life events, and emotional support in women with metastatic breast cancer: Cancer-related traumatic stress symptoms associated with past and current stressors. *Health Psychology, 18,* 555–560.

Byock, I. (1997). *Dying well: The prospect for growth at the end of life.* New York: Riverhead Books.

Cohen, J. (1988). *Statistical power analysis for the behavioral sciences* (2nd ed.). Hillsdale, NJ: Erlbaum.

Cohen, J. A. (1992). Power primer. *Psychological Bulletin, 112,* 155–159.

Dillman, D. A. (1978). *Mail and telephone surveys: The total design method.* John Wiley & Sons: New York.

Goldberg, N. (1986). *Writing down the bones.* Boston: Shambala.

Greenberg, M. A., & Lepore, S. J. (in press). Theoretical mechanisms involved in disclosure: From inhibition to self-regulation. In I. Nyklicek, A. J. J. M. Vingerhoets, & L. R. Temoshok (Eds.), *The expression and non-expression of emotions in health and disease.* Amsterdam: Harwood Academic.

Groopman, J. (1997). *The measure of our days: New beginnings at life's end.* New York: Viking.

Jung, C. G. (1927). *The structure and dynamics of the psyche. Collected Works,* Vol. 8. Berlin: Europäische Revue.

Jung, C. G. (1964). *Man and his symbols.* Garden City, NJ: Doubleday.

Kelley, J. E., Lumley, M. A., & Leisen, J. C. C. (1997). Health effects of emotional disclosure in rheumatoid arthritis patients. *Health Psychology, 16,* 331–340.

Korchin, S. J. (1976). *Modern clinical psychology: Principles of intervention in the clinic and community*. New York: Basic Books.

Kubler-Ross, E. (1969). *On death and dying*. New York: MacMillian.

Lepore, S. J. (2001). A social–cognitive processing model of emotional adjustment to cancer. In A. Baum & B. Andersen (Eds.), *Psychosocial interventions for cancer* (pp. 99–118). Washington, DC: American Psychological Association.

Lester, D. (1974). *The Collette-Lester Fear of Death Scale: A Manual*. Pamona, NJ: Richard Stockton State College.

Richardson, M. A., Post-White, J., Grimm, E. A., Moye, L. A., Singletary, S. E., & Justice, B. (1997). Coping, life attitudes, and immune responses to imagery and group support after breast cancer treatment. *Alternative Therapies, 3*, 62–70.

Ryff, C. D. (1989). Happiness is everything, or is it? Explorations on the meaning of psychosocial well-being. *Journal of Personality and Social Psychology, 57*, 1069–1081.

Schwartz, C. E., Chesney, M. A., Irvine, M. J., & Keefe, F. J. (1997). The control group dilemma in clinical research: Applications for psychosocial and behavioral medicine trials. *Psychosomatic Medicine, 59*, 362–371.

Schwartz, C. E., Feinberg, R. G., Jilinskaia, E., & Applegate, J. C. (1999). An evaluation of a psychosocial intervention for survivors of childhood cancer: Paradoxical effects of response shift over time. *Psycho-Oncology, 8*, 344–354.

Schwartz, C. E., & Fox, B. (1995). Who says yes? Identifying selection biases in a psychosocial intervention study of multiple sclerosis. *Social Science and Medicine, 40*, 359–370.

Shachter-Shalomi, Z., & Miller, R. S. (1995). *From age-ing to sage-ing: A profound new vision of growing older*. New York: Warner.

Shapiro, D. H. (1994). *Manual for the Shapiro Control Inventory*. Palo Alto, CA: Behaviordyne.

Simonton, S. S., & Sherman, A. C. (1998). Psychological aspects of mind–body medicine: Promises and pitfalls from research with cancer patients. *Alternative Therapies, 4*, 50–67.

Steinhauser, K. E., Christakis, N. A., Clipp, E. C., McNeilly, M., McIntyre, L., & Tulsky, J. A. (2000). Factors considered important at the end of life by patients, family, physicians, and other care providers. *Journal of the American Medical Association, 284*, 2476–2482.

Stuber, M. L., Kazak, A. E., Meeske, K., & Barakat, L. (1998). Is posttraumatic stress a viable model for understanding responses to childhood cancer? *Child & Adolescent Psychiatric Clinics of North America, 7*, 169–182.

Tedeschi, R. G., & Calhoun, L. G. (1996). The Posttraumatic Growth Inventory: Measuring the positive legacy of trauma. *Journal of Traumatic Stress, 9*, 455–471.

APPENDIX

Visualizations Used for Writing Exercises in the Seasons of Life Sessions

SESSION 1

Exercise: Light

Induction: I invite you to be comfortable in your seat, putting writing materials down, uncrossing legs. Allow yourself to feel the support of the seat as your body relaxes. If you are comfortable with closing your eyes you are invited to do so; otherwise, you may want to hold them slightly closed, at a soft focus. Now, let's take some deep breaths, inhaling and exhaling deeply—on the inhale taking in the healing energy that we all brought to this room and, on the exhale, allowing any tensions that remain from your day's activities to flow down from the top of your head through the tips of your toes. Continue to take a few more deep breaths. [Pause] Now, in your mind's eye, I invite you to focus on light, allowing yourself to go with the first image that comes to mind. What are its facets? Like the facets of a kaleidoscope? Are there colors? Note how the light appears. Is it bright, soft, shimmering? Does it cast a shadow? [Pause] Now focus on the light as you experienced it throughout your day. When you woke up—what was the quality of light? How did it appear as you went to work, as you came to this location? [Pause] How do you experience light in your body? Does it effect your emotions? [Pause] What lights up your mind? [Pause] Feel your soul light—what is that like, the light of your spirit? Now we'll take some moments in silence to contemplate what you're experiencing in the light. The next time you hear my voice it will be with the next instruction. Now it's time to return to the room, feeling the support of your seat, gently, softly, gradually opening your eyes, coming back to the room fully relaxed and refreshed. Now I invite you to pick up your materials and, maintaining silence, write about your experience.

Exercise: I Remember

Induction and Closing: Refer to Previous Visualization

Now I invite you to imagine, in your mind's eye, the words *I remember*. Allow the first memory that comes to mind to dwell within you. When was it? What were your surroundings? Were there people present, or were you alone? What are your thoughts as you survey the scene of this memory? I remember ___ [Pause.] Now, remember getting up this morning. What was it like to get out of bed? Was it easy? Difficult? Remember breakfast.

Remember preparing to begin the rest of your day. How did you feel? What was the scene? I remember ____ [Pause]. Scan your day. What do you remember that stands out? Were there any surprises? I remember ____ [Pause]. Now, we will take some moments in silence to allow you to once again focus on your remembrances. The next time you hear my voice will be with the next instruction. Now it's time to return to the room, feeling the support of your seat, gently, softly, gradually opening your eyes, coming back to the room fully relaxed and refreshed. Now I invite you to pick up your materials and write about your experience.

SESSION 2

Exercise: Silence

Induction

Script: Now, in your mind's eye, you are invited to focus on a silence allowing yourself to focus on the first image or thought that comes to mind. Wrap that image around you, as if you are enveloped in your image of silence. [Pause] Now, examine the silence. Is it thick, thin, light, dark? How does silence feel? Is it expectant, calm, healing? [Pause] Feel yourself feeling silence—reach out and touch it in your mind's eye. Are there any memories associated with silence? Any quiet times? [Pause] What is the sound of silence? Now we'll take some moments in silence allowing yourselves to feel the healing silence we bring to this room. The next time you hear my voice it will be with the next instruction. Exit visualization and instructions regarding materials.

Exercise: Sound

Induction

Script: Now, in your mind, focus on the first sound that comes to mind. Hear it as it resonates in your body—is it soft, loud, caressing? [Pause] What are the sounds of your day? As you rise in the morning—during your morning routine. When you leave your dwelling and go out into the world—what are the sounds that come to you? At the closing of your day as you return. [Pause] Allow yourself to feel and hear the quality and tone of the sounds that come to mind. Maybe the sound of your own voice or the voice of a loved one. What memories are evoked through sound? [Pause] Is there a sound that comes to mind in relation to your body? Is there a sound that comes to mind in relation to your emotions? Is there a sound that comes to mind in relation to your intellect? [Pause] Is there a sound that comes to mind in relation to your soul? What is the sound of your soul—what is the song of your soul? [Pause] Feel the song of your soul as it touches you reaching into eternity. Now, we'll take a few moments in silence as we listen to the unique sounds of ourselves. The next time you hear the sound of my voice it will be with the next instruction. [Pause] Now, if you are so inclined, you are invited to make one of the sounds that have come to mind as we have been focusing on sound. When you are ready allow the sound to come through your lips on the wings of your breath—the sound of your soul. Exit visualization and instructions regarding materials.

SESSION 3

Exercise: Touch

Induction

Script: Now, you are invited to lift your hand and reach over and touch your other hand. Allow yourself to feel the touch of your own hand as it caresses the other. How does it feel as you tenderly touch hands? Now, moving your hands apart, feel the contrast between touching your hands and separating from that touch. [Pause] Now, bring to your mind's eye a moment when you have been touched. How did it feel? Was it tender? Was it abrupt? What does being touched mean? [Pause] When was the last time you were touched by someone? What was that like? [Pause] Was there a time when you were longing for touch? What was that about? Do you remember the circumstances? [Pause] Have you ever felt numb—unable to be touched? What was that about? Do you remember those circumstances? [Pause] Now, bring to mind the most loving touch you can remember. What was that about? What were the circumstances? Now, we'll take some moments in silence as we allow ourselves to experience the variety of facets of ways we've been touched. The next time you hear my voice will be with the next instruction. Now, once again, lift one hand and touch the other —a tender, loving caress—feel the loving of yourself. Exit visualization and instructions regarding materials.

Exercise: Life Review

Procedure

1. We will review phases of life from birth through your current age.
2. The format will be a brief visualization with instructions to stop as we go along and jot down brief words or phrases as a memory aid.
3. We will end with full journaling and processing.

Induction

In your mind's eye you are returning to your earliest years of life from birth through toddler and early childhood. Scan those early years and note any sensations, feelings, important relationships that come to mind. Now, bring to mind your years of mid childhood and preadolescence. Scan those years and note the feelings, sensations, and significant relationships that stand out. Now, move on to the years of adolescence as a teenager. What are the highlights of those years; the feelings, sensations, and significant relationships? Now, scan the years of early adulthood. What comes to mind as you shift from childhood and adolescence to another phase of life? Now, you are entering the years of full adulthood and midlife as you scan the years culminating with the present. What comes to mind as you encounter yourself; your feelings, thoughts, and relationships? Now, we'll take some additional moments in silence as you review your life and its highlights up to now. The next time you hear my voice it will be with the next instruction. Now, slowly and gently, as you are ready, begin returning to the room —feeling the support of the seat, gradually opening your eyes—taking in your surroundings. And, maintaining silence, begin journaling.

SESSION 4

Exercise: Life Repair

Explain Procedure

Introduce format of visualization as being the same method as the visualization on Life Review in Session 3 with the exception that the journaling will be done during the exercise. Processing will occur when the exercise is complete.

Visualization

Induction

Refer to attached. Closing question: How may this particular situation be a theme or metaphor for other situations that are unresolved?

SESSION 5

Exercise: Ethical Will

Induction

Now, in your mind's eye, you are seated at a dining room table—in a comfortable seat—in familiar safe surroundings. Gradually, you see the vague outline of a figure sitting across from you—a figure you sense you have been waiting for all your life. As you watch with curiosity and anticipation, the figure becomes clear. Now you are facing your wisdom figure. When you are ready, invite your wisdom figure to share the teaching you are now ready to hear. You may have a question to ask or simply engage in conversation being receptive to the wisdom you are about to hear. We will now take a few moments in silence to hear and reflect on your inner wisdom figure. As you absorb the wisdom and teaching, in your mind's eye, extend your hand and touch your wisdom figure, feeling yourself merging together in harmony and wholeness—knowing that you have joined with your own inner wisdom and knowledge as the figure melts away. Now, remembering your inner wisdom, as you remain seated at the table, you are joined around the table by those persons you care about the most—your loved ones whom you've invited. Now, scan the table looking at their faces—thinking about what you want to say to them—what you want to teach them from your own life experience—what you may want to affirm about your lives together. We will take a few moments in silence to allow you to contemplate your loved ones. When you hear my voice next it will be with further instructions. Now, it is time to say goodbye to your guests allowing them to fade away in your mind's eye. Slowly and gently begin returning to the room, feeling your seat, becoming aware of the surroundings—remembering all that transpired—opening your eyes, returning fully relaxed and refreshed. Maintaining silence, you may begin to write when you are ready.

SESSION 6

Exercise: The Closest You Ever Felt to God and Nature

Induction

Now, in your mind's eye, you are transported to a special holy place where you feel safe, comfortable, and open. Feel yourself settling in, taking in your surroundings. When you are ready, bring to mind your image of a higher power. It could be a place in nature or God—an image that invokes your spiritual dimension. Now, scan your mind and spirit and bring to mind a time when you felt close to your image of a higher power. What were the feelings, sensations, and thoughts? We'll take a few moments in silence. When you hear the sound of my voice again, it will be with the next instruction. Now, maintaining silence, you may begin to write.

Exercise: Leaving

Induction

You are invited to bring to mind that this is the final session of this Writing Workshop for Adults with Cancer. We will be saying goodbye to each other, the room, the time we set aside for attending. What are the feelings and thoughts that arise as you contemplate leaving? Are there any physical sensations? If so, where do you feel the leave-taking in your body? We'll take a few moments in silence as we anticipate the experience of leaving. The next time you hear my voice it will be with the next instruction. Now, maintaining silence, you may begin to write.

EPILOGUE

WRITING, SOCIAL PROCESSES, AND PSYCHOTHERAPY: FROM PAST TO FUTURE

JAMES W. PENNEBAKER

In the span of 20 years, research on writing and health has evolved from a vague notion to a noble scientific enterprise. This book is both exciting and personally gratifying on several levels. On the broadest level, the field has witnessed a striking number of experiments that have demonstrated the remarkable power of translating emotional experiences into language. This relatively simple paradigm has been applied to a wide range of problems among diverse populations. Although the underlying mechanisms are still disputed, the implications for theoretical development and clinical practice are striking. On a more personal level, much of the early work surrounding the writing paradigm are intimately linked to my own professional development. Although I was involved in some of the first studies, the current research and practice associated with writing is now a broadly based undertaking.

The chapters in this book lay the basic foundations of current thinking, some of the most recent results, and describe the relevant literatures. Rather than add more data to the current discussion, this chapter is

Preparation of this chapter was aided, in part, by National Institutes of Health Grant MH52391.

more of an informal essay that gives a personal history to the writing paradigm and suggests some promising future directions for research and practice.

A VERY BRIEF HISTORY

Despite what we tell our students, some of the most interesting research projects come from intuition rather than deductive logic. The writing paradigm has been no exception. Based partly on my own personal experiences with emotional writing (and growing up in a non–self-reflective family with lots of health problems), it just made sense that having people explore their deepest thoughts and feelings would spur health changes. Prior to the first writing study, my students and I had been conducting a series of experiments exploring inhibition, autonomic activity, and health. Although I had wanted to do a writing study for years, the inhibition work gave me a theory to justify the project.

It is important to appreciate the context of the first writing study. I was a new faculty member at Southern Methodist University, just having been turned down for tenure at the University of Virginia. A beginning master's student, Sandy Beall, was eager to conduct her master's thesis right away. The department's introductory psychology classes had an extra credit option that allowed for up to 5 hours of participation time. Because of Sandy's schedule and the availability of lab rooms, the study had to be run in a week. Because of these practical considerations, we decided to have students come to the lab 5 days in a row—the first day to complete questionnaires and the remaining 4 days to do the writing. Why did we have people write about the most traumatic experience of their lives? It just felt right. And we had some preliminary evidence that people who had not talked about personal traumas tended to have more health problems.

The study worked. Because of that, we have always had people write for 3–5 days in a row for 15–20 minutes per day about traumatic or other negative experiences. Why give up a good thing? In retrospect, it is not surprising to see that so many variations on the writing paradigm have also been successful. It appears that the writing topic, the writing perspective (positive vs. negative), the number of days, and other parameters can produce positive health effects. Even the original theory on which the writing paradigm was presumably based is (appropriately) under fire. And I love it.

SEARCHING FOR THE ESSENCE

As the wide-ranging chapters in this book attest, writing about emotional topics has the power to affect peoples' lives and health. I suspect that every author who has run a writing study has been thanked by his or her participants for the opportunity to participate. One of the remarkable ironies is that people find the writing paradigm beneficial regardless of the instructions or underlying theory driving the study.

What, then, is the essence of the writing paradigm? The problem with this question is that the idea of *essence* is completely dependent on one's level of analysis. It is much like the annoying question that all colloquium speakers are asked these days, "What mediates your effects?" The answer can be culture, social context, perception, memory, neurotransmitter activity, cellular metabolism, or, best of all, a brightly colored fMRI image of a highly specific brain region. The reality is that most of these answers are true.

To me, the essence of the writing technique is that it forces people to stop what they are doing and briefly reflect on their lives. It is one of the few times that people are given permission to see where they have been and where they are going without having to please anyone. They are able to prioritize their goals, find meaning in their past and future, and think about who they are at this point in life. Unfortunately, this "essence" is inherently vague. It encompasses theoretical stances associated with self-regulation, search for meaning, creation of coherent stories about one's life, habituation, emotional awareness and expression, as well as more molecular and molar processes.

To appreciate why writing is effective, we also need to know when it is not effective. That is, what are the necessary ingredients for it to produce beneficial effects? A consideration of the various control conditions and occasional inability to replicate help to answer this question. I suspect that all of the authors represented in this book would agree that the following are necessary conditions for writing to work.

Emotional Processing

People must be given the freedom to invoke their feelings when writing about an emotional topic (see chapter 10, this volume). Emotions are part of virtually all important psychological experiences. Not allowing individuals to acknowledge them by definition restricts their exploring the impact and understanding of their topic.

Most upheavals in people's lives are associated with both positive and negative emotions. Furthermore, many of these feelings are probably contradictory. It makes intuitive sense that exploring just the positive or the negative features of an upheaval can be beneficial. I suspect, however, that giving individuals free reign to explore all of their emotions—both positive and negative—could be optimally healthy.

Creating a Coherent Story

One of the basic functions of language and conversation is to communicate coherently and understandably. By extension, writing about an emotional experience in an organized way is probably healthier than in a chaotic way. Indeed, growing evidence from several labs (see chapters 6, 7, and 8, this volume) suggest that people are most likely to benefit if they can write a coherent story. Any technique that disrupts the telling of the story or the organization of the story is undoubtedly detrimental.

Unfortunately, we are not yet at the point of being able to precisely define what is meant by *coherent, understandable,* or *meaningful* when it comes to writing about emotional upheavals. One person's meaning may be another's rumination. Many times in my research I have been struck how a person appears to be writing in a way that avoids dealing with what I see as a central issue. Nevertheless, the person's health improves and he or she exclaims how beneficial the study was. Meaning, then, may ultimately be in the eye of the writer.

Postwriting Processing

An occasional criticism of the writing paradigm is this: "How is it possible to change the lives of people when they write for only four days for 15 minutes per day; how can a total of one hour have such a huge impact?" These critics do not appreciate the fact that after writing, participants report thinking and, often, dreaming about their writing topic. Many people are psychologically in the experiment 24 hours a day for several days. In some of our most spectacular writing failures, participants have been distracted from thinking about their topic immediately after writing or have been forced to return to their classes or jobs as soon as the writing has been completed. In the more successful experiments, the writing lingers in people's minds for hours and days afterwards.

A Trustworthy Setting

From the time of Freud's transference to Roger's unconditional love, therapists have known that there had to be a basic sense of trust and security in the client–therapist relationship. Although the writing paradigm suggests a different relationship between the experimenter and participant, there is still an essence of trust. I suspect that an essential ingredient for success in the writing paradigm is that the participants believe that their writing is taken seriously, is held in confidence, and will have no adverse social effects on them.

Methodological Roadblocks

All of the above factors are probably necessary conditions for the writing paradigm to work. There are undoubtedly additional conditions that have not yet been teased out. For example, there is still some debate about the precise role of language in cementing health improvements over time. It is not at all clear when it is best to confront an emotional experience after its occurrence. Furthermore, we still do not know for whom writing is most beneficial or for what types of emotional upheavals (see chapter 5, this volume). Clearly, future research will continue to explore the basic processes underlying the writing paradigm.

Ironically, a major reason why the "process" or "essence" question has not been answered (in addition to its being an inherently unanswerable question) is because of the essential messiness of our outcome measures. Across the dozens of studies, researchers have used physician visits, immune markers, absentee rates, school grades, and other objective markers as dependent variables. Indeed, this has been a significant selling point for the disclosure paradigm. These studies are repeatedly demonstrating that writing about emotional events can influence people's lives.

An all-too-often unspoken secret about these measures is that they are terribly, terribly messy. Take physician visits as an example. At a private university where the majority of students are from out of state and live on campus (e.g., Southern Methodist University), approximately 60–70% of the students visit the student health center for illness during their freshman year. At a state university (e.g., University of Texas at Austin), only 35–50% visit the health center during the same time. This means that 30–65% of our samples do not provide helpful or harmful responses no matter how powerful the writing study. To get significant effects, then, most of us need a minimum of 20 participants per condition. Given the messiness of these measures, it is almost impossible to conduct any meaningful internal analyses. This explains why most researchers have not successfully found any self-reports or other process measures to correlate consistently with our dependent measures. Unfortunately, most biological measures are equally variable as are other real world markers that go beyond self-reports (see chapter 9, this volume).

A possible solution to the dependent measure problem is to find one or more reliable health proxy measures. One possibility may be something akin to Klein's (chapter 8, this volume) working memory measure. If such a measure can be shown to be reliably related to a health marker, it will ultimately allow us begin to detect subtle process measures. Unfortunately, as Klein notes, even working memory measures are highly variable from person to person. Furthermore, within the cognitive and neuropsychology world, there is considerable disagreement about which working memory measures are best.

The other solution requires far more work and is considerably less appealing: We need to run much larger studies with far more measures (see chapter 11, this volume). In the interim, it is wise for writing researchers to collect as many common outcome measures as possible. Although no single study is likely to determine the essence of the writing paradigm, future meta-analyses will help to point us in the right direction.

BEYOND ESSENCE: CAUSES, CORRELATES, AND CONSEQUENCES

Perhaps the most exciting feature of the writing paradigm is that it forces us to cross many of the traditional boundaries in psychology and medicine. As the chapters in this book attest, the writing paradigm has attracted researchers with interests in cognition, social processes, clinical disorders, and health and personality psychology, as well as those primarily interested in mind–body issues (e.g., chapters 2, 3, and 4, this volume).

Where is the research on the writing paradigm going to take us? I have no idea. Some of the many questions that I find particularly intriguing are described in the sections that follow.

Cognitive and Neuropsychological Issues

When people write or talk about emotional topics, it changes the ways they think and organize information. One frustration has been to try to find cognitive measures that truly tap these changes that we see in clinical settings. Until recently, most attempts have been failures. Some of the most exciting new work has been in suggesting the ways that writing appears to affect working memory. That is, after individuals write about trauma, there is an increase in the amount of working memory available. Klein's working memory findings square with Lepore's work on rumination, Smyth's findings on cognitive organization, and our own results concerning better grades and social functioning after writing.

The working memory results also are intriguing because they raise a new set of questions about the writing paradigm. Should we think of working memory as a mediator or as an outcome measure? If we assume that it is a mediator of health changes, we would expect any technique that changed working memory to also improve health. More likely, writing about emotional topics affects some more basic cognitive activity that then ultimately frees up working memory. One can't help but wonder how fast this process is. Surely, after the participant writes the final sentence of his or her disclosure essay, there is not a magical increase in working memory. Intuitively, this must take hours, days, or even longer.

To the degree that increases in working memory are reflecting basic changes in the way people organize complex emotional events, we can begin to focus on the cognitive processes themselves. And this is when we need to bring in the detail people—those neuroscientists who talk about fMRI, brain activity, cellular function, and genetic structure. In the years to come, I would love to know where in the brain these changes occur, how fast they normally occur, and how we can speed up or slow them down. However, as in our search for the essence of anything, we will still only know a small part of the puzzle even after we know all these things.

The Mind–Body Problem and Medical Implications

In many people's eyes, the real magic of the writing paradigm is that it affects such a wide range of health and biological markers. (This, of course, is only magical because most of Western culture implicitly believes in a Cartesian split between mind and body.) Furthermore, the effect sizes of some of the medical outcomes rival what is often found with more traditional interventions.

Is this a specific or general effect? In other words, is the writing intervention particularly helpful for some kinds of health problems and not others? All of the evidence would suggest that writing brings about a general reduction in biological stress. That is, when an individual has come to terms with an upsetting experience, he or she is less vigilant about the world and potential threats. This results in an overall lowering of defenses. To this point, studies have indicated that writing brings about reductions in common illness visits to physicians (e.g., upper respiratory illnesses), reductions in blood pressure, reduced use of pain medication, and long-term changes in immune function (which we frankly do not yet know how to interpret). Given the broad range of improvements in health outcomes, it would be prudent to conclude that writing provokes a rather broad and nonspecific pattern of biological changes that are generally salutary.

As a side note, social scientists should pay far more attention to objective markers of physical health. Both minor as well as major illnesses are known to be related to long-term stress levels. A person suffering from an upper respiratory infection has been infected by a particular virus but also may have a vulnerable immune system. This vulnerability may reflect hours, days, or weeks of stress. Most self-reports in the social sciences ask people to report on their stress at a given point in time or to look back and try to recall what it has been in the past. If a person is feeling happy and well today, she or he will be less likely to recall a stressful episode a week earlier or even a minor bout of a cold 2 weeks before that. Physician visits for illness or other markers of illness behavior serve as an ideal cumulative marker of stress and illness.

Although health measures are a convincing outcome measure, researchers and policy makers must also appreciate their crudeness. Some individuals (particularly poor, ethnic, or stigmatized students) are likely to never visit a university health center the entire time they are in college. By the same token, we generally find that about 20% of the students account for over 80% of student health center visits. Finally, a large percentage of people who seek medical treatment probably do not need to do so in the first place (e.g., a common virus such as a cold for which there is no cure) or go for the wrong reasons (e.g., trying to get out of an exam or get a doctor's excuse to avoid paying an airline penalty for a schedule change). Others who are extremely sick simply do not visit a physician for a variety of reasons, ranging from costs to fear. Health visits and costs, then, are simply rough proxies for true health and illness.

Despite the shortcomings of measures such as physician visits and absenteeism, they have the benefit of having significant medical and workforce costs. Some would argue that our culture pays far more attention to outcome measures that have financial implications than those that simply tap subjective distress.

Language in Writing and the Natural Environment

In the first few years of the writing research, it never occurred to us to actually explore how people wrote about traumatic experiences. Since the mid-1990s, however, it has become increasingly clear that some ways of writing are more likely to yield health improvements than others. At least three promising directions are evolving in the study of language.

The first question that must be answered to everyone's satisfaction concerns whether language use is necessary or only sufficient. By definition, all of the writing studies have required individuals to put their emotional experiences into words. Does expressing a trauma in a nonverbal way—such as through art, dance, or music—provide comparable benefits? Among highly verbal college students, we have typically found that language is a necessary condition for health changes. However, in talking informally with accomplished artists, they have frequently noted that they are able to work through complications in their lives in their work. Written words clearly work well for the literate members of our culture who are comfortable with that medium. Studies are needed that explore the role of talking about traumas among nonliterate participants and, of particular theoretical importance, of nonverbal expression among individuals who naturally express themselves without words.

A second question deals with attempts to isolate healthy versus unhealthy writing styles. That is, is the use of certain word patterns or styles more likely to yield positive results than others? And, by extension, can we train people to write in healthy ways? These questions have been at the center of my research in recent years. Across multiple studies, it is beginning to appear that individuals who develop good stories and who are able to change their perspectives from one writing session to another are the ones most likely to show health improvements (see also chapters 3 and 9, this volume). The linguistic analyses, then, suggest that people need to change or grow over the course of writing.

Assuming that one of the keys to successful writing is that the participants are able to stand back and reevaluate their lives, can we train individuals to do this in a maximally effective way? This may be a problem similar to the concerns of high school English teachers. Can we ultimately train people to construct good stories that provide meaning and structure to their lives?

A third issue about language concerns how people change in the ways they talk and communicate with others after participating in the writing paradigm. Those individuals who are most likely to benefit from writing are the same ones who tend to change in their writing style from the first to the last day of writing. Do these writing styles reflect changes in thinking styles as well as interaction styles? Much of our ongoing research explores how people naturally talk to others in their social worlds. Preliminary findings indicate that the writing paradigm does, in fact, result in differing speaking patterns and word usage in the weeks after writing. As discussed in chapter 9, this should not be too surprising. As the authors point out, traumatic experience and the writing paradigm itself are all part of a complex social system. When we write about an emotional topic, we tend to think about the topic differently and eventually convey this new thinking to our friends. In summary, writing may be as much a social phenomenon as a cognitive one.

Personality and Individual Differences

Do some people benefit more from the writing paradigm than others? As Lumley and colleagues (chapter 5, this volume) point out, this question is becoming far more complicated than was originally thought. There is mixed evidence that men and people low in alexithymia may benefit more than women and those high in alexithymia. Most of the studies we have conducted on writing have not shown any reliable individual differences that have differentially predicted health outcomes. This, of course, may be related to the crudeness and variability of health outcome measures.

A related question concerns the value of writing among people with different illnesses or traumatic experiences. For example, would cancer patients benefit more than heart disease patients? What about people who have dealt with childhood sexual abuse versus death of a parent? These are extremely important questions for which we have no answer.

Social and Cultural Dynamics

As language research now suggests, the writing paradigm may well be exerting much of its effect on people's social lives. In the years when we were first trying to understand the writing paradigm, we relied heavily on an inhibition argument. That is, having a trauma and not telling others was considered an example of active inhibition, which resulted in long-term cumulative stress. At the time, we did not appreciate how social this argument was. Keeping an important secret from others was a large part of the problem.

As the authors of chapter 9 note, emotion experiences are part of a much broader social system. A person who is keeping a traumatic experience secret from friends is probably doing it in order to maintain his or her friendship network. Furthermore, the person may harbor the belief that by telling this secret, the network will be damaged or destroyed. An extension of this reasoning is that by writing about a trauma, a person may, in fact, begin to deal with his or her social network differently (also see chapter 2, this volume). We have seen this both in lab studies as well as in real world experiences. For example, in a recent writing study, my students and I found that writing about emotional topics resulted in people changing the ways they interacted with people in the real world in the weeks after writing. Those in the experimental condition talked more with others and changed in the ways they used positive emotion words and even pronouns.

In two recent case studies, I inadvertently learned that participants in the writing technique completely changed their social lives. In one case, a woman who had been married 10 years instituted a divorce after writing. In talking with me a year later, she was deeply grateful for the opportunity to do the writing in that it forced her to deal with issues surrounding her unhappiness in her relationship. In another case, a woman who had experienced the sudden death of her husband a year earlier reported that the writing technique completely changed her social circle. Before writing, she spent time with friends who routinely referred to her as strong, courageous, and good humored. After writing, she reported that she realized that she was constantly putting on a happy face for these friends and, instead of changing her relationship with them, she sought out her old friends from childhood. Writing has the power to change the ways we think which, in turn, can affect our entire social world.

Diaries, Popular Culture, and Clinical Applications

Lori Stone, a new researcher in the disclosure world, recently conducted an Internet search for references to journaling. On amazon.com, there were over 9,000 books related to the topic. Using a standard search engine, she found more than 22,000 entries for journaling. Most of the journaling sites were people's actual journal entries.

People all over the world have traditionally written in diaries or kept journals. They have always intuitively known that putting emotional topics on paper was a good idea. It is not particularly shocking, then, to learn that writing studies are often snatched up by the media. Journals and diaries are hot topics on afternoon talk shows, women's magazines, and lifestyles sections of newspapers.

Is writing in a diary good for your health? You might think that we would know the answer to this question, but we don't. Are diary writers healthier than nondiary writers? I have never found this to be true—but, then again, people who take vitamins are not healthier than people who do not take vitamins. Like diary writers, vitamin users may actually be slightly sicker. However, both vitamin users and diary writers may be far healthier than they would have been had they not taken vitamins or written in diaries. Given the impact that writing studies are having in the media and the large number of people who keep diaries, it is incumbent on us to begin exploring how writing affects people outside the lab.

How much are our studies the product of tight experimental control? Chapters 4, 12, 13, and 14 are ground-breaking in pointing to real world applications of the writing paradigm. Projects such as the ones described in these chapters give us an idea of how powerful the writing paradigm truly is. Unlike controlled lab studies, real world projects will evaluate how writing works with a group of self-selected people—people who are naturally drawn to a writing intervention. The outcome of these projects will ultimately define the staying power of all of our work.

AUTHOR INDEX

Numbers in italics refer to listings in the reference sections.

Francis, M. E., 43, 49, *94*, 107, *116*, 123, 124, 129, *133*, 138, 147, *154*, *173*, 183, *195*, 202, *212*
Frank, A., 99, *115*
Franklin, A. J., 58, *71*
Frantz, C. M., 44, *49*
Frazier, L., *255*
Fredrickson, B. L., 103, 104, *115*, 124, *132*
Freshman, M. S., 145, *150*
Freud, S., 4, *13*, 119, *132*, 178, *192*
Freyberger, H., 90, *92*
Friedman, H. S., 101, *115*
Friedman, R., 4, *13*, 210, *213*
Friesen, W. V., 160, *173*
Frueh, B. C., 182, *192*
Funkenstein, D. H., 19, *27*

Garnick, M. B., 35, *50*
Garssen, B., 33, *48*
Garwood, G., 145, *152*
Gary, H. E., Jr., 21, *28*
Gatti, G., 186, *192*
Gaynes, B. N., *194*
Geerlings, P. J., *235*
Gendlin, E. T., 178, 180, 181, *193*, *194*
Gentry, W. D., 21, *28*
Gerin, W., 27, *29*
Geyer, S., 32, *50*
Gibb, J., *50*
Gidron, Y., 88, *92*
Giller, E. L., 187, *196*
Gillum, R. F., 211, *213*
Gilman-Sachs, A., *194*
Glanz, K., 212, *213*
Glaser, R., 34, *48*, 105, *116*, 163, 164, *174*, 183–187, *192*, *193*, *195*
Glover, D. A., 162, *174*
Glynn, L., *29*
Goldberg, D. E., *27*
Goldberg, N., 261, *271*
Golden, R. N., *194*
Goldstein, H. S., 20, *28*
González, J. L., 84, *94*, 111, *116*, 147, *153*
Goodkin, K., 33, *48*
Gordon, J., 219, *236*
Gorman, C., *51*
Gorman, J. M., 239, *255*
Gotthiel, E., 36, *50*
Gould, O. N., 150, *152*

Gould, R., 244, 248, *254*
Gravenstein, S., 186, *193*
Green, C. J., 80, *93*
Green, R. L., 243, *254*
Greenberg, L. S., 110, *115*, 178, 183, *193*, *195*
Greenberg, M. A., 3, 4, *13*, *14*, 23, 25, 28, 88, 93, 99, 105–111, 113, *115*, *116*, 121, 123, *132*, 143, 146, 147, *152*, *153*, 168, *173*, 202, 207, *213*, 259, *271*
Greenlaugh, T., 7, *13*
Greenwood, D., *193*
Greer, S., 33, 48, *51*
Greist, J. H., 223, *236*
Griffin, T. M., 56, 61, *72*
Grimm, E. A., *272*
Groopman, J., 258, *271*
Gross, J. J., 101, *115*, 160, *173*
Groves, P. M., 104, *115*
Gu, H., *194*
Guccione, A. A., 87, *93*
Guerrier, J. H., 149, *152*
Guthrie, D., *48*
Guthrie, I. K., 101, *114*

Habbal, R., 82, 85, 87, *92*
Hall, R. P., 21, *28*
Hamburg, M. A., 53, *72*
Hanewald, G., *236*
Harber, K. D., 6, *14*, 143, *152*, 209, *213*
Harburg, E., 21, 25, *28*
Harney, P., *50*
Harris, C., *50*
Harris, D. F., 142, *155*
Harris, S. D., *48*
Harrison, C. A., 220, 221, *236*
Harvey, J. H., 145, *152*, 169, *173*
Hasher, L., 137, *152*
Hayes, A., *192*
Hayes, B. E., 136, *154*
Heider, K., 160, *173*
Heim, C., 188, *193*
Helgeson, V. S., 35, 46, *49*
Hellhammer, D. H., 188, *193*
Hellstrand, K., 186, *193*
Herbert, T. B., 186, *193*
Hermans, H. J. M., 56, 57, *72*
Hermans-Jansen, E., 56, 57, *72*
Hermodsson, S., 186, *193*
Heys, S. D., *174*

King, S. H., 19, *27*
Kinner, S. A., 220, 221, *236*
Kirk, S. B., 34, *50*
Kleber, R. J., 218, *236*
Klee, M., *271*
Klein, D., 211, *213*
Klein, K., 136–139, 147, 149, *150*, *152*, *153*
Klein, M. H., 180, 181, *193*, *194*, 223, *236*
Kliewer, W., 54, 58, *72*
Klimas, N., *173*, *192–194*
Kline, J. P., 80, *94*
Klirs, E. G., 142, *153*
Kolodziej, M. E., 20, *28*
Koolhaas, J. M., 163, *173*
Koopman, C., 35, 48, 257, *271*
Korchin, S. J., 259, *272*
Korte, S. M., *173*
Koskela, K., 211, *214*
Kozak, M. J., 142, *152*, 178, 179, 182, 183, *192*, *194*
Kradin, R., 188, *196*
Kraemer, H. C., 36, *50*
Krag, D. N., *48*
Kubany, E. S., *236*
Kubler-Ross, E., 258, 267, *272*
Kucuk, O., *194*
Kumar, M., 81, 92, 147, *153*, 164, *173*, 183, 186, *192*, *194*
Kurosaki, T., *271*
Kuut, T., 232, *236*
Kuyken, W., 143, *153*

L'Abate, L., 163, *173*, 210, *213*, 216, *236*, 239–245, 247–249, 251–253, *253–256*
Labouvie-Vief, G., 92, *93*
Labov, W., 56, *72*
Lachnit, T., *236*
Lakka, T. A., *27*
Lambert, M. J., 246, *253*
Lamensdorf, A. M., 20, *28*, *29*
Lane, R. D., 92, *93*
Lang, P. J., 100, *116*, 178, *194*
Lange, A., 203, *214*, 216, 222, 224, 226–228, 234, 235, *236–238*
Langelle, C., *50*
Larsen, J. T., 100, *114*
Larson, J., 145, *153*
Laskowski, B. F., *193*

Laub, J. H., 53, *72*
Laudenslager, M. L., 188, *194*
Laughlin, J. E., 149, *152*
Lauritsen, J. L., 53, *72*
Lebowitz, B., 200, *213*
Lee, H., *271*
Leigh, H., *173*
Leirer, V. O., 149, 150, *153*
Leisen, J. C. C., 38, 49, 86, 93, 206, *213*, *259*, *271*
Lelutiu-Weinberger, C., 58, *72*
Lepore, S. J., 4, 6, *13*, 22, 23, 28, 35, 46, 49, 54, *72*, 88, 93, 99, 104–110, 113, *115*, *116*, 122, *133*, 143, 147, *153*, 207, 209, *213*, 257, 259, *271*, *272*
Leserman, J., 191, *192*, *194*
Lester, D., 264, *272*
Leupker, R. V., 211, *213*
Levenson, R. W., 101, *115*, 124, *132*, 160, *173*
Levin, D. N., 178, *194*
Levitt, M. Z., 58, *72*
Lewis, F. M., 212, *213*
Lewis, S., 44, *49*
Li, H., *174*
Li, Z., *192*
Lichtman, R. R., 125, *134*
Lightfoot, C., 58, *72*
Limbeek, J. van, *235*
Linden, W., 20, 25, *28*, *29*
Linszen, D. H., *235*
Lipman, A., 202, *213*
Liwag, M. D., 142, 145, *154*
Lolley, J., *174*
Louis, C. M., 235, *238*
Lowy, M. T., 187, *196*
Lubaroff, D. M., 169, *173*
Lumley, M. A., 38, 49, 83, 86, 89, 90, 91, 93, 206, *213*, 259, *271*
Lutgendorf, S. K., 147, 150, *153*, 164, 168, 169, *173*, 180–183, 185–187, 191, 192, *194*, *196*

MacCallum, R. C., *193*
Maccoby, N., 211, *214*
MacGregor, M. W., 21, *27*
MacLean, D., 21, *27*
Malarkey, W. S., 164, *174*, 186, 187, *193*
Mandler, G., 136, *153*
Manis, M., 19, *29*

SUBJECT INDEX

Coping
  avoidance-oriented, 36
  college, 123
Core beliefs, 110
Coronary artery disease, 101
Cortisol, 186–189
Costs
  of treatments, 4
  of writing studies, 209–211
Cultural expectations/practices, 57–58
Curriculum, social issues, 55
Cytokines, 186

Death and dying, writing intervention
    for, 257–270
  general format of, 259–263
  impact of, 263–270
  outcomes of, 264–265
  participants in, 263
  procedure for, 263–264
  results of, 265
  statistical analysis of, 265
Decision making, 149
Defensiveness, 82
Dental fears, 89
Depression, 17, 186
  and alexithymic personality, 86, 88
  in children, 58
  and cognitive restructuring, 109
  and intrusive thoughts, 105, 106
  and self-regulation, 101
Desensitization. See Habituation
Development of identity, 56
Diastolic blood pressure, 20, 24
Disasters, natural, 191
Discipline, school, 65
Disclosure model, 177–180
  immunity and effects of, 188–190
  traditional, 177
Discrimination, and children, 58
Dissemination of writing studies, 209
Distraction, and blood pressure, 22, 23
Distress
  after expressive writing, 40
  and cancer, 34, 35
  expressive writing and lowered, 42
Drivers, automobile, 149
Duchenne laughter and smiling, 124

Eating disorders, 83
EBV. See Epstein—Barr virus

EBV-VCA. See Epstein—Barr virus viral
    capsid antigen
Effectiveness studies, 211
Electronic home monitors (blood pres-
    sure), 24
Emotional competence workbooks, 249–
    251
Emotional expression, 17, 34–35. See also
    Limited emotional awareness/
    understanding/expression
  and adjustment to cancer, 34–36
  and alexithymic personality, 83–90
  controlled research on cancer and, 36–
    45
  correlational research of cancer and,
    32–36
  and immune system, 183–191
  mechanics of, 167–171
  physiological effects of, 160–161
Emotional expression workbooks, 252
Emotional processing, 34–35
Emotion. See Self-regulation of emotion
  neurophysiological-biochemical re-
    sponses, 100
  subjective—experiential responses, 100
Emotion experience, 19
Emotion expression, 19
Emotion inhibition, measurement of, 18–
    19
Emotions (term), 158
Epstein—Barr virus (EBV)
  and habituation, 107
  and repressive personality, 81
Epstein—Barr virus viral capsid antigen
    (EBV-VCA), 184–185
Ethics programs, 53–54
Evaluation of acceptable responses, 76–
    77
Examination fears, 23
  and habituation, 105
  and intrusive thoughts, 88
Experiential involvement, 180–181, 185
Exposure therapies, 104
Expression
  emotion. See Emotion expression
  perceived social context for, 77
Expressive disclosure experiments
  with cancer patients, 38–45
  sample instructions for, 41
  writing samples for, 41
Expressive therapies, 3

Expressive writing, 4. *See also* Writing
  studies
  and blood pressure, 21, 23–27
  for death and dying, 257–270
  and health, 17, 54–56
  mechanics of, 121–123
  and research with children, 59–71
  and self-presentation of children, 56–
    58
  topics for, 130–131
  and working memory, 138–140

Facilitators, 68
Fact control instructions sample, 41
Families, 34, 58
Fictional narrative (FN), 60, 66, 67
Fighting, 65
Fight or flight response, 100
Fight stories, 57
Films, stressful, 23
"Finding a new solution" technique, 67
FN. *See* Fictional narrative
Freud, Sigmund, 26

Gastrointestinal diseases, 191
Gay men, 111
Gender, 89
Generalizability, treatment, 201–207
Goals
  and cancer, 35
  writing about, 127
Grade point average (GPA), 55, 140
Group therapy, 37, 90

Habituation
  cognitive reappraisal vs., 218–222
  contradictions to role of, 123
  and self-regulation, 102–108
  response-related habituation, 105
  stimulus-related, 105
Healing, wound, 186
Health, 4, 17
  and alexithymia, 83
  and cancer, 34
  of children, 58–59
  and cognitive restructuring, 110
  and emotional disclosure, 163–167
  and positive aspects of stressors, 103
  and working memory, 149–150

Health centers, visits to, 17, 106–108
Helplessness, 25
Hepatitis B, 187, 191
Herpes viruses, 186
High blood pressure. *See* Blood pressure
HIV. *See* Human Immunodeficiency Virus
Homework, 6
Hormones, stress, 186
Hostility
  and blood pressure, 18
  in hypertensive population, 25
  and repressive personality, 82
  and self-regulation, 101
Hostility—aggression model, 20
Human Immunodeficiency Virus (HIV),
    37, 104, 186, 191
Hypertension. *See* Blood pressure
Hypertensive personality, 25
Hypertrophy, left-ventricular, 18
Hypnosis, 37

Identity
  development of, 56
  life story approach to, 125
Illness(es)
  and alexithymic personality, 83
  chronic, 7
  infectious, 101
  self-reported, 17
Immune system, 17, 183–191
  future directions, 189, 191
  and habituation, 107
  model of disclosure effects on, 188–
    190
  and self-regulation, 101
  and trauma, 187–188
Incentives to participate, 208
Infectious illnesses, 101
Inhibited personality, 77
Inhibition(s), 88–89
  active, 122
  and blood pressure, 18–19
  definition of, 77
  in hypertensive population, 25
  personal, 6
Instructions
  and alexithymic personality, 84
  samples of experimental condition, 41
  writing, 77, 206–208, 217
Interapy, 12, 224–235
  best candidates for, 231–232

ABOUT THE EDITORS

Stephen J. Lepore, PhD, is a professor in the Psychology Department at Brooklyn College and the Doctoral Programs in Psychology at the Graduate Center of the City University of New York. Since receiving his doctorate in 1991 from the University of California, Irvine, he has studied the effects of stress on mental and physical health, with an emphasis on understanding how interpersonal relationships, coping processes, and behavioral interventions can buffer persons from stress. His work, which has been funded by the National Science Foundation and the National Institutes of Health, has appeared in numerous scientific journals and books. He has received awards for outstanding research contributions from the Society of Behavioral Medicine and the Health Psychology Division (38) of the American Psychological Association.

Joshua M. Smyth, PhD, is a professor in the Psychology Department at Syracuse University. He received his undergraduate degree in Cognitive Science from Vassar College and his doctorate in Health Psychology from SUNY at Stony Brook. His research interests revolve around stress and coping processes, in particular the development and application of psychological interventions, psychoendocrinology, and the health consequences of stressful or traumatic experiences. His work on the health effects of expressive writing, funded by the Fetzer Institute and the National Institutes of Health, has appeared in top-tier medical and psychology journals. Dr Smyth has received several prestigious research, teaching, and service awards, including outstanding research awards from the American Psychological Association, the Society of Behavioral Medicine, and the American Psychosomatic Society.